William Faulkner and the Southern Landscape

CENTER BOOKS ON THE AMERICAN SOUTH

George F. Thompson, *Series Founder and Director*

WILLIAM FAULKNER
and the
SOUTHERN LANDSCAPE

CHARLES S. AIKEN

The University of Georgia Press   *Athens and London*

in association with the Center for American Places at Columbia College Chicago

William Faulkner and the Southern Landscape is the eleventh volume in the *Center Books on the American South* series, George F. Thompson, series founder and director.

Chapters 2, 3, and 7 are expanded versions of "Faulkner's Yoknapatawpha County: Geographical Fact into Fiction," "Faulkner's Yoknapatawpha County: A Place in the American South," and "A Geographical Approach to William Faulkner's 'The Bear,'" which were published in volumes 67 (1977), 69 (1979), and 71 (1981) of the *Geographical Review*. The author thanks the American Geographical Society for use of these articles.

© 2009 by the University of Georgia Press
Athens, Georgia 30602
www.ugapress.org
Set in Minion by Graphic Composition, Inc., Bogart, GA
Printed and bound by Maple-Vail
The paper in this book meets the guidelines for permanence
and durability of the Committee on Production Guidelines for
Book Longevity of the Council on Library Resources.

Printed in the United States of America

13   12   11   10   09   C   5   4   3   2   1

Library of Congress Cataloging-in-Publication Data
Aiken, Charles S. (Charles Shelton), 1938–
William Faulkner and the southern landscape / Charles S. Aiken.
        p. cm. — (Center books on the American South)
Includes bibliographical references and index.
ISBN-13: 978-0-8203-3219-2 (alk. paper)
ISBN-10: 0-8203-3219-4 (alk. paper)
   1. Faulkner, William, 1897–1962—Criticism and interpretation. 2. Faulkner,
William, 1897–1962—Homes and haunts—Mississippi. 3. Setting (Literature)
4. Yoknapatawpha County (Imaginary place) 5. American literature—Southern
States—History and criticism. 6. American literature—Mississippi—History and
criticism. 7. Southern States—In literature. 8. Mississippi—In literature. I. Title.
PS3511.A86Z566 2009
813'.52—dc22   2008037207
British Library Cataloging-in-Publication Data available

FOR MARY ANN, JOHN, CHARLES, AMY,

AND FOR AUDREY AND HER GENERATION

. . . and the host—guide—answers . . . to the best of his ability out of the . . . composite heritage of remembering that long back, told, repeated, inherited to him by his; father; or rather, his mother: from her mother: or better still, to him when he himself was a child.

WILLIAM FAULKNER, *Requiem for a Nun*

CONTENTS

ACKNOWLEDGMENTS

The genesis of this book are stories of Lafayette County, Mississippi, which were told to me in Mississippi by my maternal grandmother when I was a child. She was born at old Harmontown in the northern part of the county in 1876, where my great-grandfather owned a store. Both she and my grandfather, who died before I was born, had mothers who were members of the large Harmon family, among the first to settle in Lafayette County. My grandparents, four of their nine children, and my maternal ancestors, back to my great-great grandparents, are buried in the cemetery at Harmontown.

While in graduate school, I usually bought a magazine to read while I did my laundry on Friday nights. The *Saturday Evening Post* of March 31, 1962, contained William Faulkner's last short story, "Hell Creek Crossing," which he extracted from *The Reivers*. It was published a few weeks before his death in July 1962. As I read "Hell Creek Crossing," I not only recognized the old Memphis-Oxford Road but the iron bridge and other places that Faulkner called by their real names. I also knew that the fictitious Wyott's Crossing was really Wyatt's Crossing and that Faulkner had only slightly changed the name of Miss Ballenbaugh, who operated a store near the Tallahatchie River, from Bedenbaugh.

After my father read the story, he told me that Hell Creek was the name of an actual stream, but it was east of Oxford on the road to New Albany. The worst stream to cross on the Memphis-Oxford Road early in the twentieth century was Jim Wolf Creek, now a deep gorge with a substantial bridge. Early in the twentieth century, the U.S. Army Corps of Engineers dredged many of the streams in north Mississippi to drain the bottoms for cultivation. Interference with natural drainage caused Jim Wolf Creek and other dredged streams to cut deeper and headward, creating new major problems. Originally, Jim Wolf Creek was not deep enough where the Memphis-Oxford Road crossed it to require a bridge. My father thought that a spring up the hill from the creek kept its crossing waterlogged to the extent that, especially after a rain, a loaded wagon or a motor vehicle driven by a person who did not know how to negotiate the site could easily become stuck in mud and sand.

Approximately one-fourth of the manuscript was written in the late 1970s and early 1980s and the remainder after 2000. Some of the persons who helped me locate and interpret sources have died since I began my research, including my parents, who had great interest in Faulkner and my project and were the principal persons from whom I sought assistance. My mother helped me interpret the documents in the Lafayette County Chancery Clerk's Office. My father knew the back roads of the county and remembered the locations of houses and places that vanished long ago. He also knew Oxford well from 1915 until his death in 1991. I regret that we never made our planned winter hike into the ruins of old Wyatt.

I am especially grateful to persons who encouraged me in this project. Sanford Bederman, Thomas McHaney, and James Wheeler were among my early supporters. I thank Tom for reading and advising me on the first draft. Also, I thank several anonymous readers for their comments. I appreciate the advice and encouragement that Donald Meinig and Peirce Lewis gave me to expand what began as research articles into this book. An invitation from Lothar Hönnighausen to spend a term as a guest professor in the North American Program at the Universität Bonn provided me with new and expanded perspectives on William Faulkner and the American South. Also, I appreciate the invitation from Joseph Urgo and Donald Kartiganger to participate in the 2004 Faulkner Conference at the University of Mississippi. From the sessions, I gained new insights on approaches to Faulkner studies.

Several persons in Mississippi gave me special assistance. H. B. Swindall of Panola County took me in his pickup truck across a snake-infested soybean field to the abandoned, wasp-filled dwelling believed to have been the hunting camp of "General" James Stone. A Mr. Harmon (no relation) permitted me to use his copies of the 1925 Sanborn insurance maps of Oxford. Kenneth Akers, U.S. Army Corps of Engineers, gave me access to the Sardis Reservoir land acquisition maps. The librarians in charge of the Mississippi collection at the University of Mississippi, beginning with Dorothy Z. Oldham, who lectured me on the difficulty of research, to the congenial Jennifer Ford, who diligently searched for and found the books and documents I sought. Aston Holley of the Gathright-Reed Drugstore shared with me a number of seasoned local stories about Faulkner, some of which I had never heard. All who write about William Faulkner are indebted to Joseph Blotner for his detailed account of Faulkner's life and for publication of Faulkner's uncollected stories and many of his letters. Blotner is criticized for not revealing more about Faulkner's private and family affairs, but Blotner's extensive work forms a base from which to proceed in understanding Faulkner's life and large body of literature. For me, the history and geography of Marshall County and Holly Springs, Mississippi, have been a disjointed collection of stories filled with folklore. Hubert

McAlexander's *A Southern Tapestry: Marshall County, Mississippi, 1935–2000* offered me significant enlightenment.

Perhaps my greatest regret is not taking more advantage of my mother's and father's relatives' long association with the Falkners and the Butlers. One of my great aunts, who lived into the 1970s, appears in both of Faulkner's school pictures, which are repeatedly reproduced from the Cofield photograph collection at the University of Mississippi. I should have interviewed the sons of my great-uncle, who was a member of "General" Stone's annual November hunts to the Delta, often going ahead to set up the camp. He died at age one hundred, one year before I began my research on Faulkner. I regret not accepting an invitation from one of my mother's cousins in Oxford, who sent me a message that if I was writing about William Faulkner, *she could tell me all about him*, for she had known him all of her life.

My initial research for the Faulkner project was supported by two grants from the Graduate School of the University of Tennessee, Knoxville. Maps were drafted over several years by Will Fontanez, Director of the Department of Geography's Cartography Laboratory at the University of Tennessee, Knoxville, and by several graduate assistants who worked in the laboratory.

I appreciate George F. Thompson, founder and director of the Center for American Places at Columbia College Chicago, for his enthusiasm and confidence in my study. With his usual patience, George waited through several missed deadlines as I expanded the manuscript. He oversaw the review and editing before the manuscript went to press.

I especially thank Mary Ann, my wife, who was more than just a proofreader of the manuscript. She advised me on what to include and to omit and discussed some of the finer points of Faulkner's novels and short stories.

William Faulkner and the Southern Landscape

ONE

Faulkner's Vanishing South

Persons who visit Oxford and Lafayette County, Mississippi, to experience the flavor of Jefferson and Yoknapatawpha County are elated to have reached the storied places but are frequently disappointed in not finding all that they anticipate on the landscape, arranged geographically the way they expect. During the years since Faulkner's Yoknapatawpha saga suddenly ended with his unexpected death in 1962, sweeping geographic, social, economic, and political changes, well underway in Faulkner's time, have reached fruition in Mississippi and the South. The basic geographical framework of the Lafayette County and Oxford that Faulkner knew, including roads and place names, remain, but much of the color of his time is gone. Forests dominate the landscape that at mid–twentieth century had large expanses of cotton and cornfields surrounded by pastures. Cotton is still grown, but machines and chemicals have replaced the legions of people and mules that once toiled in the fields from daybreak to sundown from April into November.

In 2002, the fortieth anniversary of Faulkner's death, Oxford was a progressive small city of twelve thousand, not the agricultural town of thirty-four hundred the writer knew. Oxford, described by a journalist as "a picture-perfect Southern town with a long, tantalizing list of amenities," is popular with retirees and persons who commute to jobs in Memphis.[1] Tobacco-chewing farmers in bib overalls no longer flock to the courthouse square on Saturdays, and with them have vanished the dust-covered wagons and pickup trucks loaded with watermelons parked around the courthouse on hot summer days. The stores on the square that served an agrarian society are gone, replaced by businesses that cater to an affluent nonfarm population and to the University of Mississippi student body that since 1940 has grown from fourteen hundred to more than ten thousand. Faulkner's characters would have difficulty moving among businesses such as the Old Venice Pizza Company, the Kaleidoscope, and Muss Madness. Of the major retail businesses around the courthouse square when Faulkner died in 1962, only one, Neilson's department store, remained forty-five years later. Changing with the times, Neilson's has survived on the square since 1839.

Despite renovations in the 1970s and 1990s, the courthouse remains largely unchanged from the way it was at the time of Faulkner's death, from peeling white paint on the exterior to the musty courtroom on the second story. But the old jail was razed and replaced by a new one on the site in the early 1960s, and the second jail was superseded by the Lafayette County Detention Center, a much larger facility built in the 1990s two blocks west of the square. The Chancery Clerk's Office and its records vault were moved from the courthouse to a new building on the site of the old jail. Ancient annals of Lafayette County, once read by the dim glow of candles and whale oil lamps, leap to life in a bright spacious room with many windows and contemporary electric lights.

Because of a recent attitude toward preservation among Oxford's business leaders, there is little danger that the courthouse and other buildings with historical significance will be destroyed. With the university, new shopping centers, and proximity to Sardis Lake and metropolitan Memphis, Oxford has the potential to become the type of small city that at the commencement of the twenty-first century many Americans perceive as ideal. Many of the more than twenty thousand tourists who visit Oxford each year are drawn by Faulkner, and in the 1980s entrepreneurs began to discover this tourist potential. One factor in Oxford's movement to preserve buildings is recognition of their relationship to the fictional Jefferson.

However, to the visitor, few landscape symbols indicate that Oxford was the home of William Faulkner. Even after he won the 1949 Nobel Prize for Literature, Faulkner continued to live simply among his fellow Mississippians. Almost half a century after his death, no large signs advertise New Albany, Mississippi, as the birthplace of William Faulkner or Oxford as the home of the noted writer. The historical marker for St. Peter's Cemetery indicates that it is the burial place of Supreme Court justice L. Q. C. Lamar and other prominent early settlers, but the location of Faulkner's simple monument was not marked with a historical plaque until a number of years after his death. By 2000 restrained ways to capitalize on Faulkner had begun to emerge. Faulkner's home, Rowan Oak, was purchased by the university. Still secluded from the street, it is maintained much as he left it. Not until 1988 was a historical marker erected at the entrance to the property.

Faulkner buffs, both local and foreign, scout Oxford and the Lafayette County countryside in increasing numbers, trying to identify landscape sites and buildings and searching for persons who knew Faulkner or were sources for his fictional characters. They tend to forget that 1997 marked the one-hundredth anniversary of the writer's birth. During recent decades many objects of Faulkner's South have rapidly vanished from the landscape, and persons known to the writer have died. Several years ago the Illinois Central Gulf Railroad abandoned and sold its tracks that passed through Oxford. The route is now a short line, the Mississippi Central Railroad, two streaks of rust that extend from the Oxford industrial park north of the city to the Norfolk Southern Railroad at Grand Junction, Tennessee. Mississippi Central is the original name of the north–south railroad built across the state just prior to the Civil War. Because there was no buyer for the tracks past the station and the university and south of Oxford, they were torn out. With the tracks gone, the east side of the deep Hilgard Cut was graded down and the Gertrude C. Ford Center for the Performing Arts and a parking lot were constructed. The railroad station was preserved and renovated.

Almost all of the pre–Civil War plantation big houses have vanished from the Lafayette County countryside. Even most of the ramshackle tenant houses in which a multitude of blacks and whites lived in the depths of poverty at the time Faulkner wrote his major works have been razed or sit decaying in the backcountry. Like Rowan Oak, most of the few big houses that survive are renovated. With their fresh coats of white paint and neatly mowed yards, the houses do not resemble the eerie, musty, and decaying gothiclike structures among overgrown gardens that Faulkner knew (figs. 1.1 and 1.2).

The attitude of a number of local contemporaries toward Faulkner is revealed in a statement by John Cullen, among the first persons who tried to profit from their association with the writer:

> No one is interested in good and loyal citizens because they are usual. . . . But we do have 9999½ good citizens for every one Taylor or Snopes. Outsiders read Faulkner's books and think the people of our country are all ignorant and heathen. . . . It is hard for me to believe that the shy and almost prudish William Faulkner I have known could have written *The Hamlet*. This story of low-class people living in Mississippi is greatly exaggerated. . . . I wish that William had written more about some of the noble people here in our county whom I knew.[2]

But Faulkner was never the outcast in Oxford that some critics would have you believe he was. Faulkner was a member of a large, respected family and had good friends among local residents. He also had deep roots in the community (fig. 1.3). The original fifty-acre town of Oxford was surveyed in 1838 by Charles Butler, Faulkner's great-grandfather. Only when Faulkner began to publicly support equal rights for blacks did some of his fellow townsfolk abandon him. Although most residents of Oxford largely ignored Faulkner during his lifetime, they now freely discuss him. More than just a few have read Faulkner's books and short stories. Some of the rapidly vanishing older residents who knew the writer repeat well-seasoned yarns, invent new ones, and glory in having known the eccentric man some once called "Curious Bill," "Count No 'Count," and other such belittling names. Others who never knew Faulkner readily discuss "Mr. Bill." Among them was Willie Morris, the tragic young innovative editor of *Harper's*, who unintentionally resigned, lost his way, and eventually moved to Oxford. On the David Frost

Figure 1.1. The Yancey Wiley house at College Hill, Mississippi, about 1930. The house was built in 1850 by Wiley, one of the wealthiest planters in Lafayette County. Wiley in 1860 owned twenty-one hundred acres and a large number of slaves (Hathorn [1938], 223). By 1930 the house had changed ownership, had not been painted for many years, and had deteriorated structurally. The gardens were overgrown, and the lines of cedar trees along the drive leading to the house were unkempt. Symbolically, the house represented the decline of agriculture and of the elite planter class. Harmon Collection.

Figure 1.2. The Yancey Wiley house at College Hill, Mississippi, in 1987. The house was owned by James M. (Jimmy) Faulkner, William Faulkner's nephew. Renovation and modernization of Old South plantation big houses and reorganization of their grounds make them more inhabitable. But elimination of the deterioration removes the aura of the planter houses captured in Faulkner's fiction. Charles S. Aiken. Courtesy of the James M. Faulkner family.

Figure 1.3. Sketch of William Faulkner in 1934 at age thirty-seven. By 1934 Faulkner had published nine books and several short stories and was recognized as an emerging major American writer. Sketch by Sykes Kennon. *Oxford Magazine*, copy 1, April 1, 1934, 13. Mississippi Department of Archives and History.

television show in 1970, Morris concocted an anecdote about sailing around Sardis Lake with "Mr. Bill, whom he had not known."[3]

Among the factors in the new openness are the widespread changes that came to Mississippi after Faulkner's death. Faulkner and his world, with many of its peculiar characters burlesqued from reality, belong to the past.[4] Persons who may recognize models for characters in Faulkner's stories can rationally dissociate themselves from them. Also, the saga of Temple Drake, the lynching of Joe Christmas, and other Faulkner fictional episodes that shocked and outraged many Mississippians several decades ago seem bland in a more permissive age. Most of the residents of Oxford, Lafayette County, and Mississippi were born after Faulkner's death in 1962 and did not know him or his world. Younger generations campaign for more public recognition of the writer. The most overt recognition of the writer on Oxford's courthouse square is a controversial bronze statue of Faulkner sitting on a bench in front of the former federal courthouse, which is now the Oxford City Hall (fig. 1.4).[5]

In the following pages I revisit Faulkner country where I was born and where my parents, younger brother, and ancestors are buried. Four overarching geographical questions guide my venture into the world of William Faulkner. How did Faulkner convert the local geography into a fictional one? Consciously or unconsciously, did he follow certain patterns and use particular techniques? Second, did Faulkner create Yoknapatawpha County as a microcosm of the American South? Is his world the South in miniature? Third, in what ways do the historical geographies of Oxford and Lafayette County emulate those of Jefferson and Yoknapatawpha County? Faulkner's stories begin at the time of European contact with the natives of the area that became Mississippi. His Yoknapatawpha saga continues through settlement, the Civil War, and the New South era. Faulkner's death in 1962 came during the

Figure 1.4. The controversial bronze statue of William Faulkner sitting on a bench in front of the former federal courthouse (now the Oxford, Mississippi, city hall), looking across the county courthouse square. The statue was erected more than three decades after Faulkner's death in 1962. Charles S. Aiken, 2004.

transition from the New South to the Modern South, which commenced in the upheavals of the Great Depression and Second World War and continued through the turmoil of the civil rights era. During his last years, the writer struggled to come to grips with the civil rights movement and impending sweeping changes in race relations. Even though Faulkner's stories are fiction, do they accurately portray the landscape and history of the place in Mississippi where he locates Jefferson and Yoknapatawpha County? Finally, what is Faulkner's geographical legacy?

Since the 1930s, especially since Faulkner was awarded the 1949 Nobel Prize for Literature, various persons have written of parallels between the history and, to a lesser extent, the geography of Oxford and Lafayette County, and that of fictional Jefferson and Yoknapatawpha County. Such persons belong to one of three principal categories: locals, including members of Faulkner's family, who publish remembrances; amateur outlanders, some of whom readily accept almost any story about Faulkner, Oxford, Lafayette County, and the American South as fact; and serious scholars who have undertaken careful investigations of the relationship of the actual to the fiction and have guided criticism into the theoretical domain. My remembrances began with trips to Lafayette County when I was a child and the stories told to me by my maternal grandmother. My formal research into Faulkner's world began in 1974, but most of it was conducted between 2000 and 2005. My approach, methodology, and sources are primarily those of historical geography.

Scholars debate over which versions of Faulkner's works, especially his novels, should be used in literary criticism. Faulkner was deliberate in the way he wrote and employed words, sentences, phrases, and punctuation. He broke rules of grammar, spelling, and composition and had problems with editors and typesetters correcting his narratives. For this reason, Faulkner gave a specific directive for the typescript copy of *Go Down, Moses*: "Note to Printer . . . DO NOT CHANGE PUNCTUATION NOR CONSTRUCTION."[6] Although first editions of novels and stories may contain minor errors, Faulkner carefully read the page proofs of his works before they went to press. Because first editions of novels are an authentic base, I use them. Faulkner's stories, essays, and other printed material appear in various magazines, journals, and newspapers. Except where noted, I use the 1977 edition of *Collected Stories of William Faulkner* and the 1965 first printing of Faulkner's *Essays, Speeches, and Public Letters by William Faulkner*.

Those who write about the South and American race relations are confronted with the dilemma of which term to use to refer to persons of African American descent. During Faulkner's life *Negro, colored, black*, and particular derogatory terms were employed by both races. To achieve realism, Faulkner's stories contain both polite and derogatory racial language. In the 1960s *black* emerged as a word of pride in Negro culture and has continued to be used. More recently, African American and Afro-American began to be employed. Because black was the most widely accepted term when I wrote the manuscript, I primarily use it. To achieve the impact that Faulkner intends, in most quotations I leave the language that he employs.

TWO

Geographical Fact into Fiction

Vital to the interpretation of William Faulkner's work is the realization that he was raised in an atmosphere in which the past was considered a better time than the present. Faulkner was born in 1897 in New Albany, Mississippi. In 1902 his family moved to Oxford, where he lived almost all the remainder of his life.[1] Oxford was less than seventy years old in 1902, but, like a person whose difficult life has accelerated the aging process, so the inability of many persons of earlier generations to deal effectively with the tragedies of the Civil War and Reconstruction made history seem ancient. The poverty of the postwar period created a backward-looking people who, by the turn of the century, had begun to romanticize the antebellum era and the Civil War.

Fact, Basis of Fiction

Although by 1900 mythmaking had romanticized the past out of proportion, Oxford and Lafayette County achieved relative prosperity and prominence between 1840 and 1880, when Mississippi enjoyed its greatest relative prosperity and national stature. Lafayette was one of several counties created within the 1832 Chickasaw land cession. Covering all of north Mississippi and a portion of Alabama, the Chickasaw domain was one of the last large Indian tracts east of the Mississippi River. The region was topographically diverse, ranging from the poorly drained Yazoo Basin (the Delta) on the west to the undulating fall-line hills on the east. At the time of the cession, two north–south oriented areas, the Black Belt (Prairie Belt) and the Loess Plains, were considered the prime agricultural lands. Lafayette County was created one tier of counties south of the Tennessee-Mississippi border at the eastern margin of the Loess Plains (map 2.1). Under the terms of the cession treaty, land-sale proceeds went to the Chickasaws. After the area was surveyed, each Chickasaw family was assigned one or more 640-acre sections.[2] Beginning in 1836, with the federal government acting as agent, the land was sold, with the allotment deeds bearing the names of Indians as grantors. Because the Loess Plains were perceived as prime cotton lands, large numbers of immigrants soon began to arrive in Lafayette County, mostly from the Carolinas, Georgia, Alabama, and

Tennessee. Described as a "magnificent country for planters," by 1860 approximately one-fourth of the county's 913 farms were plantations, and 7,129 of the 16,125 inhabitants were slaves.[3] During the period of prominence, Oxford was chosen as the location of the federal court for the Northern District of Mississippi, and the University of Mississippi was established at the western edge of the town whose very name anticipated the university's creation.

Some Faulkner critics, many of whom were not raised in the South, fail to comprehend fully the significance and lingering impact that the Civil War and Reconstruction held for the region. Ward Miner, for example, dismisses both events as relatively unimportant to Faulkner's fiction. Although no major battles were fought in northwestern Mississippi, the Civil War's physical realities came twice to Lafayette County in dramatic fashion. In the autumn of 1862, following the battles of Shiloh and Corinth that spring, the Union army under the command of Generals Ulysses S. Grant and William T. Sherman began a movement southward through Lafayette County toward Vicksburg. In December 1862 Grant occupied Oxford, while Sherman camped with thirty thousand troops four miles to the northwest at College Hill, a prosperous Presbyterian community that focused on North Mississippi College.[4] The countryside, especially in the vicinity of College Hill, was looted and some houses were burned. However, Union forces retreated after Confederates under General Earl Van Dorn made a daring raid on Grant's storage base at Holly Springs, twenty-five miles north of Oxford, and burned his stockpile of military supplies for the Vicksburg campaign.[5] During an August 1864 campaign to locate and destroy General Nathan Bedford Forrest, Union troops under the command of General Andrew J. Smith burned a substantial part of Oxford, including the courthouse and railroad station.[6] In addition to physical destruction, the war brought financial ruin to a number of prosperous Lafayette County families who owned slaves and who had invested heavily in Confederate scrip. Moreover, many of the men who marched to war never returned. At least 260,000 southerners lost their lives in the war, including 25 percent of military-age men.[7]

The Lafayette County that Faulkner knew was a large, rectangular political unit drained in the north by the Tallahatchie and in the south by the Yocona, a river whose name was corrupted from the older Indian name "Yockeney-Patafa" or Yoknapatawpha (map 2.1).[8] The county had several incorporated places, but the only significant town was Oxford, near the center of the county on the drainage divide between the two rivers. Like other Mississippi counties, Lafayette was divided into five minor civil divisions called beats. Each beat had a constable, a justice of the peace, and a commissioner. The five beat commissioners composed the county's governing body, the Board of Police. Roads that were dirt and gravel during most of Faulkner's lifetime radiated from Oxford in all principal directions

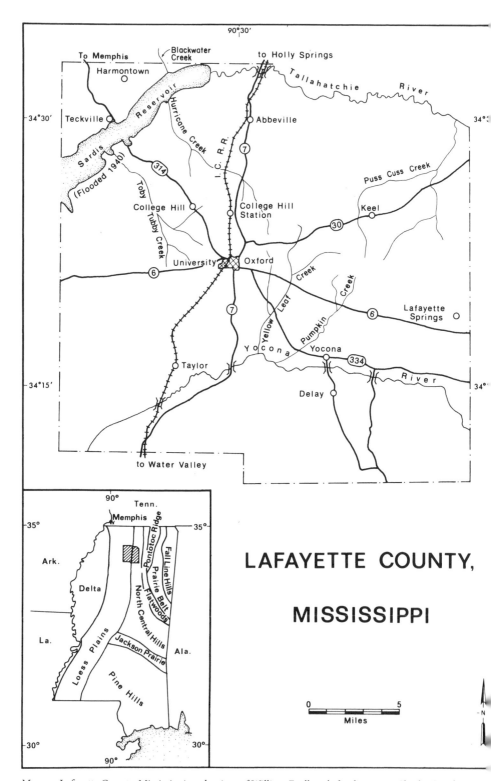

Map 2.1. Lafayette County, Mississippi, at the time of William Faulkner's death in 1962. Charles S. Aiken.

except southwest. The most important one ran northwest to Memphis, seventy miles away. In the late 1930s, Sardis Lake, a New Deal flood-control reservoir built in the Tallahatchie Valley, flooded a large portion of north Lafayette County, severing the Memphis-Oxford Road. Despite poor roads, Oxford was far from isolated. The Illinois Central Railroad, originally built in the 1850s as the Mississippi Central, crossed Lafayette County from south to north, passing through Oxford. In the heyday of rail travel, four daily passenger trains ran in each direction, giving Oxford direct service to Jackson, the state capital, and to New Orleans. Memphis could be reached in a few hours by transferring from the Illinois Central to the St. Louis–San Francisco (Frisco) at Holly Springs.

Lafayette County is marked by physical diversity. In 1860 Eugene W. Hilgard, an agriculturalist-geologist-geographer at the University of Mississippi, described Lafayette County as composed of two basic soil-physical areas, divided at a line "drawn from the N.E. corner (the mouth of Pouskous Creek [Puss Cuss Creek]) to the head of Yellow Leaf, down that creek to its mouth, and thence nearly due S" (map 2.1). North and west of this line lay the best agricultural lands of the county, ranging from the "fine cotton uplands" or "table lands" covered by two to four feet of "yellow loam" (loess) to the Tallahatchie River bottom, which "though always very fertile," was subject to frequent overflow. To the south and east of the dividing line lay the "'Pine Hill' lands" and most of the Yockeney-Patafa bottom. In the Pine Hills the loess veneer was shallow or absent, and "the sandy summits of the narrow ridges" offered "little inducement for cultivation." The Yockeney-Patafa bottom, though better than the hill lands, was considered inferior to the Tallahatchie bottom because the spring overflows drained away slowly. As a consequence the soils were "generally heavy and disposed to be 'cold.'"[9]

The agricultural settlement patterns of Lafayette County evolved against this environmental backdrop. Land speculators and initial settlers perceived the northern and western parts of the county to have the greatest agricultural potential, and these areas were quickly patented. Northern and western Lafayette County had the greatest number of plantations, the largest black populations, and the highest cotton acreages and per-acre yields.[10] The area south and southeast of Hilgard's line became primarily the domain of white farmers with small holdings. The cultural differences within Lafayette County persisted throughout the nineteenth and twentieth centuries and into the twenty-first.

Although Oxford changed during Faulkner's lifetime, the town's morphology remained basically the same. The town focused on the county courthouse square (figs. 2.1 and 2.2; map 2.2). Facing the courthouse from four sides were the principal businesses that served an agrarian society. Chilton's Drugstore, Tate Merchandise Company, Buffaloe's Cafe, Patton Hardware, Neilson's department store, the Bank

Figure 2.1. Aerial view of Oxford and the countryside to the north in 1949. "Jefferson, the center radiating weakly its puny glow into space; beyond it, enclosing it, spreads the County" (Faulkner *The Town* 1957, 315). "A Square, the courthouse in its grove the center; quadrangular around it, the stores, two-storey, the offices of the lawyers and doctors and dentists, the lodge-rooms and auditoriums above them; school and church and tavern and bank and jail each in its ordered place" (Faulkner *Requiem for a Nun* 1951, 39). Courtesy of Special Collections, University of Tennessee Libraries.

of Oxford, the Merchants and Farmers Bank, the First National Bank, McElroy's Grocery Store, and the Colonial Hotel were among the firms that came and went and, in part, survived through the twentieth century (figs. 2.3 and 2.4). The federal courthouse for the Northern District of Mississippi was on the eastern side of the square; behind it rose the town's water tower, and beyond the water tower was the Baggett cotton gin and warehouse and the Avant cotton gin. The county jail was one block from the square on the street now known as North Lamar, a thorough-fare that, like its counterpart South Lamar across the square, was lined with businesses and beyond them houses of the town's elite (fig. 2.5).

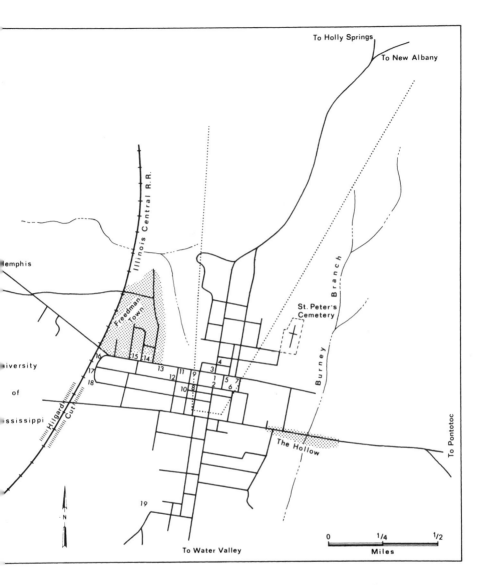

To Holly Springs

To New Albany

Illinois Central R.R.

Memphis

Freedman Town

St. Peter's Cemetery

Burney Branch

University

of

Mississippi

Hilgard Cut

The Hollow

To Pontotoc

N

19

0   1/4   1/2

Miles

To Water Valley

ette County Courthouse	11 St. Peter's Episcopal Church
:derate monument	12 First Baptist Church
ial Hotel and First National Bank	13 African Methodist Episcopal Church (AME) (black)
ette County jail	14 Second Baptist Church (black)
al courthouse	15 Baptist Church (black)
rd waterworks	16 Illinois Central railroad station
tt cotton gin and warehouse	17 petroleum tanks
movie theater	18 Oxford Electric Light Plant (not in use)
odist Church	19 William Faulkner's Rowan Oak (Shegog-Bailey house)
Presbyterian Church	

2. Oxford, Mississippi, circa 1925–1950. The dashed line outlines the area shown in fig. 2.1. Compiled
les S. Aiken from *Oxford, Mississippi, Quadrangle*, U.S. Department of the Interior, Geological Survey,
(1943), and the *Insurance Map of Oxford, Mississippi*, Sanborn Map Company, 1925.

Figure 2.2. The Lafayette County Courthouse in 1949. Constructed in the 1870s, the building replaced the original courthouse, which was burned by Union troops on August 22, 1864. Additions to the east and west sides were made a few years before Faulkner's death in 1962. Courtesy of Special Collections, University of Tennessee Libraries.

Figure 2.3. Stores on the east side of Oxford's courthouse square in 1949. Although the ownership has changed over time, Neilson's department store, Oxford's oldest business, has survived on the square since 1839. Courtesy of Special Collections, University of Tennessee Libraries.

Figure 2.4. The Colonial Hotel in 1949. The hotel was on the northwest corner of Oxford's courthouse square and for many years during Faulkner's lifetime was the town's only lodge. The building still exists but is now used for offices. The lot was originally owned by Charles Butler, Faulkner's maternal great-grandfather, who built the Oxford Inn and a livery stable on the site. The inn was destroyed when Oxford was torched by Union troops in 1864. Courtesy of Special Collections, University of Tennessee Libraries.

The Illinois Central Railroad ran along Oxford's western edge, separating the town from the University of Mississippi. For part of the distance the tracks were in the deep Hilgard Cut, and the main access to the campus was across a bridge over the chasm. Oxford's electric power plant, the railroad depot, and the bulk storage tanks of Standard Oil and other petroleum companies were at the northern end of the cut (fig. 2.6).

A few blacks lived interspersed among whites in cabins behind the houses of the elite, in the typical fashion of small southern towns that originated before the Civil War. But Oxford had one prominent black section, whose name, Freedman Town, revealed both its origin and date. Throughout most of the twentieth century Freedman Town was a crowded area of shacks among which were a few substantial dwellings of wealthier blacks. Its narrow streets were unpaved, and most houses had neither plumbing nor electricity long after most dwellings of whites had them.[11] Smaller black settlements were the Hollow, a small cluster of shacks at Oxford's eastern edge on the road leading to Pontotoc, and the community of St. Paul beyond the university on Batesville Road. Oxford's principal churches, the white

Figure 2.5. The old Lafayette County, Mississippi, jail in 1949. The building, which was a block north of the courthouse square, was razed in the 1960s and a new jail built on the site. "It was of brick, square, proportioned with four brick columns in shallow bas-relief across the front and even a brick cornice under the eaves because it was old, built in a time when people took time to build even jails with grace and care.... In fact it still looked like a residence with its balustraded wooden gallery stretching across the front of the lower floor. But above that the brick was windowless" (Faulkner *Intruder in the Dust* 1948, 49–51). Courtesy of Special Collections, University of Tennessee Libraries.

Baptist, Methodist, Episcopalian, and Presbyterian, and the black Second Baptist and African Methodist Episcopal, lay between the railroad and the square. At Oxford's eastern fringe was St. Peter's Cemetery, the town's principal burial ground. Used for both whites and blacks, the cemetery was divided into racial sections by a prominent but invisible line.

Also at the fringe of Oxford were a few houses that sat on sizable tracts; among them was a modified Greek Revival manse built in 1848 by Robert Shegog, an early merchant (fig. 2.7). The house was a decaying heap known as the Bailey place throughout half of Faulkner's life. In 1930 he purchased it for his home, named it Rowan Oak, and over the years continually attempted to renovate and enlarge it. More than 80 percent of the contents of the house at the time of Faulkner's death are still in place. The interior has a number of new features found in Oxford houses in the 1950s, from the open-flame chill-chaser gas heaters to the wall decor. There

Figure 2.6. Former Illinois Central Railroad station in Oxford, Mississippi, in 1974. The building was constructed after the Civil War by the Mississippi Central Railroad to replace the original station, which was burned by the Union army in August 1864. Charles S. Aiken.

Figure 2.7. Rowan Oak, Faulkner's home, in 1976. The house was built in 1848 by Robert Shegog, an Oxford merchant. Heated by fireplaces and without plumbing and screens on doors and windows, such houses were cold in the winter and full of vermin in the summer. A moldering ruin, the dwelling and surrounding acreage was purchased by Faulkner in 1930. A detached brick kitchen was at the rear. The narrow two-story portico is typical of houses built by planters and merchants in north Mississippi during the two decades preceding the Civil War. Compared with the townhouses of Charleston, South Carolina, and the elaborate dwellings of the Natchez district, the house is quite plain. Charles S. Aiken.

is little evidence that two costly renovations by the university were necessary to maintain the house as Faulkner left it.

In June 1929 Faulkner married Estelle Oldham Franklin, a divorced childhood friend with two children. Faulkner, Estelle, and Estelle's two children moved to Rowan Oak in June 1930. Two girls were born to the couple. Alabama arrived two months premature in January 1931 and died a few days later. Jill was born in June 1933.[12]

Fiction, Mutation of Fact

Strong parallels exist between the history of Yoknapatawpha County and that of Lafayette. Faulkner deals with the removal of the Indians, white settlement, the Civil War, the leadership decay, and the poverty of the postwar period. Geographical parallels between the real and the fictional are striking. Close examination of Faulkner's simple maps of Yoknapatawpha County, drawn in 1936 for *Absalom, Absalom!* and in 1945 for *The Portable Faulkner*, reveals minor dissimilarities, but if they are accepted for what they really are, two quickly sketched mental maps of the same area, then they are the same.[13] Comparison of the map of Yoknapatawpha with that of Lafayette County reveals obvious parallels, even to the casual observer (maps 2.1 and 2.3). Like Lafayette, Yoknapatawpha is a rectangular county drained in the north by the Tallahatchie and in the south by the Yoknapatawpha. Like Oxford, Jefferson is located on a divide, which Faulkner termed the "Pine Hills," between the two rivers. Roads radiate from Jefferson in all principal directions except southwest, as they do from Oxford. Sartoris's railroad, running north toward Memphis Junction and south toward Mottstown, crosses Yoknapatawpha County, passing through the western portion of Jefferson, as the Illinois Central crossed Lafayette County, passing through the western part of Oxford (fig. 2.8).

Like Lafayette County, Yoknapatawpha has subregions, prominent places, and landmarks, many of which are not shown on Faulkner's simple maps. Details are given for five antebellum plantations—Sutpen's Hundred, Compson's Mile, Grenier's Frenchman's Bend, the McCaslin, and the Sartoris—of which only two, the McCaslin and the Sartoris, remain viable into the twentieth century. With the exception of Grenier's, all are in the northern and western portions of Yoknapatawpha, which, as in Lafayette County, are the principal plantation areas. Acknowledging these areas as plantation country implies much more than mere ownership of land, for plantation country is where the county's traditional leaders reside. This is the idea that Gavin Stevens expresses in *The Town* when he sees the region as "the same fat black rich plantation earth still synonymous of the proud fading white plantation names whether we—I mean of course they—ever actually owned

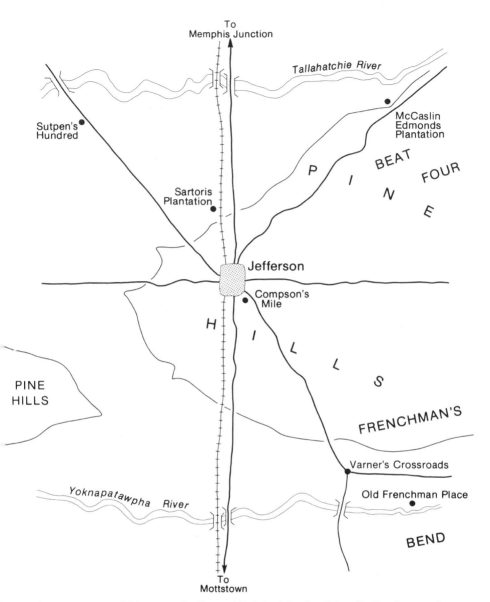

To
Memphis Junction

Tallahatchie River

Sutpen's
Hundred

McCaslin
Edmonds
Plantation

P   I   BEAT
N   FOUR
E

Sartoris
Plantation

Jefferson

Compson's
Mile

H   I   L   L   S

PINE
HILLS

FRENCHMAN'S

Varner's Crossroads

Yoknapatawpha   River

Old Frenchman Place

BEND

To
Mottstown

ap 2.3. A composite map of Yoknapatawpha County, Mississippi, developed from Faulkner's maps of
knapatawpha in *Absalom, Absalom!* 1936 and Cowley *The Portable Faulkner* 1946. Charles S. Aiken.

Figure 2.8. The Illinois Central Railroad across the lonely Tallahatchie River bottom in Lafayette County in 1941. The steel bridge over the river, which was built in the first decade of the twentieth century, is in the distance. Unidentified photographer. Courtesy of the U.S. Army Corps of Engineers, Vicksburg District Office, Vicksburg, Mississippi.

a plantation or not: . . . generals and governors and judges, soldiers (even if only Cuban lieutenants) and statesmen failed or not, and simple politicians and over-reachers and just simple failures."[14]

In direct contrast to the plantation region of northern and western Yoknapa-tawpha County are the poor-white-farmer areas of the east and southeast. Five miles east of Jefferson in the Pine Hills is Beat Four, a minor civil division of poor whites, a "region of lonely pine hills dotted meagerly with small tilted farms and peripatetic sawmills and contraband whiskey-kettles." Avoided by blacks and by white strangers, Beat Four is a "synonym for independence and violence: an idea with physical boundaries like a quarantine for plague."[15] At the southern edge of the Pine Hills and in the Yoknapatawpha River bottom is Frenchman's Bend, a ter-ritory "definite yet without boundaries." Its hub is Varner's Crossroads, a hamlet with a store, sawmill, cotton gin, school, church, and an inn known as Littlejohn's Hotel. Although the ruin of the Grenier plantation big house, known as the old Frenchman place, is nearby, Frenchman's Bend is not plantation country. After Grenier, poor whites came, including the infamous Varners and Snopes: "They took up land and built one- and two-room cabins and never painted them. . . . Their descendants still planted cotton in the bottom land and corn along the edge of the hills and in the secret coves in the hills made whiskey of the corn. . . . They were Protestants and Democrats and prolific; there was not one negro landowner in the entire section. Strange negroes would absolutely refuse to pass through it after dark."[16]

The distinctions between Beat Four and Frenchman's Bend may seem minor, but, considered in the context of relative poverty and the early twentieth-century Populist movement in Mississippi, they are profound. The families of the former region are poorer, less ambitious, and more clannish than those of the latter. Poor whites of Beat Four, though political allies of those of Frenchman's Bend, offer little political or economic threat to the old Bourbon families of the northern and western parts of Yoknapatawpha. Viewed from the northwest, Frenchman's Bend, however, with its zealous rednecks is seen as "cradle of Varners and ant-heap for the northeast crawl of Snopes."[17]

Throughout his fiction Faulkner leaves no doubt as to the exact location of Yoknapatawpha County. Like Lafayette, it is in the loess region of northwestern Mississippi east of the Yazoo Delta and south of Memphis. Faulkner frequently uses the expressions "north Mississippi" and "northern Mississippi," and in several places he indicates the distance between Jefferson and Memphis. In *The Reivers* Boon Hogganbeck, upon arriving in the city, says to Lucius Priest, "Twenty-three and a half hours ago we were in Jefferson, Missipi, eighty miles away."[18] The most vivid description of the small-scale geographical context of the county is in *Intruder in the Dust*, where, from an imaginary vantage point at the eastern edge of Yoknapatawpha, Charles Mallison sees "his whole native land, his home . . . unfolding beneath him like a map in one slow soundless explosion: to the east ridge on green ridge tumbling away toward Alabama and to the west and south the checkered fields and the woods flowing on into the blue and gauzed horizon beyond which lay at last like a cloud the long wall of the levee and the great River itself flowing not merely from the north but out of the North."[19]

The setting of Yoknapatawpha is accurate even to perception of location. In *The Hamlet* the Pine Hills are characterized as "a region which topographically was the final blue and dying echo of the Appalachian mountains."[20] Of course, Lafayette County is on the coastal plain, far removed from the Appalachian Highlands. Superficially, it appears that Faulkner is attempting to conceal the location of his county by such a statement or has simply found "dying echo of the Appalachian mountains" a pleasing phrase. Actually he is merely reiterating a commonly held belief in north Mississippi—that the prominent hills are the end remnants of Appalachia.

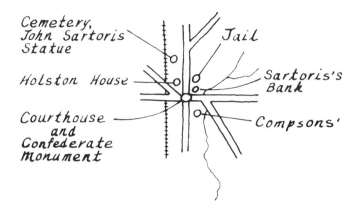

JEFFERSON, MISSISSIPPI

Map 2.4. A map of Jefferson, Mississippi, developed from Faulkner's map
in *Absalom, Absalom!* 1936. Charles S. Aiken.

Although Faulkner does not use the term "loess," his descriptions of the yellow-brown soils and local topography of Yoknapatawpha are those of the eastern edge of the Loess Plains. He is especially taken with dust. Phrases like "the thick dust of the spent summer" and "a fading cloud of yellow dust" are common, and Faulkner even uses the term "dust" in the titles of two of his novels, *Flags in the Dust* and *Intruder in the Dust*.[21] In *The Unvanquished*, when Union soldiers burned the Sartoris plantation house, the "smoke boiled up, yellow and slow, and turning copper-colored in the sunset like dust."[22]

Faulkner never published a detailed map of Jefferson, but many landscape similarities between the fictional town and Oxford are readily identifiable (maps 2.2 and 2.4). Like Oxford's, Jefferson's principal black residential area is Freedmantown, and a smaller black settlement, the Hollow, is at the eastern margin of the town. Prominent white churches are Episcopalian, Presbyterian, Baptist, and Methodist. The parallels between individual components continue, but more important is that lengthy descriptions place various components in proper relationship to one another. As Faulkner's boyhood neighbor Calvin Brown Jr. observes, "Faulkner habitually imagines his characters moving about the square and streets of Oxford and the roads, hills, and swamps of Lafayette County," and "it follows that anyone who knows the town and county well will frequently recognize these settings."[23] In *Sartoris*, Horace Benbow, returning from the First World War, left Jefferson's railroad station, passed by the town's power plant, through a residential section, and then the "hill flattened away into the plateau on which the town proper had been built . . . and the street became definitely urban presently with garages and small shops." Next came "the picture show" and finally "the square, with its unbroken low skyline of old weathered brick and fading dead names."[24] Here Faulkner gives an accurate description of a traverse along Oxford's Second Depot (now Van Buren Avenue) from the railroad station to the Lafayette County courthouse.

The courthouse square is the setting of several episodes in Faulkner's works. One finds similar courthouse squares in towns across the South, but Faulkner's details of Jefferson's square are essentially the details of Oxford's, even to the soldier atop the Confederate monument. Faulkner's soldier does not face north toward the enemy, as does almost every other Confederate monument soldier, but stares south like the one in front of the Lafayette County Courthouse. The Yoknapatawpha County jail, like Lafayette County's former jail, is one block from the courthouse and sits diagonally across from what once was the town's principal inn.[25] The fictional jail, like the county's old one, resembles a residence more than a place of detention (fig. 2.5). This alone does not prove that Faulkner had the Lafayette County jail in mind as a pattern, for many of the older southern jails were built both as places to incarcerate prisoners and as residences for sheriffs or turnkeys. From Faulkner's complete description, however, no doubt exists about the jail he used as his model. Furthermore, the old jail was diagonally across from the Colonial Hotel, Oxford's principal inn throughout most of the twentieth century (fig. 2.4).

Many analogies exist between Oxford and Lafayette County and Jefferson and Yoknapatawpha County, but close scrutiny reveals profound breakdowns in parallels between the actual and the apocryphal. The fictional Varner's Crossroads corresponds with the real community of Yocona (Cornish at the time *The Hamlet* is set), but the history and the geography of the literary community are not those of reality (maps. 2.1 and 2.3). The Sartoris plantation, with its small railroad station, is located four miles north of Jefferson. Four miles north of Oxford is College Hill Station, a former flag stop on the Mississippi Central for North Mississippi College, two miles west at College Hill (figs. 2.9 and 2.10). The Illinois Central continued the name College Hill Station for a switch.[26] Although a parallel exists between the real and the fictional railroad station, a plantation similar to Sartoris did not exist at College Hill Station. Also, there never was a 640-acre plantation on the southeastern outskirts of Oxford where Faulkner places Compson's Mile, nor an airport on the southern margin of the town where he locates Jefferson's airport. Literary critics have been quick to note that Lafayette County contains 679 square miles whereas Faulkner fixed the area of Yoknapatawpha at 2,400 square miles. The 1940 population of Lafayette County was 21,257, 40 percent of whom were blacks, but

Figure 2.9. The last days of College Hill Station on the Illinois Central Gulf Railroad three miles north of Oxford, Mississippi, in 1974. The place is Faulkner's source for the fictional railroad flag stop on the Sartoris plantation. The station was created in the 1850s on the Mississippi Central Railroad for North Mississippi College at College Hill, two miles west. An Illinois Central Railroad switch maintained the name after the college closed and the place ceased to be a station. Abandoned and sold by the Illinois Central Gulf, the site is now an industrial park at the southern terminus of the Mississippi Central short line railroad. Charles S. Aiken.

in 1936 Faulkner indicated that the population of Yoknapatawpha was 15,611, 60 percent of whom were blacks.[27]

Although Faulkner readily acknowledged that Lafayette County was the source for Yoknapatawpha, he emphasized that while one was genuine the other was apocryphal.

> Beginning with *Sartoris* I discovered that my own little postage stamp of native soil
> was worth writing about and that I would never live long enough to exhaust it, and
> that by sublimating the actual into the apocryphal I would have complete liberty
> to use whatever talent I might have to its absolute top. It opened up a gold mine of
> other people, so I created a cosmos of my own. I can move these people around like
> God, not only in space but in time too.[28]

Yoknapatawpha, then, is not an actual place but a fictional mutation with certain of its geographical components drawn from a reality that was deliberately altered. This is known, but Faulkner's process in sublimating the actual geography has never been assessed.

Figure 2.10. College Hill Presbyterian Church in 1949. Constructed in 1840, the church was the chapel for the short-lived North Mississippi College, which closed at the beginning of the Civil War and never reopened. Slaves sat in the balcony, which was accessed by two exterior stairs on the front. Declining membership was reversed in recent years by an increase in University of Mississippi students at worship services. Courtesy of Special Collections, University of Tennessee Libraries.

Faulkner's Conversion Process

Faulkner never devised a master plan around which he designed all of his works and to which he strictly adhered. Some Faulkner critics assume that he carefully researched the material that went into his fiction. Faulkner admitted several times to having a "lumber room" of people from which he built his characters. At West Point in April 1962 during one of his last interviews, Faulkner stated that he drew from three primary sources: observation, experience (which includes reading), and imagination. Faulkner did not keep precise records or remember exact sources of everything in his stories.[29] Because he depended on observation, experience, and imagination rather than on research, Faulkner refused to write most solicited articles and approached those he undertook with trepidation. Concerning his preparation for an invited article on Vicksburg for *Harper's Bazaar*, Faulkner wrote: "I get nothing from VICKSBURG yet. I dont believe I shall get anything by going there. . . . That is, I can only do an imaginative piece, and Vicksburg is not my town for me to have the right to do an imaginative piece about it." In June 1960 Faulkner declined a five-thousand-dollar offer for a five-thousand-word article for *Life's* Civil War centennial series. "Even when I was young and 'hot,' I was never much of a 'to order' writer," he replied.[30] Also, in the face of efforts by some editors to correct Faulkner's novels and stories, the writer had little interest in rectifying inconsistencies in his work after he submitted a manuscript, except for ones that detracted from the story.[31]

Superficially, from the perspective of the entire body of Faulkner's fiction, it appears that the writer began with fully developed geographical concepts of Yoknapatawpha County and Jefferson. Such was not the case. Thomas McHaney discovered that the place name Yoknapatawpha does not appear in Faulkner's earliest stories. It is not in the initial Yoknapatawpha County chronicles, including *Sartoris* (1929), *The Sound and the Fury* (1929), and *Light in August* (1932). *As I Lay Dying* (1930) is the first novel in which Yoknapatawpha appears, and it is used only once. In *Flags in the Dust*, the longer manuscript from which *Sartoris* was extracted, the county is Yocona. With the map of Yoknapatawpha County that Faulkner drew for *Absalom, Absalom!* published in 1936, he began to come to grips with the larger geographical setting of his stories. Unlike Yoknapatawpha, the name Jefferson appears with regularity throughout Faulkner's early fiction: ten times in *The Sound and the Fury*, twenty-one in *As I Lay Dying*, and 110 in *Light in August*.[32]

Even though critics have noted inconsistencies in Faulkner's geography, they primarily are amazed by its general uniformity throughout his numerous works. Faulkner could maintain geographical consistency without a master plan because the framework was always Oxford and Lafayette County deliberately altered as he wrote each novel or short story. Faulkner intentionally left a number of clues to the way in which he worked, including his office at Rowan Oak. In addition to holograph and typed copies of manuscripts, he carefully preserved the outline for *A Fable*, which he rewrote on his office wall at Rowan Oak after it was accidentally painted over.[33]

Faulkner transmuted Lafayette into Yoknapatawpha by combining the real, the modified, and the imaginary. The geography of Lafayette County and Oxford was changed in four principal ways—names were altered, components were omitted, locations were shifted, and reality was blended with fabrication. Name change is the simplest technique he used. For the name of the southern river from which the fictional county takes its name, Faulkner reverted to the Yocona River's historic title, "Yoknapatawpha." He reached back into time, not only for this term but also for "Pine Hills," an archaic name for the central drainage divide of Lafayette County.[34] Faulkner literally found "Jefferson" in a street. Jefferson Avenue (formerly Cemetery Avenue) crosses North Lamar between Adams and Madison

Figure 2.11. The closed Galloway store at College Hill, Mississippi, in 1999. The New South–era country store had virtually disappeared by the beginning of the twenty-first century. The principal replacement is similar to an urban convenience market, often owned or franchised by petroleum companies and other corporations. Charles S. Aiken.

avenues, three blocks north of the courthouse square. Seminary Hill is a short distance northwest of Jefferson. The community has a "small dingy" store that is operated by a Mr. Garroway.[35] College Hill, four miles northwest of Oxford, is the real counterpart, where for many years a Mr. Galloway operated a small store (fig. 2.11). Whiteleaf Creek, a tributary of the Yoknapatawpha River, is located between Jefferson and Varner's Crossroads, whereas Yellow Leaf Creek is situated between Oxford and Yocona. Other examples of name changes are Wylie and Wyott for the extinct town of Wyatt, Mottstown for Water Valley, and Memphis Junction for Holly Springs. Within the town proper, Oxford's Colonial Hotel becomes Jefferson's Holston House, Neilson's department store changes to Widermark's, Chilton's Drugstore is transmuted to Christian's, and the Bank of Oxford becomes the Bank of Jefferson (figs. 2.3 and 2.4). Occasionally Faulkner made a Freudian slip, using the real name when he meant to substitute the fictional. In the manuscript of *Sartoris*, for instance, he wrote that "a hillman . . . built the handsomest house in Frenchman's Bend on the most beautiful lot in Oxford," which he quickly revised to "Jefferson."[36]

Omission of details is another simple way in which Faulkner altered the geography of Lafayette County. Yoknapatawpha is a model, and despite complexities it, like all models, is less abstruse than reality. If all of Faulkner's geographical descriptions and place names were fitted together to create a total map of Yoknapatawpha County, that map would be less than the whole of Lafayette County. North Mississippi College is not considered a part of historic Yoknapatawpha County, nor is the state regional agricultural high school that operated at College Hill during the first half of the twentieth century. There is only one hamlet, Varner's Crossroads, for which Faulkner gives many details, but in Lafayette County there are several, including Abbeville, Harmontown, and Paris. Places that are fascinating, in both name and folk history, such as Greasy Creek, Piera School, and Freesprings Church, never appear. The margins and the entire southwestern quarter of Lafayette County were not significant source regions for Faulkner, and even though they are shown on his maps of Yoknapatawpha County, we are told almost nothing about them.

Faulkner deliberately omitted several essential parts of Lafayette County. The University of Mississippi, a vital part of Oxford, is excluded from Jefferson. Described in several of his works, the university is located at a fictional "Oxford" forty or fifty miles from Jefferson. Faulkner enjoyed boating and fishing on Sardis Lake, but he never made it a vital part of Yoknapatawpha County. In "Two Soldiers," written shortly after the completion of Sardis Dam, he also banished the reservoir to the fictional Oxford.[37] Several years later, in *Big Woods* and *The Reivers*, however, Faulkner conceded that much of the Tallahatchie River bottom, where he set several of his sagas, had become a government reservoir. Like the lake, the federal courthouse of the Northern District of Mississippi is acknowledged but does not have a significant role.[38] Although Faulkner indicated that Yoknapatawpha was larger than Lafayette, the omission of geographical elements makes it smaller. The apocryphal county contains neither the detail nor the area of the county from which it was sublimated.

As Faulkner moved "people around like God, not only in space but in time too," so also he moved names, places, objects, and events. Assessment of his shifting locations and his blending of the real with the imagined is more fascinating and challenging than either his name changes or his omission of elements. One must first sort out the genuine from the imaginative, then establish the location of the real that one thinks may serve as the basis of fiction.

When Faulkner altered locations, temporal and spatial shifts were made at three scales: local, from a few yards to not more than two miles; county, intracounty transfers of more than two miles; and regional, intercounty shifts. Study of Faulkner's maps reveals a definite pattern that he followed to conceal reality thinly by altering locations at the local scale. Objects were simply shifted to the opposite side. The model for the church that is shown on his *Absalom, Absalom!* map as the "Church which Thomas Sutpen Rode Fast To" is College Hill Presbyterian, a small but imposing pre–Civil War structure that Faulkner moved from the western to the eastern side of the road (fig. 2.10). Sartoris's Bank is the First National Bank, which he switched from the northwestern to the northeastern quadrant of the square. Using Faulkner's descriptions and pursuing this line of reasoning, one could conclude that the basic model for Compson's Mile, at the southeastern margin of Jefferson, was probably the Shegog-Bailey house, with its pasture, later his Rowan Oak, at the southwestern margin of Oxford (maps 2.2, 2.3, and 2.4).[39] New Hope Church and Blackwater Creek are examples of real place names that were moved at the county scale by Faulkner. New Hope Church and its adjoining cemetery are in northwestern Lafayette County; a few miles to the east is Blackwater Creek, a swampy tributary of the Tallahatchie. Faulkner transferred both names to the southern portion of Yoknapatawpha County. New Hope is a church and cemetery near the Bundren house, and Blackwater Slough is a marshy area near Varner's Crossroads. Faulkner's positioning of the Jefferson airport at the southern margin of the town is an example of intracounty object transfer. The only airport that served Oxford for many years was a grass-covered strip in the Yocona River bottom, seven miles south of the town. In certain cases Faulkner employed wry humor and clever puzzles in creating fictional names. Taylor is a hamlet a few miles south of Oxford. The Latin for tailor is *sartor*, or *sartorius* in English. The Sartoris plantation and railroad flag stop are a few miles north of Jefferson. In this case Faulkner altered the name without changing the meaning, and he switched location at the county scale.[40]

Transfers at the regional scale are more difficult to assess than those at the local and county scales, for one needs to know almost every detail of Mississippi as Faulkner knew it. The best-known examples of intercounty transfer pertain to Colonel William C. Falkner, Faulkner's great-grandfather, and the Gulf and Chicago Railroad he built after the Civil War from Pontotoc, Mississippi, to Middleton, Tennessee. Colonel Falkner, who dropped the "u" from the family name, is the model for Colonel John Sartoris, who in the 1870s built the railroad that crosses Yoknapatawpha County. As Falkner was murdered by his partner in the railroad venture, so Sartoris is killed by his business associate. And as Falkner lies buried in replete Victorian gothic in the Ripley cemetery under a statue of himself staring at the former Gulf and Chicago, so Sartoris lies buried under his statue in the Jefferson cemetery gazing at his railroad (fig. 2.12).[41]

G. T. Buckley argued that only rarely did Faulkner use Oxford as a prototype of Jefferson, citing his employment of Ripley as supporting evidence.[42] But Oxford and Lafayette County always were his context for Jefferson and Yoknapatawpha County, with additional source material shifted to this base. Like the Ripley cemetery, in *Sartoris* the Jefferson cemetery is on the railroad, but the cemetery's

Figure 2.12. Monument above the grave of William Faulkner's great-grandfather, Colonel William C. Falkner in a Ripley, Mississippi, cemetery. The writer's great-grandfather was the source for fictional Colonel John Sartoris. Falkner's eight-foot statue faces the railroad, which he built after the Civil War. Author of *The White Rose of Memphis*, the colonel stands before a stack of books, a symbol of his literary career: "He stood on a stone pedestal, in his frock coat and bare-headed. . . . His head was lifted a little in that gesture of haughty pride which repeated itself generation after generation with a fateful fidelity. COLONEL JOHN SARTORIS, C.S.A. 1823–1876, Soldier, Statesman, Citizen of the World. *For man's enlightenment he lived / By man's ingratitude he died / Pause here, son of sorrow; remember death*" (Faulkner *Sartoris* 1929, 375). Charles S. Aiken, 1974.

description, complete to the racial sections, is that of Oxford's St. Peter's. Rather than describing Ripley and the Ripley cemetery, at the regional scale he shifted his great-grandfather's monument to the Oxford cemetery and then at the local scale shifted the position of the cemetery so that it is on the railroad.

Another example of regional transfer occurs in the spotted horses episode in *The Hamlet*, set at Littlejohn's Hotel in Varner's Crossroads. The story is based on an incident Faulkner witnessed while staying overnight at a boardinghouse in Calhoun County, thirty-five miles from Oxford. General Earl Van Dorn's raid to destroy Union army supplies at Holly Springs in Marshall County is also an example of an intercounty shift. In *Light in August* Faulkner places the historic event in Jefferson rather than at Memphis Junction, his fictional place that occupies the location of Holly Springs.[43]

The combination of fabrication with fact is the fourth principal way in which Faulkner altered geographical reality. Even he had difficulty evaluating the degrees of each in his works. A few months before his death he acknowledged that he did not know precisely how observation, experience, and imagination contributed to a story. "It's like having three tanks on a collector—you open the collector valve, you don't know exactly how much comes from any one tank, so no one can say just where anything comes from—whether he imagined it, whether he saw it or read it or heard it."[44]

The problem of separating fabrication from fact is illustrated by Sutpen's Hundred, the hundred-square-mile, sixty-four-thousand-acre plantation that Thomas Sutpen created in the wilderness as Yoknapatawpha County was settled. A landholding of this size may seem bigger than life and even fiction. Both Ward L. Miner and Elizabeth M. Kerr, though acknowledging the existence of large plantations in the South, argue that Sutpen's Hundred is unrealistic in relation to its location in Yoknapatawpha County.[45] Superficially, Sutpen's Hundred appears to be totally removed from fact.

Among the earliest settlers to arrive, Sutpen is viewed with deep suspicion by Yoknapatawpha County's other inhabitants. Several factors contribute to their distrust. Among them is the way in which he acquired his land: "It was the Chickasaw Indian agent with or through whom he dealt and so it was not until he waked the County Recorder that Saturday night with the deed, patent, to the land and the gold Spanish coin, that the town learned that he now owned a hundred square miles of some of the best virgin bottom land in the country."[46]

A process in which Levi Colbert, John Love, and other Indian chiefs and agents manipulated sales was the very way that what were perceived as the best agricultural lands in the north Mississippi Chickasaw Cession initially passed into the hands of individuals, partnerships, and land companies. Thirty-three speculators acquired ten thousand or more acres in the cession. Among them were Wilson T. Caruthers of Holly Springs with 75,481 acres; Wyatt C. Mitchell, with 37,339; and James Brown of Oxford, with 30,641.[47] Faulkner gives the location of the giant plantation house built by Sutpen as twelve miles northwest of Jefferson (map 2.3). A point twelve miles northwest of Oxford along the old Memphis-Oxford Road in Lafayette County is in Section 7 of Township 7 South, Range 4 West, which ironically serves as a classic example of manipulation of Indian allotments in securing titles to the best lands. On May 13, 1836, Section 7 passed from Il Lap Pah Umbey to Edward Orne, but title to this section was not given to Il Lap Pah Umbey by the United States until October 6, 1840.[48] Orne, acting as representative for several land companies and working through Indian chiefs and agents, acquired title to 334,602 prime acres by purchasing allotments and then locating the claims.[49] Although speculators did not acquire land in hundred-square-mile blocks, and they disposed of their holdings rather than attempting to develop vast plantations, in proper geographical and historical contexts Sutpen's Hundred was not impossible.

Hell Creek Crossing

In itself each of the ways in which Faulkner transmuted actual geography into fiction appears quite simple. The total process, however, was complex, as the Hell Creek Crossing episode from *The Reivers* illustrates.[50] On a May Saturday in 1905, Boon Hogganbeck and eleven-year-old Lucius Priest steal Lucius's grandfather's new Winton Flyer and together with Ned McCaslin set out in the afternoon for Memphis along the Memphis-Jefferson Road. Four miles from town the car has difficulty negotiating the muddy approaches to Hurricane Creek. Shortly after darkness falls, the trio stops and spends the night at a store operated by a Miss Ballenbaugh. Sunday morning they cross the Tallahatchie River over "THE Iron Bridge," so called because "it was the first iron bridge and for several years yet the only one we in Yoknapatawpha County had or knew of." Now beyond Yoknapatawpha County, after passing "small white churches in the spring groves," they come to what Boon has feared since the journey began—Hell Creek bottom, infamous for its mud holes and boggy places in the road. After paying dearly for a team of mules to pull the car from the mud, they continue their journey and finally turn onto the Memphis highway.

Faulkner interrupts the narrative of the trip to Memphis with a long discussion of sequent occupance at the site of the Iron Bridge. In the days of Chiefs Issetibbeha and Moketubbe, the site was a Chickasaw Indian crossing. When Yoknapatawpha County was settled, a man named Wyott built a store and a ferryboat and named the crossing for himself. Wyott's Crossing became the head of navigation on the

Tallahatchie River, and small steamboats from Vicksburg brought to Yoknapatawpha County supplies ranging from plows to coal oil to peppermint candy and carried away cotton and furs. Memphis, however, soon diverted trade away from Wyott's Crossing because it was nearer to Jefferson by mule team than Vicksburg was by steamboat. Wyott then sold his crossing to a man named Ballenbaugh, under whom it became a rowdy "dormitory, grubbing station and saloon" for the mule skinners who operated freight wagons between Memphis and Jefferson. By 1905 Ballenbaugh's ferry was gone, replaced by "THE Iron Bridge." Just south of the bridge was the store operated by a "fifty-year-old maiden," Ballenbaugh's only child, who also farmed a quarter section of good river-bottom land in cotton and corn. In 1962, the year that an elderly Lucius Priest tells the story, Wyott's Crossing is only a name, the location of the Iron Bridge has vanished under the waters of Sardis Lake, and at the site of Ballenbaugh's store is a fishing camp.

The basic description of the old Memphis-Oxford Road across north Mississippi is accurate from the time the trio leave Jefferson until they turn onto the Memphis highway, now essentially the route of old U.S. Highway 78, at Olive Branch.[51] Four miles from Oxford the trio would have crossed a creek, but it would have been the Berry Branch of Toby Tubby Creek rather than Hurricane, which is an actual stream but is east of the Memphis-Oxford route (map 2.1). In several of Faulkner's narratives Hurricane is in its proper location, but in The Reivers he shifted the name at the county scale. On Sunday morning the travelers, after crossing from Lafayette into Tate County, would have passed several white frame churches, including the Methodist and Baptist meetinghouses at Tyro, before encountering Jim Wolf bottom, infamous for the difficult approaches to the creek until the 1930s when the road was graveled and the streambed was bridged. Superficially it appears that, for purposes of drama, Faulkner created the name Hell Creek as a substitute for Jim Wolf. Rather than inventing the name, however, he merely shifted the name at the regional scale, for Hell Creek is an actual stream that crosses the Oxford–New Albany road thirty miles from Oxford in Union County.

Shifting locations, omitting vital components, and blending reality with fabrication are all illustrated by Faulkner's discussion of the sequent occupance at the Iron Bridge. In essence, he combined the legendary and actual geography and history of two places on the Tallahatchie River and colored them with his imagination (map 2.5).

In the 1830s, during the initial settlement of Lafayette County, a Chickasaw Indian, Toby Tubby, operated a ferry across the Tallahatchie River on the Memphis-Oxford Road, or what then was the LaGrange-Hendersonville Road. Five miles upstream from Toby Tubby's ferry, Wyatt, one of the earliest incorporated towns in Lafayette County, was laid out in 1838 on the north bank of the river at the head

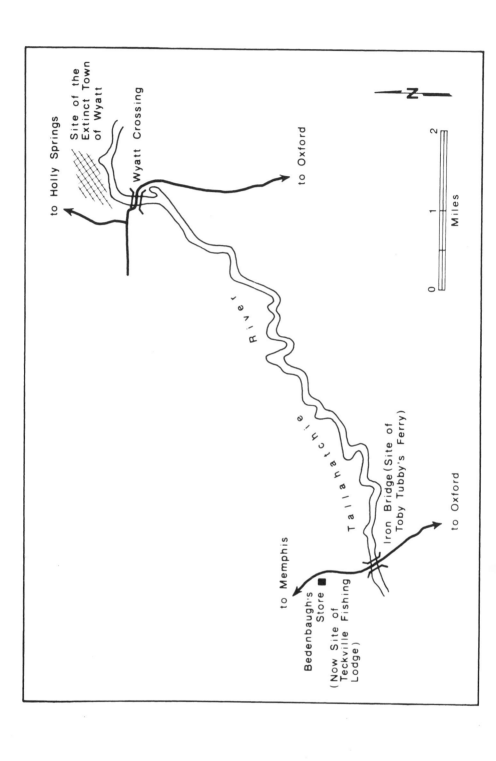

to Holly Springs

Site of the
Extinct Town
of Wyatt

Wyatt Crossing

to Oxford

N

Tallahatchie River

Iron Bridge (Site of
Toby Tubby's Ferry)

to Oxford

to Memphis

Bedenbaugh's
Store

(Now Site of
Teckville Fishing
Lodge)

0   1   2
Miles

Figure 2.13. The old Memphis-Oxford roadbed on the north shore of Sardis Lake in 1974. The lake destroyed the road as a major thoroughfare, as it made the route around the lake from Oxford to Memphis longer. Remnants of the once important thoroughfare survive as segments of county roads and state highways. The boat ramp occupies the site where the old roadbed contacts the water. Charles S. Aiken.

of steamboat navigation by Wyatt C. Mitchell and Volney Peel, land speculators and entrepreneurs. Because of its strategic location, Wyatt's promoters thought the town would become a commercial rival of Memphis. In the 1840s Wyatt had fourteen mercantile houses, a hotel, and the Brooks cotton gin factory; and five steamboats regularly made Wyatt–New Orleans runs.[52] Wyatt began to decline before the Civil War. Among the remaining traces of the town are bits of brick in an overgrown pasture, the ruins of a cemetery, and a road sign indicating that the site is "Wyatt Crossing." Although financial ruin of several of its leading citizens is usually cited as the principal cause of Wyatt's demise, Faulkner's fictional reason— the town lost significance as a port—is more correct. Competition from Memphis, together with the silting of the narrow, shallow Tallahatchie as its watershed was cleared for cultivation, quickly destroyed commercial navigation. Also, when the Mississippi Central Railroad was built across Lafayette County in the 1850s, it by-passed Wyatt five miles to the east.

Until the construction of Sardis Dam and the flooding of the Tallahatchie Valley in the late 1930s, the Memphis-Oxford Road remained the principal thorough-fare leading from Lafayette County (map 2.1). In 1906 the site of the ferry was bridged with a substantial structure that had iron trestles, and it was known by local inhabitants as the Iron Bridge.[53] Above the Tallahatchie bottom just beyond the northern end of the bridge, a stubborn, one-legged man named "Teck" Bedenbaugh for many years operated a store, assisted by a daughter, the only one of his children who never married. The site of the ferry and the Iron Bridge has been under the waters of Sardis Lake since 1940, and Bedenbaugh's store has been superseded by a fishing lodge and restaurant on the shore of the lake. The gentle grade of the old Memphis-Oxford Road rising from the Tallahatchie bottom is now a boat ramp that is part of Sardis Lake recreational facilities (fig. 2.13).

Faulkner knew the legendary histories of Toby Tubby's ferry and of old Wyatt. As a boy and a young man he hunted in the Tallahatchie River bottom and traveled the Memphis-Oxford Road, stopping occasionally at Bedenbaugh's store and encountering difficulty crossing Jim Wolf bottom. From what he observed, experienced, and imagined Faulkner fashioned the stories of Moketubbe, Wyott, Ballenbaugh, and Hell Creek Crossing.

THREE

A Place in the American South

Attempts to interpret William Faulkner's fictional Yoknapatawpha County as an entity with symbolic geographical meaning are varied. They range from that of the student in a freshman English class, who, upon encountering Faulkner for the first time, must struggle to find any, to that of Gabriel Vahanian, who calls Faulkner's world "a historical map of the Christian tradition" and "a spiritual geography of Christendom."[1] One interpretation of geographical symbolism of Faulkner's county is paramount—that Yoknapatawpha is really a microcosm of the American South. Malcolm Cowley maintains that the pattern of the Yoknapatawpha saga "can be extended to the Deep South as a whole." Elizabeth Kerr states that Faulkner's creation is a microcosm of the South. Phillip Muehrcke and Juliana Muehrcke wrote that "Faulkner created his county to contain the essence of Mississippi and of the South." Joel Williamson states that "Faulkner's Yoknapatawpha County was, of course, his own Lafayette County, Mississippi, and the surrounding counties." He continues, "Yoknapatawpha was Mississippi, and it was also all of the South."[2]

Much evidence refutes the idea that Faulkner looked upon and presented Yoknapatawpha as the South in miniature and, rather, supports the contention that he regarded his county as a specific place within the realm. Southern historians who know Faulkner's literature reject the idea that Yoknapatawpha County is a microcosm of the South. C. Vann Woodward, the preeminent historian of the South during the last half of the twentieth century, believed that "Faulkner critics have gone astray in thinking of the Yoknapatawpha novels as Southern history in microcosm, or as representing any very consistent ideas or theories about Southern history." Calvin Brown Jr., a Rhodes scholar and former head of the Department of Comparative Literature at the University of Georgia, grew up in a house on the University of Mississippi campus next to the one where Faulkner's parents, the Murry Falkners, lived while Murry was registrar. Brown also was a member of William Faulkner's Boy Scout troop. He knew Lafayette County and Oxford almost as well as Faulkner and rejected the idea that Faulkner meant Yoknapatawpha County as a miniature South.[3]

Outstanding among the geographical evidences that Yoknapatawpha is not the South in miniature are the parallels between the real Lafayette County and Oxford, and the fictional Yoknapatawpha County and Jefferson. The large-scale geography of Yoknapatawpha County is essentially the large-scale geography of Lafayette County. Here, however, I do not wish to refute the notion that Yoknapatawpha is the South in miniature by further scrutiny of geographical parallels between Yoknapatawpha and Lafayette counties. Rather, I wish to demonstrate that Yoknapatawpha is a place within the South by examining the small-scale setting of the fictional county in relation to the Upland and Lowland Souths and to the rural and urban Souths.

Yoknapatawpha and the Two Souths, Upland and Lowland

Persons who study the South have long recognized two cultural Souths. The fictional county's relationship to these two subregions is important in understanding Yoknapatawpha as a place in the South (map 3.1). At the highest level of generalization, the South may be divided into the Deep South and Border South, or the Lowland South and Upland South.[4] The Lowland South encompasses most of the South Atlantic and Gulf Coastal Plain and much of the southern Piedmont, historically areas with a plantation tradition. Rice, sugarcane, and tobacco have local importance, but the heart of the region is the old cotton belt. Slavery spread across the Lowland South with settlement, producing a large rural black population. The Upland South is physically a diverse region, ranging from the Blue Ridge Mountains and the dissected Cumberland Plateau to the fertile limestone soils of the Blue Grass and Nashville basins. Although a few plantations have existed in the basins and several other places, the agriculture of the Upland South is characterized by a yeoman-farmer tradition that emphasizes grains, livestock, and, to a lesser extent, tobacco. The black population of the Upland South has never been as large as that of the Lowland South.

In the Blue Ridge Mountains and in the dissected parts of the Cumberland Plateau in Tennessee, Kentucky, Virginia, and West Virginia, certain traits of the Upland South exist in their extremes. A distinctive "mountaineer" culture emerged in the highlands where subsistence agriculture yielded a primitive form of life. Stereotyped, the inhabitants reside in small log cabins and eke out a living by hunting and by growing patches of corn, part of which is converted into moonshine whiskey. Largely isolated, they maintain archaic customs and Elizabethan traits of speech. The highlanders, a xenophobic folk, are primarily the descendants of Anglo-Saxons and Ulster Scots. There are few blacks.[5]

The differences between the two culture areas, especially between the mountains of the Upland South and the plantation areas of the Lowland, were recognized before the Civil War and were reinforced by the conflict. Traveling across

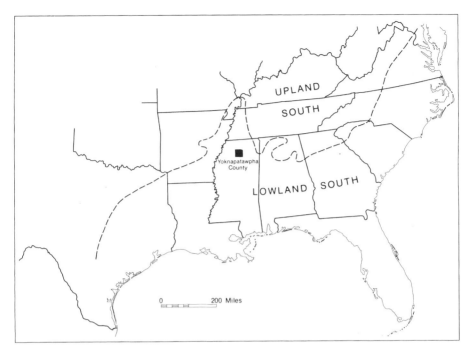

Map 3.1. The Upland South and the Lowland South. Fictional Yoknapatawpha County occupies the location of Lafayette County, Mississippi. Charles S. Aiken.

the South in 1839, the Englishman James Silk Buckingham learned that people in the mountains of northern Georgia "held the 'low-country people,' as they called them, in great contempt, thought them an indolent, luxurious, and useless race, and regarded themselves as the most important class of the productive community." Buckingham also was told that the farmers of the mountains were too poor to purchase African slaves and that the mountains were too cold for slaves during the winter.[6] Frederick Law Olmsted crossed the mountains of eastern Tennessee and western North Carolina in the 1850s. A North Carolina farmer told him that slavery was a "great cuss" and that "there ain't no account of slaves up here in the west, but down in the east part of this State about Fayetteville there's as many as there is in South Carolina." The three-fifths vote allowed for each slave gave the Lowland whites the political power in North Carolina. The farmer believed that the three-fifths clause was the basis for the strife in the state: "[P]eople out here hates the eastern people."[7] Little wonder that the highlanders of the states of southern Appalachia opposed secession, and many allied themselves with the Union rather than the Confederacy when the Civil War began.

Although the concept of the Upland and Lowland Souths has long been recognized, a precise boundary between the two culture areas is difficult to refine, especially when attitudes of people are involved. But to anyone encountering the boundary and acquainted with persons from both sides, the concept is very real. It is revealed when older blacks of the Georgia Piedmont declare that they have never gone and are afraid to go into the counties that lie a few miles to the north in the mountains of the state.[8] The boundary is reflected subtly in a university classroom when a student from eastern Tennessee mentions that she helped harvest tobacco on the family farm the past weekend, and another student, from a western Tennessee plantation, states with pretended disbelief that she has never been in a cotton field and certainly has never worked in one.

Because Faulkner's world has subregions distinguished by topographic, economic, and culture traits, one might initially conclude that Yoknapatawpha County is the South in microcosm, complete to its Upland and Lowland sections (map 2.3). The northern and northwestern parts, including the rich Tallahatchie River bottom, are plantation country, the "fat black rich plantation earth still synonymous of the proud fading white plantation names."[9] Here in the part of the county characteristic of the Lowland South are McCaslin, Sartoris, Sutpen, and Compson holdings, and here resides most of the county's black population.

Across the central part of Yoknapatawpha are the Pine Hills, the eastern part of which lies in the minor civil division known as Beat Four. The area is the "roadless, almost pathless perpendicular hill-country" inhabited by McCallums, Gowries, Fraziers, and Muirs, who speak "only the old Gaelic and not much of that."[10] Principal occupations include lumbering, farming, and making illicit moonshine whiskey. No blacks reside in Beat Four, and strangers are not welcome.[11]

If Beat Four is interpreted to represent the Appalachian portion of the Upland South, then Frenchman's Bend in the southeastern part of Yoknapatawpha County may be accepted to signify the remainder of the region. The area, "hill-cradled and remote," is located at the edge of the Pine Hills and in the Yoknapatawpha river bottom, twenty miles southeast of Jefferson. Like the Upland South, Frenchman's Bend, "definite yet without boundaries," is overt as a region but difficult to define precisely. Also, like the Upland South it is a border country, "straddling into two counties and owing allegiance to neither." Although the core of Frenchman's Bend is the ruin of the large Grenier plantation established before the Civil War, the region is not plantation country but an area of small white farmers. The farmers came in "battered wagons and on muleback and even on foot, with flintlock rifles and dogs and children and home-made whiskey stills and Protestant psalmbooks." They were not slaveholders. Not only did they not bring blacks with them, but also they lacked the other material trappings such as "Phyfe and Chippendale highboys" associated with affluent families.[12]

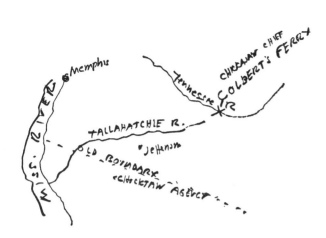

Map 3.2. A sketch map by Faulkner showing the location of fictional Jefferson, Mississippi. This simple map was drawn in 1945 in a letter to Malcolm Cowley to explain why both Chickasaw and Choctaw Indians appear in his stories (William Faulkner to Malcolm Cowley [August 16, 1945], in Cowley 1966, 24–27). Copyright 1966 by Malcolm Cowley and the estate of William Faulkner. Used by permission of Viking Penguin, a division of Penguin Group (USA), Inc.

The white occupants of Frenchman's Bend range from sharecroppers like Mink Snopes, through small landowners like Henry Armstid, to Will Varner, who "owned most of the good land in the country and held mortgages on most of the rest." Unlike the Pine Hills, a few blacks reside in Frenchman's Bend. Most are probably the descendants of the Grenier slaves, and none of them own land.[13]

Beyond this superficial description of Yoknapatawpha is an abundance of evidence that the fictional county is not a geographical microcosm of the Upland and Lowland Souths. Fundamental to assessment of Yoknapatawpha as a geographical entity is the realization that Faulkner thought of his fictional place as a specific location in the South.

Yoknapatawpha County, like Faulkner's own Lafayette County, is Lowland South (map 3.1). The fictional place is in the loess region of north Mississippi, east of the Yazoo Basin and approximately eighty miles south of Memphis. Many examples from Faulkner's writings can be marshaled to show that this is the location of Yoknapatawpha, but the most conclusive evidence is a sketch map that he drew in 1945 to explain why both Chickasaw and Choctaw Indians appear in his stories (map 3.2).[14] The importance of this hastily drawn, simple map should not be underestimated, for it shows the relationship of fictional Jefferson, Mississippi, to north Alabama and west Tennessee. The Mississippi, Tennessee, and Tallahatchie

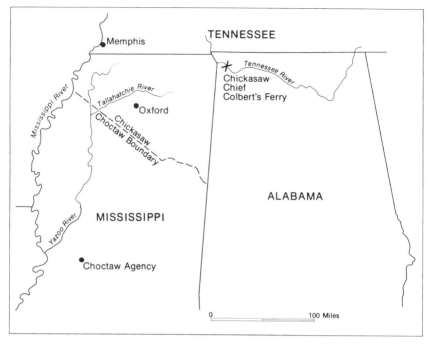

Map 3.3. An accurate version of Faulkner's sketch map. Oxford, Mississippi, occupies the location of fictional Jefferson. Charles S. Aiken.

rivers, Memphis, the site of Chief Colbert's ferry, and the boundary between the Chickasaw and Choctaw nations are displayed in their approximate relationships to one another. When the real features are plotted accurately, Jefferson occupies the location of Oxford, Mississippi (map 3.3).

Reflecting the portion of north Mississippi from which it was sublimated, Yoknapatawpha possesses such distinguishing Lowland South attributes as a plantation agricultural system, a cotton economy, and a large black population. The economic context of the Yoknapatawpha saga is an agricultural system in which cotton is an "omnipotent and omnipresent" "king."[15] Cotton is the basis for the economy not only of the plantation areas of the county but also of Frenchman's Bend and even the hill lands of Beat Four. African slaves were introduced when north Mississippi was the domain of the Chickasaws. The black population surged with the arrival of pioneer slaveholders and eventually surpassed the white population. By 1936 Yoknapatawpha had a population of 15,611—9,313 blacks and 6,298 whites.[16]

The physical, economic, and cultural diversity of Yoknapatawpha County is not a radical departure from reality. Anyone who has dealt with local geography knows that counties are diverse places, and Lafayette County upon which Yoknapatawpha is based is no exception. Although Beat Four and Frenchman's Bend appear to be in the yeoman-farmer tradition of the Upland South, close scrutiny of Faulkner's descriptions reveals that the inhabitants came from other parts of the South. The regions of origin are not what might be expected, for the clannish people of Beat Four are not mountaineers. Nor are they intended by Faulkner to represent mountaineers. They migrated, not from the mountains of Appalachia, but from Scotland to "Carolina," then from Carolina to Yoknapatawpha County. The inhabitants of Frenchman's Bend, however, came "from the northeast, through the Tennessee mountains by stages marked by bearing and raising a generation of children."[17] During the Civil War the people of Beat Four and Frenchman's Bend were not Union sympathizers but were allied with the planters and the Southern Confederacy.

Cultural distinctions between the Lowland South and the Appalachian Mountains of the Upland South are vividly presented in Faulkner's works. Although the distinctions involve economic and landscape differences, the inhabitants' attitudes, especially as they pertain to blacks, also are significant. In the novel A Fable and the short story "Mountain Victory," Faulkner reveals his perceptions of the attitudes of the poor folk of the Appalachian Mountains and the planters and blacks of the Lowland South. The country "where the corners of Georgia and Tennessee and Carolina meet" is an area "where there not only were none, but there never had been any Negroes." When the Civil War began, men and boys thirteen years and older

quitted their misty unmapped eyries . . . to engage in a war in which they had no stake and, if they had only stayed at home, no contact, in order to defend their land from Negroes; not content merely to oppose and repudiate their own geopolitical kind and their common economic derivation, they must confederate with its embattled enemies, stealing, creeping . . . by night through the Confederate lines to find and join a Federal army, to fight not against slavery but against Negroes, to abolish the Negro by freeing him from them who might bring Negroes among them.[18]

In "Mountain Victory" Faulkner brings characters of the two culture regions into intimate contact and comes as close as he ever does to using the stereotypes of southern fiction—arrogant, wealthy planter; uneducated, loyal slave; and xenophobic, moonshine-making, poverty-stricken mountaineer.[19] At the close of the Civil War Saucier Weddel, a Confederate major and a planter of Choctaw and French descent, and his black servant, Jubal, travel through the mountains of east Tennessee on their way home to Mississippi. They seek a night's lodging at the bleak and barren cabin of a family of highlanders who allied themselves with the Union. Jubal, upon discovering that the family is unfriendly, has difficulty comprehending that he is in Tennessee because the state he knows is west Tennessee of the Lowland South, not east Tennessee of the Upland South. Jubal says to Weddel:

"In Tennessee? You tole me we was in Tennessee, where Memphis is, even if you never tole me it was all disyer up-and-down land in de Memphis country. I know I never seed none of um when I went to Memphis wid yo paw dat time. But you says so. And now you telling me dem Memphis folks is Yankees?" Weddel tells Jubal that the members of the family are not Yankees but does not explain the difference between a Yankee and a Union-sympathizing southerner.[20]

To the highlanders Weddel appears haughty and arrogant, even in his tattered, faded gray cloak. He will not drink with them but gives the moonshine that he is offered to his servant. Toward the "ign'unt mountain trash," whom he considers beneath him, Jubal is intolerant and boastful. The twenty-year-old daughter of the family is awestruck by Weddel, who is "like a creature from another world with other air to breathe and another kind of blood to warm the veins." From Weddel and Jubal she learns of that other world where the family plantation, Contalmaison, is "bigger den a county to ride over," where the coffee is the finest Martinique, and where girls are ladies who wear shoes. The antipathy of the highlanders for Jubal and for Weddel, whom they suspect may be part Negro because of his dark complexion, finally leads two members of the family to ambush the pair as they leave the mountains.

The most powerful description of the distinctions between the Lowland South and the mountain core of the Upland South in Faulkner's works is in *Absalom, Absalom!* As a boy, Thomas Sutpen saw the landscape differences and experienced the clash between the two cultures. Even though he is the largest landowner in Yoknapatawpha County, Sutpen is not from the planter class. As Rosa Coldfield discerns him, "he was no younger son sent out from some old quiet country like Virginia or Carolina with the surplus negroes to take up new land."[21] Actually, Sutpen is from Virginia—mountainous western Virginia of the Upland South.

Sutpen was born in the mountains, where the people "lived in log cabins boiling with children," where "the only colored people were Indians," and where "the land belonged to anybody and everybody." As a boy Sutpen "never even heard of, never imagined a place, a land divided neatly up and actually owned by men who did nothing but ride over it on fine horses or sit in fine clothes on the galleries of big houses while other people worked for them." But the Sutpen family literally fell into such a place, "tumbled head over heels back to Tidewater by sheer altitude, elevation and gravity."[22]

In the Virginia Tidewater, young Sutpen is shocked by the differences between the mountains and his new home. Although the family lives in a cabin that is almost a replica of the one in the mountains, it is beside a broad, flat river. The crops are ones that Sutpen has never before seen, and members of the family are susceptible to strange diseases (malaria and yellow fever), unknown in the mountains, that are associated with the warmth and the dampness of the climate. His brothers and sisters seem "to take sick after supper and die before the next meal." Most important, Sutpen discovers that there is a social structure. The Sutpens are not like the prosperous whites, certainly not the ones who live in the big houses and ride horses to command workers in the fields. The Sutpens are considered white trash, beneath even the slaves who have a higher standard of living. Finally, loss of innocence and realization of his situation come to him when he is sent to the big house with a message from his father. The black butler opens the front door, looks at the barefooted child in his tattered clothes, and tells him "never to come to that front door again but to go around to the back."[23]

Although Yoknapatawpha County is Lowland South, it is no more this subregion in miniature than it is the whole South in miniature. It is a distinctive geographical entity related to, and contrasted with, other areas of the Lowland South. The areas are as diverse as the reasons for the relationships. The furniture for the Compson house at the edge of Jefferson came from French Louisiana. Colonel Sartoris's regiment marched off to fight Yankees in Virginia. When Sartoris's railroad was completed in 1876, it connected with the one that ran unbroken from Charleston, South Carolina, to Memphis.

The differences between the cultural landscape of Yoknapatawpha County and the older landscapes of the Lowland South are among the most interesting contrasts that Faulkner presents. At the time of the Civil War, portions of the South Atlantic seaboard had histories two hundred years older than that of north Mississippi, and even within the state the settlement gap was more than a century. In 1790 settlement was well advanced in areas scattered from the Tidewater of Virginia southward to Florida.[24] Along the Gulf Coast, Biloxi was established in 1699 and New Orleans in 1718. Settlement of north Mississippi, however, occurred after 1830.

The settlement gap resulted in profound differences between Faulkner's country and the older portions of the Lowland South, where in 1860 the cultural landscape was more maturely developed than in north Mississippi. Enough wealth had been accumulated so that it could be spent on elaborate houses and other luxury trappings. In north Mississippi, which was opened to extensive settlement only twenty-five years before the Civil War, most of the prosperous families were still thinking in terms of buying more slaves and of clearing more land instead of devoting capital to erect fine dwellings. Some of the largest landowners in Lafayette County in 1860 still lived in log houses. The frame and brick big houses that were erected, including the Shegog house, which seventy years later Faulkner purchased and renamed Rowan Oak, were simple boxes, two rooms over two, or four rooms over four. Most were built without the aid of an architect and were pretentious only by their size and their porticoes (fig. 2.7). The better-constructed dwellings had plastered interior walls while the more cheaply constructed ones were sealed with wood paneling.

Commenting on a portion of *Go Down, Moses* set in 1859, Faulkner observed that one purpose of the story was

> to show my country as it really was in those days. The elegance of the colonial plantation didn't exist in my country. My country was still frontier. The plantation, the columned porticoes, that was Charleston and Natchez. . . . People lived from day to day, with a bluff and crude hardiness, but with a certain simplicity. Which to me is very interesting because the common picture of the South is all magnolias and crinoline and Grecian portals and things like that, which was true only around the fringes of the South. Not in the interior, the back wood.[25]

The frontier environment comes through sharply in Faulkner's stories. Even though Grenier, Sutpen, and Compson erected large and elegant houses, the dwelling that commanded the two-thousand-acre McCaslin plantation was the more typical rural big house. It was a large dogtrot, "two log wings . . . connected by the open hallway." After the Civil War the house was modified into an imposing, but by no means refined, dwelling by Cass Edmonds when the open passageway was enclosed and the lower floor was "superposed with a second storey of white clapboards and faced with a portico."[26]

There is much pretense in the frontier environment. Miss Sophonsiba insisted on calling the Beauchamp landholding "Warwick" after the place in England she said her brother, Mr. Hubert, was "probably the true earl of."[27] Thomas Sutpen, penniless to the point that he must borrow seed cotton from General Compson to plant his first crop, was so intent on making himself part of the landed gentry that he ignored what good economic judgment and the normal settlement process dictated. He spent his first two years in Yoknapatawpha County dragging "house and gardens out of virgin swamp." Because he lacked money to purchase hardware, glass, and other manufactured items, the house that was "the largest edifice in the county, not excepting the courthouse itself," sat three years "unpainted and unfinished, without a pane of glass or a doorknob or hinge in it, twelve miles from town and almost that far from any neighbor." The construction of large houses with imposing exteriors and unfinished interiors was not uncommon on the southern frontier. In the 1920s Holly Springs, Faulkner's model for Memphis Junction, had at least one imposing, but still unfinished, antebellum house. Another dwelling was reduced to a mere bungalow after the Civil War because it was less expensive to remove the second story than to complete the interior.[28]

Yoknapatawpha and the Two Souths, Rural and Urban

The South is also rural and urban. Traditionally the area has been depicted as a rural realm where small towns and hamlets were important but cities insignificant. Like the South of this simplistic rural image, Yoknapatawpha is an area without a city. The county has one town, Jefferson, and one of its hamlets, Varner's Crossroads, is discussed in detail by Faulkner. With its courthouse square, its Confederate monument, and its biracial population, Jefferson may seem a model of all southern towns. Varner's Crossroads with its cotton gin, general store, and Baptist church may seem a model of any hamlet in the South.

The South has been considered almost wholly rural, not because it did not have cities, but because until recently scholars ignored the urban components. Standard history and geography texts treating the South devoted few pages to cities.[29] More important, cities were not considered among the factors that influenced the character of the South, and the attitude persists that if the South has cities, they must be nonsouthern places. Furthermore, a general tendency has been to regard towns and small cities as places that do not differ much from the rural countryside. Only after 1970 did a general recognition begin to emerge of an urban South that contrasts significantly with the rural South.[30]

The rate of urban development in the South began to lag behind the national rate of urbanization in 1840 and continued to trail until 1910. In 1930, when Faulkner emerged as a major writer, only one-third of the South's population was urban. Most urbanites were concentrated in towns and small cities; 37 percent resided in cities with populations greater than one hundred thousand. However, during and following the Second World War, urbanization increased at a rapid rate. By the time of Faulkner's death in 1962, more than 60 percent of the South's population was urban.[31]

Faulkner thought of Yoknapatawpha as having a definite place on the continuum between rural and urban Souths. Significant contrasts are presented in his stories between the rural parts of Yoknapatawpha County, small-town Jefferson, and southern metropolitan areas. In an interview at the University of Virginia, Faulkner identified in his works four dialectical social groups as they are related to cities. He termed them the "educated semi-metropolitan white Southerner," the "hill backward [white] Southerner," the "Negro," and the "Negro who has been influenced by the Northern cities."[32]

In his stories Faulkner presents the rural-urban continuum. To the uneducated inhabitants of the remote parts of Yoknapatawpha County, Jefferson is definitely urban, offering goods and services that cannot be obtained at Fraser's store in Beat

Four or in the hamlet of Varner's Crossroads. Mink Snopes, for example, must travel to Jefferson to purchase buckshot shells for his ancient ten-gauge gun because Varner's store does not stock them. The folk from rural areas are different from those who reside in the town, and on the streets of Jefferson even a casual observer can distinguish between the two groups. As a child Lena Grove prefers to walk into town rather than to ride beside her father in the wagon, thinking people will consider her of the town rather than from the country. Dewey Dell stops at the edge of town, puts on her shoes, and even changes to her Sunday dress, but the townspeople immediately recognize her as a country girl. Even nine-year-old Vardaman senses the difference between the two groups. "'Why ain't I a town boy, pa?' I said. 'God made me. I did not said to God to made me in the country.'"[33]

Characters in Faulkner's stories have fictional relationships with several of the South's large cities. Popeye's demise finally comes when he is arrested in Birmingham; Carothers Edmonds is unable to intercede when Lucas Beauchamp is charged with murder because he is in New Orleans for a gallstone operation. But Memphis, eighty miles northwest of Jefferson, is the primary city in Faulkner's stories. With a population that ranged from a hundred thousand to half a million during his lifetime, the Memphis that Faulkner depicts is a major city, but not one on the scale of New York or Chicago. In the first half of the twentieth century, when rural-urban differences were at a peak, Memphis with its congestion, paved streets, Irish and Italian immigrants, and second- and third-generation urban-born population was a sharp contrast to rural Lafayette County and Oxford. Even persons who had never been to Memphis knew that the city was there from the glow of its lights on the northern horizon.

In *The Reivers* eleven-year-old Lucius Priest traveled from Yoknapatawpha County to Memphis in May 1905 (fig. 3.1). As he approached the city, "civilization" became "constant." The "air was indeed urban, the very dust itself . . . had a metropolitan taste to tongue and nostrils."[34] Thirty-seven years later, in the short story "Two Soldiers," the eight-year-old younger brother of Pete Grier journeyed from a remote part of Yoknapatawpha County to Memphis to enlist in the army. On experiencing a city for the first time and having only Jefferson for a comparison, it seemed that Memphis "went on for miles." Then seeing the downtown area, the child thought that Memphis was "standing up into the air . . . like about a dozen whole towns bigger than Jefferson was set up on one edge in a field" (fig. 3.2).[35]

The contrasts between rural Yoknapatawpha and Memphis are best revealed in the comic and tragic inabilities of certain county inhabitants to function effectively in an urban environment. Although members of Yoknapatawpha County's different social groups travel to Memphis, only semi-metropolitan whites such

Figure 3.1. Main Street at Madison Avenue in downtown Memphis in 1912. "Besides the streetcars there were buggies and surreys—phaetons, traps, stanhopes, at least one victoria, the horses a little white-eyed us but still collected; evidently Memphis horses were already use to automobiles. . . . We were getting se to Main Street now—the tall buildings, the stores, the hotels, the Gaston (gone now) and the abody (they have moved it since) and the Gayoso" (Faulkner *The Reivers* 1962, 95–96). Unidentified otographer. Courtesy of the Memphis/Shelby County Public Library and Information Center.

as the Priests, Sartorises, and Stevenses make frequent trips and can comfortably conduct themselves in the city. Poor, uneducated whites like Boon Hogganbeck, Fonzo Winbush, and Virgil and Mink Snopes are overwhelmed by the city. They look and feel out of place and know only a few parts of the city, primarily the red-light district which they frequent as "young bloods" on a few "country-boy Memphis trips."[36]

Among the comical episodes in Faulkner's stories is Virgil Snopes and Fonzo Winbush's journey to Memphis about 1930 to attend barber college.[37] With their new straw hats, clean-shaven necks, and new, imitation-leather suitcases, the duo emerges from the train as hicks, fresh from the country. Even though they cannot fully comprehend or effectively function in the urban environment, they are captivated by it. Fonzo exclaims, "So this is Memphis. . . . Where have I been all my life?" Moving from the railroad station down Main Street, they plan to stay at the Gayoso, at the time one of Memphis's best hotels, but change their plans because it looks too expensive. They see another hotel that looks just as expensive as the Gayoso. Virgil says to Fonzo, "Let's look down this-a-way. Git away from all that

Figure 3.2. Downtown Memphis as viewed from near the intersection of U.S. Highways 51 and 78 in 1942. The eight-year-old Grier boy discerns Memphis for the first time that same year, "standing up into the air higher than ara hill in all Yoknapatawpha County" (Faulkner "Two Soldiers" 1942 in *Collected Stories* 1977, 93). Unidentified photographer. Courtesy of the Memphis/Shelby County Public Library and Information Center.

ere plate glass. . . . Suppose somebody broke it while we was there. Suppose they couldn't ketch who done it. Do you reckon they'd let us out withouten we paid our share?"[38]

Virgil and Fonzo then leave Main Street and at the next corner turn into a narrow street of shabby frame houses and junkyards and come to a dingy, three-story building with a latticework false entry, Miss Reba's brothel, which they mistake for a boardinghouse. They enter the house and, thinking that she is a dressmaker who has a large family of daughters, in all innocence convince Miss Reba to rent them a room. During the first night they drift into slumber as they listen to the city, "evocative and strange, imminent and remote; threat and promise both."[39]

One of the most pathetic of the poor whites who travel to Memphis is Mink Snopes.[40] In 1946, upon his release from a thirty-eight-year term in Parchman, the Mississippi penitentiary, Mink hitchhikes to Memphis to purchase a pistol with which to kill his cousin Flem. Mink is disoriented in both time and space. He has been to Memphis on only three other occasions, and the city that he recalls no longer exists. Seeing strange blinking lights, he tells himself as he enters the city, "Remember. Remember. It wont hurt you as long as dont nobody find out you dont know it." And then Memphis "engulfed him; it stooped soaring down, bearing down upon him like breathing the vast concrete mass and weight until he himself was breathless, having to pant for air. . . . It's un-sleeping, he thought. It aint slept in so long now it's done forgot how to sleep and now there aint no time to stop long enough to try to learn how again."[41]

Suddenly Mink becomes oriented and knows how he will pass the night until the next morning, when he can buy the pistol. Confederate Park on the river bluff is almost exactly as he recalls it, with its Civil War cannon and its flowerbeds criss-crossed by walkways. But a cold wind from the Mississippi River sweeps across the park benches, and he thinks of another park, Court Square, where he will be sheltered from the wind by tall buildings. Mink, however, is driven from Court Square by a policeman. He then goes to the railroad station where the trains he once rode from Jefferson arrived. The station with its "hollowly sonorous rotunda" has not changed. Mink is also ejected from the station by a policeman. He then recalls "another depot just down a cross street" but decides to spend the night wandering the streets. "A man can get through anything if he can jest keep on walking," he reasons.[42]

The next morning, after a breakfast of two boxes of animal crackers purchased at a small store, Mink approaches a pawnshop to buy the pistol. By "merely turning his head" Mink "could have seen the street, the actual house front" of the brothel that he visited on his first trip to Memphis forty-seven years earlier, an establishment that is now operated by his younger daughter, although "he didn't know it of course and probably wouldn't have recognized her."[43]

The integrity of southern rural-urban contrasts as presented in Faulkner is supported by his basically accurate, albeit fictional, description of Memphis (map 3.4). The railroad station where Virgil and Fonzo arrive and the one that Mink remembers is Union Station, accurately described to its rotunda. The other station recalled by Mink is Grand Central, and it is a short distance from Union Station, down a street that crosses Main. Faulkner's description of Confederate Park is accurate for 1946, except that the Civil War cannon were removed during a Second World War scrap drive. Likewise accurate is his description of nearby Court Square. Virgil and Fonzo would have walked down Main Street from Union Station to find the actual Gayoso Hotel. On the other side of Main Street was the Chisca, the unnamed hotel that they encountered.

The descriptions of real buildings, parks, and streets of Memphis and their relationships to one another are amazingly accurate. But what of the urban, economic, and social conditions of which Faulkner gives glimpses? The inhabitants of Yoknapatawpha County are attracted to Memphis because the city offers opportunities and services that are not available in Jefferson. The Grier boy is drawn to a

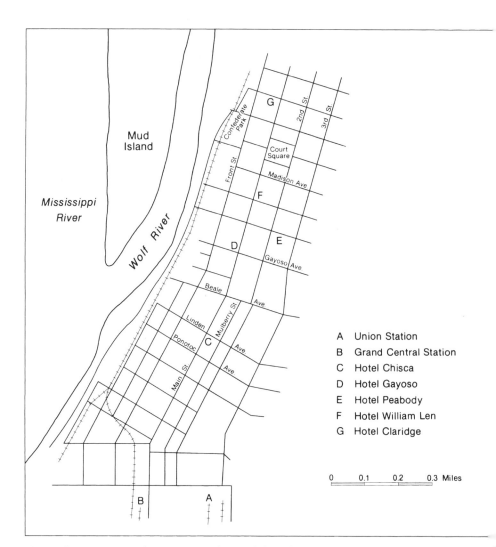

Mud
Island

Mississippi
River

Wolf River

Confederate
Park

Front St

2nd St

3rd St

G

Court
Square

Madison Ave

F

E

D

Gayoso Ave

Beale

Ave

Linden

Mulberry St

Ponotoc

C

Ave

Main St

Ave

A   Union Station
B   Grand Central Station
C   Hotel Chisca
D   Hotel Gayoso
E   Hotel Peabody
F   Hotel William Len
G   Hotel Claridge

0   0.1   0.2   0.3 Miles

B

A

Map 3.4. Downtown Memphis, 1930–1950. The area did not change significantly during the two decades. Ar
1960 economic decline and urban renewal dramatically altered downtown Memphis from the way Faulkner
knew and described it. Charles S. Aiken.

regional federal office, Virgil and Fonzo to a trade school, and Mink to a specialty shop. They also are drawn by the sense of adventure in what for them is the far country, close in space yet far removed in its environmental qualities. And like far countries, Memphis presents the opportunity to be anonymous and to engage in forbidden pleasures.

In 1930 Virgil and Fonzo would have had the opportunity to attend, among others in Memphis, the Moler College of Beauty Culture and Barbering, and in 1942 the Grier boy would have found not only an army enlistment office but the headquarters of the Second Army. Pawnshops were concentrated on Beale Avenue, and in the mid-1940s six establishments dominated the three blocks between Main and Third streets (fig. 3.3).[44] Into the fifth decade of the twentieth century, with full knowledge of public officials and city leaders, Memphis had a red-light district. In the 1920s and 1930s, it was a small, dispersed area at the southern end of the central business district. Among the infamous streets were Mulberry and Gayoso. Accord- ing to Estelle, who in 1934 asked Faulkner to show her "Miss Reba's," Mulberry was the street on which the model for the fictional establishment was located.[45] When Virgil and Fonzo left Main Street and turned again at the next corner, they would have traveled down Linden or Pontotoc for one block and turned into Mulberry. If Mink had turned his head while he walked along Beale to the pawnshop, he would have been looking down Mulberry. However, by 1946, the time of the story, the red-light district had been abolished by an edict from Memphis's political boss, E. H. Crump.[46]

Yoknapatawpha, a Universal Place

The internal evidence of Faulkner's stories and his explanations of certain seg- ments of his stories indicate that Yoknapatawpha is not a microcosm of the South. It is one thing, however, to say that Yoknapatawpha is not a microcosm of the South and another to say that this is not what Faulkner really intended for it to be. A passage in *Absalom, Absalom!* is sometimes cited to demonstrate that one of Faulkner's principal purposes was to write about the South. Upon arrival at Har- vard, Quentin Compson is besieged by questions: "*Tell about the South. What's it like there. What do they do there. Why do they live there. Why do they live at all.*"[47] To alleviate the curiosity of his Canadian roommate, Quentin relates the saga of the rise and fall of Thomas Sutpen and of the landed dynasty that he attempted to create. In his interviews Faulkner left no doubt how he perceived Yoknapatawpha as it pertained to the South. He stated repeatedly that his principal purpose was to write universally about mankind. When asked the question "To what extent were you trying to picture the South and Southern civilization as a whole, rather than

Figure 3.3. A pawnshop on Beale Avenue in Memphis in the 1930s. Colloquially known as Beale Street, the avenue was the heart of Memphis's principal shopping and entertainment area for blacks throughout the twentieth century. Culturally, Beale Street is an important place in the geography of American music. Early i the twentieth century the blues from the Yazoo Delta began the transition into the mainstream under W. C. Handy and other legendary black musicians who moved to Memphis. In the 1950s Elvis Presley learned to p the blues on Beale Street, blended this unique music with country music, and initiated the transition to rock On Beale Street, primarily at Lansky Brothers, Presley bought colorful clothes worn by blacks and changed t dress of white teenagers and young adults internationally. The original Beale Street is gone. It is no longer an avenue with businesses that cater primarily to blacks but a depressing strip of financially unstable nightclubs restaurants, and music halls inhabited largely by white tourists. Original buildings were razed and renovated in some cases leaving only the facade. The result is an artificial place promoted as the birthplace of the blues and rock and roll. Unidentified photographer. Farm Security Administration Collection, Library of Congres

just Mississippi—or were you?" Faulkner responded, "Not at all. I was trying to talk about people, using the only tool I knew, which was the country that I knew."[48] And when asked specifically if the purpose of *Absalom, Absalom!* was to portray the South, Faulkner replied: "The primary job that any writer faces is to tell you a story, a story out of human experience—I mean by that, universal mutual experience, the anguishes and troubles and griefs of the human heart, which is universal, without regard to race or time or condition. . . . I think that no writer's got time to be drawing a picture of a region."[49]

Although Faulkner did not attempt to draw a picture of the South, he took Yoknapatawpha from a geographical reality, and that reality was a part of a greater geographical whole. Certain themes, therefore, are ones common to the South. But geographically Yoknapatawpha is a microcosm within the South rather than a microcosm of the South. Literarily, however, it is much more. When we accept Faulkner's principal objective to be the telling of the universal, mutual experience of the human heart, Yoknapatawpha County becomes more than Lafayette County, Mississippi, or the South. It becomes, as John T. Irwin reminds us, "a place where we have all lived, and where some of us come from."[50]

What is the significance of recognizing that Yoknapatawpha County is not a geographical microcosm of the South but a place within the South? Accurate interpretation and full appreciation of Faulkner's stories require that they be considered within their proper historical and geographical settings. To emphasize universality in his writings, Faulkner thought the setting incidental but by no means unimportant. In a 1955 interview he stated, "I think that local color is part of the environment and no part of the environment can be more or less important than any universal truth. . . . To say that local color is merely cute . . . I can't agree with that."[51] Faulkner's use of local color both increases the complexity of interpreting his works and decreases his role as a regional authority. Critics make errors simply because of a lack of understanding of the geography of one small place in Mississippi during one short span of time. But errors of another type are made by attempts to employ Faulkner's works as general sources on the geography of the entire South.

Faulkner did not look inward and think of Yoknapatawpha County as a closed geographical model. Inhabitants of the fictional place reach toward other areas and operate within a broader spatial context. Faulkner considered the Tallahatchie and Yoknapatawpha rivers boundaries of his county. But significantly, no boundaries are shown on the two maps of the county that he drew.[52] Symbolically, Yoknapatawpha is a place with a core, but the county has no isolating walls. The interconnection of Yoknapatawpha County is perhaps best expressed by Faulkner through the perception of a child. The little Grier boy in "Shall Not Perish" comprehends his niche on earth, "that little place that don't even show on a map," as a hub that is tied to all places in a universe—"Never a one too big for it to touch, never a one too little to be remembered:—the places that men and women have lived in and loved."[53]

FOUR

Old South

Faulkner's stories and characters may be universal, but the economic and social systems in which they perform and the landscapes across which they move are not temporally or spatially generic. The historical geography of the American South and north Mississippi can be interpreted in the context of three major eras separated by two periods of rapid, dramatic change. The Old South era extended from the 1600s to 1860; the New South began about 1880 and lasted into the Great Depression of the 1930s; the Modern South is the era since 1970. The periods 1861 to 1880, the Civil War and Reconstruction, and 1940 to 1970, the Second World War and the postwar years, were times of transition when rapid geographic, economic, social, and political changes occurred.[1]

Faulkner and the Indians

North Mississippi was among the last large areas of the United States east of the Mississippi River possessed by Indians. Until the 1830s the Chickasaws and Choctaws held more than half of the state of Mississippi (map 4.1). In Faulkner's stories the Old South era begins before the Chickasaws and Choctaws ceded the last of their Mississippi lands to the United States and the northern part of the state was opened to settlement. The Choctaws relinquished their domain in north Mississippi in October 1830 at the Treaty of Dancing Rabbit Creek, and the Chickasaws ceded the last of their land at the Treaty of Pontotoc in October 1832.[2]

One scholar calls the Indians of Yoknapatawpha County Faulkner's neglected people.[3] The Indians may have been largely ignored by critics, but they are hardly overlooked by Faulkner. The Indians departed from Mississippi for Indian Territory sixty years before Faulkner was born, but the native people still had a shadowy though very real presence in north Mississippi. Few "Reds," full-blooded Indians, remained, but a number of persons, both black and white, had features that revealed Indian ancestors. "At last even the wild blood itself would have vanished," wrote Faulkner, "to be seen occasionally in the nose-shape of a Negro on a cotton-wagon or a white sawmill hand or trapper or locomotive fireman."[4] Sam Fathers, one of Faulkner's major characters, is part Indian, but he is also part black and part white, and therefore lacks a precise cultural identity.

The most significant remnants of Indians are mysterious cultural relics, which were common enough throughout Faulkner's life that a type of Saturday or Sunday afternoon outing in north Mississippi was a hunt for arrowheads, pottery, and other artifacts (fig. 4.1). The most striking landscape enigma are earthen mounds, some of which have flat tops and rise thirty or more feet above the river and creek bottoms in which the majority are located (figs. 4.2 and 4.3). North Mississippi is part of a large area in the south-central United States that had relatively large Indian populations. The greatest populations occurred during the Woodland tradition, which extended from about 1000 BC to 700 or 900 AD, and the following Mississippian tradition, which lasted until approximately the middle of the seventeenth century. Although the Woodland people began construction of mounds, the Mississippians were the primary builders, and they constructed almost all of the mounds in north Mississippi. Large platform mounds were the sites of council houses and dwellings of chiefs and priests. The large mounds are surrounded by smaller and lower burial mounds, many of which are only three or four feet high.[5] In the Loess Plains, some of the mounds are constructed of red clay, which was hauled in baskets from the hill lands. The red mounds contrast sharply with the yellow-brown soil of the creek and river bottoms.

The first encounters with Europeans were brutally devastating for the Indians. In the winter and spring of 1540–1541 the Hernando de Soto party crossed north Mississippi. The party brought a hidden catastrophe—tuberculosis and other diseases to which the Indians had little or no immunity. The diseases, together with other factors that are still not fully understood, caused a great decline in the Indian population followed by cultural reorganization.[6]

A century and a half passed before Europeans returned to the north Mississippi area. The Indian tribes, or nations, encountered in southeastern North America by the Europeans in the 1700s included the Cherokees, Creeks, Choctaws, and Chickasaws. They were coalescent societies that emerged from the fragmented descendants of the Mississippians. The northern half of Mississippi was the domain of the Chickasaws in the north and the Choctaws, a similar nation, to the south (map. 4.1). Like their Mississippian ancestors, the Chickasaws and Choctaws were agriculturalists who lived in towns, but they were not mound builders. Construction of mounds had largely ended in the interior of southeastern North America by 1600. Two centuries later the origin of the large mounds was as mysterious to the Chickasaws, Choctaws, Creeks, and Cherokees as to the white and black settlers. In the late 1700s William Bartram found the Cherokees "as ignorant as we are, by what people or for what purpose these artificial hills were raised; . . . they have

Figure 4.1. From left to right, two arrowheads, a celt, and a discoidal stone, found in a creek bed and a field. The artifacts are from Tate County, Mississippi, a few miles north of Lafayette-Tate boundary. On one side of the discoidal stone is a crude diagram of the sun with rays. The edge of the stone is well worn from Warriors of the Sun playing chungke. The artifacts are probably from the Mississippian tradition and date from 1000 to 1500 AD. Collected on the surface by the author's parents. Charles S. Aiken.

Figure 4.2. An Indian mound in 1961 in the Basket Creek bottom in Tate County, Mississippi, a few miles north of the Lafayette-Tate boundary. At the time settlement of north Mississippi began in the 1830s, the creek and river bottoms contained a number of Indian mounds. Many were destroyed by cultivation and by unwitting treasure hunters. Some mounds are protected by their use as sites for houses and cemeteries of whites or blacks. A tenant house atop this mound protected it for a number of years. Charles S. Aiken.

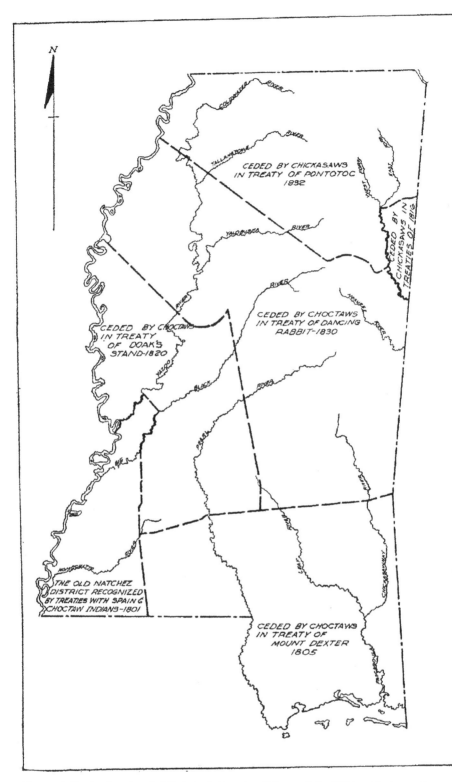

N

CEDED BY CHICKASAWS
IN TREATY OF PONTOTOC
1832

CEDED BY
CHICKASAWS IN
TREATIES OF 1816

CEDED BY CHOCTAWS
IN TREATY OF DANCING
RABBIT-1830

CEDED BY CHOCTAWS
IN TREATY
OF DOAK'S
STAND-1820

THE OLD NATCHEZ
DISTRICT RECOGNIZED
BY TREATIES WITH SPAIN &
CHOCTAW INDIANS-1801

CEDED BY CHOCTAWS
IN TREATY OF
MOUNT DEXTER
1805

Map 4.1. Indian land cessions in Mississippi, 1801–1832. U.S. wpa Federal Writers' Project 1938.

Figure 4.3. The great Winterville temple mound in Bolivar County, Mississippi, in 1963. The mound is in the midst of a temple plaza and is surrounded by sixteen smaller mounds. The site is now protected by the state of Mississippi. Charles S. Aiken.

a tradition common with the other nations of Indians, that they found them in much the same condition as they now appear, when their forefathers arrived from the West."[7]

During the early years of Faulkner's life, relatively little was known of the complex Indian culture of north Mississippi and the central South. Mounds, stone arrow and spear points, stone axes and celts, together with whole and broken pieces of pottery, were easily found if one knew where to look. Lafayette County had a number of Indian mounds, primarily in the Yocona and Tallahatchie river bottoms. Over the years, smaller mounds were modified or destroyed by cultivation and by artifact and treasure hunters. The most valuable artifact taken from a mound in Lafayette County is probably the large stone vessel with a lid that was carted off to the Hey Museum.[8] A number of mounds were inundated when the Tallahatchie bottom was flooded by the federal government's construction of Sardis Dam in the 1930s. A few mounds survive, some concealed in clear view by trees and bushes, which make them appear to be small hills or parts of hills.

Prior to the 1960s little effort was made to protect and preserve Indian artifacts and landscape sites. Just how common and unprotected were sites and artifacts during Faulkner's lifetime is illustrated by a 1910 description of the area around the large twenty-foot-high platform mound on the Abby Leatherman Plantation in Tunica County northwest of Lafayette:

Near this mound is a limited area of . . . high ground on which lay some fragments of pottery, a few flint pebbles, and much baked clay, remains of aboriginal fireplaces, broadly scattered by the plow. . . .

   The twenty-nine burials found were rather widely scattered; some were near the surface and had been disturbed by the plow. . . . It is likely that many burials have been ploughed away in the past. Fragments of human bones lay in all directions.[9]

The myth developed that a mysterious, culturally advanced race of mound builders had been slaughtered by the savages whom the British encountered in the settlement of eastern North America beginning in the 1600s. During his travels across the southeastern United States, William Bartram saw numerous mounds. Because their origin was unknown to the Indians, he concluded that the mounds were "wonderful labours of the ancients." Bartram speculated that "perhaps they were designed and appropriated by the people who constructed them, to some religious purpose, as great altars and temples similar to the high places and sacred groves amongst the Canaanites and other nations of Palestine and Judea."[10] Thomas Jefferson and Andrew Jackson were among those who believed that the mounds were built by a culturally advanced race who were killed by the ancestors of the primitive aborigines they knew. The myth influenced the Indian policies of both presidents, who believed that the red race was doomed, and thus there was no reason to assist in preservation of their savage society and primitive culture.[11]

   After the Chickasaws and Choctaws were removed, the myth of a culturally advanced race of mound builders faded. Residents of north Mississippi came to believe another myth, which holds that mounds, arrow points, pottery, and other Indian artifacts are Chickasaw and Choctaw. In his fiction Faulkner presents the widely held belief that the mounds were built by the Indians who were removed from north Mississippi in the 1830s. To have corrected the record would have undermined the authenticity of Faulkner's fiction because he drew from legend as well as from fact. Faulkner's description of a mound in the Tallahatchie bottom from the perspective of a child succinctly conveys how the mysterious earthworks were regarded by most residents of north Mississippi:

Five miles farther down the river from Major de Spain's camp . . . there is an Indian mound. Aboriginal, it rises profoundly and darkly enigmatic, the only elevation of any kind in the wild, flat jungle of [Tallahatchie] river bottom. . . . It possessed inferences of secret and violent blood, of savage and sudden destruction, as though the yells and hatchets which we associated with Indians through the hidden and secret dime novels . . . still dwelled or lurked there, sinister, a little sardonic, like a dark and nameless beast lightly and lazily slumbering with bloody jaws—this, perhaps, due to the fact that a remnant of a once powerful clan of the Chickasaw tribe still lived beside it under Government protection. . . . To us, as children, they were a little fabulous, their swamp-hidden lives inextricable from the life of the dark mound.[12]

Over the span of his life, Faulkner learned of the successive stages of Indian culture as anthropologists and other scholars excavated, mapped, and developed theories. Dr. Calvin S. Brown, the Falkners' next-door neighbor during the time they lived on the University of Mississippi campus, was an authority on Indian culture. Although archeology was not his field, Brown, who knew that the mounds were not constructed by the Chickasaws and Choctaws, in 1926 published *Archeology of Mississippi*, the first such study for a state. In addition to the book, Faulkner had access to Brown's house, which contained a number of artifacts. In his 1954 essay "Mississippi" for *Holiday*, Faulkner wrote: "In the beginning the predecessors crept with their simple artifacts, and built the mounds and vanished, bequeathing only the mounds in which the succeeding recordable Algonquian stock would leave the skulls of their warriors and chiefs and babies and slain bears, and the shards of pots, and hammer-, and arrow-heads and now and then a heavy silver Spanish spur."[13]

Faulkner employed local folklore about the death of Indians. Among them are stories of Toby Tubby, a Chickasaw who resided in the area that became Lafayette County. According to one story, Toby Tubby "went to get some whiskey in Holly Springs and was stabbed by a drunk. On his way back he stayed all night with the Rayburns. He was bleeding pretty badly [*sic*] He would not sleep in a bed and insisted that he sleep on a pallet in front of the fire. It was extremely cold that night and he caught pneumonia and died." Also, local legend holds that Toby Tubby was a very wealthy chief who owned many slaves. When he died, a slave and a great treasure were to be buried in the mound with him. Upon learning of the planned sacrifice, white settlers saved the slave's life. The story of the burial of a slave with Toby Tubby may be the basis for Faulkner's intense short story "Red Leaves." However, the slave who is to be buried with Chief Issetibbeha is not rescued from his fate by the intervention of whites. Rather than a mound, in "Red Leaves" Faulkner describes the place for burial of Issetibbeha as a "grave" that "was dug," which is in keeping with the actual custom among Chickasaws, who buried their dead in graves. A chief was inhumed in a sitting position facing east. Favorite possessions, including a pipe, war club, and bow and arrows, were interred with him. Sometimes pet animals were killed and placed in the grave, but the sacrifice of humans, once widespread in southeastern North America, appears to have been abandoned among the Chickasaws by the time the British entered their tribal lands. Toby Tubby supposedly was buried on the west bank of Toby Tubby Creek with a cedar tree planted at his head.[14]

Because Minnie Holt's 1935 account of Toby Tubby for the Federal Writers' Project was written five years after "Red Leaves" appeared in the *Saturday Evening Post*, her story that a slave was to be buried with Toby Tubby may be an example of remembered history based on Faulkner's fiction. However, there are various versions of the Toby Tubby story, some of which date from shortly after Lafayette County was settled. According to one version, Toby Tubby and his great treasure were buried in a mound in the Tallahatchie bottom close to where the Memphis-Oxford Road crossed the river. In his carefully researched biography of Faulkner, Joseph Blotner tells the version of the story in which the treasure was Toby Tubby's money from the sale of his ceded land. About 1890 a mound in the Tallahatchie bottom near the site of Toby Tubby's ferry was destroyed by treasure hunters.[15]

Over the years other mounds thought to hold treasure were demolished. In the 1930s a mound in Jim Wolf Creek bottom four miles north of the Tate-Lafayette county boundary, which according to local myth was the burial site of Chickasaw chief Jim Wolf, was leveled by the beat road supervisor. He owned the land on which the red clay mound was located and used his new motorized machinery to unearth the hidden treasure quickly. Except for a few bones and stone and clay artifacts, nothing was found.

The treasure myth also holds that if the mounds do not contain Indian objects of precious metal and gems, they are places where Lafayette County planters buried gold and silver coins, silverware, and other valuable objects to hide them from Union troops. Families in north Mississippi hid household valuables, bales of cotton, livestock, and food from the Union army, which overran Lafayette County twice during the war. Faulkner uses the burial of treasure as a component of "My Grandmother Millard and General Bedford Forrest and the Battle of Harrykin Creek."[16] The myth is not that valuables were hidden but that, for some reason, they were never retrieved. Over the years, gardens and orchards of plantation big houses were excavated; brick fireplaces and floors in the dwellings were dismantled and ripped up; and smokehouses and other farmstead buildings were thoroughly searched. Beyond big houses and their surroundings, the most obvious places for hidden treasure were entombments, planter graveyards and Indian mounds. In *Go Down, Moses* Lucas Beauchamp accidentally finds a gold coin while hiding his whiskey still at "a squat, flat-topped, almost symmetrical mound rising without reason from the floor-like flatness of the [Tallahatchie] valley." Lucas never questions his belief that the coin, the only one he found, is part of a treasure hidden in the mound during the Civil War by Buck and Buddy McCaslin.[17]

Settlement of Lafayette County

In the late 1700s the new United States of America began to take command of its unsettled western domain through a series of actions designed to control and neutralize the Indians who claimed tribal territories. Thomas Jefferson was a principal promoter of continuing a British strategy for driving the Indians farther west. The scheme was to establish in the territories privately owned trading posts at which Indians amassed debts. When forced to pay what they owed, the chiefs had to cede land. Among the reasons that the Choctaws and Chickasaws ceded the remainder of their lands in Mississippi was that the state extended its laws over the Indian domains, a deliberate ploy to force the tribes from their homelands.[18]

In 1830 the Chickasaws and Choctaws were hardly a poor primitive people, growing subsistence crops and chasing the last of the deer and other large game through the forest and across old fields. A number of the Indians in north Mississippi had adopted the tools, agricultural methods, and even lifestyles of whites, including ownership of African slaves and cotton plantations. Although only a few Indians knew English and could read and write, their lifestyle was quite different from what it had been in 1790. A federal agent reported in 1830:

> They have a plenty of Horses of superior quality . . . large herds of cattle, swine, sheep and goats, poultry of every description. . . . Cotton, beef, and pork are principal articles for exportation. . . . [They] have dry goods to render them comfortable and ornament their persons. . . . [The women are] decent and clean and in many instances particular attention is paid to fashions that are used by the whites. It is their constant practice to appear in their best apparel at their public meetings, also when they visit the country villages in the white settlements.[19]

The Indians also were interbred with whites. Some of the most powerful chiefs, including Chickasaws Levi and James Colbert and Choctaw Greenwood LeFlore, were part white. As white settlement and commerce increased across Indian lands, river ferries became important sources of income for the chiefs. Among them were James Colbert, who owned the ferry on the Natchez Trace that crossed the Tennessee River in north Alabama, and Slone Love, who had a ferry on the Tallahatchie River. Even though Toby Tubby died in 1835 or 1836, his name remained attached to the ferry on the Tallahatchie for the LaGrange-Hendersonville and Memphis-Oxford roads until Lafayette County constructed the Iron Bridge at the site in 1906. A few whites had farms, plantations, and stores in the Chickasaw and Choctaw territories before the Indians ceded their lands. Some descendants of the Harmons maintain that their ancestors settled in the area that became Lafayette County when it belonged to the Chickasaws. Dr. John Taylor, for whom the village of Taylor is named, came to Mississippi about 1810 and supposedly leased land from the Chickasaws. In 1839 it is thought that he received patents to land around Taylor signed by President Martin Van Buren.[20] It is more likely that Taylor received the right to establish a store in order to trade with the Chickasaws.

Lafayette was one of ten Mississippi counties created in the Chickasaw territory ceded by the treaty of Pontotoc Creek in 1832. The treaty provided for the land to be surveyed and sold privately and at public auctions. Following the cession, the federal government hired private contractors to survey north Mississippi using the United States rectilinear system, which was employed in the central and western parts of the nation and in Florida. Beginning at the intersect of an east–west base line and a north–south principal meridian, land was subdivided into six-mile by six-mile townships and the townships subdivided into thirty-six-square-mile sections, each of which contained approximately 640 acres.[21]

For the sale process, the land in the Chickasaw Cession was divided into two types, temporary homesteads and surplus unoccupied tracts held by the tribe. Each single adult Chickasaw and each orphan was assigned a temporary homestead. A single adult twenty-one and older received one 640-acre section. Each orphan was assigned a 320-acre half section. Families of ten or more persons received four sections (2,560 acres), families of five to nine were assigned three sections (1,920 acres), and families of fewer than five received two sections (1,280 acres). Chickasaws who owned one to nine slaves received an additional half section, and those with ten or more got an extra section. Powerful chiefs obtained more land than specified in the allotments. Title to a homestead was granted fee simple, absolute ownership with unrestricted rights of disposition. If a Chickasaw's "improvement" (a dwelling, field, mill, ferry, or other enhancement) was on a section or half section that could be farmed, the allotment had to include it. Otherwise, the allotment could be assigned to unoccupied land anywhere in the Chickasaw Cession. The Chickasaw settlement pattern before the cession was a haphazard one of clustered and dispersed improvements. Although there were exceptions, after the survey most of the allotments were assigned to the unoccupied sections desired most by the white purchasers.[22]

A variety of people intermingled on the north Mississippi frontier in the 1830s. In addition to the Chickasaws and Choctaws and their African slaves, who did not leave until five years after the 1832 Treaty of Pontotoc, the frontier teemed with federal surveyors, land speculators, agents for eastern land companies, planters seeking to purchase choice tracts of virgin soil, merchants who hastily constructed tent and log stores and saloons, and various other opportunists who sought to profit from money paid to the Indians for their land. Chickasaws who were competent to manage their affairs began to receive their wealth as soon as land was sold. The money due the uneducated ones was invested in bonds.[23] A roll of Chickasaws taken just prior to their removal in 1837 revealed 4,914 Indians and 1,156 African slaves. Because the Chickasaw Cession contained 6,422,400 acres, the sale of land brought vast sums in gold and silver to a relatively small number of people. The Chickasaw chiefs wanted a minimum of $3.00 per acre. However, the treaty specified a minimum price of $1.25 per acre ($31.23 in 2007 dollars). Speculation at auctions drove the price of the better agricultural land and land with strategic locations to much higher prices. For land that did not sell immediately, the minimum price of $1.25 per acre was reduced to $1.00 after one year and to 12.5 cents per acre after five years. By 1845 land sold in the Chickasaw Cession totaled approximately $3.3 million ($93.3 million in 2007 dollars). Despite the sale of some of the land at high prices, the average was less than $1.25 per acre, much lower than the $3.00 per acre for which the chiefs tried to bargain.[24] From the proceeds for their Mississippi domain, the Chickasaws had to pay for their new homeland in Indian Territory, for the survey and cost of selling their Mississippi land, and for the federal government to move them to their new home.

Henry Anderson and Edward Orne were principal land company agents in the Chickasaw Cession. Orne, a former ship captain from Salem, Massachusetts, represented the Boston and Mississippi Cotton Land Company, the Boston and New York Chickasaw Land Company, and the New York, Mississippi, and Arkansas Land Company. The three companies bought a total of 334,602 acres in the Chickasaw Cession. Anderson represented the American Land Company, which purchased 210,658 acres and sold them for a number of years at an office in Holly Springs (fig. 4.4).[25]

Between 1834 and 1837 Chickasaw chiefs sought a new homeland in the trans-Mississippi West. By the time tribal leaders were able to complete negotiations for an area in the southeastern part of Indian Territory (Oklahoma), large acreages of their Mississippi land had been sold, counties and towns had been created, and large numbers of settlers had arrived. In the spring of 1837, Marshall County had 8,274 whites and 5,222 blacks. The white population was the largest of any county in Mississippi. When Holly Springs was incorporated that same year, a population of 1,544 made it the third largest town in the state. Only Natchez and Vicksburg were larger.[26]

The longer they remained in their historic homeland, the more money the Chickasaws spent on various necessities and luxuries sold at outrageously high prices. A. M. Upshaw, the federal official in charge of moving the Chickasaws to Indian Territory, complained in May 1837 that the departure was hampered by "petty merchants" who wanted to keep them in Mississippi "as long as they have a cent."[27] In preparation for the move, the Chickasaws were concentrated in four

Figure 4.4. The former Holly Springs, Mississippi, office of the American Land Company, a New York joint-stock association created in 1835 to sell land purchased in the Chickasaw Cession. The building was constructed in the 1830s and is among the oldest structures in the town. Located one block south of the courthouse square, the edifice has been a residence for most of its history. The dwelling housed yellow-fever victims during the epidemic of 1878 and is known as the "yellow-fever house." Charles S. Aiken, 1999.

camps in Mississippi and Alabama. The journey, which was supposed to begin in the spring of 1837, did not commence until fall. Long trains of new wagons, slaves, horses, and cattle moved toward Memphis, from where the Chickasaws were to go by steamboat and overland to their new homeland. Bowers Reed McIlvaine, a Cincinnati insurance agent and a frontier romantic, described "a great band of the Chickasaws bound to new lands far in the West," which he encountered by chance while traveling across north Mississippi in 1837.

I do not think that I have ever been a witness of so remarkable a scene as was formed by this immense column of moving Indians, several thousand, with the train of Gov' waggons, the multitude of horses; it is said three to each Indian & beside at least six dogs & cats to an Indian. They were all most comfortably clad—the men in complete Indian dress with showy shawls tied in turban fashion round their heads—dashing about on their horses, like Arabs, many of them presenting the finest countenances & figures that I ever saw. The women also very decently clothed like white women, in calico gowns—but much tidier & better put on than common white-people—& how beautifully they managed their horses, how proud & calm & erect, they sat in full gallop.

McIlvaine comprehended the historical and geographical significance of the migration that he witnessed. The Chickasaws "are departing & their place will know them no more. . . . [L]ike the Ishmaelites they will pass from the face of the Earth, & live but in the memory of future generations, who will occupy their fields & trample their graves."[28]

The initial focus of settlement activity in the Lafayette County part of the Chickasaw Cession was not at the place that became Oxford. Rather, it was on the Tallahatchie River (map 4.2). Slone Love, a mixed-breed, rather than Toby Tubby, was the prominent Chickasaw chief in the area. Love's dwelling was on a broad natural terrace, what Eugene Hilgard called a "second bottom," in the Tallahatchie bottom a mile south of the river. In 1833 Love owned a ferry and a store on the Tallahatchie at a place federal surveyors labeled Mitchell's Bluff. Love sold the section in which the ferry and the store were located to Wyatt Mitchell and Volney Peel for $6,400 ($143,148 in 2007 dollars), $10 per acre, on May 24, 1837. The price was well above the required minimum of $1.25 per acre. The town of Wyatt was platted at the site of Mitchell's Bluff in 1837 and incorporated in 1838 (fig. 4.5, map. 4.3).[29]

On May 14, 1835, Tobo Tubby with an X as his mark transferred title to Sections 18 and 33, Township 7 South, Range 4 West, to James Brown for $3,000 ($72,836 in 2007 dollars), $2.35 per acre. On March 3, 1836, the two wives of Tobo Tubby gave title to the same sections to Brown. Apparently, Tobo Tubby died in 1835 or 1836. The site of Tobo Tubby's ferry was on the LaGrange-Hendersonville Road, later the Memphis-Oxford Road, in Section 7, which adjoins Section 33. Section 7 was one of three assigned to Il Lap Pah Umbey. On May 13, 1835, he sold Sections 5, 6, and 7 of the township to Edward Orne for $7,400 ($179,664 in 2007 dollars), $3.85 per acre. Because the creek that crosses Section 18 is named Toby Tubby and the ferry on the LaGrange-Hendersonville Road (and the Memphis-Oxford Road that replaced it) was called the Toby Tubby, it is probable that Tobo Tubby lived in the vicinity of Section 7. Unless other sections were assigned to him elsewhere, the two sections that Tobo Tubby received indicate that his household, including his two wives, numbered fewer than five. Although his ferry was a valuable asset, Tobo Tubby apparently did not have the large number of slaves or the wealth attributed to him by myth. Also, there is no evidence that he was a chief. As local tradition among whites holds, the word "Tubby" does not mean "chief" in Chickasaw.[30] Levi S. Harmon purchased Section 7 and the ferry, which continued to be called Toby Tubby. The ferry's value is revealed by the rent of $1,200 ($29,691 in 2007 dollars) paid in 1855 by Wesley Harmon to the estate of Levi Harmon, who died in 1854. Charges for ferrying were: loaded wagon 75¢, unloaded wagon 50¢, four-wheeled carriage 37½¢, man and horse 12½¢, footman 6½¢, and stock 2¢ per head.[31]

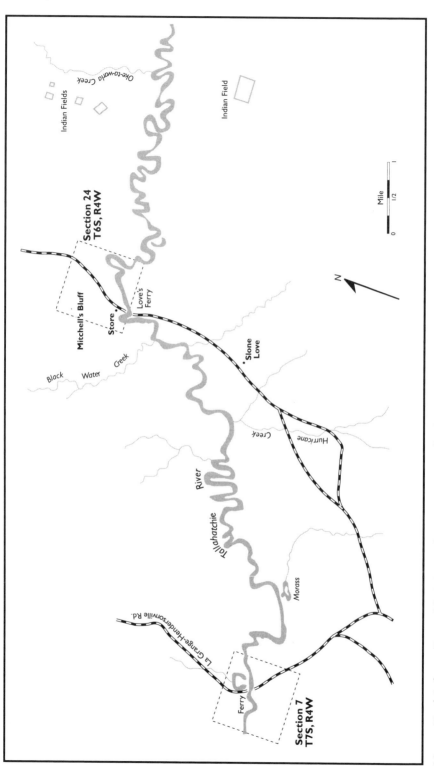

Map 4.2. North Lafayette County, Mississippi, at the commencement of settlement, 1833–1838. Developed from Chickasaw Cession Survey Maps (Township 7, Range 4 West; Township 6, Range 4 West; Township 6, Range 3 West,

Figure 4.5. Mitchell's Bluff, site of the extinct town of Wyatt on the Tallahatchie River, in Lafayette County, Mississippi, in 1980. From the river, nothing visible remains of the town, which in the 1850s had a number of commercial buildings and houses. Charles S. Aiken.

The reason that Mitchell's Bluff and Wyatt were so important at the time Lafayette County was settled is that large, bulky cargo, including four-hundred-pound bales of cotton, could be moved long distances to market at reasonable prices only by water. Roads in Lafayette County were dirt until they began to be graveled and paved in the 1930s. Small steamboats could travel from New Orleans by way of the Mississippi, the Yazoo, and the Tallahatchie to Mitchell's Bluff, which was the head of navigation. In Faulkner's stories of Issetibbeha, the front of the chief's dwelling was the deckhouse of a steamboat that had gone aground in the Tallahatchie's narrow, shallow channel when the water fell in late summer. After removing the machinery, the owners abandoned the shell. Ikkemotubbe (Doom), Issetibbeha's father, dismantled the boat and had his slaves haul it twelve miles to his ten-thousand-acre plantation south of the river.[32]

Volney Peel, who was one of the surveyors of the Chickasaw Cession, and Wyatt Mitchell, a land speculator and real estate promoter, knew that the Mitchell's Bluff site was the strategic transportation point for a large area to the north, south, and east. Wyatt maintained its strategic importance for more than two decades, losing its transportation advantage only with the construction of the Mississippi Central Railroad through Lafayette County in the 1850s. The railroad crossed the river a few miles east of Wyatt because the channel was narrower to bridge and the site was in line with Holly Springs to the north and Oxford to the south. In the 1840s, prior to the railroad, forty-five thousand bales of cotton were shipped annually

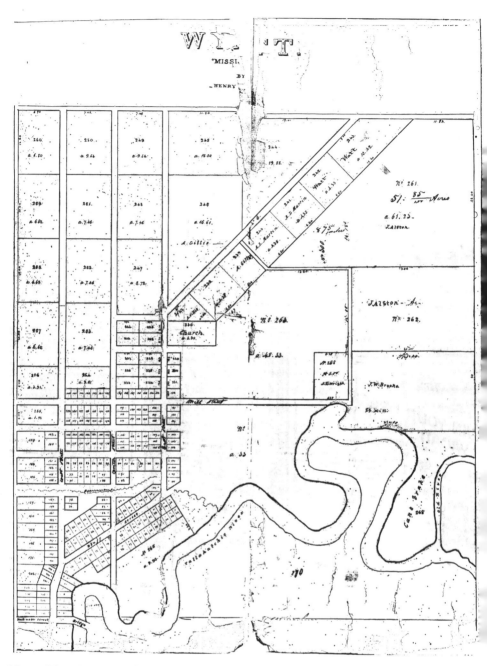

Map 4.3. Wyatt, Mississippi, about 1840. At the time it was incorporated in 1838, Wyatt was a principal river port in Lafayette County at the head of steamboat navigation on the Tallahatchie River. Bypassed by the Mississippi Central Railroad, by 1900 the town was extinct. Harmon Collection.

from Wyatt's river landing. Lafayette County was still strongly tied by rivers to New Orleans as late as 1850, for planters and businessmen maintained accounts at the city's banks. Although Wyatt began to decline in the 1850s, speculation in its lots continued into the 1870s.[33]

The place in Section 21, Township 8 South, Range 3 West that became Oxford had no strategic importance until the creation of Lafayette County on February 9, 1836. No road or Indian trace is shown in the section or township on the 1833 field survey maps. A county commission of four men, called the Board of Police, was appointed to select a location for the county courthouse. Volney Peel and Wyatt Mitchell were among the four. Although it might appear that Mitchell and Peel would have used their influence to make Wyatt the site of the courthouse, the directive from the Mississippi Legislature stated that the building had to be within a radius of five miles of the geographical center of the county.[34]

In 1835 John J. Craig built a log house with a store as an Indian trading post in Section 21, which is close to the center of Lafayette County. Craig's store was but one of the many tent and log stores and saloons that were quickly constructed by whites in the Chickasaw Cession to separate Indians from their new wealth. In 1836, the first year land could be purchased in Lafayette County, John J. Craig, together with John Chisholm of Alabama and John D. Martin, purchased Section 21 for $800 ($18,390 in 2007 dollars), the required minimum price of $1.25 per acre, from Hoka, an Indian woman to whom the 640-acre section was allotted. On June 22, 1836, the Board of Police accepted a fifty-acre tract in Section 21 that was donated for the location of the county courthouse. The gift was motivated by the opportunity to sell at greatly enhanced prices the property that adjoined the fifty acres.[35]

According to legendary history, Thomas Isom suggested the name Oxford for the new town with the idea that the state legislature would be more inclined to select it as the location for the state university. However, Isom's role in Lafayette County's history is misinterpreted. Because there is no evidence that John Chisholm ever resided in the county, and because John Craig's and John Martin's importance faded, Isom, who lived until 1902 and enjoyed a long, prestigious career, is remembered as the most important early settler (fig. 4.6). Both Martin and Isom, and probably Craig, were part of a group of Presbyterians who emigrated to Lafayette County from Maury County, Tennessee, and settled primarily in the area around College Hill. As a young man, Isom supposedly was a clerk in Craig's store. Isom later studied medicine, and although characterized by one of Oxford's long-time residents as "just an old country doctor," he became Oxford's and Lafayette County's most prominent physician, serving the leading citizens. However, Isom is mistakenly credited in some accounts as the one who established the trading

Figure 4.6. Dr. Thomas D. Isom, who was among the first residents of Oxford. He outlived the other early inhabitants of the town, dying in 1902. Unidentified photographer and date. Special Collections, University of Mississippi Libraries.

post that became Oxford.[36] A plaque at the site of Isom's office and drugstore on Oxford's courthouse square states: "Dr. Thomas Dudley Isom. Considered to be the first white settler of this region."

Selection of the site of Oxford involved more thought than what is superficially apparent from the historical records. Not only is the town near the center of Lafayette County, but it is on the drainage divide between the Tallahatchie and the Yocona rivers. At five hundred feet above sea level, Oxford is two hundred feet higher than the Tallahatchie and Yocona river bottoms. The atmosphere is slightly cooler and somewhat less humid than that in the bottoms on hot summer nights, and the mosquito population is considerably less. In the language of the nineteenth century, Oxford is high in elevation and has a pleasant, salubrious climate. Also, the early town had sources of uncontaminated water from springs and wells. The spring in Burney Branch was among several in the vicinity of Oxford, and it became the town's initial source of clean, refreshing water. Another six decades passed after Oxford's creation before it was discovered that mosquitoes are carriers of malaria and yellow fever and that contaminated water is a major source of typhoid. The diseases killed a number of Lafayette County citizens without discrimination as to race, wealth, or social status.

The physical landscape of the rolling upland areas of the north Mississippi Loess Plains is similar to that of the Piedmont of Virginia, the Carolinas, and Georgia, an area from which a number of the early settlers of Lafayette County migrated, including Augustus B. Longstreet, the first chancellor of the University of Mississippi, and L. Q. C. Lamar, his son-in-law. The site of Oxford, however, was not without problems. According to Faulkner, from the courthouse square in Jefferson ran "the four broad diverging avenues straight as plumb-lines in the four directions, becoming the network of roads and by-roads."[37] Here the description of Jefferson departs from that of Oxford. The streets within the fifty acres that comprise the original part of Oxford are not precisely oriented north–south and east–west. Unlike Jefferson, four east–west streets, rather than two, were surveyed from the courthouse square in Oxford (map 4.4). Embryonic Oxford was surveyed to conform to topography and to the arrangement of a few existing buildings, which were constructed without regard to the United States rectilinear survey (map 4.4). The courthouse square and the main thoroughfares of the town, North and South Lamar, are located on the crest of a ridge oriented north–northeast south–southwest. The land slopes away steeply from the ridge, what Faulkner calls "the plateau on which the town proper had been built."[38] The railroad and the Oxford depot are downhill to the west, fifty feet below the courthouse and outside the town's original boundaries. The legal description of the original part of Oxford is in metes and bounds, and only vaguely ties the town to the U.S. rectilinear survey. The town is "a certain piece of land Part [of] Section 21, Township 8, Range 3 West." The boundaries of the town begin "at a certain hickory tree near Craig's storehouse from thence North 80 poles, from thence east 100 poles so as to intersect the line of the South Boundary of the said described Tract at the distance of 50 poles." In 1838 the new town had six stores, two hotels, and more than a dozen dwellings. By 1860 the population of Lafayette County had grown to 8,980 whites, 7,129 slaves, and seven free colored. Marshall County, which had larger areas of desirable agricultural land, had 11,376 whites, 17,439 slaves, and eight free colored. Marshall ranked among the ten most prosperous agricultural counties in the United States.[39]

A serious topographical problem was encountered when the Mississippi Central Railroad was constructed through Oxford in the 1850s. Snaking up from the Yocona and Tallahatchie bottoms, the grades for the railroad to the town on the crest of the ridge proved too steep for early locomotives. Topography had to be adapted to the machine by excavation of a deep cut, the Hilgard Cut, through the crest of the drainage divide (fig. 4.7).

Although Faulkner obviously drew upon his father's ancestry for some of his characters, his use of his mother's family, the Butlers, for his fictional personae is more obscure. The Falkners did not move to Lafayette County until after the Civil War, but the Butlers were among the first whites to arrive. Charles G. Butler, Faulkner's great-grandfather, was hired to survey the new fifty-acre town of

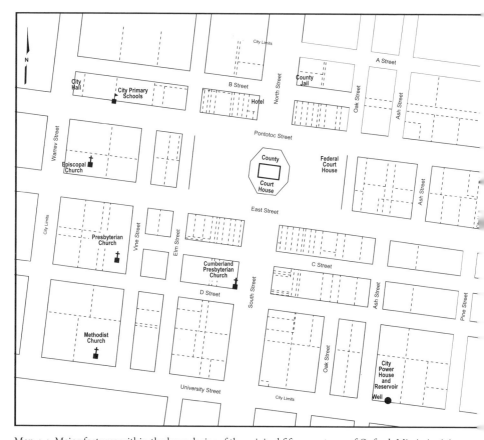

Map 4.4. Major features within the boundaries of the original fifty-acre town of Oxford, Mississippi, in 1939. The original town was surveyed by Charles Butler in 1838. Butler did not survey the streets precisely north–south and east–west. He either did not adjust for magnetic declination of the compass or tried to pl as much of the fifty-acre town as possible on the crest of the ridge dividing the Tallahatchie River and Yoco River drainage areas. Names of streets were changed over time. The original names of most of the north–south-oriented streets were for trees. Also, some streets were never fully developed and eventually were bu on. Redrafted from 1939 Oxford city map by W. L. Caldwell, courtesy of the Oxford Planning Commission. Charles S. Aiken.

Figure 4.7. Hilgard Railroad Cut looking north toward the Oxford railroad station in 1974. The cut is between the municipality of Oxford and the campus of the University of Mississippi and is among the deepest railroad incisions in nonmountainous areas of the United States. Although Eugene Hilgard, father of American soil science, is usually associated with the University of California, Berkeley, he spent the first two decades of his professional career at the University of Mississippi, where he did most of his innovative research. Hilgard studied soil profiles at railroad cuts. Charles S. Aiken.

Oxford. Butler was also the first elected sheriff of Lafayette County and a speculator in Lafayette County land and in Oxford and Wyatt lots. He bought the prime lot on the northwest corner of the courthouse square and constructed the Oxford Inn (fig. 2.4). Butler died in 1855, leaving the hotel, a livery stable, and several town lots to his wife, Burlina. With a net worth in 1860 of approximately $50,000 ($1.3 million in 2007 dollars), Burlina was one of the wealthiest women in Lafayette County.[40]

The process of settlement in northwestern Mississippi was one in which first the tablelands or plateaus of the Loess Plains were occupied, followed by the clearing of the natural terraces along the margins of the creek and river bottoms. Most of the property bought in Lafayette County during the first two years of land sales was in the northwest and north-central parts of the county. The prime areas included the tablelands around College Hill, Oxford, and Woodson Ridge, and the natural

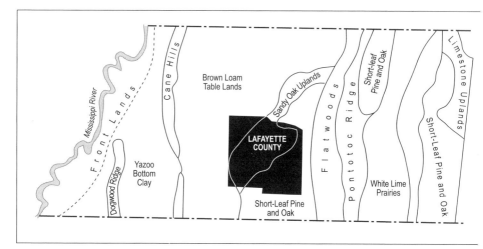

Map 4.5. Soil regions in north Mississippi as defined in 1860. Based on Hilgard 1907. Charles S. Aiken.

terraces along the Tallahatchie River (map 4.5).[41] By 1900 the alluvium along creeks and the rivers had begun to be drained and cleared. However, large areas of the Tallahatchie bottom were still forested and undrained at the time Sardis Reservoir was constructed in the 1930s.

Settlement of Yoknapatawpha County

Faulkner begins the history of Yoknapatawpha County "somewhere under the turn of the century," about 1800, when the place that became Jefferson originates as a Chickasaw agency trading post. Dr. Samuel Habersham is the post's first agent, and Alexander Holston, Habersham's groom and bodyguard, who became a tavern- and innkeeper, arrives with him. Holston may be based on Faulkner's maternal great-grandfather Charles Butler. By the time of *Intruder in the Dust*, the name Holston, similar to the name Butler, "had vanished . . . even from the county's spoken recollection: Holston merely the name of the hotel on the Square [the Holston House] and few in the county to know or care where the word came from." Jefferson begins as a "meager huddle of crude cabins set without order and every one a little awry to every other and all dwarfed to doll-houses by the vast loom of the woods which enclosed them." The first plantation is created by Louis Grenier, a Huguenot, who is the third white man in the area. Grenier acquires the first large land patent, located twenty miles southeast of the Chickasaw agency. Half of the patent is in what becomes Yoknapatawpha County and half is south of the Yokna-patawpha River in the area that becomes Grenier County. Grenier buys African slaves to work his cotton plantation.[42]

The principal Indian in the vicinity of the trading post is Issetibbeha, a Chicka-saw chief who dies between 1800 and 1808 and is succeeded by his son Moke-tubbe and then by his nephew Ikkemotubbe, who poisons Moketubbe. Mohataha, Issetibbeha's sister and mother of Ikkemotubbe, the last chief to rule the Yoknapa-tawpha area, is the local Chickasaw matriarch. In 1820 Jason Lycurgus Compson arrives at Habersham's store. In 1821 he trades his mare, with which he has won a number of races against the Indians' horses, to Ikkemotubbe for a square mile of land at the edge of the Chickasaw agency clearing. Although Compson is fic-tional, whites, including John Taylor and the Harmons, settled in the Chickasaw and Choctaw areas of Mississippi before the Indians ceded their lands. In *The Mansion* Faulkner refers to the boundary of Compson's Mile as "the old Chickasaw line," which is "the actual survey-line boundary which Mohataha, the Chickasaw matriarch, had granted to Quentin Compson in 1821."[43] Faulkner creates Comp-son's Mile thinking of a 640-acre square-mile section in the U.S. rectilinear survey system before he fully develops the fictional histories of Yoknapatawpha County and Jefferson. At the time Compson obtains his square mile in 1821, the north Mis-sissippi lands of the Chickasaws and Choctaws have not been ceded to the United States, the land surveyed into townships and sections, and sections assigned to in-dividual Indians. There is little likelihood that Compson's square mile would have meshed precisely with the U.S. rectilinear survey system. At a number of places the U.S. rectilinear and the metes-and-bounds survey systems meet, including in the Natchez area.[44] A land claim such as Compson's before cession would have had to have been legally requested and perhaps the land paid for again after the Chicka-saws relinquished their homeland.

Where the U.S. rectilinear survey system is found, most property boundaries, fences, fields, roads, and other linear landscape features are oriented north–south and east–west. Because houses front roads and property boundaries, dwellings and outbuildings usually face the cardinal directions. The federal survey system is overt throughout Faulkner's work. Yoknapatawpha County plantations, in addition to Compson's Mile, depict the system. Sutpen's Hundred is 100 sections, 64,000 acres. The McCaslin plantation is 2,000 acres, or specifically, it is three sections, 1,920 acres rounded to 2,000.[45]

Although precise conformity of his fiction with actual geography and history was never a major concern of Faulkner, in *The Mansion* he makes use of the sur-vey line for the property that the Chickasaw matriarch Mohataha had conveyed to Quentin Compson in 1821. After the Second World War a new arterial highway is to follow the old Chickasaw line. A lot that a petroleum company wants to buy for a service station had been sold by Jason Compson's father to a man named Mead-owfill. The legal metes-and-bounds description of the lot states that the boundary is "South to the road known as the Freedom Springs Road, thence East along said Road." The Freedom Springs Road has long been abandoned and is "an eroded thicket-grown ditch ten feet deep." Deeply eroded roadbeds are common in the Loess Plains of Mississippi. When loess is eroded straight down by wheels of vehicles, vertical walls are created along the roadbed. The metes-and-bounds description with the old road as the boundary means that Meadowfill's lot is thirteen feet short of the actual survey boundary of the property Mohataha had granted, and therefore is thirteen feet from the new highway, "as ponderable and inescapable a geographical condition as the Grand Canyon."[46]

Thomas Sutpen arrives at the post settlement in 1833, immediately after the Chickasaws and Choctaws cede their north Mississippi lands and Yoknapatawpha County is created. A few months after his arrival, Jefferson is chartered as a town by the Chickasaw post trader Ratcliffe, together with Jason Compson and a Dr. Peabody. Ratcliffe replaces the deceased Dr. Habersham. Dr. Peabody, who like the real Dr. Isom had a long life, appears throughout Faulkner's fiction. Dr. John Taylor, who arrived in the Mississippi Chickasaw territory about 1810, might have been Faulkner's source for Dr. Habersham. Taylor died on November 5, 1865, as federal occupation troops approached his home. The obvious origin of the name Jefferson is Thomas Jefferson, who not only authored the Declaration of Independence and became third president of the United States but also established Indian trading posts. However, Faulkner's satiric humor intercedes. The new town is not named directly for the president but for his namesake, Thomas Jefferson Pettigrew, the mail rider. The town is named for Pettigrew in order to obtain his mail pouch lock, which is needed for the door of Jefferson's first jail. By 1839, when John Sartoris arrives in Jefferson, slaves have finished the jail and are constructing a courthouse and two churches.[47]

Faulkner creates Mohataha drawing on Hoka, the Chickasaw woman who was allotted Section 21 in which Oxford is located. Mohataha comes to the trading post on Saturdays. She is "barefoot in a purple silk gown and a plumed hat, sitting in a gilt brocade empire chair in a wagon behind two mules under a silver-handled Paris parasol held by a female slave child."[48] Unable to read and write, at the agency store Mohataha signs her name with an X for the "tedious list of calico and gunpowder, whiskey and salt and snuff and denim pants and osseous candy drawn from Ratcliffe's shelves by her descendants and subjects and Negro slaves." The goods are not charged directly to Mohataha, but to the United States.[49] The federal government is to be repaid from the sale of the Chickasaw land.

Similar to other entrepreneurs who rushed into the Chickasaw Cession and quickly erected tent and log stores to separate the Indians from their new wealth, Ratcliffe is continually tempted to defraud the Indians. He "thought of that the first time he had charged the first sack of peppermint candy to the first one of old Mohataha's forty-year-old grandchildren and had refrained from adding two zeroes to the ten or fifteen cents . . . wondering each time why he did refrain." Compson buys part of the store and accepts Indian accounts to which he charges tobacco, calico, jeans, and cooking pots. To pay Thomas Jefferson Pettigrew for the lock for the jail, the initial idea is to charge it to the Chickasaw account at the agency store as fifteen dollars for axle grease to lubricate the wagon wheels for the westward trek to Indian Territory. But Dr. Peabody believes that the residents of the hamlet around the Chickasaw agency should pay for the lock. They create Jefferson and charge the lock to the municipality, which will owe the fifteen dollars into perpetuity.[50]

Faulkner's description of the exodus of the Indians from Yoknapatawpha County is less regal and orderly than the actual departure of the Chickasaws from north Mississippi described by Bowers Reed McIlvaine. The last time Mohataha comes to the agency store she "ratified the dispossession of her people forever." Mohataha asks, "Where is this Indian territory?" The reply is "West." She takes a pen, makes her X on a paper, and accompanied by a group of young men, "her household troops" who are "dressed in their Sunday clothes for traveling," she vanishes in a decrepit paintless wagon to the creak of ungreased wheels.[51]

The primary motivation for the federal government's quick removal of the Indians and the mad rush of settlers to occupy the Chickasaw Cession is cotton, a soft white fleece for which there is ceaseless demand as the Industrial Revolution gains momentum. Textiles are among the first industries for which automated machinery and the factory system are developed. The new factories with their spinning jennies and power looms require not just wool and flax but more and more cotton, "petty globules of Motion weightless and myriad even in the hand of a child, incapable even of wadding a rifle, let alone of charging it, yet potent enough to sever the very taproots of oak and hickory and gum . . . not the soaring cupola of the courthouse drawing people into the country, but that same white tide sweeping them in."[52]

FIVE

Civil War

The Civil War is central to southern history and is pivotal in William Faulkner's fiction. Although a relatively small part of Faulkner's fiction is set during the war, the conflict and its outcome haunt not only certain of Faulkner's characters but much of his work (fig. 5.1). Born in 1897, Faulkner belonged to the second generation of post–Civil War southerners. The burden of the conflict fell primarily on the two youngest of the four generations of whites and blacks who lived through the war. The youngest two included the rank and file of Confederate soldiers and their wives and sweethearts, together with persons who were children during the war. Large numbers of both generations were alive during Faulkner's childhood and early adult life. When asked in 1958 if he had known Confederate veterans, Faulkner responded:

> Yes. I remember a lot of them. I was five-six-seven years old around 1904–5–6 and 7, old enough to understand to listen. They didn't talk so much about that war, I had got that from the maiden spinster aunts which had never surrendered. But I can remember the old men, and they would get out the old shabby grey uniforms and get out the old battle-flag on Decoration, Memorial Day. Yes, I remember any number of them. But it was the aunts, the women, that had never given up.[1] (fig. 5.2)

Faulkner's family enthusiastically supported the Southern Confederacy. William C. Falkner, the writer's great-grandfather, who was known as "the old colonel," helped raise in his hometown of Ripley, Mississippi, the Magnolia Rifles, a company of volunteers that was incorporated into the Second Mississippi Infantry Regiment. In 1861 the Second Mississippi became part of General Joseph E. Johnson's Army of Shenandoah stationed at Harpers Ferry, Virginia. The regiment participated in First Manassas, the initial major battle of the Civil War, which was won by the Confederates. Falkner was a hero, but nine months later the men of the Second Mississippi, who regarded him a martinet and a reckless commander, refused by one vote to reelect him a regimental colonel. Among the Butlers, Faulkner's great-uncles William and Henry served in the Confederate army. Charles Edward Butler, Faulkner's grandfather, was a child during the war. Henry died in 1864 from wounds received at the Battle of Atlanta. William was discharged in 1862 after

Figure 5.1. William Faulkner was influenced by the life and legend of his great-grandfather, Colonel William C. Falkner. In certain respects, the colonel was always in the background, looking over the writer's shoulder as this photograph ironically depicts. Faulkner's mother, Maud Butler Falkner, painted the portrait.

he was diagnosed with tuberculosis by Dr. Thomas Isom. William was elected to Oxford's board of aldermen and participated in the initial rebuilding of the town but died in 1868.[2]

Oxford and Lafayette County contributed several companies to the Confederate army, including the Lafayette Guards and Thompson's Calvary. The best-remembered companies in the county's legendary history are the University Greys and the Lamar Rifles. The University Greys Company was composed primarily of University of Mississippi students from various parts of the state, but a number of the soldiers were from Lafayette and Marshall counties (fig. 5.3). The Lamar Rifles was a company from Oxford and Lafayette County named for L. Q. C. Lamar, noted attorney and University of Mississippi faculty member. Following the war, Lamar was a Mississippi congressman and the first southerner named to the U.S. Supreme

Figure 5.2. The vanishing army of the Confederate States of America. Sixteen survivors of the Lamar Rifles commemorated the fortieth anniversary of the formation of the company, Oxford, Mississippi, November 28, 1901. One of the former slaves who served as a company cook also attended the reunion but is not included in the photograph. Captain William G. Nelms is standing at far left dressed in his Confederate uniform. Survivors Association of Lamar Rifles [1901].

Figure 5.3. Students in front of the Lyceum at the University of Mississippi about 1860. The dress may appear to be stereotypical Old West rather than Old South, but in 1860 Mississippi was in the West. Approximately one-third of Mississippi white men ages sixteen to twenty-three lost their lives in the Civil War. Edward C. Boynton. Special Collections, University of Mississippi Libraries.

Table 5.1 The battles and skirmishes of the Lamar Rifles, Company G,
Eleventh Mississippi Regiment, Davis's Brigade, Heath's Division, A. P. Hill's Corps,
Army of Northern Virginia, 1862–1865

1861	The Lamar Rifles arrived on the war scene at the First Manassas (*First Bull Run*) battlefield after the conclusion of fighting on July 21, 1861.
1862	Seven Pines, May 31, June 1
	Gaines Farm, June 27 ⎫
	White Oak Swamp, June 30 ⎬ Three days of the *Seven Days Battle*
	Malvern Hill, July 1 ⎭
	Freeman's Ford, August 25
	Thoroughfare Gap, August 28
	Second Manassas (*Second Bull Run*), August 29, 30
	South Mountain, September 14
	Sharpsburg (*Antietam*), September 16, 17
1863	Gettysburg, July 2, 3
	Falling Waters, July 14
	Bristoe Station, October 14
1864	The Wilderness, May 5, 6
	Tolles Mill, May 10
	Spotsylvania Courthouse, May 12
	Hanover Junction, May 23
	Bethsaida Church, June 2, 3
	Weldon Railroad (Petersburg), June 18, 19
	David Farm, October 1
	Jones Farm, October 3
	Hatcher's Run, October 27
1865	Hawkes Farm (*Fort Stedman*), March 25

Source: Survivors Association of the Lamar Rifles [1901].
Note: Union names for battles are in italics.

Court. Both companies were integrated into the Eleventh Mississippi Infantry Regiment, which was composed primarily of men from the northern part of the state. The Eleventh Mississippi left for Virginia in the summer of 1861 and spent the remainder of the war as part of General Robert E. Lee's legendary Army of Northern Virginia. The University Greys, the Lamar Rifles, and the Eleventh Mississippi had distinguished military records, participating in some of the most significant and bloodiest battles of the Civil War (Table 5.1). The apogee for the Lamar Rifles and the University Greys was the third day of Gettysburg, July 3, 1863, the day that is considered the culmination of the Civil War. Men of both companies, together with others from the Eleventh Mississippi and the Fifty-fifth North Carolina, part of Davis's Brigade, successfully completed the deadly controversial charge across a mile of open ground ordered by General Lee to break the Union line. The men breached the line and reached a point forty-seven yards beyond it before being driven back, killed, or captured. The casualty rate for the University Greys at Gettysburg was 100 percent, although all who were wounded did not die.[3]

A Dead Period

Faulkner's presentation of the Civil War has two facets. On the one hand is "the unvanquished," a series of seven short stories about Colonel John Sartoris and his family set in the course of the war and published in popular magazines during the 1930s. Faulkner's primary purpose in writing the stories was to make badly needed money by capitalizing on the renewed national interest in the war stimulated by the seventy-fifth anniversary of the conflict (1936–1940). The series began with "Ambuscade," which was published in September 1934, and was followed by "Retreat" (October 1934), "Raid" (November 1934), "Skirmish at Sartoris" (April 1935), "The Unvanquished" (November 1936), and "Vendee" (December 1936). All but "Skirmish at Sartoris," which appeared in *Scribner's Magazine*, were published by the *Saturday Evening Post*. The seven stories were rewritten, an eighth, "An Odor of Verbena," was added, and the collection was published in 1938 as *The Unvanquished*.

Faulkner presents a different view of the Civil War in his other fiction. Rather than glorifying the conflict as a lost cause for the South, he gives an adverse sardonic interpretation of the war and the lingering impact during what he terms a "dead period." Faulkner opens his vendetta in *Sartoris*, the first of the Yoknapatawpha chronicles. At the beginning of the novel, the elderly Will Falls, who fought with Colonel John Sartoris, brings "the spirit of the dead man" and the war into the Merchants and Farmers Bank. Falls and John Sartoris's son Bayard, who is president of the bank, are "cemented by a common deafness to a dead period."[4]

The lingering destructive power of the Civil War is employed by Faulkner in *Light in August*. The Reverend Gail Hightower is so taken with the story of his grandfather, who supposedly was killed during General Earl "Buck" Van Dorn's raid on Jefferson to destroy a Union supply depot, that he aggressively seeks the call to be pastor of the town's Presbyterian Church. But the story so consumes him that he dwells on the raid in his sermons Sunday after Sunday. Eventually both Hightower, who loses his pastorate, and his wife, who commits suicide in Memphis, are destroyed by the long-past event from which the minister could not free himself either in the pulpit or in his private life.[5]

Initially in his Yoknapatawpha saga, Faulkner seems torn as to where to focus his Civil War stories geographically. Colonel Falkner's most significant exploits occurred while he was with the Second Mississippi regiment fighting in Virginia, and the writer at first set his Civil War stories in that state. In *Sartoris*, from the Yoknapatawpha perspective, the war in Virginia was waged in "dark and bloody obscurity."[6] However, as Faulkner developed the Yoknapatawpha saga, he focused less on Virginia and more on events in north Mississippi. In concentrating his Civil War stories on the area in and around Lafayette County, Faulkner changed what he considered minor historical facts. After fighting bravely at Second Manassas, John Sartoris lost his command when he was defeated for the rank of colonel in the regimental election of officers. Sartoris "came home and oversaw the making and harvesting of a crop on his plantation . . . got bored and gathered up a small gang of irregular cavalry and carried it up into Tennessee to join Forrest."[7]

William C. Falkner returned to Ripley, Mississippi, upon losing his command in Virginia after First Manassas and organized two groups of partisan rangers that operated briefly in west Tennessee and north Mississippi. However, there is no concrete evidence that, like John Sartoris, Falkner was ever with Nathan Bedford Forrest. In April 1863 Falkner's rangers engaged in a fight near Hernando with the Twelfth Wisconsin Cavalry, one of several Union diversionary forces moving from Memphis and LaGrange, Tennessee, south into Mississippi. The main force was seventeen hundred cavalrymen from LaGrange led by Colonel Benjamin Henry Grierson. The objective was to move across the Confederate frontier deep into the interior of Mississippi to destroy the east–west railroad to Vicksburg. Colonel Falkner's troops were severely defeated. Approximately forty men were killed and seventy-two captured. Although Colonel Falkner may not have been in command at the devastating skirmish, he bore the responsibility. After the defeat, Falkner submitted his resignation from military service, giving declining health as the reason. The remainder of his First Partisan Rangers, which in 1864 became the Seventh Mississippi Cavalry, was integrated into Forrest's army. However, William C. Falkner never served with Forrest despite myths to the contrary. Also, no clear record exists as to what Falkner did during the remainder of the war after his resignation.[8]

In the creation of his own myth, Faulkner sometimes used fiction as reality. A few months before his death in 1962, he was invited to the U.S. Military Academy at West Point. When asked if he could tell something about his grandfather, Faulkner knew that the question pertained to William C. Falkner, his great-grandfather. His answer inflated Falkner's military importance:

He went to the Mexican War as a friend of Jefferson Davis. In 1860 he organized, raised, and paid most of the expenses for the Second Mississippi Infantry. . . . He commanded, as senior colonel, the brigade with [Stonewall] Jackson until Bee arrived and took command before First Manassas. . . . In the election of officers the next year . . . his men elected his lieutenant colonel to command the regiment, and my grandfather got mad and went back to Mississippi, and got bored . . . and raised a company of partisan cavalry that was finally brigaded into Forrest, and he finished the war there as a cavalryman.[9]

Another example of Faulkner's shifting the focus of the Civil War from Virginia to north Mississippi and west Tennessee is in *Absalom, Absalom!* when half-brothers Henry Sutpen and Charles Bon enlist in the University Greys. The fictional Greys fight at the Battle of Shiloh in west Tennessee in the spring of 1862, far from Virginia where the actual company spent the war. When asked about the conflict as depicted in *Absalom, Absalom!*, Faulkner replied, "I used the Civil War . . . for my own ends there."[10]

Faulkner's shift of his focus on the war from Virginia to the Yoknapatawpha area means that he devotes little attention to Robert E. Lee, Thomas (Stonewall) Jackson, and other Confederate heroes who fought in the East. Instead, the primary officer in his stories is Nathan Bedford Forrest, one of the most able, innovative, and controversial of the Confederate generals. General U. S. Grant said of the Confederate, "for the peculiar kind of warfare which Forrest had carried on neither army could show a more effective officer than he." Faulkner refers to Forrest in eight short stories and nine novels and in several places uses him fictionally as a participating character.[11]

In north Mississippi and west Tennessee, Forrest, who had no military training and little formal education, is regarded to have been a better leader than Lee, Jackson, or any other Confederate general. Among Faulkner's comments about Lee is one he made to Shelby Foote as the two toured the Shiloh battlefield in 1952. "Lee should have taught the North not to leave folks no ground to stand on." Forrest commanded a fast-moving force of approximately two thousand cavalry and mounted infantry that struck quickly and employed innovative strategy. He passed into legend during the war. Some Confederate soldiers deserted their commands to join Forrest, who was told more than once by his superiors to purge his troops of unassigned men. Willis Lea, a member of the University Greys who was furloughed from Lee's Army of Northern Virginia to his home in Marshall County to recover from wounds, wrote his brother, Nathaniel, in July 1864 an account of Forrest's victory at Brice's Crossroads: "Our people think that old Forest [*sic*] is the greatest man of the age. He is a trump and a heavy one at that. In this last affair with the enemy [General Stephen D.] Lee and Forest attacked 18,000 Yankees (11,000 Infantry and 7,000 Cav. And Art.) with 6,000 . . . Cav. Boldness saved the day. The enemy were deceived, as to our strength, by our bold front."[12]

Figure 5.4. Bronze statue of Lieutenant General Nathan Bedford Forrest in Forrest Park, Memphis, Tennessee. Forrest, who had no military training, rose from the rank of private during the conflict to become a daring, innovative, and controversial Confederate cavalry officer. Forrest's creative tactics anticipated modern lightning warfare. He appears more a medieval knight than a modern American army officer, dramatically illustrating the great changes in warfare during the century following the Civil War. Charles S. Aiken, 2006.

Forrest spent much of his life as a Memphis businessman. After the war he resumed his planting and lumber businesses and, like Colonel William C. Falkner, became involved in railroad construction. General William T. Sherman thought that Forrest was a type of Confederate who would never surrender but instead, after the Confederacy surrendered, would engage in guerilla warfare or flee the United States. However, on May 9, 1865, Forrest announced to his soldiers that the war was over and he was going home. Forrest told his troops, "Obey the laws and preserve your honor and the government to which you have surrendered can afford to be magnanimous."[13]

Forrest died at Memphis in 1877. The general and his wife are buried in a city park named in his honor (fig. 5.4). A large equestrian statue, erected in 1905, rises above the graves. For nearly a century, July 13, Forrest's birthday, was an official holiday in Tennessee, its celebration passing only in the late twentieth century with the civil rights movement and fading memories of the Civil War. Like Faulkner, many white residents of west Tennessee and north Mississippi claim an ancestor who rode with Forrest. If the general had actually possessed an army composed of all the ancestors declared to have been with him, he would have had as large and formidable a Confederate force as Union troops often thought he had.

Forrest's reputation as an innovative and successful Confederate commander reached a peak during the years Faulkner wrote his novels and stories. After the

Second World War a myth even arose that Field Marshal Erwin Rommel, the Desert Fox who practiced blitzkrieg, had visited the United States specifically to study Forrest and his military tactics. *Rommel and the Rebel* is a novel based on the myth. Beginning in the 1960s, persons involved in the civil rights movement and revisionist historians began to depict a different interpretation of Forrest than the one presented by Faulkner and the general's early biographers. Forrest is portrayed as a guerrilla fighter who deliberately permitted the massacre of black soldiers after retaking Fort Pillow in Tennessee and as an organizer and head of the Ku Klux Klan during Reconstruction. However, Forrest fought within the command structure of the Confederate army, which was under the Confederate government. The Fort Pillow massacre story began immediately after the fight and was quickly denied by Forrest. He stated that blacks together with whites were killed in the fighting. In accordance with the policy of the Confederate government, former slaves were taken prisoner and returned to their masters. Forrest's role in the Ku Klux Klan was largely honorary. Although he initially supported the Klan, he tried to disband the organization after its violence grew.[14] Compared with Union officers, Forrest was similar to Grant and Sherman. All three understood the total war that emerged in the American Civil War, and all three remain controversial.

Total War

When questioned about the War between the States as depicted in *Absalom, Absalom!*, Faulkner replied that "Sutpen's country was wrecked by the Civil War."[15] Superficially, Faulkner's description of a destructive total war, waged on civilians as well as among soldiers, may seem not in accord with creation of his apocryphal county from the actual geography and history of north Mississippi. Disagreement exists among military scholars as to the exact definition of "total war." However, a group of historians considers the Civil War total war in the South because the Union not only sought to destroy the Confederate military but to demoralize civilians by laying waste to the southern economic infrastructure and social order.[16] The Union also abolished a nation. Despite the brief existence of the Confederate States of America, nearly a century and a half after its downfall several million Americans consider themselves its hereditary citizens.

No major battles or events that affected the outcome of the Civil War occurred in north Mississippi where Faulkner places Yoknapatawpha County. Historians have paid little attention to the conflict in the area, with the exception of events pertaining to Confederate generals Nathan Bedford Forrest and Earl Van Dorn. In his Pulitzer Prize–winning *Battle Cry of Freedom*, James McPherson hardly mentions north Mississippi.

The type of destruction associated with total war began in the Union army's fights with guerrillas in Missouri and Kansas in the summer of 1861. By the fall of 1862 total war had spread into west Tennessee and north Mississippi. In January 1863 Sergeant Alexander Downing of the Eleventh Iowa Infantry wrote in his diary that the country along the Tennessee-Mississippi border "from Memphis to Iuka, a distance of about one hundred miles, and for miles on either side . . . has been laid waste and is almost desolate. . . . Vacant houses on plantations or in towns and villages have been burned. Many of these were substantial buildings with stone chimneys, which generally remain standing. . . . These the boys hilariously spoke of as . . . 'another Tennessee Headstone,' or a 'Mississippi headstone.'" A correspondent for a New York newspaper wrote in September 1863 that between La Grange, Tennessee, and Holly Springs he discovered that only five out of fifty plantations were occupied, and buildings had been burned on most.[17] The story that great destruction occurred in Lafayette County during the war survives in official documents, private letters, diaries, and oral history. As told in 1910 by persons who experienced the war firsthand, "The county suffered greatly. . . . Wherever the Union army passed it left only poverty and destruction. All the stores in Oxford were destroyed and five residences in the town were burned. Grant's army came through the county, burning as they went. Live-stock were taken and all provisions destroyed or carried away. Many houses were plundered and destroyed."[18]

Oxford and Lafayette County became caught up in a growing war spirit in the winter and spring of 1861 and knew the conflict firsthand from the autumn of 1862 to the end of the war in the spring of 1865. By the autumn of 1862 west Tennessee and the area of Mississippi north of the Tallahatchie River had become a no-man's-land where the Union army had established fortified garrison towns and cities (map 5.1). The fortified places included Memphis, LaGrange, Grand Junction, and Jackson in Tennessee and Corinth and Columbus in Mississippi. Because large numbers of Confederate companies from Mississippi left early in the war for Virginia and the East, the Army of Mississippi was never very large, numbering less than ten thousand men. The Confederate war initiative in no-man's-land was largely confined to raids on supply lines by lightning cavalry and mounted infantry and to battles in which the Confederate army was outnumbered. The relatively safe Confederate interior of Mississippi from the beginning of the war in 1861 until the summer of 1863 lay south of the Yocona River. The Confederate frontier, which experienced repeated penetrations by the Union army beginning in the autumn of 1862, was between the Tallahatchie and Yocona rivers. Although no major battles were fought in Lafayette and Marshall counties, skirmishes, together with pillage and burning by the Union army, and even by deserters and scavengers from the Confederate army, occurred intermittently. From the arrival of the first large Union

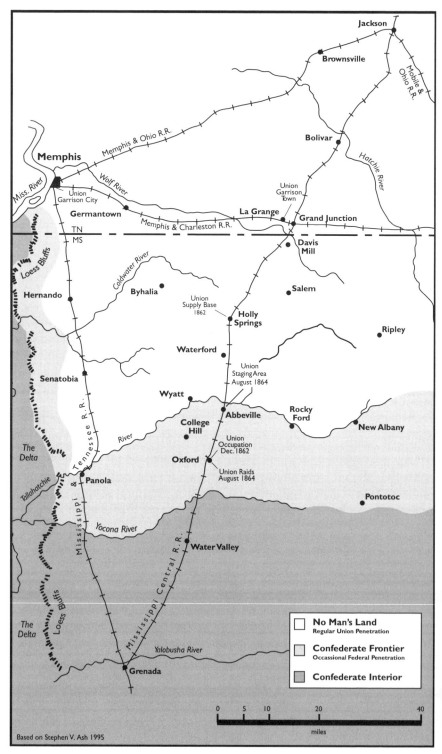

Map 5.1. Confederate and Union control of north Mississippi and west Tennessee, 1862–1865. Adapted to north Mississippi and west Tennessee by Charles S. Aiken from a concept by Stephen V. Ash 1995, 78.

armies under the command of Generals Grant and Sherman in the autumn of 1862 until August 1864, when General A. J. Smith withdrew his large force sent into north Mississippi to "kill Forrest," Lafayette and Marshall counties experienced large surges of Union troops, who confiscated food and livestock and looted and burned. During the last year of the war, north Mississippi did not have sufficient numbers of Confederate regulars or local militia to control small bands of deserters and raiders who robbed and scorched the countryside and towns. The bands were searching for anything of value that could easily be carried off, especially gold, silver, livestock, and food.

Grant and Sherman's brief invasion of Lafayette County in December 1862 was staged from Memphis and LaGrange, Tennessee, south along major roads and the Mississippi Central Railroad. The objective of the seventy-two-thousand-man army was to capture Vicksburg by land from the north and east. Grant moved his army using eighteen locomotives that pulled long trains over the Mobile and Ohio, the Memphis and Charleston, and the Mississippi Central railroads. He built a large supply depot for the Vicksburg campaign at Holly Springs. On December 1, 1862, Grant telegraphed General Henry W. Halleck in Memphis that he was advancing into Confederate frontier. "Our cavalry are now crossing Tallahatchie. . . . Sherman is up and will cross the Tallahatchie at Wyatt." Grant made Oxford his headquarters, and Sherman advanced to College Hill. Union maps reveal that Oxford was a strategic choke point where roads and the railroad converged and through which both armies would have to move (fig. 5.5; map 5.2).[19]

The large Union invasion of Lafayette County was accompanied by substantial looting and burning of houses and farmsteads. Members of the Presbyterian Church at College Hill viewed the actions of Sherman's thirty thousand troops as a "heavy clamity [sic] which God in his providence has seen fit to inflict upon our Community." "In some instances" the Yankees "forced worthy citizens to Leave . . . their homes and then Set fire to their domicils [sic]. . . . They not only robbed us of all property which they could appriate [sic] to their benefit but destroyed much which was of no use to themselves."[20]

Early in the war, both Generals Grant and Sherman officially condemned looting and destruction of property. In 1862 Grant warned his troops in west Tennessee and north Mississippi that "confiscation acts were never intended to be executed by soldiers. . . . Individuals will be summarily punished to the full extent or merely given to garrison courtmartials." Despite a few retributions, his orders were generally ignored. Sherman told his troops at College Hill, "Our mission is to maintain, not violate, all laws, human and divine. Plundering is harmful to our cause and to the honorable tone which characterizes the army of a great nation." However, before the invasion of northwest Mississippi, the secretary of war ordered Grant to

Figure 5.5. Tents of an Illinois regiment, among the troops of General U. S. Grant, camped in the yard of the Lafayette County, Mississippi, courthouse, December 1862. The troops were guarding twelve hundred Confederate prisoners confined in the courthouse. The courthouse was destroyed by fire set on August 22, 1864, by Union troops under the command of General A. J. Smith. Miller and Lanier, *Photographic History of the Civil War* 1911.

"subsist" "refugee negroes. . . . and your army on the rebel inhabitants of Mississippi." According to Grant, in retrospect, with the Confederate armies' offensives to regain territory lost through the spring of 1862, he "gave up all idea of saving the Union except by complete conquest" and decided "to consume everything that could be used to support or supply armies."[21] Succinctly, by officially sanctioned burning and plundering that affected women and children, Grant and Sherman brought total war to Lafayette County.

In the December 12, 1862, field orders to his officers, Grant remarked that "distress and almost famine hav [*sic*] been brought on many of the inhabitants of Mississippi by the march of the two armies [his and Sherman's] through the land and humanity dictate that in a land of plenty no one should suffer the pangs of hunger."

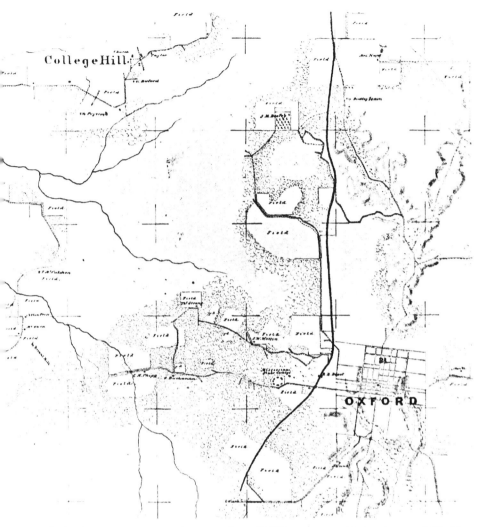

Map 5.2. Oxford and vicinity in 1862. First Lieutenant James H. Wilson, topographical engineer, and Otto H. Matz, cartographer. "The Country between the Tallahatchie River and Oxford, Mississippi," U.S. Army, Sixteenth Corps, 1862. Scale: 1 inch to 1 mile. National Archives, Washington, D.C. Wilson was one of the best U.S. Army topographical engineers (McElfresh 1999, 123–146).

Grant ordered that each army post was "authorized to keep for sale provisions and absolute necessaries for family use" for persons loyal to the Union. A fund was to be created "to supply the necessaries of destitute families gratis, either by levying contributions upon those disloyal persons who are able to pay, taxing cotton brought to their posts for sale, or in any other equitable way."[22] Looting and destruction of property in north Mississippi, which began when the Union army entered the state, continued. Families were not usually paid for what was stolen, and some families were left destitute of food.

Despite the belief that the Union army was well supplied with food, Sergeants Alexander Downing and Lucius Barber continually complained in their diaries during the summer and into the fall of 1862 about the lack of sufficient rations. Gruel, wheat flour mixed with corn meal and boiled with water in a pot, was a staple, which failed to satisfy the men's hunger. From December 6 through 18, Sergeant Downing repeatedly wrote in his diary of confiscation and destruction of food and property around Abbeville in Lafayette County without any mention of Grant's payment plan. All families were assumed to be rebels. Deep in the Confederate frontier, no one was thought to be loyal to the Union.

The following diary entries are for December 1862:

Saturday, 6th—I was on duty today with a forging party of our division, to help load the wagons with corn and cotton. We brought in seventy-five loads of cotton worth about $40,000 [$850,630 in 2007 dollars]. At one plantation some negroes were out at work picking cotton while others were bailing it in the gin house, but we drove into the houses and loaded up without asking for the privilege. The Sixth [Iowa] Division almost every day brings in from seventy-five to one hundred loads of corn or cotton. This part of the state is thickly settled and the settlements are rich. . . .

Monday, 8th—The Sixth Division is running a [grist] mill now. . . . We are now drawing full rations of meal instead of crackers and we have plenty of fresh pork and sweet potatoes. The boys have confiscated every bake oven in the country. . . . We all appreciate full rations after our fast at Grand Junction.

Tuesday, 9th—Our forging parties destroy a great deal of property unnecessarily, especially when the owner of a plantation is away with the rebel army—then there isn't much left when the boys get through.

Monday, 15th—The quartermaster of our division has brought together at this place [Oxford] about $1,000,000 [$21.3 million in 2007 dollars] worth of cotton, which is to be shipped to the North.

Thursday, 18th—We started at 6 o'clock this morning and arrived in Oxford at about 10. We were inspected by General Grant. . . . It is a fine town, on high ground and well built up with fine homes of the rich planters. A college is located here, with good buildings. The surrounding plantations are well fenced and have good buildings.[23]

In November 1862 General Grant realized that he and his seventy-two thousand troops increasingly were in a precarious situation in north Mississippi. General John A. McClenard, a political appointee, planned an expedition down the Mississippi River to capture Vicksburg and upstage Grant. To scotch McClenard, Grant ordered Sherman and his troops to return from College Hill to Memphis and to advance down the Mississippi River to Vicksburg. Another problem that Grant confronted was his extension across no-man's-land and deep into the Confederate frontier with a fragile supply line, which he was afraid that Forrest would attack and cut in west Tennessee. Despite beginning with good intentions, the actions of Grant, Sherman, and the Union army in Tennessee and Mississippi had inflamed Confederates' embitterment and hostility and even alienated persons who had been loyal citizens of the United States. On December 15 Grant wrote his youngest sister, Mary: "There are an immense number of lives staked upon my judgement and acts. I am extended now like a peninsula into an enemy's country, with a large army depending for their daily bread upon keeping open a line of railroad running one hundred and ninety miles through an enemy's country, or, at least, through territory occupied by a people terribly embittered and hostile to us."[24]

Five days later, on December 20, General Van Dorn led thirty-five hundred men on a daring cavalry raid on Grant's supply depot at Holly Springs, destroying a significant part of the stores for the Vicksburg campaign.[25] That same day, Forrest raided Jackson, Tennessee, and cut the Mobile and Ohio Railroad (map 5.3). Low on food and in immediate peril, Grant ordered additional confiscation by the Union army. Grant's forage zone was fifteen miles on each side of the Mississippi Central Railroad between Coffeeville and the Memphis and Charleston Railroad in Tennessee (map 5.4). Three decades later in his memoirs he still gloated over his revenge for Van Dorn's and Forrest's raids:

> The news of the capture of Holly Springs and the destruction of our supplies caused much rejoicing among the people remaining in Oxford. They came with broad smiles on their faces indicating intense joy, to ask what I was going to do now without anything for my solders to eat. I told them not to be disturbed, that I had already sent troops and wagons to collect all the food and forage they could find for fifteen miles on each side of the road. Countenances soon changed, and so did the inquiry. The next was, "what are *we* to do?"[26]

According to Grant's autobiography, his orders included the stipulation that "two month's supplies" were to be left "for the families of those whose stores were

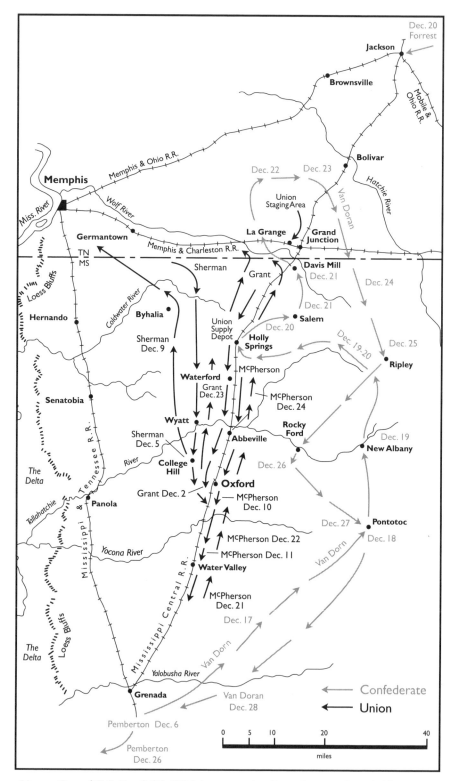

Map 5.3. General U. S. Grant's failed Vicksburg campaign, December 1862. Compiled from *Official Records* and from a map by Edwin C. Bearss 1962, 85. Charles S. Aiken.

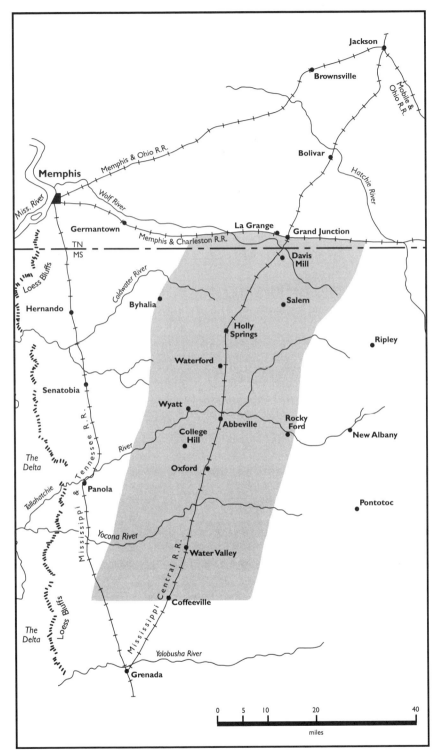

Map 5.4. General U. S. Grant's forage zone in December 1862. The description of the zone is in Grant 1885, 1:435–436. Charles S. Aiken.

taken." But in his December 25, 1862, report to Union army headquarters in Washington, D.C., Grant stated that "for 15 miles east and west of the railroad, from Coffeeville to La Grange, nearly everything for the subsistence of man or beast has been appropriated for the use of our army."[27]

Written accounts by Union soldiers and oral history of Lafayette County confirm that everything of use to the Union army, including horses, mules, and even gold, silver, and other personal property, were taken. Perhaps one of the saddest stories is one related by Sergeant Barber of the Fifteenth Illinois Infantry, who wrote in his diary near Waterford in Marshall County just north of the Tallahatchie River: "There were unprincipled soldiers who had not the least partial of humanity about them. They would rob rich and poor, old age and youth, widows and orphans, and weak and helpless alike. I have time and again seen a poor lonely woman with a house full of little ones, on her knees, begging these wretches not to take the last mouthful from her starving children, and, perhaps when they left she would be horseless and homeless, left with her little ones to starve."[28]

Families hid money, silver, food, livestock, and cotton. Some Union soldiers sought to find and steal gold and silver. According to Sergeant Barber, who was with the advanced left wing of the Union army under General James McPherson south of Oxford in November 1862, "The boys commenced an indiscriminate foraging with avidity that knew no limits. In many places gold was found which the rebels had buried before leaving for the war to prevent its falling to the hands of the Yankees, but a little coaxing would induce the head darkey on the plantation to divulge its hiding place."[29] Sarah Elizabeth Harmon's family hid part of its pork in a barrel beneath the floor of the smokehouse. A shallow depression where the barrel had been buried was visible below the ruins of the log building a century later. Union soldiers took the horse of Sarah Elizabeth who, living in a house of women and children, was a teenager during the war. Some Lafayette County inhabitants were paid in United States greenbacks for confiscated food, feed, and livestock or were issued vouchers signed by Union officers. Although loyalty to the United States was the test in deciding who received money or vouchers, it was difficult to tell a rebel from a "nationalist," as loyalists were sometimes called within the Confederacy. Don Doyle, who analyzed the postwar petitions to the U.S. Southern Claims Commission, discovered that only two hundred were filed by Lafayette County residents.[30] More claims were not filed probably because most of the inhabitants supported the Confederacy, and the majority of the initial claims were denied.

The Confederates of Holly Springs did not escape misfortune from the Union invasion. Residents who cheered General Van Dorn as his Confederate cavalry charged into the town on the morning of December 20 became increasingly dejected as the day passed. Grant's stores for the conquest of Vicksburg were housed in the large buildings of Holly Springs. In destroying the supplies, the Union officer in command of Holly Springs reported that Van Dorn left "a large portion of the business part of the town . . . in ruins." Among the buildings burned, some by accident, were the armory, the courthouse, businesses around the square, and several large dwellings.[31]

Julia Dent Grant, General Grant's wife, stopped in Holly Springs on her way to join her husband in Oxford. Julia was quartered in the Harvey Washington Walter house, a large Greek Revival mansion with neogothic towers built in 1860, which still stands. Julia owned four slaves, whom she left in Missouri, a slave state, when the Grants moved to Galena, Illinois, in 1860, because in Illinois the slaves would have been free. Accompanying Julia to Holly Springs were her son, Jesse, and Jule, identified as "my nurse and maid, a slave born and brought up at my old Missouri home." The ladies of the town found it fascinating that the wife of U. S. Grant owned a slave, calling her southern, but she corrected them, identifying Missouri as western. After a few days, Julia, Jesse, and Jule left for Oxford to join General Grant and were not in Holly Springs during Van Dorn's raid, despite a myth to the contrary.

After spending one night in Oxford, the Grants returned to Holly Springs in response to the disastrous raid as the Union army retreated to Memphis. Colonel William H. Coxe invited the Grants to stay at his new home, a Gothic Revival structure constructed in 1858. For Christmas the ladies of Holly Springs sent the Grants a turkey and other poultry.[32] They probably would not have been so generous with their delicacies had they known the severity of Grant's order for confiscation of local food supplies to feed his army. Also, despite efforts of some Union officers to prevent looting and burning in Holly Springs, Sergeant Downing reported, "The boys . . . are taking everything that they can lay their hands on, carrying to their tents couches, rockers, chairs, tables, books. . . . Some of the boys, who are the lovers of fancy books, sent home by express some of the most costly bound volumes."[33]

Kill Forrest

Forrest continued to be a major problem in Tennessee and Mississippi. In 1864, as Sherman pushed south from Chattanooga toward Atlanta, he was concerned that Forrest would cut his supply line. During the spring and summer of 1864, Union commanders sent four expeditions from Memphis into Mississippi to dispose of Forrest. In May, General Samuel G. Sturgis was unable to locate the elusive Confederate. Sturgis's second expedition into Mississippi ended with a humiliating defeat of his army on June 10 by Forrest's much smaller command at Brice's Cross-roads near Guntown, Mississippi.[34]

Following the Brice's Crossroads disaster, Sherman ordered Generals A. J. Smith and Joseph A. Mower "to pursue Forrest on foot, devastating the land over which he has passed or may pass, and make him and the people of Tennessee and Missis-sippi realize that, although a bold, daring, and successful leader, he will bring ruin and misery on any country where he may pass or tarry. If we do not punish Forrest and the people now, the whole effort of our past conquests will be lost." On June 24, 1864, Sherman telegraphed President Lincoln that he had ordered Generals Smith and Mower "to pursue and kill Forrest."[35]

Smith and Mower's first, and the Union army's third, attempt to destroy For-rest ended with a powerful Union force defeating the much smaller group of For-rest's and General Stephen D. Lee's troops at Tupelo, Mississippi. However, General Smith and other Union officers panicked over dwindling supplies and a feared counterattack. They withdrew toward Memphis, giving the Confederates a stra-tegic victory. On July 20, Sherman ordered Smith to destroy Forrest immediately. Because the lack of an adequate supply line was a major problem on his first expe-dition into north Mississippi, Smith decided to repair the Mississippi Central Rail-road and to advance over it from Grand Junction, Tennessee, to Oxford. The rail line was abandoned after Grant's withdrawal in the winter of 1862–1863 (map 5.5). Smith planned to make Oxford a supply base. From there he would strike east-ward into the Black Prairie Belt, a major source of food, cotton, and manufac-tured goods for the Confederacy. Forrest would be drawn into a decisive battle and annihilated.[36]

Smith's second expedition departed Memphis on July 29, and by August 8 he had massed ten thousand infantry and artillery troops and four thousand cavalry at Holly Springs. Three thousand black troops and three Minnesota regiments soon joined his command, increasing it to more than sixteen thousand. Confronting this formidable but unwieldy army was a Confederate force of only 5,357 men. The manpower shortage in August 1864 was due to Mississippi regiments having been deployed to Virginia and other areas of the eastern South early in the war, to the Confederate loss of the Army of Mississippi upon its surrender at Vicksburg in July 1863, and to the dispatch in May and June 1864 of much of what remained of Confederate infantry and artillery in Mississippi to reinforce General Joseph John-son in the defense of Atlanta.[37] In addition to their small force, Confederate troops in Mississippi suffered from a number of their best officers having been killed or badly wounded at Brice's Crossroads and Tupelo, including Forrest, who was shot in his right foot at Tupelo. Lack of an adequate number of weapons was another problem. Forrest wrote Mississippi governor Charles Clark concerning the grave

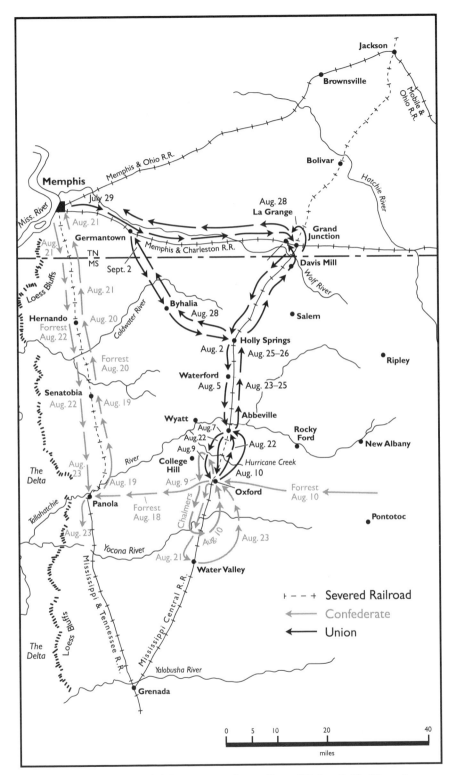

Map 5.5. General A. J. Smith's failed campaign to destroy General Nathan Bedford Forrest, July–August 1864. Compiled from *Official Records*. Charles S. Aiken.

situation: "It is plain we are to be invaded from various points, and my reliance for help in the defense of North-Mississippi is alone with the people. They must act, and act promptly, if they would save the country from devastation. Their organization is left with the officers commanding the reserves." Governor Clark responded by calling out what remained of the state militia, which was composed of old men, boys, and men who had been badly wounded. Clark complained to the Confederate secretary of war: "[We have] no arms yet. The militia was rapidly assembling," but it would be of little value because of a severe shortage of weapons.[38]

Anticipating Smith's move down the Mississippi Central Railroad, Forrest began shifting his troops toward Lafayette County. Efforts to stop the Union army at the Tallahatchie River failed. General James R. Chalmers, who commanded the troops, withdrew beyond Hurricane Creek and made it a defense line, placing four cannon on the ridge south of the stream. Unable to hold at Hurricane Creek, Chalmers withdrew to Oxford and then to a defensive position south of the Yocona River. Union troops under the command of General Edward Hatch briefly occupied Oxford on August 9 and 10. Having accomplished his goal of driving the Confederates south of the town, on August 10 Hatch returned to the Union camp at Abbeville just south of the Tallahatchie River. That evening Forrest rode into Oxford.[39]

Forrest reestablished a defense line on the ridge just south of Hurricane Creek. Realizing the significance of the location, Union forces again drove the Confederates from the ridge following heated skirmishes on August 13 and 14. When Union officers ascertained that Forrest was slowly pulling them toward Oxford with a clever collapsing defense that was taking its toll on troops, they broke off the engagement.[40]

Forrest knew that he could not stop the Union's thrust into Mississippi with adroit defensive strategy. He devised a bold plan to make Smith believe that the Confederate army was much larger than it was and about to cut the Union supply line. Forrest planned a raid on Memphis with two thousand mounted troops and three Rodman three-inch rifle guns (map 5.5). In pouring rain his force swept west from Oxford to Panola and north toward Memphis through Senatobia and Hernando, crossing swollen creeks and rivers. The Confederates struck the city shortly before sunrise on August 21. The raid was successful in the confusion that it caused but failed in a secondary objective of capturing General C. C. Washburn and other high-ranking Union officers.[41]

Forrest's ruse worked. Just as General Smith entered Oxford at the head of his large army on the morning of August 22, he received three messages from General Washburn informing him of Forrest's raid and ordering him to intercept the Confederate force leaving Memphis. Smith found Washburn's orders conflicting. In two messages Washburn correctly stated that Forrest was retiring south toward

Hernando and Panola. However, the third message said, "Captured prisoners report . . . that the enemy will retire via Holly Springs." Smith believed that Forrest's raiders left Memphis headed toward Holly Springs to cut the Mississippi Central Railroad, his supply line. When Smith ordered an immediate withdrawal from Oxford back to Abbeville, the large Union army was sloshing through the mud toward the town. Long lines of men, horses, cannon, and wagons stretched from Oxford to the Tallahatchie River.[42]

In retaliation for Forrest's use of Oxford as a headquarters and out of frustration over the Memphis raid and the failed effort to capture or kill the Confederate general, Smith ordered the public buildings to be burned, including the courthouse, railroad station, businesses around the square, and five dwellings. The University of Mississippi escaped the torch, perhaps because the buildings were used as a hospital. Smith was following Sherman's directive to "devastate the land over which Forrest passed and bring ruin and misery on any country where he tarried." The soldiers immediately set about burning and looting the town, including dwellings. However, some soldiers helped residents put out fires in houses. In addition to the courthouse, thirty-four stores and businesses and two hotels were destroyed, including the Oxford Inn owned by Faulkner's great-grandmother Burlina Butler. In burning the magnificent house of Jacob Thompson (which was across the road from the Shegog house that sixty-eight years later William Faulkner bought and named Rowan Oak), General Smith thought he was complying with the congressional act of July 17, 1862, that made it the duty of Union commanders to seize the properties of military officers and officials of the Confederate government. Thompson was the unofficial ambassador to the Court of St. James. The British, however, never recognized the Confederate States of America as a country.[43]

Forrest's raid on Memphis, which is told by historical markers and remembered locally as a heroic story of the Confederacy, was actually in vain. Without Forrest's feint, Smith and most of his force would have shortly left Oxford and north Mississippi. In need of more troops for his assault on Atlanta, on August 19, two days before Forrest's raid, Sherman telegraphed Washburn in Memphis that he wanted Smith and a large portion of his force to join him in Georgia. Sherman's telegram was not received by Washburn until August 23, two days following Forrest's attack and one day after Smith withdrew from Oxford. On August 27 Smith began the withdrawal from Mississippi. The large Union army was gone from Holly Springs and north Mississippi by the end of August.[44]

A Confederate woman's letter and a telegram by General Sherman give contrasting insights into Smith's second effort to destroy Forrest. Willis Lea's mother, Sarah, of Holly Springs, wrote in September 1864 to her son Captain Nathaniel Lea in Virginia:

We have had a terrible raid on us. . . . We were not hurt much, but of all that has been amongst us, they are the most low-down, out-breaking demons I have ever seen. . . . The people on the [out]skirts and for three miles of town are perfectly torn to pieces—clothing, bed-clothing, beds and provision all gone. Many of their houses all burnt, most of the negroes in town have left. . . . I long for peace. . . . Forrest's men fight well, I tell you. William joined Capt. Sanders' company from the [Tallahatchie] bottom. Brave fellows! they were of much service to our neighborhood, followed them up to the R.R. and took some prisoners.[45]

Sherman, whose primary purpose was to keep Forrest distracted in Mississippi while his army drove into the heart of Georgia, put the Memphis raid in the perspective of the war. He telegraphed Washburn, "If you get a chance send word to Forrest. I admire his dash but not his judgement. The oftener he runs his head against Memphis the better."[46]

The Unvanquished

Against the backdrop of the local clashes between Confederate and Union armies, in *The Unvanquished* Faulkner presents the home front in Yoknapatawpha County and north Mississippi, creatively drawing on actual events. According to Faulkner, *The Unvanquished* should be the first of his novels to approach because "it's easy to read." This is among the reasons *The Unvanquished* is considered a lesser work and is not taken as seriously as his other books. However, Faulkner did not mean that the story is simplistic. *The Unvanquished* is easy to read "compared to the others."[47] At first glance, the book appears to be the adventures of two boys who during the war encounter a series of serious events underlain with humor. Initially, *The Unvanquished* also seems more dated than Faulkner's other books, a Great Depression period piece in its vocabulary and its presentation of blacks and slavery. The novel is actually about the brutality and the destructiveness of war presented through the perceptions of Bayard Sartoris, a white boy of the planter elite, and Rango, a black companion, who seems an equal but actually is a slave. The boys mature from ages twelve to fifteen as the war is waged in Yoknapatawpha County.

Events associated with both of the major invasions of the Union army into north Mississippi are depicted in Faulkner's fiction, but he never attempts to present them accurately or to clearly distinguish Grant and Sherman's thrust into Lafayette County in the fall and winter of 1862 from the invasion by A. J. Smith in the summer of 1864. In *The Hamlet* Faulkner mentions that Louis Grenier supposedly buried his money "when Grant overran the country on his way to Vicksburg," a reference to the general's aborted movement south through Oxford toward the river

city in the fall of 1862. And in *Sartoris* the elderly Will Falls tells a more historically correct account of "Van Dorn ridin' into Holly Springs" and "burnin' Grant's
stos" than the version in *Light in August*. In *Requiem for a Nun* Faulkner uses the
August 9, 1864, skirmish at Hurricane Creek—"a sudden battle centering around
Colonel Sartoris's plantation house four miles to the north, the line of a creek held
long enough for the main Confederate body to pass through Jefferson to a stronger
line on the [Yoknapatawpha] river heights south of the town." But he combines the
brief occupation of Oxford by Union troops on August 9 and 10, 1864, with the second brief occupation on August 22 that culminates in the burning of the town. The
major skirmish at Hurricane Creek in August 1864 in which General Forrest commanded a cannon battery on the ridge overlooking the stream is not in Faulkner's
work. However, a fictional battle at the stream on April 28, 1862, is invented by the
fictional Forrest in "My Grandmother Millard and General Bedford Forrest and
the Battle of Harrykin Creek."[48]

In *The Unvanquished* Yoknapatawpha County is behind the Confederate frontier into 1863, the third year of the Civil War. Relatively isolated on the Sartoris
plantation north of Jefferson, Bayard and Rango continually play war, taking turns
at being Confederate and Yankee. The boys have seen only two Confederate officers in uniform, one of whom is Colonel John Sartoris, Bayard's father. They do not
see a Yankee until one day in 1863 from a cedar grove at the edge of the plantation
the boys spot a Union officer in the road looking at the Sartoris big house through
field glasses. Without realizing that the officer is in advance of a large army, the
boys shoot at him with an old musket, killing his horse. The incident initiates a
series of events that ends with the Yankees' burning the big house after they fail to
capture Colonel Sartoris, who escapes on a horse saddled and waiting at the rear of
the dwelling. All that remains of the house is an "ash pile and chimneys standing
up out of it."[49]

The Yankees take from Sartoris two mules and a chest full of silver. Two of the
slaves run away. In trying to discover who killed the horse, one of the Union officers, Colonel Nathaniel G. Dick, suspects the truth but does not tell. Because
of Dick's kindness, Rosa Millard, John Sartoris's mother-in-law, and the boys set
out to find him to obtain a written order for recovery of the silver, the mules, and
the two slaves. Colonel Dick leaves Mississippi for Alabama. During the six-day
journey to Alabama to find him, they see widespread destruction caused by the
war. As told by Bayard, Granny Millard says: "'The Yankees have already been
here.' Then we saw it too—a burned house like ours. . . . We went on . . . burned
houses and gins and thrown-down fences on either side. . . . [T]he sun rose up
and we went on . . . along that broad empty road between the burned houses and
gins and fences. Before, it had been like passing through a country where nobody

lived; now it was like passing through one where everyone had died at the same moment."[50] The landscape of Yoknapatawpha County becomes as war-torn as the one in Alabama. The Yankees burn Jefferson just before Christmas in 1864. "For three years the country had been full of Yankees, and then all of a sudden they were gone." The inhabitants "now . . . lived in a world of burned towns and houses and ruined plantations and fields."[51]

In *The Unvanquished* Faulkner gives insight into a major problem that developed pertaining to slaves. One of the most striking scenes is a large body of slaves in Alabama, who trudge throughout the night past the burning big house on Hawkhurst plantation. The slaves are without food or specific direction except to follow the advancing Union army toward a river, which the slaves believe is the Jordan, over which they will cross into the biblical allegory of the Promised Land and freedom. Bayard remembers:

> They began to pass in the road yonder while the house was still burning. We couldn't count them; men and women carrying children who couldn't walk and carrying old men and women who should have been at home waiting to die. They were singing, walking along the road singing. . . . The dust didn't even settle for two days, because all that night they still passed. . . . [A]nd the next morning every few yards along the road would be the old ones who couldn't keep up any more, sitting or lying down and even crawling along, calling to the others to help them; and the others—the young strong ones—not stopping, not even looking at them. I don't think they even heard or saw them. "Going to Jordan," they told me. "Going to cross Jordan."[52]

The Union officers are unable and unwilling to deal with such a large body of homeless people and hold the slaves just short of the river while the army crosses. Then they remove the temporary bridge, abandoning the slaves. Faulkner probably bases this incident on an actual event during General Sherman's infamous sixty-mile-wide march across Georgia from Atlanta to Savannah during the summer and fall of 1864. Freed slaves began following Sherman's army and became a major problem. They slowed the army and created a constant issue as to how to feed them. Near Savannah, the Union army crossed deep and swollen Buck Head and Ebenezer creeks on pontoon bridges early in December. The slaves following the army were held back on order of General J. C. Davis and the temporary bridges were removed, leaving masses of blacks on the banks. In remembrances, Union officers blamed the abandonment of the slaves on Sherman. In his autobiography, Sherman explained the abandonment on the slaves having fallen asleep, which agrees closely with Faulkner's fictional description.[53]

Some scholars believe that large numbers of slaves following the Union army did not become a problem until Sherman's march across Georgia in 1864. However, the refugee, or "contraband," issue actually began after the Battle of Shiloh in the spring and summer of 1862 when Generals Grant and Sherman were preparing for their advance to Vicksburg along the Mississippi Central Railroad. In the LaGrange–Holly Springs area along the Tennessee-Mississippi boundary, a large number of slaves left plantations and began following the Union army. Rootless and helpless, the slaves jammed the roads and Union army camps looking for food and shelter. As the large Union army under Grant moved southward from Tennessee into Mississippi, Sergeant Alexander Downing was struck by the nature of the slave refugee problem. On November 29, 1862, he wrote in his diary: "There are thousands of negroes, women and children, of all shades of color gathered at Holly Springs. The roads by which we marched were lined with them. The best of the negro men have been taken South by the rebels to work on their fortifications." To deal with the refugee situation, Grant appointed Chaplain John Eaton of the Twenty-seventh Ohio to establish camps to feed, clothe, and provide medical care and find work for the contraband slaves, not so much to care for them as to protect the Union troops from disease and demoralization. Eaton established the first such camp, the beginning of what became the Freedmen's Bureau, in 1862 near Grand Junction, Tennessee, just east of LaGrange. Located at the place where the Mississippi Central Railroad crossed the Memphis and Charleston Railroad, the campsite was strategic for receiving food and medical supplies and transporting the former slave refugees from the region.[54]

In *The Unvanquished* Granny, Bayard, and Ringo at last find Colonel Dick. Granny tells him that Union soldiers took a chest of silver, two slaves, and two mules: "I have come to get them." Colonel Dick replies, "Have them you shall." His orderly writes an order, which Colonel Dick takes to the Union general in command.

> Field Headquarters,
> —th Army Corps,
> Department of Tennessee,
> August 14, 1863.

> To all Brigade, Regimental and Other Commanders: You will see that bearer is repossessed in full of the following property, to wit: Ten (10) chests tied with hemp rope and containing silver. One hundred ten (110) mules captured loose near Philadelphia in Mississippi. One hundred ten (110) Negroes of both sexes belonging to and having strayed from the same locality.

> You will further see that bearer is supplied with necessary food and forage to expedite his passage to his destination.

> By order of the General Commanding.[55]

A significant part of *The Unvanquished* revolves around Granny Millard's illicit trade in mules. She forges orders to acquire additional mules from the Union army, which she sells through a group of Confederate deserters and thieves led by a man named Grumby. Granny gives the money and some of the mules to whites and blacks who are destitute because of the war. Eventually, Granny is murdered by Grumby, and her death is avenged by Bayard and Rango, fifteen-year-old boys. Superficially, this part of *The Unvanquished* seems implausible. In the place of a Confederacy of gallant whites who are dedicated to what is right, Faulkner depicts one in which a genteel planter woman engages in subterfuge and theft, law and order breaks down, and southern whites rob and kill, not just Yankees but their fellow compatriots, including women.[56]

Because a severe shortage of horses and mules developed in north Mississippi, both Union and Confederate armies confiscated the animals. Large numbers of horses and mules were killed in action and died under the burdens of war and from the lack of adequate feed. An elderly southern woman and two boys appropriating mules from the Union army with what seemed an official document would have been suspicious, but not outlandish, in north Mississippi during the final months of the war. Even General Grant issued an order in November 1862 similar to one by fictional Colonel Dick's commanding general.

SPECIAL ORDERS, } HDQRS. 13TH A. C., DEPT. OF THE TENN.,
No. 31.   } La Grange, Tenn., November 27, 1862.

It having come to the knowledge of the general commanding that certain ladies living in the vicinity of Henderson's Station, Tenn., did, after a raid by guerrillas upon that station, turn out with buckets and extinguish a fire which had been kindled by these lawless persons, threatening a railroad bridge important to the Government, and by their exertions save it, desires that this patriotic conduct shall not go unnoticed or unrewarded. It is therefore directed that the commanding officer of the District of Jackson shall have the names of these ladies enrolled and direct that they be protected in their property and the quit of their homes, and also that rations be issued to them from time to time free of charge if necessity requires it, and that every facility be given them to purchase every article of necessity for use of themselves and families.

By order of Maj. Gen. U. S. Grant:

JNO. A. RAWLINS
Assistant Adjutant-General[57]

Southern cotton was just as important to the Union as it was to the Confederacy. Northern agents, including Jesse Grant, General U. S. Grant's father, entered north Mississippi with the Union army in 1862. Throughout the remainder of the war, from Memphis as the principal base, agents roamed "the cotton garden of the world," stealing and buying the staple and selling it to Union textile mills at substantial profits. Because southern ports were blockaded by the Union navy, planters readily sold cotton to the northern agents for lack of any other market and were paid in United States money, usually paper greenbacks rather than gold or silver.[58] The United States money, more valuable than the almost worthless Confederate scrip, helped to sustain the Confederacy through the purchase of medicine, flour, salt, coffee, arms, and munitions. As the war progressed, overland trade and blockade running by northern and southern speculators and merchants became more complex and eventually involved horses, mules, food, and other basic necessities. The price of food was driven so high that the Union army tried to set maximum prices. In August 1864 prices for barrels of flour and pork were capped at sixteen dollars and fifty-seven dollars. The price for a pound of bacon was thirty-three cents, a bar of soap fifteen cents, and a bushel of salt four dollars.[59]

By the beginning of 1865, with the defeat of the Confederate army and the collapse of the Confederate government imminent, law and order in north Mississippi began to break down. The report of the Confederate officer at Oxford following withdrawal of troops after the town was burned in August 1864 portended the collapse: "I have no guards or supporting force, as the troops used here were returned to the reserve corps. . . . The country is swarming with deserters, and without a force of regular troops I fear little can be done to break up these clans of tories. . . . Blockade-running and intercourse with the enemy has been quite common here."[60] Forrest was concerned about the number of "roving bands of deserters, absentees, stragglers, and horse-thieves, and robbers, who consume the substance and appropriate the property of citizens without remuneration, whose acts of lawlessness and crime demand a remedy, which I shall not hesitate to apply, even to extermination."[61]

Within the lawless milieu of the collapsing Confederacy, Bayard and Rango, together with Uncle Buck McCaslin, spend weeks in the winter of 1864–1865 hunting Grumby, who killed Granny at a cotton compress near the Tallahatchie River, and Ab Snopes, who led Granny to Grumby. The three follow Grumby's trail of robbery and revenge across the north Mississippi countryside. Because Granny was Colonel John Sartoris's mother-in-law, Grumby's band does not dare kill Bayard, his son. They know that Sartoris and his partisan cavalry will hunt and kill them. In hopes that Bayard, Rango, and Uncle Buck will give up the chase, Grumby's band gives Ab Snopes to them by tying him to a tree. Snopes is let off lightly with a thrashing, but the boys continue hunting Grumby. After additional days chasing Grumby, the boys suddenly encounter a gruesome scene. An elderly black man was lynched and left hanging in their path as a warning. Eventually, the outlaws deliver Grumby to Bayard and Rango. After killing Grumby, the boys nail his body to the door of the compress where Granny was murdered. As another symbol of their revenge, Bayard and Rango cut off one of Grumby's hands, take it to Jefferson's cemetery, and wire it to Granny's grave marker. Now she can rest in peace.[62]

Failure of the Southern Confederacy

The crucial aspect of the Civil War was the southern states' failure to successfully secede from the United States and create the Confederate States of America. Historians have long debated the causes of the South's lack of success. James McPherson divides the reasons why the South lost the war into four categories.[63] First, from the beginning of the conflict the Confederate States confronted overwhelming odds. The North had three times the white population of the South, a much larger economy, and considerably more manufacturing capability and diversity. A major source for the belief that the South was doomed to fail is Robert E. Lee's farewell address to the Army of Northern Virginia. Throughout the seven decades following the war, the speech was repeatedly published, and many southern schoolchildren were required to commit to memory and to recite Lee's address with its stunning words: "After four years of arduous service marked by unsurpassed courage and fortitude, the Army of Northern Virginia has been compelled to yield to overwhelming numbers and resources."[64] Surviving members of the Lamar Rifles, who in 1901 viewed the war from the retrospect of four decades, essentially restated Lee's reasons for the defeat: "After four years of gallant resistance in defense of her constitutional and inherent right to independence, the South was overwhelmed by superior numbers and resources of the North, aided by the world, upon which she drew largely for both men and material."[65]

A second argument for the South's loss is that the Confederacy was weakened by internal divisions. Many southern whites either failed to support the cause or lost the will to fight. In his "Book of Reminiscences" Thomas P. Buford, a graduate of the University of Mississippi and a member of the Lamar Rifles, wrote that the war was lost because "the ardor and enthusiasm of the South in the beginning of the struggle were not maintained. The South lacked the staying qualities."[66] The respected southern historian E. Merton Coulter believed that "the forces leading up to the defeat were many but they may be summed up in this one fact: The people did not will hard enough and long enough to win. The Confederacy never developed a civil and military esprit de corps."[67] The internal divisions interpretation became especially popular among historians during the 1970s and 1980s in the wake of the United States' failure to adequately support South Vietnam and the subsequent loss of the country to communist North Vietnam.

A third reason for the South's loss of the war is poor leadership within the Confederacy. President Jefferson Davis, a graduate of West Point and former U.S. army officer, continually intervened in Confederate military strategy. Robert E. Lee performed well in defending Virginia but never seemed to have a comprehensive view of the war. Generals George E. Pickett, John Bell Hood, Braxton Bragg, Earl Van Dorn, and other Confederate commanders were incompetent at critical times. A prevailing Confederate belief was that the primary military strategy should be defensive rather than offensive. The South could win the war by not losing, but for the North to win, it had to defeat the Confederacy. The Confederate army failed to pursue the disorganized, retreating Union army toward Washington following its stunning defeat at First Manassas (First Bull Run). General Joseph E. Johnson fought retreating battles from Chattanooga to Atlanta rather than taking the offense against the Union army advancing into the heart of the Confederacy under Sherman. After capturing Atlanta, Sherman in the late summer of 1864 began his infamous march across Georgia to Savannah along a sixty-mile front. General John Bell Hood took the main body of the Confederate army in Georgia and Alabama, forty thousand strong, into Tennessee, opposite the direction of Sherman. At the Battle of Franklin, Hood ordered his troops to march into withering Union gunfire and needlessly destroyed much of his army, the last formidable Confederate force in the west.[68]

A fourth reason that the South lost the war is what James McPherson terms "the dimension of contingency," the role of chance in uncertain, fluid conditions. Despite the emphasis that some historians, popular writers, and cinema and television documentaries place on Gettysburg, the Civil War did not have a decisive battle. At several critical times during the conflict, events could have gone in favor of the South or the North. James McPherson believes that four major junctures determined the eventual outcome—the counteroffensive of Jackson and Lee in Virginia and Bragg and Kirby Smith in the west during the summer of 1862, the battles of Antietam and Perryville in the autumn of 1862, the battles of Gettysburg, Vicksburg, and Chattanooga during the summer and autumn of 1863, and large numbers of Union casualties combined with little military progress followed by major Northern success with the capture of Atlanta and the Shenandoah Valley in the summer of 1864.[69]

Grant's failed attempt to take Vicksburg by movement of large armies through Lafayette County and across Mississippi in the fall and early winter of 1862 can be added to the resurgence of the Confederacy. Grant's defeat coincided with growing concern in the North that the South, though smaller, was much stronger militarily than Union leaders and common soldiers initially believed. The war was not a trivial matter that was over by Christmas of 1862. The Union soldiers were not going home; more northern men were being inducted. As Grant's substantial army retreated from Mississippi, Sergeant Downing, in retrospect, wrote in his diary for December 27:

The days of the latter half of . . . December were the darkest we had seen up to that time and, as it proved, they were the darkest days of the entire Union army during the whole four years of war. Our armies, all along the line, East and West, had not been successful. The second 600,000 men had been called during the summer, and the loyal men of the North responded. . . . But there was an element in the North holding nightly meetings and declaring that the war was a failure; there was also talk of England's recognizing the Confederacy; then there were discouraging letters from the home folks to the men in the field, for the times were hard and the situation looked very bad to them. They would, in writing to us, ask what we thought of the outlook, and almost to a man, the reply would be that we would push ahead until we were successful, for our loss already had been too great to give up the struggle short of going to the bitter end.[70]

It is not surprising that in Faulkner's large, complex body of fiction are incidents and statements that support all four major reasons for the South's loss of the war. Faulkner's interpretation of the war hinges on the impact of defeat. The myth of the war as a Southern Lost Cause was at its height when Faulkner was a child and a young man, and the idea that the Confederate cause was doomed to fail, even by Providence, is overt in his fiction. The concept of the Lost Cause began to develop immediately after the war, promoted primarily not by Confederate soldiers but by their sweethearts, wives, children, and grandchildren, especially their daughters and granddaughters. Many of the southern women who lived through the war and Reconstruction, particularly ones such as Rosa Coldfield who were of marriageable age, viewed the conflict not as a glorious lost cause but as a "holocaust." The war took from Rosa, who was twenty in 1865, the security of her father. The young men from among whom she could have found a husband "were dead on lost battlefields."[71]

Faulkner chronologically employs the Lost Cause and its idioms in his historical fiction before the concept and the term actually developed. The first use of "Lost Cause" is in a history of the Civil War published in 1866. In *Absalom, Absalom!* just before the end of the war in 1865, Henry Sutpen crosses paths in Carolina with his father, Colonel Thomas Sutpen, whom he has not seen for four years. Henry says to his father, "God quit us four years ago only He never thought to tell us; no shoes nor clothes and no need for them . . . and when you don't have God and honor and pride, nothing matters." In a prayer during the war Rosa Millard addresses God concerning the Confederacy's "holy cause": "You have seen fit to make it a lost cause." And in *Absalom, Absalom!* Faulkner expresses the "Forget? Hell!" aspect of the Lost Cause myth, which developed after 1890, in what Wash Jones says to Thomas Sutpen during the war: "Well, Kernel, they kilt us but they aint whupped us yit, air they."[72]

A detailed study has never been made of Unionists, or "nationalists" as some preferred to be called, in the Confederate States of America. The number of dissenting southerners behind Confederate lines varied from relatively few in plantation counties such as Lafayette, Mississippi, to more than half the population in east Tennessee, which was largely inhabited by white yeoman farmers. A significant number of southern families, even slaveholding ones, did not support secession. However, they sided with the Confederacy because they had too much to lose if the fledgling nation was defeated. Dr. Thomas Isom, a slave owner who along with L. Q. C. Lamar represented Lafayette County at Mississippi's cession convention, voted against withdrawal from the United States. However, once Mississippi was committed to the Confederacy and its war for independence, Isom became a surgeon in his new nation's cause.

An example of the lack of support for the Confederacy in Yoknapatawpha County is Goodhue Coldfield, Rosa's father. Goodhue is a Jefferson merchant whose other daughter, Ellen, marries Thomas Sutpen. At the commencement of the Civil War, Coldfield, who is both a Unionist and a conscientious objector, closes his store and hides in the attic of his house to escape the possibility of being conscripted into the Confederate military or having to support the Confederacy in any way. Food, which he pulls up into the attic by a rope, is taken to him daily by Rosa. Coldfield dies in his self-imprisonment in 1864.[73]

Somewhat surprising, perhaps, is Faulkner's recognition of contingency. On the third day of Gettysburg, the outcome of the battle rested on Robert E. Lee's decision to break the Union line and force retreat. A Confederate cannon barrage was followed by a disastrous infantry charge across a mile of open ground in which a large part of Lee's army was killed or badly wounded. In *Intruder in the Dust* young Charles Mallison thinks of the battle:

> For every Southern boy fourteen years old, not once but whenever he wants it, there is the instant when it's still not yet two oclock on that July afternoon in 1863, the brigades are in position behind the rail fence, the guns are laid and ready . . . and the furled flags are already loosened to break out . . . and it's all in the balance, it hasn't happened yet . . . it not only hasn't begun yet but there is still time for it not to begin . . . yet it's going to begin, we all know that, we have come too far with too much at

stake and that moment doesn't need even a fourteen-year-old boy to think *This time. Maybe this time* with all this much to lose and all this much to gain: Pennsylvania, Maryland, the world, the golden dome of Washington itself to crown with desperate and unbelievable victory the desperate gamble.[74]

Of the four reasons for the South's loss of the Civil War, Faulkner's primary one is a part of an overriding theme throughout his apocrypha, leadership failure. Faulkner indicates both directly and indirectly that the Confederacy was defeated because of deficiency in its leaders. Bayard Sartoris sacrificed his life, not for the Confederacy but in "a hare-brained prank." Prior to the battle of Second Manassas, Bayard, Colonel John Sartoris's twenty-three-year-old brother, together with thirty-year-old General Jeb Stuart, came upon Union general Pope and his staff at breakfast. Responding to a taunt from a captured Union major, Bayard returned under fire to "capture" some anchovies and was killed by a Union cook.[75]

Through frequent retelling, Aunt Virginia Du Pre reconstructs the foolish act in the myth of the Lost Cause, raising it to "a gallant and finely tragical focal point . . . altering the course of human events and purging the souls of men": "Mr. Stuart went on and Bayard rode back after those anchovies, with all Pope's army shooting at him. He rode yelling 'Yaaaiiiih, Yaaaiiiih, come on boys!' . . . and jumped his horse over the breakfast table and rode it into the wrecked commissary tent."[76]

The incident is an allegory. Southerners provoked a war they knew they could not win, needlessly threw away the lives of thousands of young men, and wrecked the South economically. Bayard gave his life in an act that has no significance to the war, the Confederacy, or posterity. Faulkner's use of anchovies at first may seem humorous, but their purpose is to underscore the senselessness of both Bayard's act and the war. By inclusion of actual cavalry general Jeb Stuart in his fiction as Bayard's buddy, Faulkner obliquely attacks the revered Confederate who was "the eyes" of General Lee's Army of Northern Virginia.

Another example of the senseless acts is that of Reverend Gail Hightower II's grandfather. The Civil War exploits of Gail Hightower I—which obsess and eventually destroy the grandson—are not true. Hightower I did not die gallantly during General Van Dorn's cavalry raid that destroyed Grant's supplies but was killed in a henhouse by a blast from a shotgun while he was stealing chickens. "They didn't know who fired the shot. . . . It may have been a woman, likely enough the wife of a Confederate soldier. . . . Any soldier can be killed by the enemy in the heat of battle, by a weapon approved by the arbiters and rulemakers of warfare. Or by a woman in a bedroom. But not with a shotgun, a fowling piece, in a henhouse."[77]

In *Absalom, Absalom!* Faulkner places blame not just for the South's defeat but for the prolonged agony of the war and its aftermath on the Confederate leadership:

[I]t was '64 and then '65 and the starved and ragged remnant of an army having retreated across Alabama and Georgia and into Carolina, swept onward not by a victorious army behind it but rather by a mounting tide of the names of lost battles . . . battles lost not alone because of superior numbers and failing ammunition stores, but because of generals who should not have been generals, who were generals not through training in contemporary methods or aptitude for learning them, but by divine right . . . conferred upon them by an absolute caste system.[78]

Among Faulkner's fictional characters who should not have been generals is Confederate Brigadier Jason Lycurgas Compson II, "who failed at Shiloh in '62 and failed again, though not so badly, at Resaca in '64."[79] General Van Dorn's military triumph in stopping Grant's move south toward Vicksburg along the Mississippi Central Railroad in 1862 by burning the Union supply depot at Holly Springs was overshadowed by his death at the hands of a fellow southerner with whose wife he was having an affair. To Faulkner, Buck Van Dorn depicted a particular type of Confederate leader, a person who "on one night with a handful of men would gallantly destroy a million dollar garrison of enemy supplies and on the next night would be discovered by a neighbor in bed with his wife and be shot to death."[80]

The idea that the South initiated a war, a glorious Lost Cause, that Confederate leaders could not win is employed by Faulkner in *Go Down, Moses*. Isaac McCaslin, who was born just after the Civil War, thinks, "'Who else could have declared a war against a power with ten times the area and a hundred times the men and a thousand times the resources, except men who believed that all necessary to conduct a successful war was not acumen or shrewdness . . . not even integrity . . . but just love of land and courage.'"[81]

Through Isaac's thoughts, Faulkner uses actual incidents to expose the type of Confederate leadership he believed contributed to the South's defeat. Robert E. Lee's battle order for Sharpsburg (Antietam) is found by a Yankee intelligence officer on the floor of a saloon where it had been thrown by a Confederate officer who had wrapped it around "a handful of cigars." In the actual incident, a copy of General Lee's detailed orders for his army was discovered in a field by two Union soldiers before the Battle of Sharpsburg. The Confederate officer who lost the orders had wrapped them around three cigars. After receiving the Confederate plan, an excited General George McClellan devised a strategy to "whip Bobbie Lee." However, a Maryland Confederate discovered that McClellan had Lee's orders and told Jeb Stuart, who informed Lee. McClellan's tendency for caution and delay gave Lee adequate time to save his army. Stonewall Jackson is killed when he "is shot from among a whole covey of minor officers and in the blind of night by one of his own patrols." Like Jackson, General James Longstreet is "shot out of the saddle by his own men in the dark by mistake" but is not killed. And in *Go Down, Moses* Faulkner continues his attack on Jeb Stuart's judgment and abilities, which he began more than a decade earlier in *Sartoris*. Stuart is a "gallant man born apparently . . . already knowing all there was to know about war except the slaughter and brutal stupidity of it." At Gettysburg Stuart fails to warn Lee of the size and position of the Union army because he is "off raiding Pennsylvania hen-roosts." Stuart rides "his whole command around the biggest single armed force" ever on the North American continent, but the eyes of the Army of Northern Virginia never lets Lee know the size and position of the Union army the Confederates are about to confront.[82]

Aftermath

The settlement of Lafayette County, Mississippi, the creation of Oxford, and the holocaust of the Civil War passed into legendary history. Faulkner had little concern for sorting out that which was true from that which was false, even though he knew much more about actual history and geography than is usually conceded. In most instances legend was more intriguing than fact. By the mid-twentieth century what were considered the critical events in local history were summarized in a few succinct phrases strung together in an ironically Faulknerian sentence fragment, stamped on a metal plaque, and posted on the Oxford city hall for all to read:

THE CITY OF OXFORD

A TRADING POST IN THE WILDERNESS OF THE CHICKASAW COUNTRY BEFORE THE TREATY OF PONTOTOC IN 1832 INCORPORATED BY THE LEGISLATURE IN 1837 HOME OF THE UNIVERSITY OF MISSISSIPPI SINCE ITS FOUNDATION IN 1844 BURNED BY THE INVADING ARMY OF THE UNITED STATES ON AUGUST 22, 1864 RESTORED BY THE COURAGE AND GENIUS OF HER PEOPLE TO BECOME A PROGRESSIVE CITY AWAKE ALIKE TO PRESENT CHANGE AND TO THE RICH CULTURE AND TRADITION OF THE OLD SOUTH.

SIX

New South

One of the grandest creations of the New South was a mythical concept of an Old South. The heyday of the Old South era was relatively short in north Mississippi, lasting only about twenty-five years from the beginning of settlement in the 1830s until the commencement of the Civil War in 1861. When Faulkner published the first of his Yoknapatawpha novels in the 1920s, Lafayette County and Oxford were less than one hundred years old. However, the north Mississippi landscape contained elements that made the region seem ancient. Cultural landscape relics and fossils of a plantation economy and society suggested a bygone age that was more prosperous and more elegant, with people who were more noble. Not just the history but the burden of an ancient past were conveyed from the older generations to the younger ones.

Throughout Faulkner's work are translucent and opaque references to the ever-present past. Superficially, the story of Cecilia Farmer, the Jefferson jailer's daughter, who at the beginning of the Civil War scratched her "significantless" name and the date, "April 16th 1861," on a glass windowpane of the jail with a diamond ring, seems to have no importance. Jefferson preserves the glass because it is part of a love story from Civil War lore. In 1864, as the Confederate army retreated through Jefferson past the jail, after failing to hold the Union army at the Sartoris plantation and "the line of a creek," a lieutenant saw Cecilia berating them for leaving the town defenseless. At the end of the war, the Confederate officer returned and, without ever speaking to Cecilia, married her. The fiction is based on the story of Jane T. Cook, who with a diamond ring scratched her name on a windowpane in the Henry Tate house on Johnson Avenue south of the courthouse square. Jane scolded Confederate troops as they retreated south through Oxford after failing to stop the large Union force at Hurricane Creek in August 1864. Among the troops was William Montgomery Forrest, the son of General Bedford Forrest. Impressed by Jane's spunk, William returned after the war and married her. When the Tate house was razed in the 1950s, the windowpane with Jane's name was saved and placed in the Buie-Skipworth Museum. Faulkner realized that the incident not only has meaning in isolated local history, but it also has universal significance.

You know again now that there is no time: no space: no distance: a fragile and work-less scratching almost depthless in a sheet of old barely transparent glass, and . . . there is the clear undistanced voice as though out of the delicate antenna-skeins of radio, further than empress's throne, than splendid insatiation, even than matriarch's peaceful rocking chair, across the vast instantaneous intervention, from the long long time ago: "*Listen, stranger; this was myself: this was* ***I***."[1]

The Lost Cause

Faulkner was fascinated with the stories of affluent whites who settled in Oxford and Lafayette County. However, even though he was a grand pretender, he was repulsed by pomposity, especially that of older women whom he labels "maiden aunts." Faulkner employs "maiden aunts" as a generic term. The group includes older married women as well as spinsters and widows. Also, most were "aunts" in a generic sense. A fading custom in the plantation South is for a younger person to call an older woman "aunt" though she may be only distantly related. Members of Faulkner's family were maiden aunts, including his mother, Maud Butler Falkner, who became increasingly demanding and difficult as she aged, dying only two years before her noted son.

The recent past of Lafayette County and north Mississippi seemed ancient, in part, because of the way in which local history and geography were interpreted by the maiden aunts. The aunts whom Faulkner knew were composed of three gen-erations. The one born from the mid-1830s through the late 1840s knew the Old South and suffered through the war and Reconstruction as young adults. The gen-eration born in the 1850s and in 1860 and 1861 knew the war and Reconstruction as children and teenagers. Members of the generation born during the last three years of the war and Reconstruction (1863–1876) thought that they remembered the Old South and experienced the Civil War firsthand because of the vivid stories they were told. Isaac McCaslin, born in 1867, is a member of the third generation. He is exposed to tales of the conflict to the extent that "even at almost eighty" he was "never . . . able to distinguish certainly between what he had seen and what had been told him."[2]

Many of the females of the two older generations suffered dreadfully from the war—robbed of fathers, young husbands, and the men whom they would have married, and also deprived of wealth in slaves and land that would have sustained them at economic levels well above either the gut-wrenching poverty or the genteel poverty that many experienced (fig. 6.1). More than one-third of the seventy-eight thousand troops Mississippi contributed to the Confederate military died. About twelve thousand were killed or succumbed to battle wounds and approximately

Figure 6.1. An unidentified Oxford, Mississippi, woman resplendent in
the summer dress of affluent southerners on the eve of the Civil War. The
long-sleeved dress and broad-brimmed hat are to ensure that no sunrays
reach the skin. Skin reddened and tanned by the sun was a mark of
low-class whites. The woman is thought to be the daughter of Edward C.
Boynton, a professor at the University of Mississippi, who was dismissed
from the faculty in 1861 "for want of attachment to the government of
the Confederate states." Boynton and his family moved to New York, but
he left behind a trove of glass photograph negatives documenting the
university at the close of the Old South era. Special Collections, University
of Mississippi Libraries.

sixteen thousand died of disease.[3] The extent of physical destruction during the Civil War varied across the Confederate states. Except for the loss of men and general economic disruption, the Confederate core throughout the war suffered little impact of the conflict on the landscape (map 5.1). But other areas, such as no-man's-land and the Confederate frontier, which were large territories in Mississippi, revealed the destruction wrought by total war. In 1901 James W. Garner described the outcome of the war in Mississippi:

> The people were generally impoverished; the farms had gone to waste . . . ; the fields were covered with weeds and bushes; farm implements and tools were gone . . . ; there were barely enough farm animals to meet the demands of agriculture . . . ; banks and commercial agencies had either suspended or closed on account of insolvency; the currency was in wretched condition . . . ; there was no railway or postal system worth speaking of . . . ; the [slave] labor system in vogue since the establishment of the colonies was completely overturned . . . ; about one-third of the white breadwinners of the state had either been sacrificed in the contest or were disabled for life. . . . Another class of dependents were the widows and orphans. . . . Many of the women had never been accustomed to perform domestic service, and consequently found themselves at a great disadvantage in the struggle which now ensued.[4]

In 1860 real estate and personal estate in Lafayette County had assessed values of $5.9 million and $10 million, respectively, a total of nearly $16 million ($410.6 million in 2007 dollars). In 1870 the assessed values of real and personal estates were $1.5 million and $1.9 million, a total of $3.3 million ($54.7 million in 2007 dollars) and a decline of 79 percent from 1860.[5] The 81 percent decline in personal property was primarily the result of President Lincoln and the Reconstruction Congress freeing slaves without compensation to owners. The 75 percent decline in real estate was due in part to the loss of farm animals and the destruction on farms and plantations and in Oxford and Lafayette County hamlets. But other factors also contributed to the decrease in wealth. What is not considered is that slavery added to the value of land in the southern states because the area of the nation where bondage was legal was finite and had a limited amount of arable land. Even northern families found it profitable to own slave plantations in the states where thralldom was legal. Abolishment of slavery resulted in southern landowners' loss of this comparative advantage. Southern land values suddenly were determined by competition in the national market, and prices dropped. Also, as the farming frontier expanded, the acreage of land in farms in the United States increased from 407 million in 1860 to 838 million in 1880.[6]

Families' loss of wealth can be documented through estate records of the Butlers and the Harmons, among the first families to arrive in Lafayette County. Faulkner's great-grandmother Burlina Butler had provisions, horses, and feed confiscated by Grant's army in December 1862, and her inn and livery stable were among the buildings torched by General Smith on August 22, 1864. Burlina's petition to the U.S. Southern Claims Commission for financial restitution was denied because she was unable to prove Union loyalty. In 1870 Burlina's real estate and personal wealth was $1,500 ($24,586 in 2007 dollars), compared to $50,000 ($1.3 million) in 1860. After the war Burlina sold the inn site and several of her other Oxford lots, and she gave additional property to her children.[7]

Wesley Harmon, who owned a plantation in Lafayette County north of the Tallahatchie River, died in 1860, leaving four minor children and an estate of approximately $30,000 ($771,744 in 2007 dollars). His widow received one-third of his 785 acres of land. From 1860 until his youngest daughter became twenty-one in 1870, the remainder of the estate was managed by an administrator. The primary source of income to support Harmon's family was the annual rent from his estate's twenty-six slaves and remaining 524 acres. The estate lost money in the exchange of U.S. currency for what became worthless Confederate scrip and when one hundred bales of cotton were shipped in 1860 and 1861 to a Memphis merchant who never paid for them. With ratification of the Thirteenth Amendment to the U.S. Constitution in December 1865, the estate's slaves were freed. What had been a "large estate, real and personal" in 1860 was one "insufficient to pay the debts" by 1866. With sale of the estate's 524 acres in 1866, the last source of income was lost. At the final settlement in 1871, the estate's assets were $5,883 ($103,023 in 2007 dollars) and the debts were $4,341 ($76,019). DeWhitt Stearns, a carpetbagger who was appointed Lafayette County chancellor during Reconstruction, charged court costs of $1,000 ($17,512), or 3.3 percent, on the prewar estimate of an estate valued at $30,000. Stearns also charged an attorney's fee of one hundred dollars ($1,751) in addition to the forty-dollar fee already assigned. Court costs and the additional attorney's fee left the estate with only $372 ($6,515), half of which Stearns paid to the administrator as his fee. Wesley Harmon's wife and four children received $37.20 ($652) each.[8]

Faulkner's grandparents were members of the last Old South generation, and his parents belonged to the first generation born following the conflict. Faulkner did not particularly admire his parents' postwar generation. He characterized its members as belonging to a time when "nothing was happening." "There would be little brush-fire wars that nobody paid much attention to, . . . the time of travail and struggle where the hero came into his own had passed. From '70 on to 1912–14, nothing happened to Americans to speak of. . . . There was nothing that brought the issue . . . to be brave and strong or dramatic." The persons of this period "had to be there for the simple continuity of the family."[9] Faulkner's ideas about the first post–Civil War generation underlay his beliefs concerning leadership failure. His father, Murry, was born in 1870 and his mother, Maud Butler, in 1871. Murry was an alcoholic who failed in several business ventures, including a livery stable and a hardware store. When he died in 1932, his estate was only large enough to care for Maud for one year. William assumed financial responsibility for his mother from 1933 until her death in 1960.[10]

During Faulkner's lifetime, the maiden aunts were the primary collectors, recorders, interpreters, and embellishers of local history. The aunts preserved a substantial amount of historical material, but their endeavors also contributed to the creation of the myths of an Old South and enhancement of the failed Southern Confederacy into a glorious Lost Cause. Today, Lost Cause and Southern Confederacy are frequently used interchangeably. However, to equate the two fails to consider how the Lost Cause was interpreted from the 1890s until after the First World War. The term "Lost Cause" originated in the title of a history of the Confederacy published immediately following the war.[11]

Reconciliation of former Confederates with defeat in the Civil War evolved through several stages. Despite the early appearance of the term Lost Cause, its use as a synonym for the failed Confederacy was not immediately accepted but was embraced increasingly over the decades following the Civil War. As a boy during the first decade of the twentieth century, Faulkner knew the Lost Cause at its crescendo, by which time it had assumed religious overtones. As a young man, he witnessed its gradual decline. However, Faulkner did not know firsthand the conditions in the South that led to the idea of a Lost Cause. Immediately after the war southerners had to deal with loss. In the spring and summer of 1865 families of Confederate soldiers had to discover what had happened to men who did not return home. Were they so badly wounded that they lingered in a Union prison, hospital, or someone's home? If they were killed, where were their graves? National cemeteries were established by the Union army in or near the battlefields where the war was fought, primarily in the South. However, the national cemeteries were not for Confederates, who often were buried in unmarked mass graves. Individual graves either were unmarked or were identified by wooden boards, sometimes with "Rebel" or "Traitor" the only word written on a grave marker. Lincoln's Gettysburg address dedicated "hallowed ground" for fallen Union soldiers, not for dead Confederates. After the war the federal government continued its policy of maintaining national cemeteries only for Union soldiers, even though graves of Confederates were within the burial grounds or nearby. The Grand Army of the Republic had enough political power to prevent placement of flowers and flags on Confederate graves at Arlington National Cemetery on Decoration Day (southern Memorial Day) until the election of President William McKinley, who in 1898 ended the exclusion of southerners.[12]

The task of establishment of cemeteries for Confederate soldiers fell primarily to local Ladies Memorial Associations, which evolved into creation in 1894 of the large, well-organized national United Daughters of the Confederacy (U.D.C.) with headquarters in Nashville. Although the monuments to the Confederate dead began to be erected shortly after the war, the initial ones usually were relatively simple single-shaft memorials, such as the one in the middle of Broad Street at the main entrance to the University of Georgia in Athens. By the 1890s the South had recovered enough financially to invest in elaborate memorials to the Confederacy. Most of the Confederate monuments were erected between 1900 and 1917 and included ones to Confederate women, such as the ornate memorial on the lawn of the Mississippi capitol in Jackson. Also, most of the monuments with soldiers atop them were erected during this period. Some soldiers were generic, sold for monuments in the North as well as in the South. The two Confederate monuments in Oxford, Mississippi, have soldiers atop them and were erected after 1900. Blacks are depicted in some of the more elaborate Confederate monuments, including the one in Arlington National Cemetery, which features a mammy and a servant. Slaves often accompanied their young masters to war as servants and cooks. Many Confederate companies, including the University Greys and the Lamar Rifles, included several slaves who cooked meals, washed clothes, maintained camps, and built fortifications. Only in the fall of 1862 did President Lincoln fully realize that the Confederacy, which had a much smaller white population than the Union, was not collapsing, despite the loss of major battles such as Shiloh. The South had mobilized its large slave population for the war effort. At least fifty thousand slaves were involved directly in the war. Blacks were so outraged that slaves were included on some Confederate monuments that in the 1920s black-owned newspapers sarcastically promoted the erection of mammy monuments.[13]

Charles Wilson emphasizes that remembrance of the war and the failed effort to create a new nation became a quasi religion as southerners sought to maintain the Confederate identity and sacrifice. The religious phase of the Lost Cause was brought to a conclusion by the national effort to win a global war. In 1917 President Woodrow Wilson, a southerner and devout Presbyterian, led the United States into the First World War, which hastened sectional reconciliation.[14] Also, by the time of the United States' entry into the First World War, most of the widows and spinster sweethearts of Confederates killed in the Civil War, among the most devoted keepers of the Lost Cause, were a rapidly vanishing generation of old women. A woman who was twenty in 1865 was seventy-three in 1918. To Faulkner the "aging unvanquished" women were like "old unordered vacant pilings above a tide's flood." They had "an illusion of motion," which to Faulkner meant life, but they were "facing irreconcilably backward toward the old lost battles, the old aborted cause, the old four ruined years whose very physical scars . . . had annealed back into the earth; twenty-five and then thirty-five years; not only a century and an age, but a way of thinking died."[15]

During the religious phase of the Lost Cause, great emphasis was placed on Confederate Decoration Day (Memorial Day) and on local, state, and regional reunions of Confederate veterans. Monuments to Southern soldiers were erected in almost every county courthouse town in the South. Efforts were also begun in both the North and the South to preserve major battlefields and to construct elaborate memorials in them. The largest and most significant battle fought close to Lafayette County was Pittsburgh Landing, which increasingly became known by its Union name, Shiloh. At Shiloh, important landscape features were preserved or recreated. The sunken road, the peach orchard, the infamous bloody pond, and the oak tree under which General Albert Sidney Johnson rapidly and unknowingly bled to death after a Minié ball severed an artery in his leg, were more significant than monuments.

The death of a Confederate veteran, particularly a high-ranking officer or a soldier who had exhibited unusual bravery, was a special religious experience of the Lost Cause. Ritual surrounded the funeral and burial. A Confederate battle flag usually was draped over the coffin and "Dixie" was played or sung. A particular group of hymns quickly became part of the service, including "How Firm a Foundation," which was sung at the funerals of Thomas "Stonewall" Jackson and Jefferson Davis. "Nearer My God to Thee," "Soldiers of Christ, Arise," "Abide with Me," and "Let Us Pass Over the River, and Rest Under the Shade of the Trees," the latter based on last words of Stonewall Jackson, were especially popular.[16]

Although several organizations were created for Confederate veterans, the United Daughters of the Confederacy remained the most dedicated and persistent guardian of the Lost Cause. From Reconstruction into the early twentieth century, older U.D.C. members, often costumed in black silk dresses accented with white lace at formal occasions, were striking. One good black silk dress for all social and religious occasions was an inexpensive means of continuous mourning and a pretense of the status and symbol of wealth, even if lost. Just how serious and far the religion of the Lost Cause was taken by some members of U.D.C. is revealed in their rituals to maintain the memory of the Confederacy. Meetings began with a ritualistic prayer, and "How Firm a Foundation," the official hymn of the U.D.C., was sung.[17] It is not surprising that from such meetings came resolutions to condemn history books used in the local public schools on the grounds that they contained little discussion of the Southern Confederacy or an incorrect interpretation of the South's heroic role in the Civil War. Until after the Second World War publishers offered alternate editions of textbooks for southern schools that supported sectional interpretations of the Civil War and race relations. But members of the U.D.C. also campaigned for state pensions and medical care for Confederate veterans, raised funds to create and support Confederate soldiers' homes and college scholarships for the descendants of soldiers, and continued to maintain cemeteries and burial plots of Confederate soldiers. Ultimately, members reached out beyond the Lost Cause and became active participants in national endeavors that were not directly related to the Civil War.

As mentioned before, one must not interpret "maiden aunts" to mean just spinsters. The most successful female keepers of Confederate heritage were married. A woman needed education, financial security, political influence, and social standing to rise within the U.D.C. Mary Forrest Bradley, the daughter of Jane Taylor Cook and Captain William Montgomery Forrest, served as president and honorary president of the Tennessee Division of the United Daughters of the Confederacy. She also was awarded a citation by President Wilson for her work with the Parents-Teachers Association during the First World War and received a national service pen for more than two thousand hours of volunteer activities during the Second World War.[18]

Southerners born after the First World War did not know the religious overtones of the Lost Cause. After the Second World War, Decoration Day, Jefferson Davis's and Robert E. Lee's birthdays, and other Confederate holidays ceased to be celebrated in the Confederate states. As a child and young man, Faulkner knew the cold, dark shroud of the lingering Confederacy, and he witnessed the vanishing religious rites of the Lost Cause:

> [T]he town itself wrote the epilogue and epitaph: 1900, on Confederate Decoration Day, Mrs. Virginia Depre, Colonel Sartoris's sister, twitched a lanyard and the spring-restive bunting collapsed . . . leaving the marble effigy—the stone infantryman on his stone pedestal . . . epilogue and epitaph, because apparently neither the U. D. C. ladies who instigated and bought the monument, nor the architect who designed it nor the masons who erected it, had noticed that the marble eyes under the shading marble palm stared not toward the north and the enemy, but toward the south, toward . . . his own rear—looking perhaps, the wits said (could say now, with the old war thirty-five years past and you could even joke about it . . .), for reinforcements.[19]

Faulkner's description of Jefferson's Confederate monument leaves the impression that on all such monuments the soldiers face north toward the Union states

Figure 6.2. Confederate monument erected by the Albert Sidney Johnson Chapter of the United Daughters of the Confederacy on the University of Mississippi campus in 1906. The monument differs from ones depicting Confederate soldiers in uniform. The soldier is dressed as a scout, facing into the rising sun with his left hand shading his eyes. Symbolically, he anticipates the approach of a large Union army crossing the Tallahatchie River into the Confederate frontier. Charles S. Aiken, 2004.

from which the enemy came. A Confederate soldier who faces south, with his back toward the enemy, is thought atypical. John Windberry discovered that there are four basic locations of Confederate monuments: battlefields, cemeteries, lawns of state capitols, and local sites in towns and cities, including lawns of courthouses and other public places. Monuments with soldiers atop them accounted for 49 percent of the 666 he studied. Of the 362 monuments located on courthouse lawns, 62 percent have soldiers atop them. Only 45 percent of the soldiers face north. The direction that a courthouse faces is the primary factor in determining the direction that the soldier faces.[20]

All or parts of only four of the Confederate states were surveyed using the United States rectilinear system, which was employed in the Chickasaw and Choctaw cessions. Faulkner was reared in a part of Mississippi surveyed in townships six miles by six miles partitioned into thirty-six sections one mile by one mile. The local geography in which the four cardinal directions are paramount led him to believe the myth that soldiers atop Confederate monuments always face north.

The monument erected on the University of Mississippi campus in 1906 by the Albert Sidney Johnson Chapter of United Daughters of the Confederacy has a soldier atop it (fig. 6.2). The Confederate warrior differs from most. He is not in uniform and does not stand at rigid attention or at parade rest. The monument faces east and greets visitors entering the campus. The soldier is dressed in the apparel of a Confederate scout with his left hand shading his eyes from the sun as though he anticipates the imminent approach of Union troops. Because two large Union armies invaded Lafayette County in 1862 and 1864, the campus monument is more in keeping with local Civil War history than many memorials to the Confederacy, including the one at the Lafayette County courthouse described by Faulkner.

By the Great Depression of the 1930s the religious fervor of the Lost Cause had faded, but the role of women in the interpretation of southern and local history was extant. Rather than a small, immature, and rowdy planter and university town on the southern cotton frontier, Oxford of the Old South was reinterpreted as a place of charm and culture, an Arcadian intellectual paradise that was destroyed by the Civil War. The description of Oxford in the 1938 Federal Writers' Project guide to Mississippi is an example of the tendency to fantasize:

> [The University of Mississippi] under the administration of Dr. Augustus B. Long-
> street . . . drew some of the South's most brilliant minds to Oxford, and until the
> outbreak of the War between the States, a society of culture and gaiety flourished. . . .
> Young men held tilting tournaments that resembled in their color and pageantry the
> jousts of Scott's romances. Sober-minded scholars divided their attention between
> their books and addresses to the crowds gathered on the courthouse square.[21]

Characterization of the Old South as an era of bold southern knights who engaged in tilting tournaments is actually part of the Lost Cause myth, which places the failed Confederacy in the context of the unsuccessful Scottish rebellion presented in Walter Scott's novels. Although the University of Mississippi improved academically, especially after Frederick Augustus Porter Barnard became chancellor, only eleven of the seventy-four "sober-minded scholars" in the first class, that of 1848, graduated.[22]

Faulkner's reaction to the Lost Cause and the enhancement of local history was to make the stories antithetical. He was not particularly kind to the female keepers and embellishers of the annals of Oxford, Lafayette County, and north Mississippi. Distinguished families from Virginia and the Carolinas, handsome men, lovely women, lush plantations, opulent houses, and loyal docile darkies, became grist for *The Sound and the Fury*, *Light in August*, *Absalom, Absalom!*, and other stories. The burden of the past is often conveyed by Faulkner's employing the maiden aunts and potent descriptions of pungent odors. Throughout Faulkner's stories are snippets directed at old women. The "big decaying wooden houses of Jefferson . . . set . . . in shaggy untended lawns . . . seemed to be spellbound by the shades of women, old women still spinsters and widows." Even in the 1940s "the women, the ladies, the unsurrendered, the irreconcilable, . . . would still get up and stalk out of picture houses showing *Gone with the Wind* for reinforcements." At the University of Virginia in 1958, Faulkner revealed that his aunt went to the theater in Oxford to see *Gone with the Wind* and got up and left when the word "Sherman" appeared on the screen. The animosity against Sherman in Oxford was directed at his troops burning and looting in Lafayette County in 1862, rather than at his burning Atlanta and pillaging across Georgia in 1864. However, Sherman did not burn Wyatt, a myth that persists.[23]

"A Rose for Emily" is among Faulkner's most derisive and widely read stories, and a poor introduction for a novice to one of the great twentieth-century writers. Not only does the tale have a gruesome gothic surprise about Miss Emily's private life, but Faulkner's description of her is hardly flattering. She "looked bloated, like a body long submerged in motionless water. . . . Her eyes, lost in the fatty ridges of her face, looked like two small pieces of coal pressed into a lump of dough." And yet Faulkner had compassion for Emily, even though he did not reveal it in her story. In a class at the University of Virginia, Faulkner stated that her life was "simply another manifestation of man's injustice to man." Emily's father did not wish for her to marry because he wanted his daughter to be his housekeeper rather than to find love, marry, and have a family.[24]

Particular old women of Jefferson, such as Caroline Bascomb Compson, cannot confront reality. In the decaying Compson big house, Miss Caroline lies on a bed in a room that is kept dark all day, and the air is saturated with the reek from a camphor-soaked cloth across her brow. To Faulkner, Miss Caroline is "cold and weak," filled with the pretense of family status and delicate health. The intense-smelling camphor is more a prop to elicit sympathy than a treatment for a malady. Miss Caroline has traits similar to those of Rosamond Alston Stone, the mother of Phil Stone. Stone believed that his mother's hypochondria was caused by her childhood during the Civil War spent almost entirely in isolation with slaves and two spinster aunts. He remembered his mother as a person who "enjoyed bad health all her life and never suffered any pain less than 'agony,' never had a serious illness until she was eighty-three years old, slept with all windows closed, got as little sunshine as possible, lived largely off of molasses and [corn] bread and fatback, . . . and when she died from a broken hip at eighty-five she still had half of her own teeth . . . and could read a newspaper without eyeglasses."[25]

In certain respects *Absalom, Absalom!* is Faulkner's response to the Lost Cause. The novel, published in 1936, is set in 1909 and 1910. The date of the story of Thomas Sutpen, as retold, is deliberately precise in relation to the Civil War. By 1909 a number of older persons who survived the war were still alive. Women who were in their late teens or early twenties in 1861, prime marriage age, were spinsters approaching seventy. The religion of the Lost Cause was at its crescendo. In an attempt to ensure that her version of the story of Thomas Sutpen endures, Rosa Coldfield, a spinster dressed in "eternal black" since 1866, calls Quentin Compson, who in the summer of 1909 is leaving for Harvard, to the hot "dim coffin-smelling gloom" of her darkened house. When Miss Rosa enters the room there comes "the rank smell of female old flesh long embattled in virginity." Miss Rosa, in desperation, could have married Thomas Sutpen, her deceased sister's husband. But Sutpen's crude proposal of marriage was crushing. By fate and hate she remains unwed. Miss Rosa's voice does not cease, and Quentin thinks that he is two distinct persons listening to her, "the Quentin Compson preparing for Harvard in the South, the deep South dead since 1865 and peopled with garrulous outraged baffled ghosts, listening, having to listen, to one of the ghosts . . . and the Quentin Compson who was still too young to deserve yet to be a ghost."[26]

The New South Cotton Plantation Landscape

While the Lost Cause cast its gloom over certain aspects of southern life, after the Civil War the South changed economically, socially, politically, and geographically. The economic context of Faulkner's Yoknapatawpha saga is an agricultural system in which cotton, "a king," is "omnipotent and omnipresent."[27] A distinct type of cotton production system corresponds with each of the three periods of the American South: the Old South slave era, which in north Mississippi extended from the 1830s through 1865; the New South era of tenant farming that lasted from about 1880 until shortly after the Second World War; and the Modern South era of mechanized farming.[28] The first two-thirds of Faulkner's life corresponded with the mature phase of the New South era, which extended from about 1900 through the 1930s. Although Faulkner treats the Old South and touches upon the transition period to the Modern South, most of his Yoknapatawpha stories are set in the New South.

The Falkners were not a planter family but were small-town businessmen engaged in enterprises of the agrarian infrastructure. Although William Clark Falkner, the old colonel, was finished as a soldier before the Civil War ended, he arose as a New South promoter, politician, builder of railroads, and novelist who wrote *The White Rose of Memphis*. That his life was suddenly and romantically terminated when he was murdered in 1889 by a former business associate with whom he was feuding solidified his myth. J. W. T. Falkner, William Clark Falkner's son and William Faulkner's grandfather, known as the young colonel, sold the family's profitable Gulf and Chicago Railroad in 1902. Murry, Faulkner's father, lost his job with the family enterprise. He moved the family from Ripley to Oxford and purchased a livery stable. Oxford had a population of only 2,014 in 1910, but with its arc streetlights, numerous stores, and the University of Mississippi on its western edge, the town seemed cosmopolitan compared to Ripley, which was only one-third as large.[29]

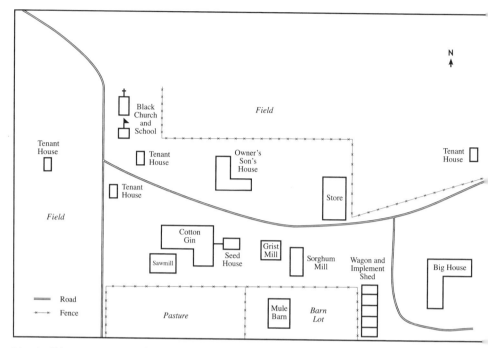

Map 6.1. Diagrammatic map of the headquarters of a New South plantation at a crossroad in north Mississippi. Charles S. Aiken.

Throughout the New South era, as throughout the Old, cotton was the primary underpinning of Lafayette County's economy. Cotton not only was a king that beat back the wilderness and drove out the panther, bear, and deer, but it also was a master that enslaved all, whites as well as blacks, to the rhythm of its production, from plowing in late winter through harvest in autumn. Holidays, payment of taxes, school terms, church revivals, and the daily rhythm of farm and town life were set by the fluffy white sovereign. Cotton was a

> white surf crashing against the flanks of gin and warehouse and ringing like bells
> on the marble counters of the banks: altering not just the face of the land, but the
> complexion of the town too, creating its own parasitic aristocracy not only behind
> the columned porticoes of the plantation houses, but in the counting-rooms of mer-
> chants and bankers and the sanctums of lawyers, . . . but finally nadir complete: the
> county offices too: of sheriff and tax collector and bailiff and turnkey and clerk.[30]

The Yoknapatawpha County countryside contrasted sharply with Jefferson. The New South cultural landscape was reorganized and greatly expanded from that of the Old South. A plantation labor force composed of black and white tenant farmers replaced the slaves of the Old South. The New South rural settlement

Figure 6.3. Nolan's store at the junction of the old Memphis-Oxford Road and old Helena Road in Tate County, Mississippi, in 1966. The store was built in 1918 by a furnish merchant to replace a smaller one constructed shortly after the Civil War. The store was part of a New South family-owned agribusiness complex that also included a steam powered cotton ginnery, grist mill, sawmill, and large sorghum mill. Charles S. Aiken.

pattern consisted of hamlets at strategic locations including major road junctions. Although historians have placed much emphasis on stores of merchants who furnished tenant farmers on plantations and yeomen who barely made a living on small hard-scrabble farms, the principal hamlets also had cotton gins, gristmills, sawmills, and sorghum mills, which were important components of the New South agrarian infrastructure (map 6.1; fig. 6.3).[31] One or more white churches, cemeteries, and a public school for whites were elements of hamlets. Churches, cemeteries, and schools for blacks usually were on plantations and within enclaves of black landowners.

Yoknapatawpha County has several rural communities, but Frenchman's Bend, which sprawls across the Yoknapatawpha River into Grenier County, is developed in the greatest detail by Faulkner. In certain respects Frenchman's Bend is atypical of the type of New South hamlet found in the Lowland South. Although the ruin of Frenchman's Bend, the giant plantation of Louis Grenier, is the site of the community, the plantation's blacks are superseded by white tenant farmers and yeomen. Hardly any blacks remain in the community; none own land. The few blacks who work for affluent whites are regarded with suspicion and antagonism by white tenants and yeomen. Grenier's estate is "parceled out . . . into small shiftless mortgaged farms" held by Jefferson banks, which sold the mortgages to Will Varner. Varner was a beat supervisor in Yoknapatawpha County, a justice of the

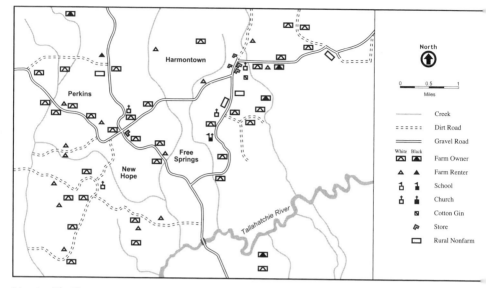

Map 6.2. The Harmontown community in north Lafayette County, Mississippi, in 1941. Redrafted from a map in Nichols and King 1943. Charles S. Aiken.

peace in Grenier County, and an election commissioner in both. "He owned most of the good land in the country and held mortgages on most of the rest."[32]

Although Will Varner is from poor white yeoman stock, he technically is a planter with considerable land. However, he is never identified as a planter by Faulkner. Varner is simply an unscrupulous white who has amassed considerable wealth. And the wealthy Varner sarcastically rejects identification as a planter. He does not live in Grenier's great house, but occasionally he sits in the overgrown lawn before the decaying ruin. "I like to sit here" says Varner. "I'm trying to find out what it must have felt like to be the fool that would need all this . . . just to eat and sleep in."[33]

Varner's Crossroads is the focus of the Frenchman's Bend community. Varner's businesses include a store, a cotton gin, a gristmill, a blacksmith shop, and a livery barn. The hamlet also has a schoolhouse, a church, and an unpainted rambling log and frame house called Littlejohn's hotel, identified by the sign "ROOMS AND BORD." About three dozen dwellings are within the sound of the school and church bells.[34]

Among the various New South communities of Lafayette County was Harmontown just north of the Tallahatchie River (map 6.2). The hamlet began before the Civil War on the LaGrange-Hendersonville Road as a center for the Harmons, one of Lafayette County's principal Old South families. The family included George,

Levi, Wesley, and J. W. Harmon, who owned several thousand acres within and along the edges of the Tallahatchie River bottom. The family's plantation headquarters with big houses and cotton gins was on the plateau land above the flood-prone and mosquito- and snake-infested river and creek bottoms.

During the New South era, Harmontown developed 4.5 miles west of the dying town of Wyatt around the Harmon family cemetery and a union church building. During its heyday from the 1880s until 1940, when construction of Sardis Reservoir flooded north Lafayette County's best farmland and cut the Memphis-Oxford Road, Harmontown had three furnish merchant stores, a cotton gin, a gristmill, a service station, and a Baptist church, which replaced the union building. The Harmon family cemetery became a community burial ground. In the 1930s and 1940s, the primary store was Cook and Hale, a cradle-to-grave furnish business, which also owned the cotton gin. Free Springs Methodist Church was one mile to the south of Harmontown. Bedenbaugh's store was moved to the crossroads, where the road to Como crosses the Memphis-Oxford Road, because the reservoir caused the removal of most of the close customers. In 1940 Perkins, a small eleven-grade consolidated public school for whites, and Oak Grove Christian Church (Church of Christ) were three miles west of the hamlet. A Methodist church and two ramshackle one-room schools with four grades each served blacks. In 1940 the Harmontown community had seventy-six white and thirty-six black households, considerably less than the numbers in 1930 before construction of the reservoir.[35] At the beginning of the twenty-first century, the cemetery, the Baptist church, and a few houses were all that remained of the New South Harmontown hamlet. A new community of whites called Harmontown developed two miles west of the old hamlet around the intersection of new State Highway 310 (the former Como Road) and the old Memphis-Oxford Road. New Harmontown has a public water system, two stores, and a number of dwellings on small lots. Because of the lack of county zoning and enforced building codes, modest new houses, mobile homes, and a hodgepodge of shacks called fishing camps are strung out along Highway 310 and the old Memphis-Oxford Road.

Yoknapatawpha County, like Lafayette, contains small rural enclaves of black farmers (figs. 6.4 and 6.5). Farms of blacks are small, often less than fifty acres, and clustered. Usually farms are comprised of land that whites do not want because of poor soil or severe erosion. In addition to purchasing inferior land, blacks acquire land from their "white folks," families of former masters, who sell or will property to their former tenants, descendants of slaves, and mulatto kin. Carothers Edmonds's father deeded his Negro first cousin and his heirs a house and ten acres on the McCaslin place, "an oblong of earth set forever in the middle of the two-thousand-acre plantation like a postage stamp in the center of an envelope." The

Figure 6.4. A double-pen log house of a black landowner in east Tate County just north of the Tate-Lafayette County boundary in 1964. The dwelling is partly whitewashed. "A weathered paintless dog-trot cabin . . . on a rise of ground above a creek-bottom cotton patch" (Faulkner *The Mansion* 1959, 398). Charles S. Aiken.

Figure 6.5. Elderly farm owners in south Marshall County, Mississippi, in 1964. The mules are a matched pair of prime animals. A wagon pulled by two mules was a common method of travel by southern black and white yeomen until motor vehicles began rapidly replacing it after the Second World War. The equivalent of the versatile pickup truck, a wagon could carry more children and relatives than a buggy or surrey, and it hauled farm crops and supplies. In addition to pulling wagons, mules drew field implements and were ridden. William Faulkner's tribute to the noble mule is in *Sartoris* 1929, 278–279. Charles S. Aiken.

Figure 6.6. The poorly maintained dirt road between College Hill and College Hill Station, Lafayette County, Mississippi, in 1974. The road was barely passable in an automobile in dry weather even after it was graded. After blacks began to vote in large numbers, the road was paved with asphalt. Almost all of the recently built houses along it are occupied by blacks. Charles S. Aiken.

larger rural enclaves of blacks had a church, a school, and sometimes a store. Most enclaves were geographically and culturally isolated. Some did not have electric power or telephones until long after whites received them. Until the restoration of voting rights to Mississippi blacks by the 1965 Voting Rights Act, roads through the enclaves were not well maintained by the beat supervisor unless they were major thoroughfares. The typical route through an enclave is described by Faulkner in *The Mansion*, which is set in 1946. It was "a Negro road, a road marked with many wheels and traced with cotton wisps, yet dirt, not even gravel, since the people who lived on and used it had neither the voting power to compel nor the money to persuade the Beat supervisor to do more than scrape and grade it twice a year" (fig. 6.6). Southern towns also have black enclaves, some of which are just outside municipal boundaries. Residential areas of whites usually are segregated from those of blacks by one or more boundaries, including the business district, a major thoroughfare, a stream, or the railroad. The principal black enclave of Jefferson, as in Oxford, is Freedmen Town, also called Freedman Town (map 6.3). In *Light in August* Faulkner concisely describes the place in 1932 through the thoughts of Joe Christmas. "He was in Freedman Town, surrounded by the summer smell and summer voices of invisible negroes. . . . [H]e saw himself enclosed by cabinshapes, vague, kerosenelit."[36]

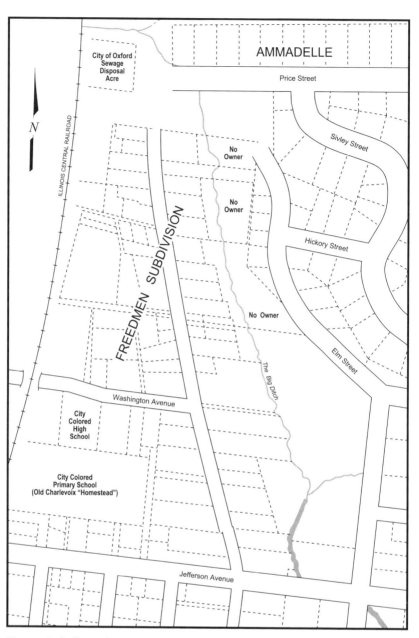

Map 6.3. Oxford's Freedmen Town in 1939. The area of black settlement developed at the edge of Oxford following the Civil War. Although called a subdivision, Freedmen Town was not initially platted as a planned residential area. Freedmen Town began haphazardly in the area of small lots near its center where former slaves squatted on land they did not own. By 1939 the area had been annexed by Oxford and a city high school for blacks had been established. However, as was customary in southern towns, Freedmen Town was segregated from white residential areas. The Big Ditch, the railroad, and Jefferson Avenue isolated Freedmen Town from white residential areas. There probably was no serious attempt to sort out and establish ownership of lots until after the Second World War. In the 1970s the city government used federal block grants to clear the area of shacks, establish and pave streets, and construct water and sewage lines. Today, Freedmen Town contains new privately owned housing and federally funded housing. The area is less densely populated than in 1939. Redrafted from 1939 Oxford city map by W. L. Caldwell, courtesy of the Oxford Planning Commission. Charles S. Aiken.

ıre 6.7. Cotton harvest in Jim Wolf Creek bottom in Tate County, Mississippi, in November 1961. ause the bolls of traditionally planted cotton varieties opened at different times, a field was hand ·ested two or three times from August into December. In this field, the best cotton had been harvested; ·t remained was "scrap." The term for the last harvest was "scrapping." In 1961 hand harvest was being ·dly replaced by mechanical pickers. Charles S. Aiken.

Although Faulkner does not focus intently on the techniques of New South cotton culture, he gives perceptive insights into black and white tenant farmers caught up in the agricultural system. Traditional cotton culture required from 160 to more than 200 hours of labor per acre, integrated into three phases—plowing and planting in the spring; thinning and weeding in late spring and early summer; and harvesting in late summer and autumn (fig. 6.7).[37] The 1930s was the acme of southern tenant farmers in both numbers and public attention given to them. Never before or after was as much media and scholarly attention focused on southern tenants, especially sharecroppers, as during the Great Depression. The fictional literature is so extensive that an entire genre of sharecropper novels is recognized.[38] The best-known works include Erskine Caldwell's *Tobacco Road* and John Steinbeck's *The Grapes of Wrath*. Documentaries with photographs and text encompass James Agee and Walker Evans's *Let Us Now Praise Famous Men* and Dorothea Lange and Paul Taylor's *An American Exodus*. Faulkner's most significant works that treat tenant farmers, *The Hamlet* and *Go Down, Moses*, were published at the conclusion of the Great Depression. However, because the tenant farmer theme is overpowered by more potent ones, Faulkner's works are not always included among the sharecropper novels. Within the scope of southern literature, *The Hamlet*, which concerns lower-class poor whites, and *Go Down, Moses*, which treats the relationship between white planter families and their black slaves and tenants, some of whom are relatives, are capstones to the conclusion of the New South era.

The critical characteristics of New South farm tenancy are vividly described by Faulkner, including the nature of the furnish system, the way cotton acreage is assigned, and the condition of tenant houses. The tenant furnish system is one in which a landlord advances cash and/or food and clothing to a tenant through a store he or she owns or through the store of a local merchant. The size of a family and the ages of its members determine the cotton acreage that can be worked.

One of the first questions Jody Varner asks Ab Snopes, who comes to Varner's store in Frenchman's Bend to rent a farm, is, "How much family you got?" Ab responds with a vague answer. When pressed by Jody Varner as to whether the family is five, six, or seven, Ab knows the question pertains to the number old enough to work. He replies, "I can put six hands in the field." The term "hand" means a worker. Ab then asks about the amount of rent for the farm. Jody responds, "Third and fourth. . . . Furnish out of the store here. No cash." "I see," replies Ab. "Furnish in six-bit dollars." "That's right," answers Jody. Furnish in six-bit dollars means that a landlord or a merchant practices usury and charges one dollar for every seventy-five cents of food and clothing purchased on credit.[39] Ab's question is sarcastic, implying that, like most white and black tenant farmers, he understands that he is victimized. Jody's reply to the question is equally caustic, for he knows that there are more tenants who want to rent than there are farms. The questions and answers are cuttingly oblique, a conversation technique still used in the plantation South for discussions about chicanery. Essentially, Jody tells Ab that he is going to exploit him and there is not a damn thing that he can do about it.

The amount of rent that Ab is to pay is one-fourth or one-third of the cotton and corn crops. These are the amounts charged to farmers who legally are "share tenants." Share tenants owned work stock, usually mules, and farm implements, including a wagon and plows. In addition to land, a landlord furnished a share tenant a house and the right to cut trees from a wood lot for cooking and heating. In north Mississippi the standard rent paid by a share tenant was one-fourth of the crops. One-third was considered exorbitant, usually paid for highly productive land or by tenants without recourse. "Sharecroppers," or "croppers," were tenants who did not own work stock or farm implements. Because mules and plows were furnished by the landlord, a sharecropper paid more rent than a share tenant, usually one-half of the cotton and corn crops.[40]

The tenant house into which Ab and his family move is a "sagging broken-backed cabin set in its inevitable treeless and grassless plot and weathered to the color of an old beehive." The windows do not have sashes, glass, and screens—only shutters. The yard is barren, scraped stark of vegetation with hoes. Rubbish, ashes, broken pottery, and cans are strewn across the yard.[41]

The furnish and the house for the Edgar Brownlees, a black tenant family, are representative of the prevailing conditions at the time *The Hamlet* was published (table 6.1; fig. 6.8). In 1943 the Brownlees and their eight children lived on a plantation on the Memphis-Oxford Road a few miles north of the Lafayette County–Tate County boundary. Brownlee, a sharecropper, paid one-half of his cotton and corn crops. No rent was paid for vegetables grown in a garden and peas planted among the corn in the field. Brownlee's milk cow grazed the pasture without charge. The family was furnished from a store, which once was part of the plantation but had been sold. Brownlee was more resourceful than most sharecroppers, for he borrowed less money from the landlord and charged less at the store than most tenants (table 6.1).

Although the north Mississippi landscape Faulkner knew was that of the New South plantation, it had a few cultural relics and fossils from the Old South. Most striking residuals of the Old South were houses of planters, few of which had ever been elegant, but many of which seemed to have been grand, even log dwellings, because of their great size and imposing porticos (figs. 1.1 and 6.9). Throughout Faulkner's lifetime, most of the houses sat unpainted. Some were occupied by black tenant families; others were abandoned and decaying. Of the big houses that were maintained, the interiors of a few, at least their parlors, were kept as they were in 1865. Occupied big houses were filled with musty odors and what Faulkner calls the smell of "old flesh"; miasmas permeated furniture, floors, and walls. Almost all the big houses had legends about the people who had built them. The story of the Coxe family's Galena, a six-section, 3,840-acre plantation twenty miles north of Oxford in Marshall County, is one of the earliest examples of a local legend restated in context of Faulkner's fiction (fig. 6.10). In 1938 the story of Galena was described "as bizarre as any William Faulkner . . . told":

Low and broad . . . [the house] is but one story high and rambles into a sturdy yet graceful H, its broad porch extending across the center hall and front rooms. . . . The gray of the frame walls is so drab and blotched that even the remaining chips of paint are practically drained of color. Dulled to a lifeless blue are the heavy blinds that run the length of the many stained windows to shut out all light of the outside world. The original furnishings are in disorder, as if thrust aside in haste a half century ago when the house was vacated. Massive oak and walnut furnishings possess each room. In the front parlor an oil portrait of William Henry Cox [*sic*] looks down from above the heavy mantel upon a lovely old secretary and an old fashioned piano.[42]

Table 6.1 The Brownlee family's furnish list for 1943

Date	Expenditure	Amount
March 7	Amount from Jan. 1943	$75.15
March 7	Amount from Feb. 1943	29.63
March 7	Cash to Frank	6.14
March 7	4 bunches of onions	1.40
March 7	30 lbs. Seed potatoes	.60
March 15	Account at store	2.65
March 18	Cabbage plants	.40
March 20	Feb. light bill	1.50
March 25	Cabbage plants	.40
March 26	Sugar and lard	2.35
April 4	50 lbs. flour & 8 lbs. lard	4.10
April 17	Cash	2.00
April 19	March light bill	1.50
April 24	Account at store	5.30
May 3	Account at store	4.10
May 12	Account at store	3.40
May 22	Account at store	5.35
May 29	Account at store	6.35
June 16	Cash	5.00
June 16	April light bill	1.50
June 17	Account at store	6.35
June 17	May light bill	1.50
June 30	Account at store	5.00
June 30	Cash	.50
July 15	June light bill	1.50
Sept. 6	Account at store	4.10
Oct. 8	Sub-total	180.00
Oct. 8	10% Interest	18.00
Oct. 8	TOTAL	198.00
Nov. 1	Account paid in Full	00.00

Daybook of William Thorn, 1943–1949.

Figure 6.8. An unoccupied tenant house on a plantation on the Memphis-Oxford Road in Tate County, Mississippi, in 1966. The Brownlees, a sharecropper family, lived in the dwelling during the 1940s. At the time the house was constructed in the 1920s, it was surrounded by fields. Restrictions on cotton acreages beginning in 1933 with the Agricultural Adjustment Act resulted in the area encircling the house being devoted to pasture. The dwelling was wired for electricity in 1940 when the Tallahatchie Valley Electric Power Cooperative began the distribution of electricity from Tennessee Valley Authority in the area north of Oxford. Charles S. Aiken.

Figure 6.9. The Tate house in Oxford, Mississippi, in 1949. The house had two, two-over-two-room wings in the shape of an L, rather than four rooms over four. It was larger than the Wiley and Shegog (Rowan Oak) dwellings, but the porticoes of all three were similar. The Tate house was razed in the 1950s. Courtesy of Special Collections, University of Tennessee Libraries.

Figure 6.10. The Coxe family's Galena plantation big house near Chulahoma in Marshall County, Mississip in the 1930s. The fully furnished house, which was built in the 1840s, had not been occupied for a number c years. The dwelling may have originally been a dogtrot with the Greek revival wings added later. Courtesy c Chesley Thorne Smith.

Figure 6.11. Graves of a planter family in an abandoned north Mississippi cemetery in 1974. Although the graves appear to have been robbed, the destruction probably was caused by animals and fallen trees. Charles S. Aiken.

According to local oral history, William Henry Coxe, a Scotsman who lived in Georgia, sent his five handsome sons with several hundred slaves to establish a new plantation in Marshall County, Mississippi. The complex of Galena's slave quarters and other buildings was so large that travelers frequently asked the name of the village. But the Coxe brothers came to Faulknerian ends. William Henry Jr. in a drunken spree attempted to ride his horse up the front steps but fell and broke his neck. Toby, also drunk, killed his bride in the house and then committed suicide. Another brother drove a team of horses off the river bluff at Memphis into the Mississippi.[43] The big house on Galena plantation was closed about 1890 and never reoccupied. Because of the nuisance of curious persons visiting the unoccupied house, the owner of Galena razed the dwelling sometime after 1938.

Even the cemeteries presented to Faulkner a bygone age of affluence. Rural cemeteries of the planters contained large tombstones for those who died in a flush time before the Civil War, while the small postwar monuments and the unkempt condition of cemeteries attested to a poverty and a loss of pride (fig. 6.11).

To most local persons, the landscape cultural relics and fossils of the Old South seemed common, and they sat among newer, ordinary landscape features. Many occupied and unoccupied big houses, such as Galena, were on landholdings that were still viable plantations. Only a person such as Faulkner, a sensitive and discerning observer, questioned what the past implied. In the apocrypha that Faulkner developed from the reality, he wrote that, similar to William Henry Coxe's Galena, all that remained of the domain of Louis Grenier was "nothing but the name of his plantation and his own fading corrupted legend like a thin layer of the native ephemeral yet inevictable dust on a section of country surrounding a little lost paintless crossroads store."[44] And from the reality Faulkner created a stunning description of Quentin Compson's view of the ruins of the fictional Sutpen's Hundred. "He looked up the slope before them where the wet yellow sedge died upward into the rain like melting gold and saw the grove, the clump of cedars on the crest of the hill . . . the cedars beyond which, beyond the ruined fields beyond which, would be the oak grove and the gray huge rotting deserted house half a mile away." In the grove of cedars was the unkempt, abandoned Sutpen cemetery with "two flat heavy vaulted slabs . . . cracked across the middle by their own weight" and beside the horizontal monuments were "three headstones leaning a little awry."[45]

In north Mississippi, even the land overtly indicated decay. The hill lands of the north Mississippi Loess Plains during Faulkner's lifetime were among the most severely eroded areas in the United States (figs. 6.12 and 6.13). The ease with which loess erodes in combination with careless tillage practices introduced by the initial settlers resulted in sheet and rill erosion that led to gullying. In 1860, at the end of the Old South era and less than thirty years after the settlement of north Mississippi

Figure 6.12. Gullied land in Lafayette County, Mississippi, photographed in 1936 by Walker Evans. "[I]t was a region of scrubby second-growth pine and oak . . . where not even a trace of furrow showed any more, gutted and gullied by forty years of rain" (Faulkner *The Hamlet* 1940, 196). Farm Security Administration Collection, Library of Congress.

Figure 6.13. An aerial view of severely eroded land northeast of Oxford, Mississippi, in 1938. Cultivated patches are among gullies in former large fields. Today, much severely eroded land has been graded and planted in grass or is hidden in pine forests. O. S. Welch. Soil Conservation Service Collection, National Archives.

began, Eugene W. Hilgard punningly warned that Oxford and other towns of the Loess Plains were "in danger of going, in the most literal sense, '*down hill*.'"[46] Accelerated erosion, however, went largely unchecked for seven more decades and climaxed in the 1930s just prior to the introduction of aggressive conservation measures under President Franklin Roosevelt's New Deal. By the early 1930s most gullied land had been abandoned for crops and either had reverted to scrub forest or lay barren. The Federal Writers' Project guide to Mississippi incisively states, "A great many crumbling mansions, built during the flush times of the 1830s and 1840s, desolately face the encroaching gullies. These houses, gradually moldering away as the earth slides from beneath them, are unpainted with sagging porches and rotting pillars; they are often occupied by Negro families" (fig. 6.14).[47] But a few of the big houses, including the one on the Parks plantation near Coldwater in Tate County, continue to be maintained (fig. 6.15).

Although accelerated erosion no longer is a serious problem in north Mississippi, the hills and plateaus that Faulkner knew were riddled with scars. His descriptions of soil erosion are among the most vivid in American literature. The southern edge of the Pine Hills north of Varner's Crossroads is "a region of scrubby second-growth pine and oak among which dogwood bloomed . . . and old fields where not even a trace of furrow showed any more, gutted and gullied by forty years of rain and frost and heat into plateaus choked with rank sedge and briers . . . and crumbling ravines striated red and white with alternate sand and clay."[48]

Although William Faulkner's grandfather owned a cotton farm north of Oxford, the family was never directly dependent upon either cotton or farming. Indirectly, though, the family was economically tied to the staple through its business interests. In 1938 Faulkner purchased a 320-acre farm seventeen miles northeast of Oxford as an investment. He named his half-section Greenfield Farm. In his fiction Faulkner is antagonistic toward cotton. He believes that slavery of the Old South and tenant farming of the New are abusive, not only to people, but also to the land. The people who are caught up in the New South cotton system, whites as well as blacks and planters as well as tenants, were tightly tied to the land and the plantation system and could not escape. Despite what Faulkner wrote about cotton, the agricultural infrastructure of Oxford and Lafayette County dictated that it was the most valuable crop that he could grow. Continually in need of money, Faulkner compromised and grew cotton on Greenfield Farm. He employed four black tenant families and even played the role of furnish merchant by opening a commissary. For a few years, Faulkner's brother John lived on the farm and managed it. If Greenfield had had a fifth tenant farmer, it would have met the *1940 Census of Plantation Agriculture* definition of *plantation*. Faulkner was no farmer. He bought a used Fordson tractor, an obsolete machine, to break the land for spring planting.

Figure 6.14. Former plantation big house on the Memphis-Oxford Road occupied by a black family in 1980. The dwelling was razed in the 1990s. Charles S. Aiken.

Figure 6.15. The big house on the 950-acre Parks plantation near Coldwater in Tate County, Mississippi, in 1961. Maintained in immaculate condition by Mrs. Parks, the owner, the house illustrates the commonality town and rural big houses, including Faulkner's Rowan Oak, built throughout north Mississippi during th two decades prior to the Civil War. Most were designed and constructed not by architects but by carpente who followed pattern books. Charles S. Aiken.

The tenants cultivated their crops with mules.[49] The commissary was never able to achieve the economies of scale necessary to provide the complete stock of goods required by tenant farmers. Cans of peaches, tomatoes, and other food went out of date while tenants traveled to Oxford for most of their necessary supplies.

Mink Snopes is among the poor whites trapped in farm tenancy, living a meaningless life in a rotting shack in Frenchman's Bend and sensing that his life is being drained away by hard work that returns nothing but mere existence. Abner (Ab), patriarch of the Snopes family, set the precedent for his clan's use of fire as a reprisal instrument shortly after the Civil War, when he burned the barns of Major de Spain and a Mr. Harris.[50] Ab's kinsman Mink directs his outrage toward the land with fire:

[T]he ground, the dirt which any and every tenant farmer and sharecropper knew to be his sworn foe and mortal enemy—the hard implacable land which wore out his youth and his tools and then his body itself. . . . *You got me, you'll wear me out because you are stronger than me since I'm jest bone and flesh. I cant leave you because I cant afford to. . . . And not just me, but all my tenant and cropper kind. . . . But we can burn you. Every late February or March we can set fire to the surface of you until all of you in sight is scorched and black, and there aint one . . . damn thing you can do about it.*[51]

However, to persons who understand fire, it is a management tool. North American Indians set fires in the forest and fields in late winter and early spring to destroy the accumulated tinder of leaves, grass, limbs, and fallen trees, creating a parklike landscape. The pinewoods across the lower South, including south Mississippi, are dependent on fire for their continued existence. Use of fire as an ecological management tool also is entrenched in the cultures of Europe and Africa, and whites and blacks continued the practice in North America.[52] As the boll weevil moved across the southern cotton regions between the 1890s and 1923, fire became an important instrument in controlling the insect. Burning harvested fields and surrounding grass, weeds, and bush borders destroys the insects and their wintering places. In the early twentieth century, when Faulkner began his Yoknapatawpha saga, only a few persons, mostly planters, comprehended fire as a land management tool. Ironically, Faulkner, an outdoorsman and farmer, did not grasp fire's ecological significance in the southern environment. In 1953 Faulkner and the writer and photographer Bern Keating, on the way to a party at the country club in Greenville, Mississippi, passed a field that had been burned. Keating said, "Those damn peasants." Faulkner muttered, "You'll never stop it. That's one difference between our peasantry and the European peasant. The European peasant loves the land. These people burn it because they hate it."[53]

Like Yoknapatawpha County, the Yazoo Delta became a land Faulkner sees as "warped and wrung to mathematical squares of rank cotton" because it is "too rich for anything else, too rich and strong to have remained wilderness." The tenant plantation, with its great economic and social cleavage between those who own and those who till the land, diffused throughout the Delta, and cotton spread with it. The New South cotton system with its planters and tenants is part of a larger economic system that perpetually operates on borrowed money, with tenants in debt to planters, planters in debt to small-town banks, small-town banks in debt to Memphis banks, and Memphis banks in debt to financial institutions in northern cities. The Delta is a place where "cotton grows man-tall in the very cracks in the sidewalk, mortgaged before it is ever planted and sold and the money spent before it is ever harvested, and usury and mortgage and bankruptcy and measureless wealth all breed and spawn together until no man has time to say which one is which, or cares."[54]

The Plantation and Responsibility

Faulkner thought that the consequence of man's replacement of the wilderness by the slave plantations of the Old South, followed by tenant plantations of the New South, was that the shameful agricultural system would be destroyed from within. Faulkner's idea that change originates within a land-use system alludes to a controversial concept held by Derwent Whittlesey, Preston James, Robert Platt, and other prominent American geographers during the first half of the twentieth century. The concept of sequent occupance, which places emphasis on the dynamic character of landscape in which successive stages of human habitation occur, served American geographers as an important research paradigm from the 1920s into the 1950s. In explaining sequent occupance Whittlesey stated, "Human occupance of an area, like other biotic phenomena, carries within itself the seed of its own transformation. . . . The American farmer, inaugurating a stage of occupance by plowing and planting virgin soil, sets in motion agents which at once begin subtly or grossly to alter the suitability of his land for crops; in extreme cases the ground deteriorates to a point where it must be converted into pasture or forest, or even abandoned; when either of these events occurs, human occupance of that area has entered upon a new stage."[55]

Whittlesey's idea that a stage of occupance has within itself the seed of its own transformation was never seriously debated or questioned.[56] That this idea was rejected by most geographers as too narrow and deterministic is demonstrated in that the majority of sequent-occupance studies recognize that external factors as well as internal ones produce landscape change. By 1960 the sequent-occupance paradigm had largely vanished from geographical research. As originally conceived, sequent occupance placed emphasis on static snapshots of the landscape through time. The process of landscape change, the primary key to understanding alteration of geography, was not emphasized. For the southern cotton plantation, processes of change occurred rapidly during two periods. The first, between 1865 and 1880, saw a change in the labor force from slaves working in gangs and squads to one of farm tenants. The second period, between 1935 and 1970, was a shift from the labor-intensive work force of farm tenants to tractors, mechanical cotton harvesters, combines, and weed- and grass-control herbicides.[57]

Absalom, Absalom! exemplifies Faulkner's idea of change caused by forces from within, especially as they pertain to abuse of land. The novel is the complex story of the landed dynasty that Thomas Sutpen attempts to create. In a letter written at the time he conceived *Absalom, Absalom!* Faulkner states that the book's theme is that of "a man who outraged the land, and the land then turned and destroyed the man's family." The same idea is expressed in *Go Down, Moses* and *Big Woods*. Near the end of the "Delta Autumn" section of *Go Down, Moses*, Isaac McCaslin thinks that the ravaged woods and fields and devastated game are the "consequence and signature" of man's "crime and guilt, and his punishment." Succinctly put, Isaac believes that "the ruined woods . . . don't cry for retribution. The very people who destroyed them will accomplish their revenge."[58]

Faulkner's idea that a system of land occupance is destroyed from within is tied to his theme of landscape decay. Soil erosion, soil exhaustion, and land abandonment in the South's cotton and tobacco regions traditionally have been interpreted as direct results of plantation agriculture. Faulkner, however, achieves with his fiction what most scholars of the American South have never emphasized in fact. He reveals the ultimate cause of landscape decay is not the cotton plantation per se but the decline in agricultural leadership and land management.[59]

A principal theme throughout Faulkner's works is the decline of elite pre–Civil War families such as the Sartorises, Compsons, Greniers, Habershams, and McCaslins and the assumption of leadership by families such as the Varners and Snopeses. Of the five Yoknapatawpha plantations whose histories are developed by Faulkner—Grenier's Frenchman's Bend, Compson's Mile, Sutpen's Hundred, Sartoris, and McCaslin-Edmonds—all but McCaslin-Edmonds are destroyed, and they fall primarily from within. After the Civil War one 640-acre section is all that remains of Thomas Sutpen's one-hundred-section domain of sixty-four thousand acres. By 1905 the only descendant of Grenier is a pathetic alcoholic who drives the hack for one of Jefferson's livery stables. The dysfunctional Compson family dwindles to essentially nothing. By the 1940s two of the three male heirs are dead, one by suicide, and the third, the last of the line, is a confirmed bachelor. The

640-acre Compson's Mile was still intact at the conclusion of the Civil War. However, former Confederate Brigadier General Jason Lycurgus Compson II spent the thirty-four years between 1866 and his death in 1900 selling fragments from the square mile to pay the mortgage on what was left. Eventually, Flem Snopes buys what remains of Compson's Mile at the edge of Jefferson and subdivides it into small lots for veterans' housing.[60]

Houses, fictionalized from reality, are among the landscape images that Faulkner uses to convey impressions of the leadership decline and failure (figs. 1.1, 6.9, and 6.10). The ruin of the Grenier house, the old Frenchman place, is "a gutted shell of an enormous house with its fallen stables and slave quarters and overgrown gardens and brick terraces." After the abandoned house and part of Grenier's domain pass into the hands of unscrupulous Will Varner, Will gives the dwelling to Flem Snopes upon marriage to his daughter, Eula. Flem salts the yard of the house with a few silver dollars, supposedly part of a fortune Grenier buried to conceal it from the Union army, and sells the dwelling and ten acres at an inflated price to gullible buyers.[61] Union troops burn the Sartoris's house during the Civil War, but the "monstrous tinder-dry rotten shell" of Sutpen's Hundred stands until 1910 when Clytie, Sutpen's mulatto daughter, sets it ablaze: "The house collapsed and roared away." In 1910 all that is left of Compson's Mile is a "fragment containing the house and the kitchen garden and the collapsing stables and one servant's cabin." The house is a scene of disillusionment: "weedchoked traces of the old ruined lawns and promenades, the house which had needed painting too long already, the scaling columns of the portico where Jason III . . . sat all day long with a decanter of whiskey and a litter of dogeared Horaces and Livys and Catulluses, composing (it was said) caustic and satiric eulogies on both his dead and his living fellowtownsmen."[62]

Underlying the theme of decline of the elite families is Faulkner's overarching theme of responsibility and the refusal to face it and the desire to escape it. Among Faulkner's most vivid examples of the tendency to escape responsibility, especially responsibility for land and plantation, is Isaac McCaslin. Significantly, Isaac, who was born in 1867, is a member of the first post–Civil War generation, the one Faulkner believed belonged to an era when "there was nothing that brought the issue . . . to be brave and strong or dramatic." Although Isaac comes to a realization of the evils of slavery and of the abuses associated with the tenant system, he does not take control of the two-thousand-acre McCaslin plantation and assume an aggressive role in land-tenure reform. Rather, Isaac seeks escape from responsibility by refusing, at the age of twenty-one, his inheritance, which is given to his older cousin Cass Edmonds. Isaac squanders the remainder of his life subsisting on what he makes from piddling carpenter jobs, a hardware store that he sells to Jason Compson, and the small monthly "pension" given to him by Cass.[63]

Isaac, especially as a boy and after he ages and becomes Uncle Ike, is a likable character who has been treated favorably by a number of Faulkner critics. Born in the harsh Reconstruction period of an elderly bachelor who marries a spinster, Isaac is orphaned by the age of twelve and is reared by Cass, who is hardly much older than he. If this is not enough to create compassion for him, a superficial acceptance of Isaac's repudiation of the evils of his heritage does. Also, Isaac's experiences in the wilderness, where he learns to appreciate nature, are ennobling. Although Faulkner depicts Isaac as a likable, universal character filled with disillusionment, he has no sympathy for him. In a seminar at the University of Virginia, Faulkner commented on Isaac's repudiation of his heritage:

> Well, there are some people in any time and age that cannot face and cope with the problems. There seem to be three stages: The first says, This is rotten, I'll have no part of it, I will take death first. The second says, This is rotten, I don't like it, I can't do anything about it, but at least I will not participate in it myself, I will go off into a cave or climb a pillar to sit on. The third says, This stinks and I'm going to do something about it. McCaslin is the second. He says, This is bad, and I will withdraw from it. What we need are people who will say, This is bad and I'm going to do something about it, I'm going to change it.[64]

The Masks of Faulkner

Faulkner's eccentric behavior was partly associated with his being a role player. He wore various masks, a concept in literary criticism that has received increasing attention. Lothar Hönnighausen explores the masks of Faulkner and correctly argues that role playing was essential to the writer's creative achievement. During the 1920s and 1930s Faulkner occasionally appeared at social gatherings in Oxford wearing the blue lieutenant's uniform of the Royal Air Force (RAF). Faulkner was in ground school for flight training in Canada when the First World War ended. He did not receive his wings and was not qualified to wear an officer's uniform. However, members of his class were commissioned honorary lieutenants in the Royal Air Force. If recalled to duty, he would have been a second lieutenant. More than a decade later, in the early 1930s, Faulkner earned a private pilot's license by taking lessons in Memphis.[65]

As Faulkner grew in stature as a writer, increasingly he received various honors and invitations to give addresses. When notified that he was to be awarded the

Howells Medal by the American Academy of Arts and Letters, Faulkner wrote that he would be unable to come to New York to accept it because he was a farmer and would have no money until he harvested his crops. In declining an honorary Doctor of Letters degree from Tulane University in 1952, Faulkner played the illiterate backwoods novice, whom some unwary critics still accept, and replied that he did not deserve an honorary degree for he did not graduate from grammar school. Faulkner also played the role of planter, and not with just the pretense of Rowan Oak. Greenfield Farm had the trappings of a New South plantation complete to a name, a manager, four black tenant farmers, and a commissary.[66]

For all his roles, the mature Faulkner always knew who he actually was, a largely self- but well-educated member of the Mississippi small-town planter-business elite and a distinguished writer of international renown. Despite a few rogues, the Falkners and the Butlers were old established Mississippi families whose members had surveyed the town of Oxford, built a railroad, founded a bank, and created other business enterprises. The Falkners and Butlers always performed their military duty, supporting both the Confederacy and the United States. Families such as the Falkners and the Butlers enjoyed the luxury of tolerating a few rascals such as Charlie Butler, Faulkner's grandfather who stole Oxford's tax money and vanished,[67] and eccentrics such as Bill, supposedly a famous author, but locally largely unread and undistinguished. Among the reasons Faulkner always returned to Oxford and spent most of life there is that his niche was defined and within certain social and economic constraints allowed him to do essentially as he pleased. Short of murder, he would never have been arrested on the streets of Oxford or the back roads of Lafayette County. If discovered publicly drunk, Faulkner was taken home rather than to jail. When a state game warden caught Faulkner and his neighbor William Baker, who was not a native Mississippian, hunting ducks in the Tallahatchie bottom, Baker produced his hunting license. To Baker's astonishment, Faulkner, a distinguished author of hunting stories, did not have a license. "I tried my best to get the game warden to put him in jail," recalled Baker, a priggish retired army colonel, "but he didn't do it, we came on home."[68]

Meta Carpenter Wilde, Faulkner's largely unknown love in Hollywood until she revealed the details of their almost thirty-year relationship several years after his and Estelle's deaths, in certain respects understood the writer better than any other person. She described Faulkner's ability to adapt to different surroundings:

[H]e possessed an acute and affecting sense of place, and that he changed as he moved into new ambiences. The variations of New York, where he quickened his pace and fell into a crisper speech pattern, were different from the alterations that came over him in Hollywood, where his posture was straighter, his dress less haphazard,

Figure 6.16. William Faulkner in 1955. This photograph is representative of the way in which Faulkner dressed much of the time in Lafayette County. Although he may appear to be in the costume of a farmer, the khaki pants and shirt are the dress of a middle-class rural Mississippian. Faulkner never was photographed wearing overalls, the uniform of laborers and tenant farmers.

even on the natty side at times. I could picture him after the first few days in Oxford taking on the gait of townspeople, slowing his speech, falling into vernacularisms, hanging up his city clothes for trousers and jacket that he would wear over and over.[69]

In a planter-dominated society, dress and decorum at social events are among the symbols of caste and class (fig. 6.16). Although much has been written about Faulkner's apparent disregard for his appearance, major social occasions revealed the real person. In preparing for a 1954 trip to South America as a cultural representative for the U.S. Department of State, Faulkner wrote Saxe Commins, his editor at Random House in New York, about the clothing he needed. Faulkner's instructions for shoes were detailed and specific. "I want English shoes, Church is the maker. . . . The shoes will be 6½, B width or C, that is, not too narrow. . . . Not pumps: lace shoes, patent leather evening shoes, with lace-up fronts." In preparing for Jill's wedding to Paul Summers in 1954, Faulkner wrote Commins that he would "need money, probably a ghastly amount. Am solvent now, but I will suggest you send $5000.00 . . . as Jill and her mother seem bent on making a production out of this, and her trousseau wedding stuff, bridesmaid's dresses, champagne etc will run quite a piece of jack." Despite his comment about Jill and Estelle spending too much, for the wedding reception at Rowan Oak Faulkner hired black waiters in red coats from Hotel Peabody, Memphis's most exclusive lodge and a regional center for planter society.[70]

In 1952 for a four-hundred-dollar honorarium, Faulkner accepted an invitation for an address in Cleveland, Mississippi, to the Delta Council, an organization of planters and other businesspersons that controls the agriculture of the Yazoo Delta and the adjoining Loess Plains.[71] The manner in which Faulkner appeared before this group of Mississippians, whom he considered more Snopes and Varners than members of the old landed elite, and what he said to them reveals his attitude toward most contemporary planters.

Faulkner addressed the Delta Council wearing seersucker trousers, an old belted jacket, and a shirt with a badly frayed collar. A handkerchief was stuck into his sleeve, English-style, and in his lapel was his French Legion of Honor rosette.[72] Although Faulkner contrasted sharply with the Delta planters in their new expensive suits, apparently he decided to go as one of the historic Mississippi planter-business elite and master of Rowan Oak, a member of an old southern Bourbon family fallen into genteel poverty but having lineage and credentials that gave him higher status than those whom he addressed.

To many of those present, Faulkner's speech came off as an attack on the federal government with its welfare programs and bureaus seeking regimentation and as a patriotic call for a return to an America as its founders envisioned it. The theme of respect for but independence from the federal government had appeared in Faulkner's stories for more than a decade. The five thousand who heard the speech gave Faulkner a standing ovation, and the Delta Council issued his address as a pamphlet. Hodding Carter, editor of the liberal Greenville, Mississippi, *Delta Democrat-Times*, commented that "the prophet . . . was not without honor in his own country."[73]

Analysis of the speech reveals the overriding theme is not an attack on the federal government, but a theme persistent throughout Faulkner's work—responsibility. Faulkner observed that the founders of America had left the Old World and come to the New World seeking "a place, not to be secure in" because they had just repudiated that, but "a place to be free in, to be independent in, to be responsible in." "That's what I am talking about: responsibility. Not just the right, but the duty of man to be responsible, the necessity of man to be responsible if he wishes to remain free; not just responsible to and for his fellow man, but to himself, the duty of a man, the individual, each individual, every individual, to be responsible for the consequences of his own acts." Faulkner went on to state that "we no longer have responsibility." He took a swipe at "those who misuse and betray the mass of him for their own aggrandisement and power," a direct but opaque reference to some planters' exploitation of their tenants. Faulkner ended by announcing that he believed that the heirs of the "old tough durable fathers" are "still capable of responsibility and self-respect, if only they can remember them again."[74]

Faulkner stated repeatedly that he used southern settings for his characters only because the South was the place that he knew best. He took the local, ordinary, and thought of it in terms of the universal. In the speech to the Delta Council, Faulkner did the reverse; he took the universal and meant it in the local sense. The speech with its theme of responsibility had a universal flavor, not directed toward Mississippians or the Delta planters. Yet the theme ties directly to Faulkner's plantation stories where an overriding theme is failure to be responsible.

SEVEN

Geographical Interpretation of "The Bear"

"The Bear" is among the most complex of William Faulkner's stories set in the New South era. It is also among the most read and analyzed. One collection identifies eight critical approaches to "The Bear," but a geographical perspective is not among them, despite Faulkner's overt and symbolic use of geography.[1] The story has two overt interrelated geographical themes. One is Faulkner's sources for the fictional setting; the other is the theme of landscape change.

"The Bear" is a part of *Go Down, Moses*, which was published in the spring of 1942. A few days after the book was released, a short, simplified version of the story appeared in the May 9 issue of the *Saturday Evening Post*. With one of its five sections omitted, "The Bear" was republished in 1955 as a section of *Big Woods*, a collection of Faulkner's hunting stories.[2] Of the three versions of the story, critics consider the one in *Go Down, Moses* to have the greatest intellectual depth.[3] Critics focus on two major themes. One is the wilderness theme, which is found primarily in parts 1, 2, 3, and 5. The second is the racial theme, the relationship between the McCaslin family and their slaves and descendants, which is presented largely in parts 4 and 5.

Sources for the Setting

"The Bear" is the story of the pursuit of a legendary bear each November and of the final hunt in which the beast is slain. The complex saga is set during the 1880s in the Tallahatchie River bottom in northern Yoknapatawpha County. Members of the hunting party include Major Cassius de Spain, who owns the camp and the surrounding land; General Jason Lycurgus Compson, a former Confederate officer and head of the Compson family; and McCaslin Edmonds, the young manager of the two-thousand-acre McCaslin plantation. The principal characters of the story are Isaac McCaslin, Edmonds's sixteen-year-old cousin who owns the plantation; Isaac's hunting mentor, Sam Fathers, an old man who is the son of a quadroon slave woman and a Chickasaw Indian chief; Boon Hogganbeck, a boy in the body of a forty-year-old man; Lion, a large dog; and Old Ben, the legendary bear.

Much of the action of the hunts occurs in and around de Spain's hunting lodge, "a paintless six-room bungalow set on piles above the spring high-water."[4] To heighten the suspense of what is to be the final hunt, Faulkner interrupts the action with a trip to Memphis by Isaac McCaslin and Boon Hogganbeck. The hunting party has been in camp for more than two weeks and would have departed except that the climax of the November trip, the annual, ritual chase of Old Ben, has been postponed by unusually cold weather. The men have exhausted the whiskey, and Isaac and Boon are sent to Memphis to purchase more. A railroad owned by a timber company passes close to the camp. Isaac and Boon catch the early-morning outbound log train to Hoke's, the timber company's sawmill camp on a mainline railroad to Memphis. They return to Hoke's by sunset and take the inbound log train to de Spain's camp.

De Spain's hunting camp appears on both maps of Yoknapatawpha County that Faulkner drew (map 2.3).[5] However, the timber company's railroad, which runs through the Tallahatchie bottom, is not shown. From an examination of Faulkner's maps the log line should connect with Sartoris's railroad, which runs northward from Jefferson. But close analysis of Faulkner's descriptions reveals that this spatial relationship does not exist. When Isaac and Boon board the log train for the journey from the camp to Memphis, the engine comes "up out of the woods under the paling east."[6] This description implies that Faulkner did not think of the log train traveling eastward past de Spain's lodge toward Sartoris's railroad, but westward toward another rail line that is not shown on his maps. Isaac and Boon's itinerary is further evidence of a second mainline railroad west of Yoknapatawpha County. In all journeys by train from the county to Memphis, except for the one in "The Bear," a change of trains is necessary at Memphis Junction. In "The Bear" Isaac and Boon travel directly to Memphis from Hoke's without interruption.

Clarification of the fictional setting of "The Bear" is provided through analysis of the actual geography from which the apocryphal was developed. As explained in chapter 2, Faulkner modeled most of the geographical components of his fictional county after Lafayette, but he took other landscape elements from surrounding Mississippi counties and mentally shifted them to the Lafayette base. The fictional setting of "The Bear" comes only in part from the real Tallahatchie River bottom in Lafayette County.

Faulkner loved the forest. As a child, he learned the Tallahatchie bottom where his father, Murry, hunted. The site of de Spain's camp in fictional Yoknapatawpha is close to the location in Lafayette County of the Cain plantation that Murry liked to visit (map 7.1). John Faulkner remembered the plantation as "Bob Cain's place,

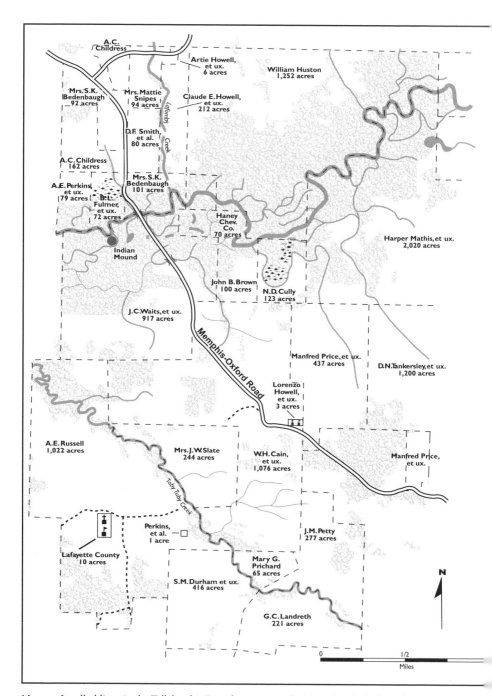

Map. 7.1. Landholdings in the Tallahatchie River bottom near the Memphis-Oxford Road in 1936. Boundaries of the Cain plantation are for 1925. From Sardis Reservoir land acquisition maps, U.S. Army Corps of Engineers, Vicksburg District Office, Vicksburg, Mississippi. 1936. Charles S. Aiken.

down in the bottom." Cain's name was Cornelius Franklin, not Robert or Bob. He usually was called by the nickname Tince. Cain owned stock in the First National Bank of Oxford, the financial institution begun in 1910 by J. W. T. Falkner, William Faulkner's grandfather. The land that adjoined the Cain plantation on the east was owned by Manfred Price, which is the origin of the name of the fictional Manfred de Spain, son of Cassius de Spain. Parts of the Cain plantation remained forested. Into the last two decades of the nineteenth century, bears and even panthers still roamed through the densely wooded Tallahatchie bottom.[7]

During the 1920s and the 1930s, most of Faulkner's hunting experiences occurred at the camp of "General" James Stone. Like the Cain plantation, Stone's camp was near the Tallahatchie River but on the edge of the Yazoo Delta in Panola County, thirty miles west of Oxford (map 7.2).[8] To reach the hunting lodge, one traveled from Oxford to Batesville and then rode to Stone's Stop on the Batesville Southwestern Railroad, a timber company line built in 1910. The log line ran southwestward into the Delta from a large planing mill near the Illinois Central Railroad at Batesville. Stone's Stop initially was in the heart of the wilderness. The hunting lodge was a small bungalow half a mile north of the railroad and three-quarters of a mile south of the Tallahatchie River.

A map of northwestern Mississippi showing Oxford, Batesville, the Tallahatchie River, and the railroads helps to clarify Faulkner's method of blending two actual places to create a fictional place (map 7.3). Faulkner thought of Jefferson as having the approximate location of Oxford. To reach Memphis from Oxford by railroad, one needed to change trains at Holly Springs from the Illinois Central to the St. Louis–San Francisco (Frisco) line (fig. 7.1). In fiction, travel to Memphis from Jefferson required a change of trains at Memphis Junction, Faulkner's name for Holly Springs.

The Illinois Central Railroad had four main lines across north Mississippi. One ran through Holly Springs and Oxford; another went southward from Memphis through Batesville. To reach Memphis from Stone's camp, one could ride the Batesville Southwestern Railroad to Batesville and from there take one of the several Illinois Central daily passenger trains that went directly to the city. The itinerary was that of Isaac and Boon's journey to Memphis with two principal alterations. To place the log railroad in Yoknapatawpha County, Faulkner mentally rotated the Batesville Southwestern Railroad at the junction with the Illinois Central so that the former went eastward up the Tallahatchie River valley rather than westward into the Yazoo Delta. And to comply with the chronology of *Go Down, Moses*, Faulkner shifted the Batesville Southwestern from the early twentieth century to the latter part of the nineteenth.

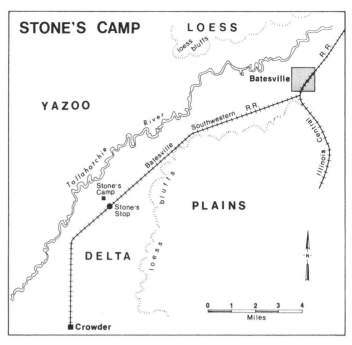

Map 7.2. Situation of "General" James Stone's camp. Compiled by field survey and from data on the *Crowder, Mississippi, Quadrangle*, 1:62,500, and the *Sledge, Mississippi, Quadrangle*, 1:62,500 (Washington, D.C.: U.S. Geological Survey, 1935). Charles S. Aiken.

Figure 7.1. The former Illinois Central Railroad depot and hotel at Holly Springs, Mississippi, in 1974. The depot was partly destroyed during the Civil War. Expansion and reconstruction by the Mississippi Central Railroad was completed in 1886. Charles S. Aiken.

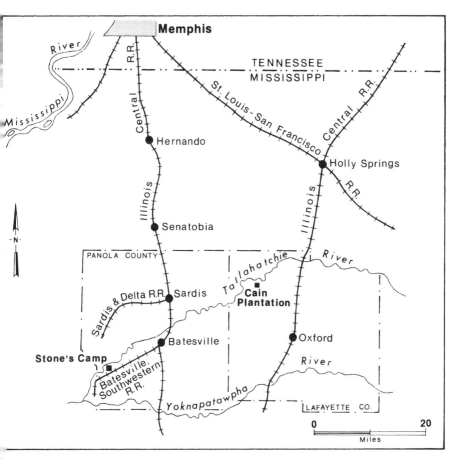

Map 7.3. Railroads in northwest Mississippi in 1925. Compiled from *Hammond's Complete Map of Mississippi* 1925. Charles S. Aiken.

Landscape Change Theme

Beyond Faulkner's use of real landscape objects to create the fictional setting for "The Bear," the search for geographical meaning reveals a story that deals with obsolescence produced by change and the futility of attempting to arrest change to preserve something. Four components of the story have outlived their time and are obsolete. Old Ben is no longer "a mortal beast" but "an anachronism indomitable and invincible out of an old dead time, a phantom, epitome and apotheosis of the old wild life."[9] Sam Fathers, who shares more traits with the romantic forest Indian than a person born a Negro slave, also has outlived his time. Sam is not only old but also alone in his native Chickasaw homeland. He has "no people, none of his blood anywhere above earth that he would ever meet again."[10] Sam's death closely follows that of Old Ben at the end of the last hunt.

The third obsolete component of the story is the wilderness, the demise of which is symbolically linked to the deaths of Old Ben and Sam Fathers. Although "the wilderness, the big woods," is "bigger and older than any recorded document," it, like the Indian and the bear, belongs to a bygone time. Men who fear the wilderness doom it by gnawing at its edges with axes and plows. The fourth outmoded element of the story, one overlooked by critics, is the Lord-to-God bird, for it is never seen or described, only heard. However brief its role, the large, beautiful black, white, and red ivory-billed woodpecker is a critical part of the story. Faulkner uses the legendary "big woodpecker called Lord-to-God by negroes" to create the dramatic setting in which Isaac McCaslin, a boy on his first hunt in the big woods of the Tallahatchie bottom, encounters Old Ben face-to-face. Isaac hears the drumming of the ivory-billed woodpecker but never sees the elusive bird at a place in the wilderness where "frail and timorous man had merely passed without altering it, leaving no mark nor scar." When the woodpecker's steady drumming stops short, Isaac knows that the bear is present, peering at him. Suddenly he realizes that Old Ben is gone, for the woodpecker resumes its hammering. The ivory-billed woodpecker, called the "Lord-by-God" bird by some ornithologists, is thought to have become extinct in 1944, about the time *Go Down, Moses* was published.[11] Although Faulkner is writing of events set in the Tallahatchie bottom in the 1880s, he actually is describing the Yazoo Delta in his present, the early 1940s. Faulkner's knowledge of the big woods provides evidence in his fiction that there were more ivory-billed woodpeckers in the parts of the Delta wilderness not invaded by timber companies than ornithologists realized in 1944.

Unlike Sam Fathers, Old Ben, and the ivory-billed woodpecker, who are doomed, it seems for the moment that a portion of the wilderness can be saved, or at least its disappearance can be arrested. The instrument for prevention of landscape change is an incorporated hunting club proposed by General Compson and Walter Ewell.[12] The club will lease the camp and hunting privileges in the surrounding woods from Major de Spain. The underlying motive is to persuade the major to return to the camp in the hope that when he relives the hunts, the semiannual pilgrimages to the wilderness will resume. The hunts were in June and November until the major sold his first camp. After the sale, the hunt became an annual November event. De Spain, however, knows that the past is dead and that nothing will bring it back. After the bear is killed, de Spain never sees the hunting camp again.

Young Isaac McCaslin returns to the camp in June 1885, just before the timber company is to begin cutting de Spain's part of the doomed wilderness. Passing through Hoke's, he finds that the lumber camp is much larger. A new planing mill

covers two or three acres, and beside it are stacked miles and miles of new track rails. Isaac surveys the scene in shocked and grieved amazement. Then he realizes that the forces altering the landscape were introduced years before. The innocent log train that took the hunting party to and from the wilderness for so many seasons, with its "diminutive locomotive" and "shrill peanut-parcher whistle," was a principal agent in the destruction of the big woods and the alteration of the landscape (fig. 7.2).[13] Isaac now knows why Major de Spain has not returned to the camp and realizes that he, too, will never return. It is impossible to go back to what was.

Faulkner was so deeply influenced by the past that throughout his life he sought to preserve bits and pieces of it. He advocated the preservation of objects that seemed quite undistinguished and ordinary long before such efforts became fashionable. Writing in 1947 to the editor of the *Oxford Eagle*, Faulkner questioned a proposal to raze the old courthouse and to erect a new one:

> Bravo your piece about the preservation of the courthouse. I am afraid your cause
> is already lost though. We have gotten rid of the shade trees which once circled the
> courthouse yard and bordered the Square . . . all we have left now to distinguish
> an old southern town from any one of ten thousand towns built yesterday from

Kansas to California are the Confederate monument, the courthouse and the jail. . . . Your cause is doomed. They will go the way of the old Cumberland [Presbyterian] church. . . . They call this progress. But they don't say where it's going; also there are some of us who would like the chance to say whether or not we want the ride.[14]

Faulkner's theme in "The Bear"—that landscape change cannot be halted or even arrested once a land use is outmoded and altering forces are set in motion—was based in part on his attempt to preserve the past at Stone's camp. By the mid-1930s only a few large areas of wilderness remained in the Yazoo Delta, one of which surrounded Stone's camp. The western portion of Panola County and the adjoining parts of Quitman and Tallahatchie counties were among the last sections of the Yazoo Delta to be drained and cleared. Destruction of the forest and over-hunting caused much of the game to disappear. In a "Notice to Hunters" published in the Batesville weekly newspaper in November 1934, James Stone warned that no trespassing or fishing was permitted on his lands in Panola County. Apologetically, he added "trespassing in the past" had cost him "considerable" and that he had been "driven to this course."[15] Because of the lack of game and his financial problems, the elderly Stone began to lose interest in his hunting domain.

In a sentimental attempt to preserve something in which he had spent so many enjoyable hours, Faulkner, together with R. L. Sullivan of Oxford and Whitson (Whit) Cook of Harmontown, organized the Okatoba Hunting and Fishing Club, which received a charter of incorporation from the Mississippi secretary of state in January 1935. The purpose of the club was "to aid and assist in the preservation of game and fish on the lands on which the corporation shall acquire hunting and fishing privileges."[16] James Stone transferred to the club hunting and fishing rights on his land in the Delta west of Batesville. Faulkner's plan was to have a man, who would be paid a modest salary and appointed a deputy game warden, live in the camp throughout the year.[17] Because of the lack of money, the deputy game warden was never hired, and because a hunting club, even one with a name as mystical as "Okatoba," could never bring back the past, the scheme failed. In 1937 the Stone family disposed of the land on which the hunting camp was located, the timber rights were sold, and the wilderness was logged.[18]

Faulkner developed "The Bear" from a previous story. During the spring of 1935 at the height of his interest in the Okatoba Hunting and Fishing Club, he wrote "Lion," which was published in *Harper's*.[19] Despite similarities between "Lion" and "The Bear," several differences exist. In "Lion," Major de Spain refuses to return to the hunting camp after Old Ben is killed, but his reason is not developed. Also, the other members of the hunting party do not consider organizing a club. In "The Bear," written six years later, Faulkner drew richly on his own experience and termed the fictional hunting-club scheme to arrest change "an invention doubtless of the somewhat childish old General but actually worthy of Boon Hogganbeck himself." Even the boy Isaac McCaslin "recognized it for the subterfuge it was: to change the leopard's spots when they could not alter the leopard, a baseless and illusory hope."[20] Nearly twenty years later at the University of Virginia, a reflective Faulkner, commenting on "The Bear," gave his opinion of landscape alteration and attempts to prevent it:

> What the writer's asking is compassion, understanding, that change must alter, must happen, and change is going to alter what was. That no matter how fine anything seems, it can't endure, because once it stops, abandons motion, it is dead. It's to have compassion for the anguish that the wilderness itself may have felt by being ruth-lessly destroyed by axes, by men who simply wanted to make that earth grow some-thing they could sell for a profit, which brought into it a condition based on an evil like human bondage. . . . [B]ut they [the big woods] were obsolete and had to go. But that's no need to not feel compassion for them simply because they were obsolete.[21]

Faulkner's idea that the wilderness was ruthlessly destroyed only to be super-seded by an inferior land use in which men grow cotton for profit by exploiting other persons is intimately tied to part 4 of "The Bear." Part 4 is puzzling to most readers who encounter the story for the first time. At the University of Virginia Faulkner stated that part 4 is a component of the novel but not a component of the story "The Bear." Part 4 should be understood in the context of the whole of *Go Down, Moses*.[22] Critics and anthologists, however, believe that part 4 is vital to "The Bear" because its removal dilutes the story.[23] Part 4, which chronologically occurs after part 5 and seems to have only an indirect relation to the other parts of the story, concerns the relationships between the McCaslin family and their slaves and descendants. The section explains why Isaac, who rejects his inheritance of the McCaslin plantation, is a failure as a responsible man. From notes in the plantation commissary ledgers, Isaac learns of miscegenation by his grandfather. He comes to believe that the land is cursed. His grandfather and the other slaveholders who used their chattel to clear the wilderness to grow cotton brought the curse to the land: "the land which old Carothers McCaslin his grandfather had bought with white man's money . . . and tamed and ordered or believed he had tamed and or-dered it for the reason that the human beings he held in bondage and in the power of life and death had removed the forest from it and in their sweat scratched the surface of it to a depth of perhaps fourteen inches in order to grow something . . . which could be translated back into the money."[24]

The Civil War and emancipation did not end the curse because the sharecropper and share tenant systems by which cotton plantations continued to be operated became new forms of bondage. The sharecroppers and share tenants were tied to the land through their poverty and indebtedness to the plantation commissary, "the square, galleried, wooden building squatting like a portent above the fields whose laborers it still held in thrall '65 or no." From the commissary, recorded in the same ledgers that recorded the provisions for the slaves, moved "the slow outward trickle of food and supplies and equipment which returned each fall as cotton made and ginned and sold." The flows were "two threads frail as truth and impalpable as equators yet cable-strong to bind for life them who made the cotton to the land their sweat fell on."[25]

At the time Faulkner wrote "The Bear," the Yazoo Delta with more than one and a half million acres in cotton was one of the most intensely farmed monoculture regions in the United States. Eighty-nine percent of the farmland in the Yazoo Delta was in plantations worked by 58,592 tenant families, 88 percent of whom were blacks. The Yazoo Delta was primarily a cotton region of the New rather than the Old South. Most of the land was cleared of wilderness during the twentieth century. Cotton acreage increased from 652,000 in 1899 to 1,626,000 in 1929. The fertile alluvial crescent was "deswamped and denuded and derivered in two generations so that white men . . . [could] own plantations and commute every night to Memphis and black men own plantations and ride in jim crow cars to Chicago to live in millionaires' mansions on Lakeshore Drive." But on the plantations, the white tenant farmers lived like Negroes and the Negro sharecroppers lived like "animals."[26]

The sharecropper was the principal type of tenant farmer in the Delta. Houses of sharecroppers dotted the fields, and cotton production was so intense that the crop was literally planted to the doorsteps. The owners of some plantations did not permit sharecroppers to have even a small vegetable garden. More than sixty-four thousand sharecroppers were in the Yazoo Delta in 1930. Because sharecropping was a family system that employed even small children and because most sharecropper families were large, approximately three hundred thousand persons in the Yazoo Delta were part of the tenure system. The physical and social isolation and the economic plight of sharecropper families are vividly revealed in documentaries of the 1930s. Sharecroppers were among the American serfs who lived out their lives in the depths of poverty.[27]

Faulkner witnessed a recurrent sequence in the Delta: logging of the wilderness, drainage of the land, and establishment of plantations. He saw the wilderness around Stone's camp cleared and the land planted in cotton as happened on so much of the Yazoo Delta's land. Although Faulkner was not opposed to change and learned from his feeble attempts that change could not be prevented, he believed that the land-use alterations in the Delta brought something that was less desirable than the wilderness. At the University of Virginia, Faulkner observed that "change if it is not controlled by wise people destroys sometimes more than it brings. That unless some wise person comes along in the middle of the change and takes charge of it, change can destroy what is irreplaceable. If the reason for the change is base in motive—that is, to clear the wilderness just to make cotton land, to raise cotton on an agrarian economy of peonage, slavery, is base because it's not as good as the wilderness which it replaces."[28]

Delta Autumn

Faulkner developed the transformation of the Yazoo Delta from wilderness to New South plantations more fully in "Delta Autumn." In the context of the landscape-change theme, this story is the epilogue to "The Bear." As he did for the setting of "The Bear," Faulkner drew on his personal experience in creating the setting for "Delta Autumn." After the Stone family lost their Panola County lands in the late 1930s, Faulkner and his party of hunters traveled farther south in the Delta to find virgin wilderness. In November 1940 the party's camp was close to the Big Sunflower River near Anguilla, Mississippi, almost 150 miles from Oxford (map 7.4). The party drove to the Big Sunflower in motor vehicles and then traveled eight miles by boat to reach an isolated place where the men pitched tents. Shortly after he returned from the 1940 hunt, Faulkner mailed the short story "Delta Autumn" to his literary agent. More than a year later, the narrative was published by *Story* after unsuccessful attempts to sell it to better-paying magazines.[29] Considerably revised, "Delta Autumn" became the section of *Go Down, Moses* that follows "The Bear."

"Delta Autumn" opens when the party of hunters once again enters the Yazoo Delta to begin the annual November ritual. The year is 1940; more than half a century has passed since the events of "The Bear." Isaac McCaslin is now approaching eighty and is known as Uncle Ike to his companions, the sons and the grandsons of hunters in "The Bear." Each autumn, for most of his life, Isaac has followed the retreating wilderness and the diminishing game: "Soon now they would enter the Delta. The sensation was familiar to him. It had been renewed like this each last week in November for more than fifty years—the last hill, at the foot of which the rich unbroken alluvial flatness began as the sea began at the base of its cliffs. . . . he would look ahead past the jerking arc of the windshield wiper and see the land flatten suddenly and swoop, dissolving away beneath the rain as the sea itself would dissolve, and he would say, 'Well, boys, there it is again.'"[30]

As Isaac rides through the gray November day and as he lies awake in the tent at night, he recalls how it once was. Game was so abundant that a man shot a doe or

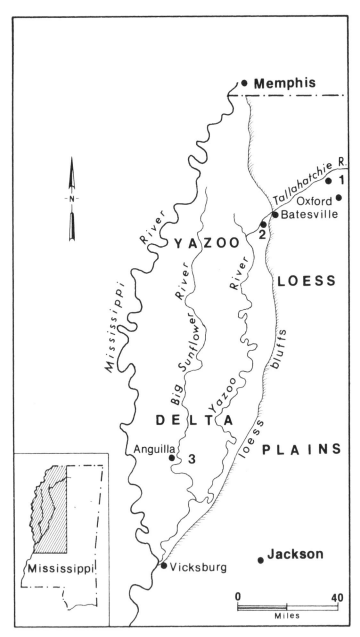

Map 7.4. Location of Faulkner's hunting experiences. Charles S. Aiken.

a fawn as quickly as he did a buck, and turkeys were shot with pistols to test skills in stalking and marksmanship. Isaac also remembers how through the years the wilderness retreated, increasingly distant from Jefferson. Now, in an automobile, he must travel two hundred miles from the town almost to the Delta's southern extreme. He fondly remembers the events of "The Bear," the apex of his life. In the days of Major de Spain and Sam Fathers, the hunting party had a permanent camp with a house. The camp is now ephemeral, only pitched tents.

Isaac also contemplates the land-use changes in the Delta during his lifetime. What is anticipated in "The Bear" has occurred by the time of "Delta Autumn." When Isaac was a child, the only settlements of the Yazoo Delta were on the fringes, along the Mississippi River on the west and the loess bluffs on the east. With the passing of years, the interior, "the impenetrable jungle of water-standing cane and cypress, gum and holly and oak and ash," became patches of cotton, then fields, and then plantations. The land now "lay open from the cradling hills on the East to the rampart of levee on the West, standing horseman-tall with cotton for the world's looms." The land clearing continues. To reach the river landing where the boats are launched, the caravan of two automobiles and two trucks passes through an area that was logged during the previous year. The new, "ruthless mile-wide parallelograms wrought by ditching the dyking machinery" in the flank of the wilderness index the endless clearing and drainage of the land as the Delta wilderness retreats southward.[31]

Isaac's view of the changes is that of a disillusioned old man who is a detached observer. Although of the Delta wilderness, Isaac is not of the Delta agricultural region, and he does not consider himself a part of the landscape alteration he has witnessed. There are two reasons for his detached status. Yoknapatawpha County is not located in the Delta but is several miles to the east in the Loess Plains. As a Yoknapatawpha County resident, Isaac has the attitude toward the Delta of a Mississippian from the older Loess Plains plantation area to the east. The malaria-infested, flood-prone Delta is thought to be a region that largely attracted not planters but primarily opportunistic poor whites, some of whom created great plantations through exploitation of black tenants lured from the older plantation regions with promises of larger cotton yields and less work. An example of such a person is Big Daddy in Tennessee Williams's *Cat on a Hot Tin Roof*, who is the son of a penniless derelict. Big Daddy eventually owned a "kingdom—twenty-eight thousand acres of th' richest land this side of the Valley Nile!"[32] Isaac condescendingly calls such whites "Delta peckerwoods."[33]

Isaac also is not a part of the Delta and the landscape changes that he has witnessed because he is disconnected from the land. At the age of twenty-one he removed himself from responsibility for what happened to it. Having lived most of his life in a small house in Jefferson, Isaac is "no farmer, not even a countryman save by his distant birth and boyhood" on the McCaslin plantation. The desire to repudiate his inheritance was not changed, even by what he experienced when he returned to de Spain's hunting camp that final time. He had never wished to own any piece of land, "not even after he saw plain its ultimate doom."[34]

The landscape-change theme in "Delta Autumn" is overshadowed by the more powerful but interconnected theme of the relationships between whites and blacks. The miscegenation of Isaac's grandfather, Carothers McCaslin, comes full circle. The mulatto descendant of the union between McCaslin and one of his slaves has given birth to a child by Roth Edmonds, the last white male descendant. The woman comes with the child to the hunting camp, and, unable to find Roth, confronts Isaac, Roth's cousin, who has been like an uncle to him. "'You spoiled . . . [Roth]' she said. 'You, and Uncle Lucas and Aunt Mollie. But mostly you.' 'Me?' he said. 'Me?' 'Yes. When you gave to his grandfather that land which didn't belong to him, not even half of it by will or even law.'" Isaac, finding himself in a situation in which he must act responsibly, demonstrates toward the woman and the child the same attitude he has shown toward the land. "He cried, not loud, in a voice of amazement, pity, and outrage: 'You're a nigger!' 'Yes' she said. 'James Beauchamp— you called him Tennie's Jim though he had a name—was my grandfather. I said you were Uncle Isaac.'" Unwilling to deal with the problem, Isaac agrees that the woman should return to the urban North where she was reared and marry a black man. "'Get out of here! I can do nothing for you! Cant nobody do nothing for you!'" In addition to money, Isaac bestows another gift on the child, the hunting horn that was left to him by General Compson. The horn, which is covered with the unbroken skin of a buck's shank and fastened with silver, is a valuable possession, but it has lost its meaning as the wilderness of the Delta has vanished in the wake of the cotton plantation.[35]

Epilogue

In *The Reivers* Faulkner provides a final example of his keen geographical sense when he synthesizes the retreat of the hunting camp across space through time. The wilderness surrounding de Spain's original camp, which is the setting of "The Bear," was not quite as immense as it appeared to the youthful Isaac McCaslin. The camp, with its lodge, stables, and kennels, was situated in only four or five sections of virgin river-bottom wilderness that de Spain purchased after the Civil War from the one-hundred-square-mile estate of Thomas Sutpen. The Tallahatchie wilderness in northern Yoknapatawpha County merged with the vast expanse of wilderness of the Delta, and the bottom was an eastern gateway to the swamp and jungle

Figure 7.3. The house believed to have been "General" James Stone's hunting lodge in 1980. The abandoned dwelling, now gone, was located on a tract of land west of Batesville, Mississippi, in the edge of the Yazoo Delta near the state highway that follows the route of the Batesville Southwestern Railroad. Charles S. Aiken.

that extended westward to the plantations and the towns along the Mississippi River. The original camp was less than twenty miles from Jefferson, and the hunting party could leave at midnight and be on a deer or bear stand by sunup. After Major de Spain sold the original camp, he created a new one in the wilderness approximately forty miles west of Jefferson. A narrow-gauge railroad that was built by a northern lumber company ran close to the new camp, just as a railroad ran close to the old one, and the major was provided with a courtesy stop for his guests. The site of the second camp was still virgin wilderness in 1905.

By 1925 it was apparent that the forest in the vicinity of the second camp was doomed. All members of the old hunting party, except Isaac and Boon, were dead. Manfred de Spain, who unlike his father was not a hunter, sold the timber and the land. By 1940, the time of "Delta Autumn," the hunters had to load their gear in motor vehicles and drive two hundred miles on paved highways to find enough wilderness in which to pitch tents. With the major long dead, the annual camp is no longer known as de Spain's but is named for the oldest hunter and called "McCaslin's."[36]

Gone is the geographical reality from which Faulkner developed the fictional setting of "The Bear," but landscape relics survive. The forest remnants on the Cain plantation in Lafayette County were cut in the 1930s and the land disappeared beneath the waters of Sardis Reservoir when the Tallahatchie River was dammed. But a few miles farther west at the edge of the Delta in Panola County, longtime residents relate that the highway between Batesville and Crowder follows the route of the old "dummy line," the Batesville Southwestern Railroad. The highway traverses a landscape with agricultural diversification. Cotton is still an important crop, but soybeans and wheat grow in abundance. With the passing of the New South plantation, sharecroppers have vanished; there have not been any in the Delta since 1970.[37] Although nothing along the highway marks the place once known as Stone's Stop, a half-mile north of the old railroad bed at the edge of a snake-infested soybean field is the site of a house. The house, which stood into the 1990s, is believed to have been Stone's hunting lodge (fig. 7.3). The large oaks beside the house were among the last remnants of the big woods.

Preservationists might decry what happened to Faulkner's landscape sources for the setting of "The Bear," but change itself was a source for the story. Landscape change continues, and punctuates one principal theme in "The Bear."

EIGHT

Toward the Modern South

The Last Cotton House

"Jewel and I come up from the field following the path in single file," states Darl Bundren at the beginning of *As I Lay Dying*.

> The path runs straight as a plumb-line, worn smooth by feet and baked brick-hard by July, between the green rows of laid-by cotton, to the cottonhouse in the center of the field. . . .
>
> The cottonhouse is of rough logs, from between which the chinking has long fallen. Square, with a broken roof set at a single pitch, it leans in empty and shimmering dilapidation in the sunlight, a single broad window in two opposite walls giving onto the approaches of the path.[1]

The scene with which Faulkner opens *As I Lay Dying*, his third Yoknapatawpha County novel, was at the time a common one across the New South cotton landscape (Fig. 8.1). At the beginning of the twenty-first century, cotton is still grown in Lafayette County, but other key components of the scene described by Faulkner have vanished from the landscape. "Green rows of laid-by cotton" remain, but cotton houses together with brick-hard paths worn smooth by feet began to disappear within a decade of Faulkner's description, and by 1970 they had largely vanished from southern cotton fields.

The cotton house scene may seem enduring, but within the context of the historical geography of Lafayette County and the South, the landscape is New South. Cotton houses were so ordinary that few persons gave any thought to their preservation, and today they are as rare as slave houses of the Old South. Prior to mechanization, extending back to the commencement of commercial cotton culture during the late eighteenth century in the Sea Island region along the South Carolina–Georgia coast, paths trodden smooth and hard became the lowly thoroughfares of the South's cotton regions. The narrow passageways signified two features of traditional cotton culture—unremitting poverty and backbreaking toil. One detractor sarcastically noted that poverty clung to cotton like iron filings to a

Figure 8.1. A cotton house and cotton field in Lafomby Creek bottom in north Lafayette County, Mississippi, in September 1980. Cotton houses have almost disappeared from the southern landscape, for mechanical cotton harvesters made them unnecessary relics. The last cotton crop was planted in the field in 1999, and the cotton house was razed in 2000. A nonfarm dwelling and yard occupy the site. Charles S. Aiken.

magnet.[2] The poor black and white households that comprised the labor forces on fertile alluvial river-and-creek-bottom plantations and small hardscrabble yeoman hill farms of the New South walked because they could not afford to own, borrow, or wear out mules, horses, wagons, and buggies. Also, because traditional cotton culture required more than 160 hours of labor per acre, feet, usually bare feet, pounded paths to, from, and through fields from the commencement of plowing in late winter until the end of harvest in late autumn.

The cotton houses that dotted fields were minute, unassuming landscape features in which tenant farmers and small landowners stored their harvested cotton until they could obtain a wagon and team of mules to haul it to a gin. On plantations a cotton house was often on each tenant tract.[3] Some houses were named, often for tenants who used them for many years. One named for a fondly remembered black tenant might be designated "Uncle George's cotton house." Some cotton houses were decrepit buildings, which like the Bundrens' stood in "shimmering dilapidation," but others were well-built structures. Cotton houses were important buildings that had roles other than the storage of cotton. To Faulkner the small structures were places of sanctuary and sin. Without other shelter, Vernon Tull, his wife, and his four daughters spent a winter in an old cotton house on the McCaslin plantation. Wesley Snopes, who looked like a schoolteacher and was admired for his singing at church revivals, was tarred and feathered and run out of Yoknapatawpha County after he was caught with a fourteen-year-old girl in a cotton house.[4]

When International Harvester Farmalls and other brands of tricycle-type all-purpose tractors began to appear in southern cotton fields in the 1930s, the amount of labor needed to produce a five-hundred-pound bale of ginned cotton began to diminish. Tractors for planting and plowing were followed by mechanical harvesters in the late 1940s and herbicides for grass and weed control in the mid-1950s. At first, adoption of the new technology and reduction of labor was slow and cautious. In 1940 Lafayette County had 69 tractors; in 1950 it had 579. Mississippi had almost no mechanical cotton harvesters in 1948, the year they began to be mass produced at an International Harvester factory in Memphis. By 1955 the state had 2,600, and in 1965 there were 4,750. Between 1949 and 1960 the amount of Mississippi's cotton crop harvested with machines increased from 4 to 40 percent. In 1967, 87 percent of the state's cotton crop was harvested mechanically. Three years later 99 percent was picked by machines.[5] In the era of mechanized agriculture, the labor force is paid a set weekly wage or paid according to the number of days a person works.

By 1960 cotton acreage had declined across several great regions of the South that failed to adopt the new technology, including the Piedmont and the Alabama-Mississippi Black Belt. Increasingly, other lagging regions, including parts of the Mississippi Loess Plains, were at a competitive disadvantage in producing the crop. In 1930 Lafayette County farmers harvested 35,900 acres of cotton; in 1950 they harvested 19,670. By 2002 the acreage had dropped to 6,109. Cotton houses began to disappear from fields with the introduction of tractors because they interfered with efficient use of machinery. Their disappearance accelerated with the further adoption of new machinery and the decline in the number of tenant farmers. Tenant farmers' numbers in Lafayette decreased from 2,450 in 1935 to 1,463 in 1950, 642 in 1959, and 367 in 1964.[6] Nearly all cotton houses had vanished by 1970 with almost total mechanization of the harvest.

The McGehee plantation, located a few miles northwest of Oxford in Panola and Tate counties, has remained in the same family since the Old South era (map. 8.1). The four-over-four big house was constructed in the 1850s. Stark Young was a relative of the McGehees, and he used the plantation as the setting for his novel *Heaven Trees*. In 1945 the 960-acre McGehee plantation was worked by fifteen black sharecropper families. By 1961 the landholding was well advanced in the transition from

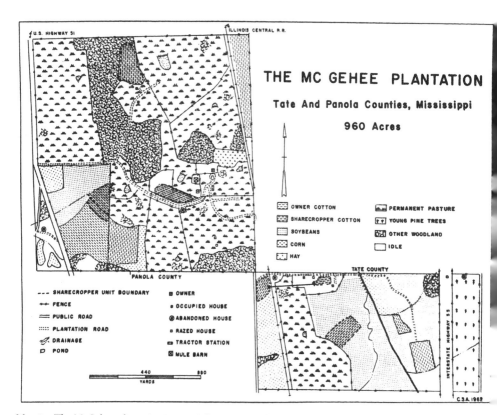

Map 8.1. The McGehee plantation in 1961. The 960-acre plantation is located in Tate and Panola counties, Mississippi. In 1961 the plantation was in transition from a New South–era landholding farmed by black sharecroppers using mules to a fully mechanized neoplantation of the Modern South. Not only did Interstate Highway 55 take more than ten acres from the plantation, but the new thoroughfare isolated about fifty acres from the main part of the landholding. The distance to the isolated acreage was five miles. The owner planted the isolated part in pine trees. By 2000 crop farming was discontinued and the entire plantation was planted in pine. Charles S. Aiken, 1962.

a labor-intensive sharecropper to fully mechanized plantation. The labor force had declined to six black sharecropper families. The smaller labor force was evidenced by four vacant tenant houses and five sites where houses had been razed. Approximately 110 acres were planted to cotton, 100 acres to corn, and 100 to soybeans. Four hundred acres were in improved pasture, and the remainder were woods. Three tractors were used to prepare and plant all of the cropland. Fifteen acres of cotton and five acres of corn were worked by three middle-aged sharecroppers using the plantation's ten aged mules. The other three sharecroppers were younger, and their primary occupation was tractor driver. Each of the three part-time sharecroppers had only five acres of cotton, which were weeded and harvested by their wives and children. Herbicides were used to control grass and weeds on the remainder of the cotton and on the corn and soybeans. All of the crops, except the thirty acres of sharecropper cotton, were harvested with mechanical cotton pickers and combines.[7] By 2000 row-crop farming on the old plantation had ceased. Almost all the land was planted in pine trees, illustrating the exodus of a number of planter families in Faulkner country from cotton and row-crop agriculture. The large capital investment in farm machinery and labor and the low financial return from cotton, soybeans, and other crops require greater economies of scale than can be achieved on a farm of several hundred acres.

In *Requiem for a Nun*, published in 1951, Faulkner succinctly captures the rapid transformation of cotton culture that was under way:

> Negro and white both . . . an entire generation of farmers has vanished . . . the machine which displaced the man . . . left no one to drive the mule, now that the machine was threatening to extinguish the mule . . . both gone now: the one, to the last of the forty- and fifty- and sixty-acre hill farms . . . the other to New York and Detroit and Chicago and Los Angeles ghettos, or nine out of ten of him that is, the tenth one mounting from the handles of a plow to the springless bucket seat of a tractor, dispossessing and displacing the other nine just as the tractor had dispossessed and displaced the other eighteen mules to whom that nine would have been complement.[8]

The great migration of blacks from rural Mississippi to cities, northern and southern, began with the arrival of the boll weevil in the Natchez district in the first decade of the twentieth century and substantially accelerated with mechanization of agriculture that commenced in the mid-1930s. The Ohio River became symbolic of the River Jordan, which blacks, like the children of Israel, crossed over into the Promised Land. Blacks, who took segregated Greyhound and Trailways buses and Illinois Central trains from Oxford, Senatobia, Clarksdale, and a host of Mississippi towns to Chicago, Detroit, and other northern cities, found that after buses and trains crossed the Ohio or Mississippi River from Kentucky and Missouri into Illinois, the drivers and conductors announced that passengers could sit wherever they wished. A few bold blacks at the back of segregated buses and in Jim Crow cars on trains hesitantly moved to seats among whites.

Kinship ties played a significant role in the migration in that, often, entire families went to the same metropolis. However, family members sometimes migrated to several cities. The experiences of the Brownlees, the black sharecropper family who in 1943 lived in a shack on a plantation a few miles north of the Tallahatchie River, were similar to those of thousands of black and white households from the rural South. All of the Brownlees' eight children were alive when Edgar died at age eighty-one in 1981. Three were in Chicago, one each in Detroit and Memphis, and three were with Edgar in the Golden Land. Edgar left instructions that his body was to be transported from Los Angeles back to Mississippi for burial beside Ollie, his wife, who died in 1968. In addition to their eight children, in 1981 Ollie and Edgar had forty-two grandchildren and twenty-seven great-grandchildren.[9] The substantial headstone that marks the graves of Edgar and Ollie in the Independent Tyro Baptist Church on the Memphis-Oxford Road bespeaks a wealth undreamed of in 1943 when the Brownlees' most valuable material possessions were a wood-burning iron cookstove, a secondhand refrigerator, and a radio.

The Vanishing New South

Faulkner's most productive period coincided with the Great Depression. In 1929 he published *Sartoris* and *The Sound and the Fury. As I Lay Dying* appeared in 1930, *Sanctuary* in 1931, *Light in August* in 1932, *Pylon* in 1935, *Absalom, Absalom!* in 1936, *The Unvanquished* in 1938, *The Wild Palms* in 1939, and *The Hamlet* in 1940. The publication of *Go Down, Moses* in 1942, a few months after the United States entered the Second World War, concluded most of Faulkner's innovative works. Six years passed before *Intruder in the Dust* appeared in 1948. Within the context of southern historical geography, *The Hamlet*, which concerns lower-class poor whites, and *Go Down, Moses*, which treats the plantation and the relationship between white planter families and their black slaves and tenants, some of whom are relatives, are capstones to Faulkner's fiction of the New South era.

The last third of Faulkner's life (1941–1962), which corresponded with the transition from the New South to the Modern South, was a period of rapid change. The New South era came to a close in the upheavals of the Great Depression and the Second World War. The period was as traumatic and transforming as was the one that terminated the Old South in the tragedies of the Civil War and Reconstruction. By 1945 thousands of rural and small-town black and white Mississippians had been uprooted in the great American war mobilization. Many were pulled from farms and plantations by the military draft. Others moved from the land, not just to nearby Memphis and New Orleans but to metropolises in the North and West, drawn by the labor shortages in factories and incomes that were spectacularly higher than those eked from agriculture. The migration continued during the economic boom that followed the war. Between 1940 and 1970 more than one million whites and almost one million blacks migrated from Mississippi. Between 1940 and 1950, 1,172 blacks and whites, 7.3 percent of the population, left Lafayette County, and 3,671, 21.1 percent, migrated between 1950 and 1960.[10] Most migrants told relatives and friends that they would be back. However, except for occasional visits, few left their new homes to return to Mississippi.

Blacks who served in the armed forces during the Second World War, though segregated, did not encounter the degrees of discrimination they knew in the plantation South. Neil McMillen describes how surprised black soldiers were when in other sections of the United States and in foreign countries they discovered just how segregated and discriminated against they were in the South. Dabney Hammer of Clarksdale told McMillen that "the only time in my life I felt like a man was in Europe." To keep blacks in their place, white racists deliberately treated those who had served in the military with contempt. Admiring the large number of medals on Hammer's uniform, a white Clarksdale man said there was one thing the war hero should not forget—"You're still a nigger."[11]

Shortly after the war, President Harry Truman decreed an end to segregation in the military. Although in 1950 blacks still did not have the freedom to vote in most of the plantation South, they were emerging as a new national political force as a result of population redistribution. Acceleration of migration to cities during and after the war made blacks significant voting blocs in a growing number of urban congressional districts. The Supreme Court's decision in *Brown v. Board of Education of Topeka, Kansas* in 1954 marked the beginning of the end of legal racial segregation in public schools and initiated the civil rights movement, which extended through the 1960s.[12]

Some scholars contend that the relatively unproductive six-year gap between 1942 and 1948 was one in which Faulkner was written out, and his remaining talent was co-opted by a lengthy and devastating contract with Warner Brothers as a motion-picture scriptwriter.[13] Faulkner's exiles in Hollywood were not quite as bad as he pretended in his letters to family and friends. Faulkner was an elitist. Elitists are attracted to and must be close to similar people. Faulkner especially liked women, not just women but attractive, highly intelligent young women. From the time he was a teenager, William Faulkner had a special friendship with Estelle Oldham, a neighbor. Estelle was intelligent and relatively well educated. Supposedly, Estelle wanted to marry Faulkner. However, Faulkner was only twenty, had no money, and did not believe that he was ready for marriage. Also, Faulkner knew that both his family and the Oldhams, who were small-town social snobs, were opposed to the marriage. Estelle reluctantly married Cornell Franklin, a lawyer who was a graduate of Ole Miss. After several years of living in Hawaii and China and two children, the couple divorced. Estelle returned to Oxford where she and Faulkner renewed their friendship and married in 1929. Estelle was a fragile, injured woman when she came back to Oxford. The strained marriage to Franklin, the stress of living in China, the divorce, and rearing two small children had taken its toll. Faulkner had little money when they married, and he moved Estelle and her children into a decaying pre–Civil War house that initially lacked plumbing and electricity. Estelle's social drinking escalated. By the mid-1930s Faulkner's marriage had become tedious and strained, in part due to Estelle's heavy drinking bouts and her failure to adequately see to the house and her family. However, a stable home for the couple's daughter, Jill, other family commitments, and Faulkner's eventual rediscovery of his love for Estelle helped to keep the couple together until his death.[14]

On his trip to Hollywood in 1935–1936, Faulkner met Meta Doherty Carpenter, a twenty-eight-year-old woman who was director Howard Hawks's secretary. Meta was a small, lovely woman with blond hair. Born and reared in Memphis, she considered her real home to be a family plantation in Tunica County, Mississippi, in the Yazoo Delta. Just out of high school, Meta married a man named Carpenter, and they moved to California, where the marriage floundered and the couple divorced. Meta was intelligent, quiet, and kind. Her upbringing in Memphis gave her an urban sophistication that Oxford and other small-town girls usually lack. Most important, Meta was from Mississippi. Faulkner fell in love with Meta the moment he met her. He told her she was the one person for whom he had been looking his entire life, and if he had met her before Estelle, he would have married her. Mississippi may be the only state where place of birth means an instant bond between two persons who do not know each other. During the days following their initial meeting, Faulkner repeatedly reminded Meta "that we were both from Mississippi and therefore different by upbringing and outlook from anyone else for miles around."[15]

Meta initially resisted Faulkner's invitations to go to dinner with him, probably knowing where it would lead, straight into his bed, where she slept off and on during his Hollywood trips over the next fifteen years. Howard Hawks assigned Meta to type Faulkner's movie scripts, even though he knew that Faulkner could type, because he probably considered her a suitable companion for the lonely writer. At least, Faulkner's companionship with Meta would help to control his binge drinking. At best, the relationship might blossom into a romance, which would give the writer an inner peace that Hawks sensed Faulkner needed. Despite Meta's additional marriages and divorces, she always returned to Faulkner. Although they last slept together in 1951, the two corresponded almost up to the time of Faulkner's death in 1962. Meta's letters were sent to Faulkner via Phil Stone's office in Oxford or Random House in New York. Meta refused to be interviewed by Joseph Blotner for his indispensable but incomplete, almost day-by-day account of Faulkner's life. If Blotner had access to any letters between Faulkner and Meta, he did not use or publish them. In 1976, after Faulkner's and Estelle's deaths, Meta published *A Loving Gentleman: The Love Story of William Faulkner and Meta Carpenter* (with Orin Borsten). She gave as her reason "to protect the truth and beauty of our relationship from those who stand ready to exploit it immediately upon my demise."[16]

According to Meta, one of the primary reasons that Faulkner was so unhappy in Hollywood during his lengthy contract with Warner Brothers in the 1940s was that he was paid such a small salary, starting at only $300 per week, compared with $1,250 that he had been paid in the 1930s. Faulkner said that he had to take the job because he needed the money. Faulkner returned to Oxford in the winter of 1944–1945 but was back in Hollywood the next summer. In dialogue she acknowledges is remembered, Meta asked, "Was it the studio? Did they put pressure on you to come back?" "No, honey love. I could have stayed on and handled the Warner lawyers. There's only one reason I'm here. You." But Meta always knew that Faulkner would not remain with her. "The pull to Oxford and the Faulkner way of life was greater than me. Everything at Rowan Oak, even the wife whose body he did not touch, whose weaknesses bound him to her, drew him away from me."[17]

Despite his relationship with Meta and the contract with Warner Brothers, the years 1942–1947 would still have been a relative void in Faulkner's primary work. The productivity gap was a time in which Faulkner sensed that an era of the South was ending. He had largely exhausted his unique and innovative approaches to his southern material, and he had not fully conceived how to deal with or incorporate the rapid changes into new lengthy works of fiction. Faulkner had written of the destruction of plantations and the decadent planter class, of poor whites, and of blacks. He also had produced a book about the Confederate frontier in the Civil War. With "Delta Autumn" in *Go Down, Moses* he concluded the story of the vanishing Mississippi virgin wilderness. Also, what is generally not understood is that the Second World War caused Faulkner more distress than his contract with Warner Brothers. The military, in which he tried to enlist, did not want him, even for a desk job at any rank. While going back and forth between Mississippi and California, Faulkner was trying to finish *A Fable*, a book about war. On April 22, 1944, Faulkner wrote to Harold Ober from Hollywood:

Yes, I am back again. I have not done anything more with the story. . . .

I don't know when I shall get back at it. . . . War is bad for writing, though why I should tell you. This sublimation and glorification of all the cave instincts which man had hopes that he had lived down, dragged back into daylight, usurping preempting a place, all the room in fact, in the reality and constancy and solidity of art, writing. Something must give way; let it be the writing, art . . . will happen again. It's too bad I live now though. . . . I have a considerable talent, perhaps as good as any coeval. But I am 46 now. So what I will mean soon by have is had.[18]

The horrendous Second World War was fought so rapidly between December 1941 and August 1945 and so overwhelmed the nation that nothing in the rural and small-town South seemed universal to the Japanese surprise attack on Pearl Harbor or to the great battles of Midway, Guadalcanal, North Africa, Sicily, Salerno, Anzio, Normandy, Leyte, the Bulge, Iwo Jima, and Okinawa. Not only did the war effort uproot millions of southerners, but it also produced domestic rationing of gasoline, tires, sugar, meat, shoes, and other basic necessities. The war, which for Americans began with the attack on Pearl Harbor, ended less than four years later with the dropping of two secretly built cataclysmic bombs that destroyed entire Japanese cities. At the war's end devastating atrocities by the Germans, the Japanese, and the Soviets were revealed. Fifty-five million persons, most of them civilians, were killed during the war. Millions of others suffered lifelong physical and mental wounds. Adjustments from the warfare of the 1940s to the cold war economy, society, and politics of the 1950s were especially unsettling and difficult, despite the rapid growth in prosperity for millions of Americans, including Faulkner.

Immediately following the Japanese attack on Pearl Harbor, Faulkner wrote the timely and poignant "Two Soldiers." The *Saturday Evening Post* purchased the story for one thousand dollars, which the writer desperately needed. Despite Faulkner's efforts to interject the war into "Knight's Gambit" and "Snow," the short stories were rejected by *Harper's* for being complex and obscure. *Go Down, Moses*, published in 1942, received mixed reviews. Random House reported that the book, which later would be recognized as one of Faulkner's important works, was not selling well. In May 1940 Faulkner wrote Robert Hass of his financial responsibilities and problems. "Beginning at the age of thirty I . . . began to become the sole, principal and partial support . . . of my mother . . . [a] brother's widow and child, a wife of my own and two step children, my own child; I inherited my father's debts and his dependents, white and black without inheriting yet from anyone one inch of land or one stick of furniture or one cent of money." Unable to support the large flock for whom he had financial obligation, Faulkner signed the lengthy contract with Warner Brothers. He believed his talent was wasted in this endeavor. But without the Faulkner touch, Howard Hawks's *Air Force*, *To Have and Have Not*, and *The Big Sleep*, and Jean Renoir's *The Southerner*, for which Faulkner made revisions without Warner Brothers' knowledge, might not be cinema classics.[19]

Faulkner's recognition of the rapid changes initiated by the war and his attempts to deal with them in his fiction continued with the "Compson Appendix," which he wrote for *The Portable Faulkner*. The 1946 Malcolm Cowley project helped to revive public interest in Faulkner's fiction and to stimulate the writer, who was approaching fifty. Although the appendix deals with the history of the Compsons, it has glimpses into the present. Caddy appears in a magazine picture riding in a car with a Nazi staff general. Frony and Dilsey become parts of the great migration of blacks. They move to Memphis after Jason evicts them from the Compson place.[20] As early as the summer of 1943 Faulkner realized that the war was initiating profound changes in American and southern societies, especially alterations in race relations. In a letter to stepson Malcolm Franklin, who was a Navy pilot, Faulkner wrote:

> There is a squadron of negro pilots. They finally got congress to allow them to learn how to risk their lives in the air. They are in Africa now, under their own negro lt. colonel, did well at Pantelleria, on the same day a mob of white men and white policeman killed 20 negroes in Detroit. . . . [Y]ou come back down and are told that 20 of your people have just been killed by a mixed mob of civilians and cops at Little Poo Poo. What would you think?
>
> A change will come out of this war. If it doesn't, if the politicians and the people who run this country are not forced to make good the shibboleth they glibly talk about freedom, liberty, human rights, then you young men who live through it will have wasted your precious time, and those who dont live through it will have died in vain.[21]

Perhaps Faulkner's greatest postwar local public achievement was his insistence that the names of the Negroes from Lafayette County who were killed in the war should be listed on the monument with the names of the whites who gave their lives. Whites' lack of official recognition of blacks, who were condemned to anonymity in death, is as old as African American slavery. Graves of black slaves in planter family and community cemeteries are at the rear, marked in Faulkner country with nameless sandstone rocks. Out of habit, and without thought of blacks, the committee that designed the monument in 1947 remembered only the fifty-three white Lafayette County residents killed in the war. Faulkner, together with James Silver and a Mrs. Duke, protested the failure to include the names of the blacks who died. The committee agreed to include the blacks and even accepted the inscription for the monument that Faulkner suggested:

Dec. 7, 1941 Sept. 9, 1945
THEY HELD NOT THEIRS, BUT ALL MEN'S LIBERTY
THIS FAR FROM HOME, TO THIS LAST SACRIFICE

Ironically, the design of the monument is a geographical model of the planter cemetery, with the whites in front and blacks in the rear. But what is usually an invisible line separating the races in a cemetery, as in Harmontown's and Oxford's St. Peter's, is a deliberate boundary on the monument. Below the line of words "OF THE NEGRO RACE" are the names of the seven Lafayette County blacks who were killed.[22]

Noel Polk observes that of the major southern writers at the time of the Second World War and the immediate postwar era, Faulkner is the only one who treats the conflict and its aftermath. Faulkner's ventures into the Second World War are short stories and parts of novels. None of the older southern writers, including Faulkner, produced Second World War novels of the magnitude of Irwin Shaw's *The Young Lions*, Norman Mailer's *The Naked and the Dead*, Joseph Heller's *Catch-22*, and James Jones's *From Here to Eternity*.[23] Faulkner's major twentieth-century war story is *A Fable*, which was published in 1954. The novel is set during the First World War, the war of Faulkner's generation, and is about the second coming of Christ. Despite some critics viewing the novel as a lesser Faulkner work, *A Fable* was awarded the 1955 Pulitzer Prize for Literature.

Faulkner never came to grips fully with the rapidly changing post–Second World War South in his fiction. Most of his books and stories written after *Go Down, Moses* are extensions of previous works and begin or supposedly are set before the Second World War. Although the lives of poor white tenant families are vividly described in *The Hamlet*, published in 1940, their stories are explored in greater depth in *The Town* and *The Mansion*, the second and third parts of the Snopes trilogy, which appeared in 1957 and 1959. *Requiem for a Nun*, published in 1951, continues the *Sanctuary* story of Temple Drake, who marries Gowan Stevens. The couple have two children. The younger one, an infant, is murdered by its black nurse. Written as a play, sections that more fully explain the histories of Jefferson and Yoknapatawpha County are interspersed between the acts, including the Second World War:

Then Pearl Harbor and Tobruk and Utah Beach . . . young men who had never been farther from Yoknapatawpha County than Memphis or New Orleans . . . now talked glibly of street intersections in Asiatic and European capitals, returning no more to inherit the long monotonous endless unendable furrows of Mississippi cotton fields, living now (with now a wife and next year a wife and child and the year after that a wife and children) in automobile trailers or G.I. barracks on the outskirts of liberal arts colleges.[24]

Faulkner's insistence in 1947 that the names of blacks from Lafayette County killed in the war be included on the Second World War monument inaugurated a new proactive involvement with racial issues that dominated the remainder of his life. Race, not the Second World War, gave new energy and direction to the writer. Knowing that he would be called a traitor to Mississippi and the South, Faulkner deliberately struck out on a course as an advocate of equal rights for blacks. Among his most direct early statements of his new challenge are two letters to the editor of the *Commercial Appeal* in 1950 condemning the life and ten-year sentences, rather than death, given to three white men in Attala County, Mississippi, who murdered three black children: "I, a native of our land and a sharer in our errors, just happened to be on the spot in time to say it first."[25]

Intruder in the Dust

Intruder in the Dust, published in 1948, is a discontinuity with Faulkner's prewar Yoknapatawpha novels. At the beginning of 1948 Faulkner's seeming creative drought ended. On January 15 he put "the big mss [*A Fable*] aside." Still grasping for a title, by February 1 he had sixty pages of *Intruder in the Dust* and rapidly finished the manuscript during the winter and spring. With renewed enthusiasm Faulkner wrote Harold Ober at Random House that he was at work on a short novel, "a mystery-murder though the theme is more relationship between Negro and white." Faulkner confronted and made a degree of peace with the decline in his creativity spawned by increasing age, heavy consumption of alcohol, and family responsibilities. Early in 1948 he confided to Robert Hass, "I seem to write so much slower, have to do so much more rewriting before sentences come exactly right than I used to."[26]

According to Faulkner, *Intruder in the Dust* was conceived as early as 1940 and is set "about 1935 or '40." It continues the Yoknapatawpha saga with Gavin Stevens, Charles (Chick) Mallison, Lucas Beauchamp, and other characters whom Faulkner had previously introduced. Lucas is falsely accused of killing Vinson Gowrie. The Gowries lead a mob of poor whites from Beat Four to Jefferson to take Lucas from the jail and lynch him. The actual murderer, Vinson's older brother, Crawford, is leader of the mob. Gavin Stevens, Lucas's attorney, resigns himself to the black man's guilt and his fate at the hands of the lynch mob. However, Chick, together with Aleck Sander and Miss Eunice Habersham, reject the predestined lynching and prove Lucas innocent of the murder. Despite what Faulkner says about the date of the novel, the powerful race theme and the dialogue of *Intruder in the Dust* place it explicitly into the immediate post–Second World War phase of the transition from New South to Modern South. Thomas McHaney observes that "Faulkner's books are reactions to the present, and . . . Faulkner set the great majority of his books when he began to write them, in the immediate present and portrayed dramatically the effect or impact or enduring weight of the past upon these present moments."[27]

Some critics dismiss Faulkner's works after *Go Down, Moses*, with the exception of *The Mansion*, as second rate and essentially unimportant. Thadious M. Davis does not include *Intruder in the Dust* in his *Faulkner's "Negro,"* because Faulkner "attempt[s] to explain, or perhaps expiate, the South's irresponsible and peculiarly selective morality." Daniel Singal characterizes *Intruder in the Dust* as "an inferior work, marked by a sharp drop-off in imaginative powers and by that apparently unstoppable virus of moral preaching." Critics continue to berate Faulkner with such statements as *Intruder in the Dust* "includes more than its share of clumsiness and embarrassment."[28] However, such a view of Faulkner's latter work is myopic, a narrow perspective based on literary interpretive value for a select few rather than upon the broader historical importance of his fiction to critical facets of the human experience. Malcolm Cowley is among the critics who perceptively comprehend Faulkner's post-1942 works:

> Though none of his later books was on a level with *The Sound and the Fury* or *Go Down, Moses*, none of them made concessions to other people's tastes. . . . Some of Faulkner's best writing is in passages of *Requiem for a Nun* and *Intruder in the Dust* and especially . . . in the Mink Snopes chapters of *The Mansion*. In retrospect I should judge that he solved the problem of keeping alive his genius better than any other American novelist of our century.[29]

Intruder in the Dust may not rank among Faulkner's best works, but it had greater public impact than *The Sound and the Fury, Light in August*, or any other of his pre–Second World War novels, including the infamous *Sanctuary*. *Intruder in the Dust*, together with its movie version, are parts of a significant body of postwar creative literature, cinema, and media that helped an important group of whites, especially young southerners, grasp racism and the actual conditions of blacks in southern and American society. From the end of the Second World War in

1945 through the end of the cold war at the conclusion of the twentieth century, race was a paramount theme in both world and United States history. World colonial empires fell, sweeping socioeconomic reforms occurred in the United States, and communism swept certain countries and then began to fail. Nowhere was the downfall of communism greater than in the Soviet Union and its empire, both of which split apart. Even though some of Faulkner's beliefs and predictions concerning national and world events were incorrect, he was among the vanguard who grasped that the American South was on the cusp of sweeping alterations in race relations. In his study of the South during the twenty years that preceded the civil rights movement, John Egerton discusses *Intruder in the Dust*'s significance beyond narrow literary criticism. Egerton titles his study *Speak Now Against the Day*, a prophetic phrase from Faulkner's 1955 address to the Southern Historical Association. According to Egerton, in *Intruder in the Dust* "Faulkner the scout, the explorer, [was] formulating his report to the advancing South, telling us in lines too cryptic for our understanding—or his—what was waiting just over the mountain." Why did Faulkner write the novel? "Was this Faulkner for a mass audience? Not quite. Was it Faulkner in a studied attempt to be current and contemporary? Perhaps. Was it Faulkner in a struggle with his own conscience and the conscience of the South? Undoubtedly."[30]

In 1951 C. Vann Woodward (1908–1999), the most influential southern historian during the latter half of the twentieth century, published *Origins of the New South*, a revisionist interpretation of the post–Civil War era. Woodward also wrote *The Strange Career of Jim Crow*, which Martin Luther King Jr. called the bible of the civil rights movement. Woodward credited William Faulkner, whom he did not read and whom he criticized early in his career, with teaching him fundamental lessons about the South and interpretation of its history. Later Woodward confessed, "To my embarrassment I find myself as a very junior instructor parroting [New York] metropolitan wisdom back in 1938, shamelessly remarking that William Faulkner seemed to draw his subjects out of abandoned wells." At the urging of Cleanth Brooks and Robert Penn Warren, Woodward eventually read Faulkner. In his autobiography Woodward wrote,

The history of the South had too often been written defensively. . . . I took heart, however, from the example set by Southern men of letters. . . . [T]he great novelists often wrote about the obscure, the provincial, the eccentric, the tormented, and the humble—the uncelebrated. Yet one of those writers had populated a single Mississippi county of his own imagining with characters known throughout the literate world. If obscurity and provinciality of subject matter proved no obstacle to literature, why should they prove so to history? If Southern novelists, poets, and playwrights could, as Robert Penn Warren admonished us, "accept the past and its burden" without evasion or defensiveness or special pleading, why should Southern historians not profit from their example? And if they could break through the veils of myth and illusion that obscured their own history, might they not help penetrate the legends of success and victory and innocence that obscured the ironic implications of national history?[31]

Among the things that both Faulkner and Woodward teach is that history is change, change is motion, and motion is life. In his important 1956 interview for *Writers at Work*, Faulkner stated, "Life is motion. . . . The aim of every artist is to arrest motion . . . by artificial means and hold it fixed so that a hundred years later, when a stranger looks at it, it moves again. . . . Since man is mortal, the only immortality possible for him is to leave something behind him that is immortal since it will always move." Woodward presumed that not only is history in motion, but those who interpret it are also in motion.[32] It follows that the definition of "southern" is in motion, which means that what defines the South, including attitudes about race, change through time. To find examples of changes in the definition of the South, one must discover that which is important to southerners. Read stories on front pages of southern newspapers from before the Civil War to the present. The discussions at the dinner tables of L. Q. C. Lamar, Nathan Bedford Forrest, and William Clark Falkner in the 1850s were hardly the same topics of conversations at the dinner tables of their descendants in the 1950s or the topics in the first decade of the twenty-first-century South.

Intruder in the Dust was Faulkner's first successful book in immediate sales, and it brought the author the most public attention he had received since the publication of *Sanctuary* in 1931. *Intruder in the Dust* sold more than fifteen thousand copies in the trade edition, close to the number Random House expected for a book by one of its popular authors. In response to the large sales, Random House reissued *Go Down, Moses*, *The Wild Palms*, and *The Hamlet*. Metro-Goldwyn-Mayer quickly purchased the film rights to *Intruder in the Dust* for fifty thousand dollars, the type of sale Faulkner had been trying to make to Hollywood for two decades. After Random House and Faulkner's agent took their shares, the writer had forty thousand dollars ($344,422 in 2007 dollars), the largest sum he had ever received for a work.

As he labored to finish *Intruder in the Dust*, Faulkner was in debt to the extent that he asked Robert Hass for an advance of thirty-nine hundred dollars to pay his 1944 federal income tax and five hundred dollars for his 1947 Mississippi taxes. The large amount of cash from *Intruder in the Dust* solved Faulkner's immediate financial problems. With publication of the novel and sale of the film rights, Faulkner entered a new financial era. A flow of money from prizes, books, stories, speeches, and movie and television rights kept him in relatively comfortable but hardly luxuriant financial circumstances for the remainder of his life. In the late 1950s and early 1960s his annual income averaged about ten thousand dollars ($70,000 in 2007 dollars). However, occasionally he had to scrounge for cash for special events and to purchase costly items. At the time of his death in 1962, Faulkner was making arrangements to buy Red Acres, an expensive 250-acre farm nine miles from Charlottesville. Faulkner did not plan to sell Rowan Oak, but he wanted a second home near Jill and her family.[33]

Race relations, segregation, and discrimination were hardly new themes in Faulkner's works. The relationships between blacks and whites are predominant topics throughout. The themes are strongly presented in *The Sound and the Fury, Light in August, Absalom, Absalom!*, and *Go Down, Moses*. However, in these and other works written prior to 1942, the attitude of elite whites toward discrimination and injustice to blacks is largely passive, despondent, and ineffectual.

The nuances of unwritten segregation codes of the New South were bizarre and paradoxical, but they were strongly rooted in basic dogma that whites held about blacks from Europeans' first contacts with sub-Saharan Africans. Fundamental to the creed were the beliefs that blacks were intellectually inferior to whites and that they were immoral and unclean.[34] In a drinking bout with two poor whites and three Negroes, planter elite Bayard Sartoris and the other whites drink from a jug of moonshine, but without thought or challenge they do not let the blacks' lips touch the container. In desperation to include the Negroes, the only vessel that Bayard can find is the cap from the automobile breather pipe. "It'll taste a little like oil for a drink or two. But you boys won't notice it after that."[35] Luster sleeps in the bed with mentally retarded Benjamin Compson. A long board is placed between the boys by Dilsey, Luster's mother. The board is explained to Benjy, who is told, "Stay on your side" because "Luster little, and you don't want to hurt him." But in a segregated society, a black and a white sleeping together is taboo. The board is both a physical barrier and a figurative symbol segregating black and white, even though Benjy is cared for by black servants and often sleeps in a bed in their cabin behind the Compson big house.[36] In these examples from *Sartoris* and *The Sound and The Fury* Faulkner does not attack segregation outright but reveals its inherent hypocrisy.

Faulkner's elite whites escape blacks and the burden of segregation not just by physical barriers but also by mental flight. Isaac McCaslin responds to miscegenation and the racial quagmire created by his ancestors by repudiation of his inheritance, the McCaslin plantation, but his efforts toward monetary compensation of his black relatives are feeble failures. When Isaac discovers that the woman whom

Roth Edmonds, the last white McCaslin, might marry is part black, he confronts the possibility of a legal interracial union, something he cannot accept. Isaac thinks to himself, *"Maybe in a thousand or two thousand years in America. . . . But not now! Not now!"*[37]

Like Isaac McCaslin, Jason IV, the last Compson male, seeks deliverance from responsibility by renunciation. Jason has his retarded brother, Benjy, castrated in 1913 after he attacks a female child. Following his mother's death in 1933, Jason sells the Compson big house and its lot, all that remains of Compson's Mile; has Benjy committed to the Mississippi asylum; and turns out Dilsey, the last of the blacks who have long and faithfully served his family. "'In 1865,' he would say, 'Abe Lincoln freed the niggers from the Compsons. In 1933, Jason Compson freed the Compsons from the niggers.'"[38]

The civil rights movement usually is considered the period between the U.S. Supreme Court's 1954 decision on school desegregation in *Brown v. Board of Education* and the assassination of Martin Luther King Jr. at Memphis in 1968. However, the movement actually began in the global social, economic, political, and geographical upheavals of the Great Depression and the Second World War, the period in which Faulkner wrote his most significant works laying bare the seamier, intimate aspects of southern race relations. *Light in August*, published in 1932, includes a riveting indictment of lynching, encompassing its relentless haunting of the participants. After shooting Joe Christmas, Percy Grimm castrates him while he is still alive. "Then . . . from out the slashed garments about his hips and loins the pent black blood seemed to rush like a released breath. It seemed to rush out of his pale body like the rush of sparks from a rising rocket; upon that black blast the men seemed to rise soaring into their memories forever and ever. They are not to lose it, in whatever peaceful valleys, beside whatever placid and reassuring streams of old age."[39]

No one attempts to stop the fanatical Percy Grimm from lynching Joe Christmas. In *Intruder in the Dust*, which appeared sixteen years later, Faulkner presents a new version of the historically persistent clash between southern elite whites and poor whites over blacks. Elite whites risk danger to themselves as intercessors, ultimate intruders, to protect a black man from poor whites. Gavin Stevens, Chick Mallison, and Miss Eunice Habersham not only aggressively intercede to prevent the lynching of Lucas Beauchamp, but Chick and Miss Habersham diligently work to prove him innocent of the murder of Vinson Gowrie. In retrospect of more than half a century, a story about whites actively working to save a Negro from being lynched as an approach to solving America's race problem may seem absurd. However, the campaign to prevent lynching of blacks is where the effort began, which eventually became the civil rights movement that ended legal segregation and restored voting rights to blacks.

Lynching is a method of false justice from antiquity. During the colonial period and the first century of the United States, lynching occurred primarily in frontier areas with inadequate legal and law enforcement systems. Until 1886 whites were lynched in greater numbers annually than blacks. As slaves, blacks were protected by their masters. However, after freedom blacks lost protection, except from their "white folks," planters who safeguarded their tenants and whites who sometimes defended descendants of their families' slaves and their mulatto relatives. The largest number of persons who were victims of mob justice after records began to be kept occurred in 1892, when 161 blacks and 69 whites were lynched, primarily in the South.[40]

Violation of the taboo on sex between black men and white women, especially by rape or attempted rape, is usually thought to be the principal reason blacks were lynched. However, Faulkner's reason poor whites from Beat Four want to lynch Lucas Beauchamp, the murder of a white, is the primary motive blacks were lynched. Between 1882 and 1968 alleged homicide was the inciting factor in 40.8 percent of the 4,743 blacks and whites who were lynched, while alleged rape was the provoking factor in 25.3 percent. Also, contrary to the large number of photographs that indicate death by hanging or burning, most of the 4,743 victims were executed with firearms.[41]

Ida B. Wells was initially overlooked in civil rights era literature, but the crusade to end lynching in the United States was begun in 1892 by this petite woman. Wells, who was born a slave in Holly Springs, Mississippi, in 1862, was the granddaughter of her master. She eagerly sought to educate herself and to improve her social skills. Wells moved to Memphis in 1879 and taught school in Woodstock, a suburban hamlet. Under the name "Iola," she wrote articles on the role of women and on racial segregation for black-owned newspapers. The lynching of three blacks who owned a prosperous Memphis grocery store by whites who resented the competition provoked Wells to write *Southern Horrors: Lynch Law in All Its Phases*, which was published in New York in 1892. To protest the treatment of blacks in Memphis, Wells initiated a boycott, a tactic that remains a weapon by which blacks protest injustice. She originated the boycott of public transportation in Memphis more than half a century before Martin Luther King Jr. used the same nonviolent economic leverage in 1955 to end segregation on buses in Montgomery, Alabama.[42]

The anti-lynching crusade begun by Wells had a major impact. By the time the National Association for the Advancement of Colored People was organized and began its well-known effort against lynching in 1909, the number of murders of blacks by white vigilantes had declined from 161 in 1892 to 82. Mob justice continued to decrease after the First World War. Fewer than twenty-five blacks were lynched annually in the mid-1920s and fewer than ten in the mid-1930s.[43] Between January 1889 and December 1966, 464 persons were lynched in Mississippi, including three in Lafayette County. By the late 1940s a lynching in which elite whites would knowingly stand by and let poor whites kill a black man, as depicted in *Intruder in the Dust*, was uncommon. This probably was among the reasons Faulkner set *Intruder in the Dust* a decade prior to the time of its publication. The last lynching in Lafayette County occurred in 1935 when a party of seventy-five white men broke into the jail during the trial of Elwood Higginbotham, who had confessed to killing Glen Roberts. Higginbotham, who was taken from the jail and hanged from a tree on a county road, was one of eighteen blacks lynched in the United States that year. Only one black was lynched in the United States in 1948, the year Faulkner wrote *Intruder in the Dust*. Since 1952 few lynchings have occurred in the nation.[44]

In older southern plantation counties, which after Reconstruction had few outsiders moving into them, most blacks through long established paternalistic relationships, and kinship, had white protectors. In Yoknapatawpha, Carothers Edmonds is the protector of Lucas Beauchamp, not only because he is his relative but also because he is his landlord. *In Intruder in the Dust* Faulkner removes the possibility of Edmonds's intervention by placing him in New Orleans for a gallstone operation.[45] The social standing and education of Gavin Stevens, Chick Mallison, and Eunice Habersham give them authority over and protection from the Gowries and other poor whites when they intervene on Lucas's behalf. All three are the descendants of slaveholders and have had close associations with blacks throughout their lives. Miss Eunice may be poorer than the Gowries. She drives an old secondhand pickup truck and peddles chickens, eggs, and produce on the streets of Jefferson. But she is an elite with authority. Miss Eunice is a member of one of the town's oldest families. Her house is without electricity and plumbing and in need of paint, but it is a large colonial dwelling. Miss Eunice also exhibits status through her dress. Although she wears cheap cotton stockings and print dresses from Sears Roebuck, her shoes and gloves are expensive, custom made for her in New York. The small antique gold watch pinned on her chest by a gold brooch is a badge of social rank.[46]

Customarily in the segregated South, conversations about racial matters between blacks and whites, and even among whites, were oblique. However, in *Intruder in the Dust* the discussions of racial issues are unusually candid for the time. Gavin Stevens and Chick Mallison ponder why they are drawn into Lucas Beauchamp's problems and deliberate their responsibility, not just to him, but to blacks.

Unfortunately, rather than accepting the fictional dialogue as authentic and quite advanced for the period, some critics dismiss Stevens and Mallison's discussions about race as "preaching" by an intellectually drained Faulkner. But this dialogue is some of the most genuine in Faulkner's fiction, contemporary to the time in which it was composed by an author who was torn by conflicts in what he traditionally believed and what he knew was right. Cleanth Brooks wrote that Gavin Stevens's "arguments do reflect a very real cultural situation, and the reader could learn from them a great deal about the problem of the South."[47]

The conversations between Gavin and Chick are more historically authentic than the one in *Absalom, Absalom!* between Thomas Sutpen and his son Henry near the end of the Civil War. The Sutpens' dialogue is cast in the language of the Lost Cause, a concept that developed later. There is a double filter for the Sutpens' conversation, first through Faulkner's dialogue written in the 1930s employing fictional characters' imagined conversations of the Civil War era and then through the dialogue of fictional Quentin Compson and Shreve in 1909–1910, who employ the language of remembrance.

Faulkner perceptively realized that he could be accused of preaching in *Intruder in the Dust*. In a 1948 letter to Harold Ober, he states that the "premise" of his "short novel" is "that the white people in the south, before the North or the govt. or anyone else, owe and must pay a responsibility to the Negro. But it's a story; nobody preaches in it."[48]

Among Faulkner's fictional characters, Stevens comes the closest in expressing what the writer personally stated about segregation, equal rights, and the relationship between blacks and whites. Stevens says to Chick:

> I'm defending Lucas Beauchamp . . . from the North and East and West—the out-
> landers who will fling him decades back not merely into injustice but into grief and
> agony and violence too by forcing on us laws based on the idea that man's injustice
> to man can be abolished overnight by police. . . . I only say that the injustice is ours,
> the South's. We must expiate and abolish it ourselves, alone and without help nor
> even (with thanks) advice.[49]

According to Stevens, what southerners are defending in resisting outsiders, especially northerners, is "the privilege of setting . . . [Negroes] free ourselves. . . . [G]oing on a century ago now the North tried it and have been admitting for seventy-five years now that they failed." He tells Chick:

> Someday Lucas Beauchamp can shoot a white man in the back with the same
> impunity to lynch-rope or gasoline as a white man; in time he will vote anywhen
> and anywhere a white man can and send his children to the same school anywhere

the white man's children go and travel anywhere the white man travels. . . . But it wont be next Tuesday. Yet people in the North believe it can be compelled even into next Monday by the simple ratification of votes of a printed paragraph: who have forgotten that although a long quarter-century ago Lucas Beauchamp's freedom was made an article in our constitution and Lucas Beauchamp's master was . . . beaten to his knees . . . yet only three short generations later they are faced once more with the necessity of passing legislation to set Lucas Beauchamp free.[50]

Chick does not have the aloof detachment of Uncle Gavin. By placing the events of *Intruder in the Dust* during the last half of the 1940s, the time into which the novel fits, rather than in the 1930s, the time Faulkner intended, Chick belongs to the generation of white southerners who have to confront inherited misconceptions about and prejudice against blacks more directly than Stevens's generation. Chick's generation is composed of teenagers and younger children in 1948. His generation bears the brunt of desegregation and equal rights for blacks more directly than any other. Chick's journey toward his predestined encounter with equality begins at the age of twelve when he attempts to make Lucas acknowledge his inferiority. Chick tries to pay Lucas for rescuing him from hypothermia and giving him his dinner after he falls into the icy waters of Nine Mile Branch on the McCaslin plantation. Chick is near the age of transition from child to adult. In the South's plantation society this passage is often awkward and difficult for both whites and blacks. President Jimmy Carter is among the rural white southerners who experienced the traumatic passage from child to man in the now-vanished traditional plantation society. According to Carter, when he was fourteen, the day came when his black childhood playmates opened a pasture gap, stood aside, and let the emerging white adult enter before they did. The unwritten segregation codes required that adult whites were to precede inferior blacks.[51]

In traditional plantation society adult blacks and even black children were expected to care for white children. Reprimand of white children was part of the responsibility of adult blacks. From Lucas's perspective, he merely cares for a white child who has fallen into an icy creek and is in danger of becoming ill. Chick understands this. "He could no more imagine himself contradicting the man striding on ahead of him than he could his grandfather . . . because like his grandfather the man striding ahead of him was simply incapable of conceiving himself by a child contradicted and defied." The underlying problem in the encounter is not Lucas being an uppity Negro, but Chick's inability to comprehend and react appropriately to a situation he confronts for the first time. The emerging man in Chick interprets Lucas's refusal of payment for his dinner to mean that he has been a guest in the house of a black, an inferior. Also, the food, collard greens, a piece of pork side-meat dipped in flour and fried, heavy lard biscuits, and a glass of buttermilk are "nigger food."[52] White families often eat items of the same fare but usually do not eat them together as a meal. Also, Chick has to eat from a plate and drink from a fruit jar from which Negroes have eaten and drunk. Even though blacks may cook for whites daily, elite whites do not eat from the same dishes or use the same forks, spoons, and knives as blacks. Such utensils are considered unclean no matter how many times they are washed.

The encounter over the payment culminates in arrogant rage when Chick hurls the coins on the floor and commands Lucas, "Pick it up!" Lucas understands the encounter and tells Aleck Sander, "Pick up his money." Still the one in charge, Lucas patently and forgivingly says to Chick the child, "Now go on and shoot your rabbit. . . . And stay out of that creek." Chick the child-man later thinks: "*We got to make him be a nigger first. He's got to admit he's a nigger. Then maybe we will accept him as he seems to intend to be accepted.*"[53]

Novels are not the only works to address race relations. A genre of Hollywood "message films," which depict social realism, were made following the Second World War. Prejudice is among the themes they portray, ranging from discrimination against war veterans (*The Best Years of Our Lives*), Jews (*Gentlemen's Agreement*), Native Americans (*Devil's Doorway*), and blacks. *Intruder in the Dust* is one of five films concerning "the Negro question" made in 1949 and 1950. The others are *Home of the Brave* and *Lost Boundaries*, released by United Artists, and *Pinky* and *No Way Out*, produced by Twentieth Century-Fox. Although blacks found the films less than satisfactory in presenting segregation and the other problems they confronted, from its founding the National Association for the Advancement of Colored People realized that publicizing the plight of blacks was "of the highest strategic importance to the Negro people. . . . Determination to expose injustices rested on their belief that a democratic society would respond constructively if only it had the facts at its disposal." Despite their shortcomings, the postwar message films were better than no publicity. One of the highest compliments paid to the film version of *Intruder in the Dust* by blacks was that at least in theaters no one laughed.[54]

The 1949 motion picture version of *Intruder in the Dust* was made by Clarence Brown, a graduate of the University of Tennessee and one of Metro-Goldwyn-Mayer's distinguished directors. Brown began his film career in 1920 and was nominated for the Academy Award for best director six times. After reading the galley proofs of *Intruder in the Dust*, Brown insisted that MGM purchase the film rights to the book. Louis B. Mayer, long the autocratic head of MGM, did not like liberal causes, Faulkner, or the novel. But Mayer and Brown had long been close friends, and the friendship kept the mogul from objecting to the film.[55]

In interviews Clarence Brown stated that he had witnessed the 1906 Atlanta race riots and had never been able to forget them. He wanted to make a film about race problems in the South. In an interview with the Memphis *Commercial Appeal* Brown said: "As a Southerner, I believe this motion picture can be a great accomplishment toward nationwide better understanding of the true relationship between the races in the South and of the gradualism which is solving this very old problem. Mr. Faulkner's book is the first thing ever written upon that theme." Brown thought that chapter 7 is "the most eloquent statement as to the true situation in the South."[56] Essentially, as Faulkner and the fictional Stevens, Brown believed that "gradualism" should be the approach to solving the South's and the nation's race problem.

To achieve authenticity, Brown insisted on filming *Intruder in the Dust* in Oxford and Lafayette County. Although location cinematography dates from the beginning of the movie industry, in 1949 it was unusual for a director to film 90 percent of a motion picture on location, as was the case with *Intruder in the Dust*. Brown also cast southern actors and local residents in the film. In the current permissive age of cinema and television when southern states and communities actively solicit media companies with no concern as to topics or content, the opposition that Brown initially met in Lafayette County and Mississippi to a film about a lynching may seem strange. Brown won local leaders through his wit and charm at presentations to Oxford's board of aldermen and chamber of commerce, and by his indirect threat to make the movie in Hollywood and depict the town as he pleased.[57]

Clarence Brown may have had another motive for wanting to make a movie of *Intruder in the Dust*. His recent films staring children had done well at the box office. In 1944 Brown directed Enid Bagnold's *National Velvet*, starring Mickey Rooney and Elizabeth Taylor, and in 1946 he made a movie based on Marjorie Rawlings's *The Yearling*. Both films are in Technicolor and were immensely popular. *The Yearling* stars Gregory Peck, Jane Wyman, and Claude Jarman Jr., whom Brown discovered in a fifth grade classroom in Nashville while looking for a southern child to play the part of Jody. Jarman won a special Academy Award as outstanding child actor for his performance.[58] Brown was searching for another film for Jarman, a tall fourteen-year-old, who was the right age and size for the role of Charles Mallison (fig. 8.2).

Intruder in the Dust was an inexpensive movie. It was filmed similar to a documentary, in black and white and without major stars. Rather than using high-contrast black and white film, as is the case with some racially charged movies, Brown chose various shades of gray, a blending of black and white. The closest player to a star is David Brian, a competent actor who is miscast as Gavin Stevens and called John in the film. Brown meant for the film to be carried by Claude Jarman

Figure 8.2. William Faulkner and Claude Jarman Jr. during the filming of *Intruder in the Dust* in Lafayette County, Mississippi, in the winter of 1949. Courtesy of Special Collections, University of Tennessee Libraries.

Jr. and talented character actors, who include Elizabeth Patterson as Miss Habersham, Will Geer as Sheriff Hampton, and Porter Hall as Nub Gowrie. In the novel Charles Mallison is the main character. Juano Hernandez, a talented Puerto Rican actor cast in his first cinema role, delivers a first-rate performance as the independent, "uppity" Lucas Beauchamp and is the film's dominant character (fig. 8.3).[59]

Faulkner and Brown got along well (fig. 8.4). Brown was a pilot during the First World War, and, like Faulkner, thought of himself as a farmer. Faulkner rewrote a few scenes, suggested one change in the cast, helped Hernandez with his accent, and even leased his horse to MGM. He was not paid or given credit for work on the film because he was still under contract to Warner Brothers.[60]

In retrospect of more than half a century, the motion picture based on *Intruder in the Dust* seems conventional and even quaint, but both Faulkner and Brown were complimented for their bravery for venturing into the volatile topics of race and mob lynching. Brown received commendatory letters from major movie directors and producers such as Jerry Wald and John Huston.[61] *Intruder in the Dust* received good to excellent reviews and is the best of the 1949–1950 message films concerning blacks. Also, *Intruder in the Dust* remains among the best cinema adaptations of a Faulkner novel. However, the film did not do well at the box office. The race theme was hardly new by the time *Intruder in the Dust* appeared in October 1949. *Home of the Brave*, *Lost Boundaries*, and *Pinky* preceded it. Because

Figure 8.3. "'Strip off,' the man said. So he stripped off the wet unionsuit too and then he was in the chair again in front of the now bright and swirling fire" (Faulkner *Intruder in the Dust* 1948, 11). Still photograph of scene 76 from *Intruder in the Dust*. Claude Jarman Jr. plays Charles (Chick) Mallison and Juano Hernandez plays Lucas Beauchamp (MGM 1949). Courtesy of Special Collections, University of Tennessee Libraries.

Figure 8.4. William Faulkner and Clarence Brown discuss the filming of a rural scene in Lafayette County, Mississippi, for *Intruder in the Dust* in the winter of 1949. Courtesy of Special Collections, University of Tennessee Libraries.

the lynching theme was thought derogatory to the South, some southern theaters rejected the film. But the very strict Memphis censorship board, headed by the "wacky and screwy" Lloyd T. Benford, approved it. The Oxford premiere was at the Lyric Theater on Tuesday, October 11, 1949, which Mississippi governor Fielding Wright unenthusiastically proclaimed "William Faulkner Day." The motion picture opened the following evening at the Loew's Palace in downtown Memphis. Although not an official premiere, opening night in Memphis at the larger and grander theater was as important as the Oxford event. Clarence Brown, Elizabeth Patterson, and a charming Porter Hall, who stole the festivities in Oxford and Memphis, attended both openings. Claude Jarman was unable to attend because he was in the midst of the filming of a new movie.[62] The audience was composed especially of Mississippians who had moved to Memphis.

Intruder in the Dust suffered from the lack of a major star to attract audiences. Brown became depressed over the film's failure to attract a large audience. It is a gloomy film that featured the cold, bleak Mississippi late-winter countryside, ill-kempt antiquated stores around Oxford's square, mud-splattered cars and trucks, the medieval jail, and an attempt to exhume a body from a grave. Brown thought of *Intruder in the Dust* as a first-rate picture, a status it now holds. However, he made it like a B movie, which it quickly became at theaters, the lesser second film of a double feature. Although Brown won the best director award given by the British Academy, the American Academy of Motion Picture Arts and Sciences did not nominate the picture for a single Oscar. With its teenage star and horror ambience, the film appealed as much to children and teenagers as to adults. Its role in filling out a double feature actually caused more people to see *Intruder in the Dust* than would have seen it as a single feature.

Both the novel and the movie played significant roles in the era that immediately preceded the civil rights movement. In his study of the Hollywood message movie, Thomas Cripps wrote of the acceptance of *Intruder in the Dust* at theaters:

[E]xcept for a few . . . they almost unanimously read it as its makers intended: as an assertion of the thrust of liberalism in a particular time, and on a human scale that avoided the purely political and therefore offered change as a prospect rather than a program. . . . The *Oxford Eagle* and the *California Eagle*, the former white and rural, the latter black and urban, agreed on the movie, the former for its "groping for fair play and tolerance" while avoiding mere "indictment," the latter calling it "a smashing weapon against intolerance." Together they constituted a striking consensus of black and white agreement on newly defined terms of postwar racial arrangements rooted neither in empty nostalgia nor interventionism, but rather in the shared nonceword *tolerance*.[63]

The most prophetic review of the film version of *Intruder in the Dust* is by George Harmon of Mississippi's *Jackson Daily News*:

> The film triumphs in that the lynching never takes place, in that the Negro improperly accused of murdering a white man is given his freedom and in that the happy ending comes about through the intelligent endeavors of a few Southern whites pitting themselves against a less intelligent mob guided by centuries of tradition and custom.
>
> The film is not a plea for abolition of segregation. It is not even a plea for tolerance.
>
> It's not a plea for anything—just a story of an episode which took place in a Southern town and as an objective presentation of attitudes of people involved.[64]

At the midpoint of the twentieth century, a few southern whites, especially a few who were children and teenagers at the time the novel and the movie appeared, remembered *Intruder in the Dust* when, a little more than a decade later, as young adults, they were directly confronted with the underlying race message. They had to make a decision whether or not to act responsibly, as had Chick Mallison, Miss Habersham, Aleck Sander, Gavin Stevens, and Sheriff Hampton, or conform to a mob guided by centuries of tradition and custom.

NINE

From Yoknapatawpha County to the World

After publication of *Intruder in the Dust*, Faulkner increasingly became involved in the national civil rights debate. The civil rights era was divided into three distinct phases: mobilization, 1954 into 1960; confrontation, 1960 through 1965; and white acquiescence, 1966 through 1972.[1] During the mobilization phase, Mississippi quickly moved into the forefront of blacks' quest for equal rights. In August 1955 whites lynched Emmett Till, a Chicago teenager visiting relatives in Tallahatchie County in the Yazoo Delta. Till allegedly made a sexual remark or gesture to the wife of one of the men. The Till affair was the first major incident of the civil rights era to attract international media attention. Comments and actions of local whites, especially by Sheriff Clarence Strider, were an embarrassment and made Mississippians appear absurd. Roy Bryant and J. W. Miliam, two of Till's killers, were indicted but were acquitted by an all-white Tallahatchie County jury. Shortly after the verdict, the two confessed to murdering the black youth in an article sold to *Look* magazine.[2]

After winning the 1949 Nobel Prize for Literature, which was awarded in December 1950, Faulkner became less of an eccentric semi-recluse and assumed public responsibilities, which he believed were decreed by his renown (fig. 9.1). He who had repeatedly exposed leadership failure in fiction could not elude his civic responsibilities and become an Isaac McCaslin in fact. The public Faulkner began to emerge at an impromptu interview he gave at the Colonial Restaurant a few hours before the October 1949 premier of *Intruder in the Dust* at Oxford's Lyric Theater. Drinking club soda over ice, Faulkner fielded a variety of questions from reporters about the movie and about himself with baiting responses and seasoned stories. The writer's relaxed public confidence probably resulted more from the lack of pressing financial problems than the prestige heaped on him by the movie premiere. Shortly before the program at the Lyric was to begin, Faulkner created a family panic when he revealed that he had given away his tickets.[3]

Faulkner knew that his day as a "young and hot" writer was past and his best, most innovative work was done. Not without adjustment problems, in 1948 he began to come to grips with being an aging artist. However, after the excitement of the filming of *Intruder in the Dust* in Lafayette County, Faulkner became depressed and began

Figure 9.1. Under gray skies with sleet falling, William Faulkner told Estelle good-bye as he and Jill boarded an American Airlines plane in Memphis to fly to New York on December 6, 1950. From New York Faulkner and Jill flew to Stockholm, Sweden, where he was presented the 1949 Nobel Prize for Literature. Symbolically, this photograph marked Faulkner's emergence as a public figure, who increasingly commented on race and other controversial contemporary issues. Photograph courtesy of the *Commercial Appeal*.

a drinking binge. Despite renewed writing, Faulkner continued to worry about decline in his ability. Beginning in 1936 Faulkner entered Wright's Sanitarium in Byhalia, Mississippi, during alcohol binges. However, in April 1949 Faulkner sought additional help for depression from psychiatrists at Gartly-Ramsay Hospital in Memphis. Also, in 1949 another young woman, twenty-year-old Joan Williams, came into his life. The relationship, which lasted through 1953, was based on misconceptions that both eventually did not believe. Joan wanted Faulkner as a mentor. A great writer could teach her to be a great writer. Faulkner thought that a love relationship with a young woman could alleviate his loneliness and help rejuvenate him.[4]

Go Slow Now

After Faulkner was awarded the Nobel Prize for Literature, he endeavored to settle into his place as a writer who enjoyed significant recognition in his waning years.

Figure 9.2. William Faulkner with two students at the University of Virginia during 1957–1958 when he was writer-in-residence. The writer lived long enough to enjoy the acclaim and awards bestowed on a great author. On formal occasions Faulkner's dress usually was not eccentric. He enjoyed tweed jackets, and, like every competent aviator, he wore a good wristwatch. Special Collections, University of Virginia Library.

During the 1950s Faulkner traveled to various foreign countries as a cultural representative of the U.S. Department of State. He also gave speeches, wrote essays, published public letters, and served as writer-in-residence at the University of Virginia (fig. 9.2). At the time of the U.S. Supreme Court's 1954 decision in *Brown v. Board of Education*, Faulkner had written of intimate southern race relationships for a quarter of a century. The *Brown* decision, the Till murder, his growing renown as the great southern writer, and his decision to take a public stand on racial injustice drew Faulkner further and further into the public debate over equal rights and desegregation.

A number of Faulkner's statements on discrimination and segregation are bold and open minded. He commenced his address to the Southern Historical Association in Memphis with, "To live anywhere in the world of A.D. 1955 and be against equality because of race or color is like living in Alaska and being against snow." Faulkner's conclusion to his address was a response to a speech made three months earlier by Mississippi's powerful U.S. senator James O. Eastland to a group of citizens at Senatobia, a town forty miles northwest of Oxford. Eastland, who chaired the Senate's Judiciary Committee, encouraged the audience of two thousand whites gathered at Northwest Mississippi Junior College to defy federal court decrees. "There is not a single legal reason for . . . [the Supreme Court's *Brown* decision]. It is immoral, infamous and illegal and . . . deserves no respect from us. . . . If a suit is filed to integrate the schools of this community, don't obey it. Your future depends on your ability to resist." Faulkner's retort to his fellow Mississippian was: "We speak now against the day when our Southern people who will resist to the last these inevitable changes in social relations, will, when they have been forced to accept what they at one time might have accepted with dignity and goodwill, will say, 'Why didn't someone tell us this before? Tell us this in time?'"[5]

Other statements by Faulkner concerning blacks and desegregation are conservative, contradictory, and patronizing. In retrospect, Faulkner was an outspoken moderate, who envisioned himself as liberal going "upstream or against the current." In conservative, staunchly segregated Oxford and Mississippi, where almost no blacks voted, he had the reputation of a trouble-making liberal who even Miss Maud, his mother, thought was stirring people up. In 1956 two boys asked Faulkner what it was that made him different from other people. Faulkner told them to "ask around," report what people said, and he would tell them if the perceptions were correct. A few days later one of the boys told him that he had asked two people, "and all I could find out was you're a nigger-lover." A teary-eyed Faulkner replied, "I guess that's better than being a fascist."[6]

Although Faulkner's work was on the cutting edge of twentieth-century fiction, in certain respects he was a nineteenth-century man. Faulkner was reared among blacks, and they served him and treated him as a superior throughout his life. He was never able to fully achieve in fact that which he overcame in his fiction. At the age of thirty Faulkner inherited the responsibility of caring for, not just members of his family, but two blacks who were born in slavery, Uncle Ned Barnett and Mammy Callie (Caroline) Barr. Uncle Ned, who habitually called Faulkner "Massa," had belonged to his great-grandfather, and "ownership" passed to the writer when he became the head of the Falkner clan. *Go Down, Moses* was dedicated to Caroline Barr, who died at age one hundred in 1940 and was a second mother to Faulkner and his brothers.[7]

Despite his wisdom and insightfulness, Faulkner's day-to-day experience with blacks throughout his life lured him into the trap of considering himself an authority who understood the innermost person. "I have known Negroes all my life and Negroes work my land for me. I know how they feel." This quagmire of smug miscomprehensions has ensnared white Americans from conservative racists to liberal integrationists. The malady is not unique to Faulkner or to southerners, for other respected white Americans, including William Alexander Percy and General William Sherman, have fallen into the same trap.[8]

It is paradoxical that, in spite of a perceptiveness that revealed people's innermost hidden feelings as well as any writer, Faulkner did not fully comprehend that plantation blacks' seeming incompetence was partly a pretense learned during slavery and carried over into the New South. In a letter to Estelle in January 1960 concerning a serious brief illness, Faulkner complained about Andrew Price, who together with his wife lived and worked at Rowan Oak. "Andrew was probably squatting over the fire in their cabin as he always is when something happens on the place that he should stop or at least know about." Ironically, the Faulkner who understood that the Negro demeanor was part charade also believed that the attitude was evidence of irresponsible behavior that had to change if blacks were to be accepted by whites. In a 1958 public address at the University of Virginia, Faulkner stated that "the white man has forced the Negro to be always a Negro rather than another human being . . . and therefore the Negro cannot afford, does not dare, to be open with the white man and let the white man know what he . . . thinks. . . . We, the white man, must take him in hand and teach him . . . responsibility. . . . He must learn to cease forever more thinking like a Negro and acting like a Negro."[9]

Faulkner believed the idea expressed in *Intruder in the Dust* that blacks, northern whites, and the federal government were pushing integration on southern whites too fast. He adopted the idea that persons promoting integration should "go slow now." This belief seemed in accord with the vague instructions of the U.S. Supreme Court in *Brown II* that there should be a "prompt and reasonable start" of school desegregation, and it was to proceed "with all deliberate speed." In a 1956 interview Faulkner stated, "The Negroes have had ninety years . . . [of discrimination and segregation] and now that they are winning it would take a lot of wisdom to say 'Go slow.' Perhaps it is too much to ask of them, but it is for their own sake."[10]

Faulkner also held the belief stated in *Intruder in the Dust* that blacks had to "earn" freedom and equality by demonstrating that they could be a "responsible" people. A 1960 letter Faulkner wrote to Paul Pollard, who with his wife had been employed as servants by the Faulkners in Charlottesville, reveals the writer's personal demeanor toward blacks. Pollard wrote to Faulkner and asked him to donate the amount of money required for a lifetime membership for him in the National Association for the Advancement of Colored People (NAACP). In reply Faulkner did not address Pollard by his first name, even though in the letter he called Pollard's wife "Elizabeth." Habitually Faulkner did not address a black as "Mr."— rather, his salutation was one he used not just for blacks but also for whites whom he did not know very well. It was simply "Dear Pollard," similar to his salutation to Ernest Hemingway, "Dear Hemingway." Faulkner responded that he could not send the money for a membership because the NAACP, which he once believed in, now condoned "actions which will do your people harm." Invoking Booker T. Washington and George Washington Carver, whom some young blacks in the civil rights movement labeled "Uncle Toms," Faulkner revealed that he believed in the doctrine of accommodation, a widely held and cherished racial dogma among middle- and upper-class white Southerners. "As I see it, your people must earn by being individually responsible to bear it, the freedom and equality they want and should have. As Dr. Carver said, 'We must make the white people need us, want us to be in equality with them.'" Faulkner concluded by moralizing, "If the individual Negro does not . . . [get] himself educated and trained in responsibility and morality, there will be more and more trouble between the two races."[11] In sum, Faulkner accepted and promoted equality for blacks, but he could not escape his belief in *equal but separate.*

The Path to Wreck and Ruin

In his 1955 address to the Southern Historical Association, Faulkner again assumed the role of an authority on blacks and stated that he was "not convinced that the Negro wants integration in the sense that some of us claim to fear he does." Faulkner also warned of two dangers that threatened America and the South in a time of great political and social change. The cold war was well under way. Drawing on his global travels as a goodwill ambassador for the Department of State, Faulkner warned of communism and issued a dismal prediction. "Inside the last two years I have seen . . . Japan, the Philippines, Siam, India, Egypt, Italy, West Germany, England and Iceland. Of these countries, the only one I would say definitely will not be communist ten years from now, is England." Faulkner also cautioned lest "our native land, the South, . . . wreck and ruin itself twice in less than a hundred years, over the Negro question."[12] Faulkner became increasingly concerned about the accelerating civil rights movement leading to violence as southern whites were pushed into a position in which they had to accept racial integration. In "A Letter to the North" in the March 5, 1956, issue of *Life,* Faulkner wrote,

> From the beginning of this present phase of the race problem in the South, I have been on record as opposing the forces in my native country which would keep the condition out of which this present evil and trouble has grown. Now I must go on record as opposing the forces outside the South which would use legal or police compulsion to eradicate that evil overnight. . . . [T]he South will go to any length, even that fatal and already doomed one, before it will accept alteration of its racial condition by mere force of law or economic threat.[13]

Mississippi was a vortex during the confrontation period of the civil rights era. Medgar Evers, the state field representative for the NAACP, was murdered as he entered his home one night in 1961 by fanatical racist Byron de la Beckwith.[14] On the last day of September in 1962, the major armed confrontation over desegregation, which Faulkner feared, happened, ironically, at Oxford.

The significance of the 1962 "battle of Oxford" as the major clash between federal and state governments over integration during the civil rights era should not be underrated. It remains the largest mobilization of the United States military to deal with a domestic crisis since the Civil War. Troop deployment was larger than for the 1794 frontier whiskey rebellion, the 1894 Chicago Pullman strike, the 1932 veterans' "bonus army" tragedy, and the 1957 confrontation over the integration of Little Rock's Central High School. President John Kennedy mobilized 31,000 troops to deal with the Oxford crisis, 11,000 Mississippi National Guardsmen, and 20,000 U.S. Army soldiers. Half of the 31,000 troops were deployed in Oxford and vicinity. The 2,700-man Mississippi 108th Cavalry Regiment and two units of the Mississippi 155th Infantry Division were sent to Oxford. An additional 12,000 U.S. Army troops were also deployed in the city and the surrounding area, including ten airborne groups; two infantry units; and medical, engineer, quartermaster, and signal corps support units. The last troops were not withdrawn from Oxford until July 24, 1963.[15]

Ironically, this critical clash at Oxford during the civil rights movement, a major event in the nation's history, is largely forgotten. It is overshadowed by the United States' discovery a few days later that the Soviet Union had intercontinental ballistic missiles in Cuba and the effort of President Kennedy to force their removal. The Cuban missile crisis was the closest that the United States and the Soviet Union came to nuclear catastrophe during the cold war.

The Oxford tragedy began as a deliberately engineered racial charade by Mississippi's demigod governor Ross Barnett that spun out of control. Barnett pretended that he would prevent the enrollment of James Meredith, the first black student, at the University of Mississippi. On September 13 Ross Barnett addressed the citizens of Mississippi on television and radio, presenting the enrollment of James Meredith as an impending crisis. He warned, "There is no case in history where the Caucasian race has survived social integration. . . . We must either submit to the unlawful dictate of the federal government or stand up like men and tell them, 'Never.'"[16] The Mississippi Board of Trustees of Institutions of Higher Learning wanted to admit Meredith but were opposed by Barnett, who at a meeting on September 19 berated the members with a vulgar redneck tongue lashing.[17]

Despite his public defiance of the federal court order to admit James Meredith, Barnett secretly pledged to President Kennedy and his brother, Attorney General Robert Kennedy, that he would go on television and radio stations on Sunday night, before the enrollment of Meredith on Monday morning, and acquiesce to federal authority. Although he promised to keep Mississippi highway patrolmen in Oxford on Sunday, September 30, and Monday, October 1, to maintain law and order, Barnett withdrew most patrolmen and left the few who remained without specific orders. On the evening of September 30, the scheming and naive Barnett made his speech. "I urge all Mississippians and instruct every state official under my command to do everything in their power to preserve peace and to avoid violence in any form. . . . To the officials of the federal government I say, 'Gentlemen, you are trampling on the sovereignty of this great state. . . . You are destroying the Constitution of this great nation. . . . May God have mercy on your souls.'"[18]

Distrusting Barnett to enforce the federal court order that James Meredith be enrolled, on Saturday, September 29, President Kennedy federalized the eleven-thousand-member Mississippi National Guard, ordering the soldiers to report to their armories. He also sent five hundred troops of the 720th Military Police Battalion from Fort Hood, Texas, to Memphis. On Sunday, four hundred federal marshals and deputized border and prison guards arrived in Oxford. Nicholas Katzenbach, deputy attorney general, in retrospect, admitted that he made a mistake when at 4:00 p.m. he placed a ring of marshals around the Lyceum, the building that has been the focus of the campus since before the Civil War.[19] Katzenbach created a flash point on which a mob could focus, and he underestimated the size of the mob and the degree of violence that was about to erupt. I can understand how Katzenbach failed to perceive the situation correctly. On Sunday afternoon, my father and I were in Oxford, which is close to our family's farm. When we left about 4:00 p.m., both the town and the campus were peaceful. There was little evidence that a large group of outsiders had descended on Oxford or that a mob was about to form.

At 7:00 p.m., as Barnett made his speech on television and radio, a bloody riot was under way on the Ole Miss campus. The melee was inflamed by retired U.S. army general Edwin Walker, who had commanded the 101st Airborne troops employed by President Dwight Eisenhower at Little Rock in 1957 to enforce the integration of Central High School. Walker told the mob that he was on the wrong side at Little Rock but on the right one at Ole Miss. The mob had a few students, but it consisted primarily of persons who came to Oxford, heeding Ross Barnett's fraudulent earlier plea to resist federal tyranny and defend the southern way of life. A construction project on campus provided the mob with bricks, concrete blocks, and a bulldozer. In addition to the mob confronting the marshals, there were several hundred curious onlookers from Oxford, nearby towns, and the rural countryside. University of Mississippi chancellor J. D. Williams, campus policemen, student leaders, and faculty members circulated among the mob in a futile attempt to disperse them.[20] A number of students fled from the campus. Others barricaded themselves in their dormitories and fraternity and sorority houses. The occasional firing of guns was especially frightening to the students. The riot spilled over from the campus into Oxford and reached the courthouse square and the yard of the house in which Maud Falkner had lived. Secluded, Rowan Oak remained relatively safe.

The melee was filled with irony. During the night the Lyceum began to fill with bloody victims, resuming the hospital role it had had during the Civil War following the April 1862 Battle of Shiloh. The wounded were tended by Oxford's Dr. L. G. Hopkins, who assumed the duty held a century earlier by Dr. Isom. Although the riot was hardly the Armageddon predicted by Faulkner as a result of blacks' immediate demand for civil rights, two persons were killed, and 166 marshals, 48 soldiers, and 20 students were treated for wounds. One estimate placed the total number of persons injured at more than 350.[21]

The primary unknown as to the outcome of the confrontation at Oxford was the Mississippi National Guard. Promptly after the riot began, President Kennedy ordered the closest Mississippi National Guard units to reinforce the federal marshals, who were about to be overrun. John and Robert Kennedy and Nicholas Katzenbach wondered if the National Guard would actually respond and confront a mob composed mostly of fellow Mississippians. The first unit to arrive at the campus was Troop E of the 108th Armored Cavalry Regiment at Oxford. The unit was commanded by Captain Murry C. Falkner, the thirty-three-year-old nephew of the writer. Murry was representative of one of the generations of whites who bore the brunt of the civil rights movement. He was nineteen in 1948 when *Intruder in the Dust* was published. Earlier on the evening of September 30, two guardsmen refused to assist a marshal who came to the Oxford armory for gas masks. Murry Falkner told the guardsmen, "This is a court-martial offense. . . . We're now federal troops. . . . It had better not happen again." There was no opposition when the guardsmen were loaded into trucks. Armed with rifles and pistols, but without ammunition or tear gas, the Mississippi guardsmen were welcomed by the outnumbered federal officers as they filled in among them around the Lyceum. The soldiers were cursed and attacked by the mob, even after they identified themselves as Mississippians. Despite the pain in his left arm, which was broken by a brick thrown at him in front of the Lyceum, Murry remained in command.[22]

All eleven thousand Mississippi National Guardsmen reported for duty, including lieutenant Ross Barnett Jr., the governor's son.[23] When I asked one national guardsman I know his reaction in having to confront fellow Mississippians, he replied, "When people are trying to kill you with bricks, it puts everything in a different perspective." A number of Oxford residents and University of Mississippi students and faculty were glad to see the National Guard and U.S. Army roll into the town and campus and restore order.

Large numbers of soldiers had not been in Oxford since a century before when in August 1864 Union troops under the command of General Andrew Smith burned the courthouse, businesses around the square, and several homes in revenge over their failure to defeat or capture General Bedford Forrest. Ironically, blacks were not principal targets for attacks by whites. The confrontation was one of white against white. No black person was killed or seriously injured. A black woman walked unmolested through a mob. One group of blacks sat in amused patience on their front porches and watched white fight white over "the Negro question,"[24] an issue of contention as old as African American slavery.

The irony continued. The aftermath of the "battle of Oxford" was in certain respects similar to the end of the Civil War. Of the more than three hundred persons arrested or detained, only twenty-five were University of Mississippi students. Despite utterances of treason, sedition, inciting a riot, and murder, most of the three hundred were released for lack of evidence. None of the twelve who were charged with insurrection and conspiracy went to trial. Except for eight students who were disciplined by the university for unbecoming conduct, no one was punished. All of the marshals who were injured recovered.[25] No one was charged with murdering either of the two whites who were killed. It is assumed that they were victims of stray bullets fired by marshals, who were armed with .38 caliber pistols.

Faulkner did not live to see the violent confrontation that he anticipated. In June 1962 the writer fell from his horse and injured his back. He began drinking whiskey and taking pain medicine to relieve his agony, initiating a process that had long been his nemesis. On July 5 Estelle and Jimmy Faulkner, his nephew who adopted his spelling of the family name, took him to Wright's Sanitarium at Byhalia. Although Faulkner had been to the sanitarium a number of times, on this trip he did not recover. Officially, on July 6 Faulkner succumbed to heart failure. However, rumors of the exact nature of his death persist. The gossip is fueled in part by family members, including Jimmy, who on more than one occasion stated, "Brother Will had never had any sign of heart trouble."[26]

Faulkner's prediction that the South would be torn apart over integration proved to be as erroneous as his belief that most countries he visited as a goodwill ambassador for the Department of State would soon be communist. The writer's great talent, marvelous body of literature, and Nobel Prize did not make him an infallible prophet of national and world events. Contrary to popular belief, the majority of white southerners, and even white Mississippians, were not hard-bitten racists who would "go to any length and against all odds . . . to justify and . . . defend segregation." Only about one-fourth of white southerners were. Opposing them were one-third of the southern whites who were either liberal or moderate and who supported, or did not oppose, integration. The eventual outcome of the civil rights encounter, however, depended on the "large majority," about 40 percent of white southerners. During the confrontation stage of the civil rights movement in the 1960s, most members of the large majority were unwilling to let the South "wreck and ruin itself . . . over the Negro question," and sided with the moderates and liberals.[27] According to William Doyle in his thorough, award-winning study of the 1962 crisis at Oxford, "the vast majority of white Mississippians, when forced to choose between a full-scale revolt and obeying the law, chose law and order." Among the messengers of peace were the eleven thousand Mississippi National Guardsmen, several hundred of whom risked their lives to help restore peace in the largely forgotten riot at Oxford.[28]

Faulkner may have been led to his dismal predictions by his prolonged periods of relative isolation in Oxford and Charlottesville, which at the time were two small southern university towns where there was no escape from constant discussion of what would happen if the segregation barriers were suddenly removed. James Silver's *Mississippi: The Closed Society* is a discussion of the defiant anti-integration and anti–federal government atmosphere that prevailed in Oxford and Mississippi during the 1950s and early 1960s. And, paradoxically, both Silver and his book were products of the paranoia. Under Barnett, the Mississippi State Sovereignty Commission quickly focused on collecting information on Silver and other Mississippians who repeatedly criticized the governor and state legislature and supported the admission of blacks to the white colleges and universities. Because its publication in 1964 corresponded with the disappearance of three civil rights workers during Mississippi Freedom Summer, Silver's book quickly became a best seller for the unknown historian, who had been at the University of Mississippi since 1936 without any distinguished published scholarship. Silver asserts that white Mississippians are a distinct, homogenous, backward people. Their uniformity of thought extends beyond race, even to fondness for white and cream-colored cars. "This, then, is the essence of the closed society. For whatever reason, the community sets up the orthodox view. Its people are constantly indoctrinated—not a difficult task, since they are inclined to the accepted creed by circumstance. . . . With a substantial challenge from the outside . . . the society tightly closes its ranks, becomes inflexible and stubborn, and lets no scruple, legal or ethical, stand in the way of the enforcement of the orthodoxy." In his "Letters from the Closed Society," Silver advises one of his children to "read the various *New York Times* accounts of everything because they are more informative than everything else." Ironically, Turner Catledge, a graduate of Mississippi State University and a native of Neshoba County, where the three civil rights workers were murdered, was the managing editor of the *New York Times*.[29]

Through his novels, public letters, and speeches, Faulkner was among a small number of white southerners who wrote and spoke about giving equal rights to blacks. His works are filled with the "struggle with his own conscience and the conscience of the South" over race. Also, Faulkner is more widely read by south-erners than is often believed. Among the Mississippi National Guardsmen and the U.S. Army regulars were men who knew Faulkner's literature. In a convoy of military police that rolled into Oxford at 4:00 a.m. on October 1, 1962, near the end of the night of rioting, was William Parris, a specialist fourth class who was born in Virginia. Upon seeing the courthouse and the square filled with soldiers, he wondered what the writer would have thought of the spectacle.[30]

Critics continue to speculate about how Faulkner would have responded to the impending crisis at the University of Mississippi and to the riot. One critic believes that "he probably would have seen [it] as the tragic result of increased meddlesome federal intervention."[31] I believe that Faulkner's response would have been quite different. A few days before his death and a few weeks before the riot, Faulkner placed the blame for the impending crisis where it belonged, on the conniving Governor Ross Barnett, whom the writer thought was elected largely by persons similar to those in Yoknapatawpha County's Beat Four. Faulkner viewed the crisis in the context of his life's work, a continuation of the historic confrontation between southern planter and business elites and poor whites. When he was asked, a few days before his death, if there would be trouble over the enrollment of James Meredith, the writer responded, "If we do, it will be because of the people out in Beat Two who never went to the University or never intended to send their children to the University." Asked how Barnett was elected governor, Faulkner answered, "Eighty-two Beat Twos," that is, voters in Mississippi's eighty-two counties.[32]

Most of the inhabitants of places like Beat Two are not sophisticated or well educated enough to comprehend the charades of southern politicians and fall prey to demagogues such as Barnett. A "nigger" was to be enrolled in the state university, and the governor of Mississippi in an address on television and radio had called on white citizens to prevent it. Faulkner would have seen irony in the Meredith affair; it was similar to the theme of *Intruder in the Dust*. A black man was going to be lynched in Oxford, not Jefferson, by people from Beat Two, not fictional Beat Four, but there were no imaginary Chick Mallisons, Miss Habershams, or Gavin Stevenses to prevent it, only Falkners, other members of prominent families, and the Mississippi National Guard. Had Faulkner lived, despite being beyond what Joseph Blotner terms "the public man stage 1953–1957," he probably would have responded to Barnett's September 13 speech with public letters to the Memphis *Commercial Appeal*, a Scripps Howard regional newspaper that circulates over the northern half of Mississippi. At the least, Faulkner's letters would have stimulated more serious public discussion over Meredith's enrollment, which might have reduced the size of or prevented the mob in Oxford. At best, the letters might have motivated Mississippi officials to have persuaded Barnett to send more highway patrol officers to Oxford on September 30 and to give them specific orders to aid federal officials in keeping the peace on the university campus and in Oxford.

In sarcastically arguing the futility of northerners' appeasing blacks with additional federal legislation in *Intruder in the Dust*, Gavin Stevens is wrong, but he is prophetic. By 1962 the civil rights movement had been under way for almost a decade. In Mississippi and other parts of the Deep South the movement had achieved only token desegregation of schools and had made little headway in obtaining unrestricted voting rights for blacks. After extension of the civil rights movement into the rural and small-town plantation South, beginning in 1961 in Mississippi, blacks finally achieved federal legislation that they sought.[33] The Oxford riot and other racial incidents in the South motivated President Lyndon Johnson to propose the 1964 Civil Rights Act and the 1965 Voting Rights Act. Congress passed the legislation and brought to blacks the second and final freedom. The sweeping 1964 Civil Rights Act abolished segregation in all facilities and places that served the public, and the 1965 Voting Rights Act restored the ballot to disfranchised blacks.[34] Speaking to the nation, but primarily to white southerners, upon signing the 1965 Voting Rights Act President Johnson used language strikingly interlaced with Faulknerian-type phrases:

It is difficult to fight for freedom. But I also know how difficult it can be to bend long years of habit and custom to grant it. There is not room for injustice anywhere in the American mansion. But there is always room for understanding toward those who see the old ways crumbling. And to them today I say simply this: It must come. It is right for it to come. And when it has, you will find that a burden has been lifted from your shoulders too. It is not just a question of guilt, although there is that. It is that men cannot live with a lie and not be stained by it.[35]

A Better Man

Faulkner realized that he could not fully overcome in life that which certain of his characters were able to surmount in fiction. In *Intruder in the Dust*, despite Chick Mallison's attempt to make Lucas Beauchamp a "nigger," he demonstrates that his racial attitude and tolerance go beyond his Uncle Gavin's. Faulkner thought that he could do nothing to change Gavin Stevens, but young Chick is sensitive and malleable. According to Faulkner, Stevens "was a good man but he didn't succeed in living up to his ideal. But his nephew, the boy, I think he may grow up to be a better man than his uncle. I think he may succeed as a human being."[36]

An Oxford boy who was sixteen in 1948 would have been in his twenties in the mid-1950s. He would have had to make a decision about whether or not to join the

Citizens' Council, the white-collar racist organization that fought desegregation and equal rights in the courts and through punitive economic retribution against blacks. Under Governor Ross Barnett, the Citizens' Council contributed to racial turmoil and briefly assumed control of Mississippi's government, giving the State Sovereignty Commission secret police powers. Eventually, the Citizens' Council resorted directly and indirectly to violence. A man the age of Chick also would have to confront the lynching of fourteen-year-old Emmett Till in Tallahatchie County in 1955, the assassination of NAACP representative Medgar Evers in Jackson in 1961, and the murder of three civil rights workers in Neshoba County at the beginning of 1964 Mississippi Freedom Summer. In the fall of 1962, a man the age of Chick Mallison in 1948, would have been thirty. As a member of the Mississippi National Guard, he would have gone onto the Ole Miss campus to restore order, corralling and arresting fellow Mississippi whites who resorted to mob violence.

The children of persons the approximate age of Chick were the first generation of whites to attend Mississippi public schools with blacks. Parents had the choice of the integrated public schools or private schools, many of which were hastily organized when massive desegregation finally came to Mississippi public schools during the winter of 1970.[37] The public school systems of Oxford and Lafayette County were among the few in Mississippi that did not experience massive white flight. In 1990 the Oxford public school system had 2,702 students, 49 percent of whom were blacks. Because of interregional migration of blacks from Lafayette County to cities and intraregional migration within the county from rural areas to Oxford, blacks comprised only 39 percent of the 2,070 students in the Lafayette County school system.[38] During the first decade of the twenty-first century, the second generation of whites was attending the integrated Oxford and Lafayette County school systems, and blacks had access to public places and to a considerable range of jobs not open to them in 1962 when Faulkner died. In the late 1960s blacks began to be elected to public offices in the South. Although most held minor offices, by 1990 Mississippi had the largest number of black elected officials in the nation.[39]

It took more than a quarter of a century for the University of Mississippi to recover from the 1962 riot. Both students and faculty fled the institution. By the end of the 1962–1963 academic year thirty-seven faculty members had resigned. The university lost most of the Chemistry Department and the entire faculty of the Philosophy Department.[40] Memphis State University, now the University of Memphis, benefited from the disaster at Ole Miss. In addition to a number of students who were permitted to transfer from the University of Mississippi and register late for the 1962 fall semester, Memphis State gained the dean of its new College of Engineering, its first geologist, and several other faculty members.[41]

A decade after the Ole Miss riot, the campus, even to the football uniforms, depicted neglect and loss of pride. By the beginning of the twenty-first century, the university was well into recovery. Buildings had been renovated and new ones constructed. The general appearance of the campus had improved. An increasing number of blacks followed James Meredith and enrolled at Ole Miss. The university also began to actively recruit blacks. Not without much debate and protest, Confederate flags, which began to appear in increasing numbers after the 1954 Supreme Court *Brown* decision, began to disappear from the campus, even from football games. The contributions of the university to the Confederate cause began to be deemphasized without removal of campus symbols of the role of the university in the Civil War. The stained glass windows in the old library to the memory and sacrifice of the Confederate Greys are protected by transparent sheets of plastic, and the monument of the Confederate scout with his eyes shaded by his hand, looking and waiting for a Union army, still greets visitors arriving at the main entrance to the campus. However, little is said in university brochures about symbols of the Lost Cause. Ole Miss, which endured until after the civil rights movement as the last major unvanquished southern university, increasingly looks beyond the past, beyond the distant gaze of the Confederate soldier toward the world.

On September 30 and October 1, 2006, forty-four years after the riot, an aging James Meredith was invited back to the university from which he was the first black to earn a degree. A bronze statue of Meredith was unveiled, dedicated to his brave role in the history of the university. In his remarks, Meredith quoted Faulkner's well-known reckoning of the past, the present, and the future. "Tomorrow is just another name for today. . . . But tomorrow is today also. Yao. Tomorrow is today."[42]

TEN

Faulkner's Geographical Legacy

William Faulkner was hardly the first writer and not the last to create fictional places based on actual ones. What sets Faulkner apart from most creators of place is the depth and complexity of his Yoknapatawpha saga, combined with the thin but opaque veil between the apocryphal and the actual. A crucial turning point in Faulkner's career came with his realization that the stories he based on the local ordinary were not only interesting original creations but were accepted by some of the best literary critics as innovative and challenging fiction. One of Faulkner's most frequently quoted utterances concerning his awareness of the depth of his geographical creation is in his important 1956 interview for Malcom Cowley's *Writers at Work*. "Beginning with *Sartoris* I discovered that my own little postage stamp of native soil was worth writing about . . . and by sublimating the actual into apocryphal I would have complete liberty to use whatever talent I might have to its absolute top."[1] This articulation is both revealing and canceling.

Geographically, Faulkner's stories do not fully define his "little postage stamp of native soil." Compilations of all of Faulkner's descriptions of Jefferson and Yoknapatawpha are not constructions of a complete town and an entire county. On the other hand, Faulkner depicts Yoknapatawpha as an entity that is not just part of the South but a place in America and the world. In *Sanctuary* Faulkner conveys a sardonic cultural bond between the decaying plantation of deceased Louis Grenier and Paris. The story of Temple Drake opens at the abandoned big house "known as the Old Frenchman place, built before the Civil War." The plantation dwelling is a "gutted ruin rising gaunt and stark out of a grove of unpruned cedar trees." The place is located not just in an isolated area of the rural South but in a remote part of Yoknapatawpha County. The conclusion of *Sanctuary* is set in the Luxembourg Gardens of Paris. Faulkner probably composed the short piece with which he ends the novel as a descriptive fragment written while in Paris in 1925. He wrote Aunt Bama that he lived "just around the corner from the Luxembourg Gardens. . . . I write there, and play with the children, help them sail their boats."[2] The urban gardens with "the pool and the opposite semicircle of trees where at sombre intervals the dead tranquil queens in stained marble mused" are about as distant in setting and culture from the remote area of rural Yoknapatawpha County, Mississippi, as one could get in first-world countries in 1931. Although both places are in first-world countries, Frenchman's Bend seems third world compared to the high first-world culture of Paris and the Luxembourg Gardens. Nevertheless, Paris is joined to Yoknapatawpha not just by a deceased Frenchman's overgrown plantation but by affluent southerners who knew both places.

Some fiction writers, such as James A. Michener and John Steinbeck, conduct research for their fiction, but others, including Faulkner, do little formal investigation.[3] Faulkner tossed out many letters but saved ones he considered significant. In addition, he preserved most of his holograph and typed manuscripts, realizing their value, and he gave a number of interviews. However, Faulkner left no autobiography, autobiographical novel, or lengthy journal that would give more complete insights into how he found and kneaded his material and conducted his writing. Also, Faulkner never wrote what he called his "last book . . . the Doomsday Book, the Golden Book, of Yoknapatawpha County" after which he would "break the pencil and . . . have to stop." "The Golden Book of Jefferson and Yoknapatawpha County in Mississippi" was an idea that emerged in 1932. Faulkner began the book with a five-page biography of John Sartoris, then set it aside. The Golden Book idea reemerged thirteen years later in Faulkner's correspondence with Malcolm Cowley. In response to Cowley's 1945 letter saying, "It's gone through, there will be a Viking Portable Faulkner," an exuberant Faulkner wrote, "By all means let us make a Golden Book of my apocryphal county." *The Portable Faulkner*, however, was not the Golden Book. The Golden Book, a project for Faulkner's "old age," was an illusion that always lay beyond the writer's immediate horizon.[4]

At the time of his unexpected death in 1962 at age sixty-four, Faulkner had no plans to stop writing (fig. 10.1). He was in the process of committing himself to Random House for future novels to obtain money with which to buy Red Acres, a farm near Jill and her family in Charlottesville, Virginia. Faulkner did not plan to sell Rowan Oak, which he deeded to Jill on her twenty-first birthday.[5]

Ken Ringle was an undergraduate student and a library assistant at the University of Virginia during the time Faulkner was a writer-in-residence in 1957–1958. Ringle, curious about how Faulkner researched and wrote, later confessed:

> Stalking him for clues became a passion. Once, on my job shelving books at Alderman Library, I borrowed the key to the room in the stacks where he wrote. He'd just finished *The Mansion* and I thought the pictures on the wall, the books he used for reference, his general writing environment would give me clues on how to be a writer.
>
> I found the answer, but not the one I expected. The room was absolutely bare. There was nothing in it but one of the library's standard oak tables and a chair, an

Figure 10.1. William Faulkner on the lawn of the University of Virginia, probably in the winter of 1958. Faulkner continued to publish and to live an active life after he turned sixty. His death occurred without warning at age sixty-four in July 1962. Special Collections, University of Virginia Library.

upright Underwood typewriter and a big stack of writing paper. Nothing else. No books, no pictures or posters on the wall, no jottings, no comfy sweaters, not even a dictionary. It was all in his *head*.[6]

One of Faulkner's most revealing statements about how he worked discloses that some of his best stories originated with landscape images. "With me a story usually begins with a single idea or memory or mental picture. The writing of the story is simply a matter of working up to that moment, to explain why it happened or what it caused to follow." *The Sound and the Fury* "began with the picture of the little girl's [Caddy's] muddy drawers, climbing that tree to look in the parlor window with her brothers that didn't have the courage to climb the tree waiting to see what she saw." Faulkner envisioned the Snopes trilogy "at once like a bolt of lightning lights up a landscape and you see everything."[7]

Faulkner and the Natural Landscape

Faulkner's fiction is filled with vivid descriptions of the natural landscape that are accurate to north Mississippi. Most of his accounts of the physical environment consist of short but poignant phrases. The area north of Jefferson is "upland country, lying in tilted slopes against the unbroken blue of the hills . . . the road descended sheerly into a valley of good broad fields." In 1860, just after initial settlement, Eugene Hilgard described the same area as "fine cotton uplands lying between the creeks forming the immediate confluents of the Tallahatchie, in N. W. Lafayette."[8] Because a sudden change can occur from warm to cold days, late autumn is a time in north Mississippi that can seem the coldest of the year. Faulkner captures a dark, cold day in the phrase "a slow drizzle of November rain just above the ice point." And a local philosopher in a rural store might be heard to pronounce his view of the weather in terms similar to Dr. Peabody's: "[T]he one trouble with this country: everything, weather, all, hangs on too long."[9]

Shelby Foote witnessed Faulkner's keen grasp of the natural landscape. On a Sunday in April 1952, Foote stopped at Rowan Oak and asked Faulkner if he would like to accompany him to Shiloh for commemoration of the ninetieth anniversary of the battle. Foote had meticulously studied the geography of battlefields for his trilogy on the American Civil War. That day in April he observed Faulkner's careful analysis of the contours of Shiloh battlefield and quick comprehension of what to some historians and military strategists is a confusing topography. Foote succinctly proclaimed, "He had a good eye for terrain." Foote told Faulkner that once he picked up a stick about the size and weight of a Civil War musket and "went charging up and down gulleys" [sic] to see what it was like to have been a soldier. Faulkner replied, "That's just the way I do it. You did right."[10]

Summers in north Mississippi are long, hot, and humid, and winters are cool to cold and wet. Days when temperatures rise above 90 degrees Fahrenheit are common from June into September, and temperatures over 100 degrees are not unusual in July, August, and early September. Much of the rain in the summer is from local convectional showers and the passage of an occasional cold front or warm front. Before air-conditioning became common in homes after 1960 and in motor vehicles, tractors, and mechanical cotton pickers after 1970, persons lay awake on hot, humid summer nights hoping that distant thunder meant that a convectional shower with its downdraft of cool air, or perhaps even a cool front, was approaching. Cotton farmers worry about unusually cool temperatures in summer rather than very hot ones. Long, hot days with late afternoon or evening showers are good cotton weather. In *As I Lay Dying* Faulkner accurately describes the passage of an especially severe cold front across north Mississippi in July with unusually heavy rain that caused the Yoknapatawpha River to flood. "The sun, an hour above the horizon, is poised like a bloody egg upon a crest of thunderheads; the light has turned copper: in the eye portentous, in the nose sulphurous, smelling of lightning."[11] Light the color of copper and the sun the color of a bloody egg, which means that one can look directly at it, are the result of dust, usually from the Great Plains, in the upper atmosphere. No mention is made in *As I Lay Dying* of a hurricane, but hurricanes downgraded to tropical storms, which occasionally move inland from the Gulf of Mexico, can produce an excess of precipitation, especially if the rain is accompanied by high winds. A summer deluge so great that it overflows the Yocona, Tallahatchie, and other streams usually results from a hurricane that has moved inland from the Gulf. The military events associated with General Smith's invasion of Lafayette County and General Forrest's feint raid on Memphis in August 1864 were conducted in heavy rain that persisted over several days. General James R. Chambers, Confederate Army, reported from Oxford on August 20, "Rains every day, roads terrible, and streams swollen."[12]

Critics have long speculated over what Faulkner means by the title *Light in August* for one of his best novels. He was asked at the University of Virginia, "Is it true . . . the title *Light in August* came from a colloquialism for the completion of a pregnancy." The question referred to a myth that because August is so hot, women in the South plan pregnancies so that babies are born before August. Faulkner's response, "No, I used it because in my country in August there's a peculiar quality to light and that's what the title means," is a contrived answer. A few months later Faulkner concocted a different answer.

> About the middle of the month when suddenly there's a foretaste of fall, its cool, there's a lambence, a luminous quality to the light, as though it came not from just today but from back in the old classic times. It might have been fauns and satyrs and the gods and—from Greece, from Olympus in it somewhere. It lasts just for a day or two, then it's gone, but every year in August that occurs in my country, and that's all that title meant.[13]

According to Joseph Blotner, Faulkner was searching for a title for the novel, and his working title, "The Dark House," did not seem appropriate. While sitting on the east gallery late one afternoon, Estelle commented, "Bill, does it ever seem to you that the light in August is different from any other time of the year?" "That's it," responded Faulkner. Without explanation he went into the house. On his manuscript he marked through the title "Dark House" and wrote "Light in August."[14] For his amusement, Faulkner initially told Hal Smith and others who inquired about the title that in the South a pregnant woman anticipated her delivery before the hottest days of summer and said that she wanted to be "light in August." Eventually Faulkner admitted that the title has nothing to do with the content of the novel. However, near the end of *Light in August* the lonely Reverend Hightower has the recurring twilight vision in which the orange light at the end of day is combined with his remembrance of his life's scope.[15]

One of Faulkner's great geographical legacies is his disturbing interpretation of the destruction of the natural environment, from the vanishing virgin wilderness to soil erosion. Destruction of the wilderness in the Yazoo Delta has continued since Faulkner's death. Meander scars and oxbow lakes formed by the Mississippi River and its tributaries as their channels shifted are among the final vestiges of the wilderness. These important small ecological areas are the last to be drained and placed in cotton, soybeans, rice, and catfish ponds. In remaining oxbow lakes and meander scars vegetation is killed by grass and weed herbicides, which in 1962 were in their initial stages of use in American agriculture. The chemicals wash from surrounding fields into the basins. Destruction of the hardwood forests, the dominant indigenous vegetation of north Mississippi, has been especially devastating. Mississippians and Americans are rapidly losing their great heritage of hardwoods because timber companies, the U.S. Forest Service, and university schools of forestry promote rapidly growing pine. Much of the land in the Loess Plains that was open fields and pastures at the beginning of the Second World War is now pine. Superficially, this would seem a restoration of wilderness, but the land is planted primarily in loblolly pine, a tree that is not native to north Mississippi. Also, trees often are planted in unnatural rows parallel to north–south and east–west property boundaries that follow the U.S. rectilinear survey lines.

Control of the severe soil erosion that Faulkner described is a positive change in the natural environment. Serious control of erosion began in the 1930s as part of Franklin Roosevelt's New Deal. Even many of the deep gullies have been bulldozed over or are hidden by pine and kudzu. Hailed in Faulkner's day as a solution to erosion, kudzu is now regarded as a weed that is out of control and does little to prevent soil loss.

Small mammals and reptiles native to north Mississippi, including rabbits and squirrels and snakes, are abundant. The deer population has recovered almost to historic levels. Sightings of panthers, and even bears, are continually reported. Bears are being reintroduced into certain wilderness areas of Mississippi, but despite repeated alleged sightings and stories of phantom panthers, the animals probably have vanished from north Mississippi.

Since Faulkner's death, new challenges to the natural environment have emerged, including the arrival of fire ants, coyotes, and armadillos in Lafayette County. The coyotes have diminished quail, or bobwhite, which Faulkner hunted during the winter. Coveys have been driven from fields to gardens, orchards, and yards of houses in seeking protection from the wily predators. Illustrating the confusion over amelioration of the natural environment is *National Geographic*'s 2006 map of unconfirmed sightings of the big, beautiful black, white, and red Lord-to-God bird in the Tallahatchie River valley in 1988, the Yazoo Delta in 1987 and 1988, and the Pearl River valley in 1999 and 2005. However, the ivory-billed woodpecker may really be extinct, for it can be confused with the similar pileated woodpecker.[16]

Faulkner and the Cultural Landscape

Because most of his fiction is set in the New South era, another of Faulkner's great geographical legacies is vivid descriptions of people, places, objects, and actions that have vanished. Through powerful descriptions he demonstrates that the ordinary, seemingly insignificant, has meaning. Prior to Faulkner's death, the influence of his literature began to move beyond narrow literary criticism, helping to sway social and political events. After Faulkner was awarded the 1949 Nobel Prize for Literature, his stories were included in more college and high school textbooks, and his novels appeared more frequently on literature course reading lists. Students had the opportunity to venture beyond the gothic "A Rose for Emily," the Faulkner story frequently included in anthologies.

Faulkner is regarded as one of the authorities on the cotton plantation South. For many white and even some black southerners, he provides their first journeys into that world. As strange as it may seem, millions of white southerners live in a largely blackless South, and a number of blacks live in isolated rural and urban communities where they have little contact with a variety of whites. In the Upland South, most whites have essentially no acquaintance or only passing contact with blacks. At the opposite extreme, until well into the twentieth century, most of the nation's blacks were trapped and isolated in the rural plantation regions. Blacks knew only the paternalism and/or harshness of whites under whose control they remained long after they were legally free from thralldom. The early efforts of the civil rights movement were deliberately conducted in cities where boycotts, marches, attempts to desegregate public places, and confrontations with white mobs and police were covered by the media, especially television. Into the early 1960s Martin Luther King Jr. and other influential civil rights leaders believed that campaigns in towns, small cities, and the rural countryside would attract little media attention or notice by the president and Congress. However, not until the early 1960s, when the struggle was taken into the small towns and rural South, led by the Student Nonviolent Coordinating Committee (SNCC), did the reality of blacks' segregation and lack of voting rights begin to be fully comprehended at the national level. Places such as McComb and Neshoba County, Mississippi, and Camden and Selma, Alabama, became landmarks in the civil rights struggle.[17]

James Rufus Agee, a contemporary of Faulkner, although twelve years younger, was from Knoxville, Tennessee, in the Upland South. In 1938, as he and Walker Evans headed toward Alabama and destiny to research a story on sharecroppers for *Fortune*, Agee admitted in his journal that he "knew little or nothing about the cotton country . . . beyond some passages in Faulkner." Agee and Evans were not fully prepared for the social, racial, and economic conditions they encountered in the Lowland South of Alabama. Their naivete caused inclusion of seemingly insignificant details and personal confessions in the innovative *Let Us Now Praise Famous Men*, the documentary book that was written from material for the sharecropper story that *Fortune* refused. A quarter of a century later, guileless young urban blacks and whites, who took the civil rights movement into the rural plantation South, were equally unprepared for the conditions they met.[18]

Faulkner's life and work, like Agee's, overlapped in varying degrees with those of Tennessee Williams, Eudora Welty, Erskine Caldwell, Thomas Wolfe, Flannery O'Connor, Carson McCullers, Richard Wright, Robert Penn Warren, and Lillian Smith. All presented a South different from the one most people perceived. Many southerners considered these writers' stories to be derogatory and false, even though they daily observed, but apparently did not grasp, the people, places, and conditions of which the authors wrote. Creative writers' revelation of a South that most Americans did not see is what C. Vann Woodward meant when he advised historians to take "heart . . . from the example set by Southern men of letters. . . . great novelists often wrote about the obscure, the provincial, the eccentric, the tormented, and the humble—the uncelebrated."[19]

But the South's great writers of fiction were not alone in fathoming the lower depths of the realm. Led by Howard Odum at the University of North Carolina, a detailed revisionist picture of the South from geographical and sociological perspectives began to emerge during the 1930s. Arthur Raper, Ralph J. Bunche, Thomas Jackson Woofter, Charles Johnson, John Dollard, Hortense Powdermaker, and Rupert Vance are among the revisionist interpreters of the South who created a new professional research literature. Also, journalists such as Wilbur Cash and Jonathan Daniels wrote important books that presented amended versions of the South. Another significant work is *An American Dilemma: The Negro Problem in America*, by Gunnar Myrdal, a foreigner. Myrdal's analysis was among the evidence that convinced the U.S Supreme Court that separate schools for blacks in the South were not equal to those of whites and that under the U.S. Constitution segregated schools should be abolished. In the 1950s Woodward began to take the interpretation of southern history into confronting and exposing contemporary problems, what Robert Penn Warren meant when he admonished southerners to "'accept the past and its burden' without evasion or defensiveness or special pleading."

Woodward led the way for historians with *The Strange Career of Jim Crow*, which exposed the myth that blacks and whites in the South had always been segregated by law.[20] Ironically, the most revealing visual documentation of economic, social, political, and geographical conditions in the South at the time Faulkner was at his creative apogee came from the most conservative of federal agencies, the U.S. Department of Agriculture. During the Great Depression an underpaid staff of photographers from the Farm Security Administration moved across the southern and other landscapes of the nation to document what novelists, educators, and journalists described. Under the direction of Roy Stryker, the group included Marion Post Wolcott, Dorothea Lange, Walker Evans, Arthur Rothstein, Jack Delano, and Russell Lee.[21]

Faulkner's work stands apart from both the fiction and nonfiction of his contemporaries in its power of expression. His power of expression, more than his material, distinguishes it. Shelby Foote believed that what Faulkner "does superbly" and "quite possibly . . . the thing that will last longest about Faulkner's writing—is his uncanny and highly artistic ability to communicate sensation." Foote cites as an example Faulkner's ability to convey the sensation of what it is like for a boy to fall into a creek of ice water in November, including the feel of his clothes as he scrambles up the bank.[22]

Faulkner's ability to convey sensation extends to odors, which often are overlooked but are very much a part of the geography of a place and the persons who inhabit it. When asked by a student at the University of Virginia about his various uses of "smell" in *Sartoris* and *The Unvanquished*, Faulkner seemed taken aback by the question. His initial response was, "I can't say unless smell is one of my sharper senses. . . . There's no reason, there's certainly no deliberate intent." Faulkner added that smell is "a part of the environment which the writer is trying to describe."[23] Faulkner opens the Yoknapatawpha chronicles in *Sartoris* with a distinctive fragrance. Eighty-four-year-old Will Falls, who lives at the county poor farm, brings the deceased John Sartoris into Jefferson's Merchants and Farmers Bank "like an odor, like the clean dusty smell of his faded overalls, the spirit of the dead man." Faulkner closes the narratives with a unique blend of odors. At the end of *The Reivers*, a crying Lucius Priest is comforted by his grandfather. Lucius remembers, "I could smell him—the starch and shaving lotion and chewing tobacco . . . and always a faint smell of whiskey."[24]

Between *Sartoris* and *The Reivers* Faulkner liberally employs aromas to convey mood, personality, and culture. Jason Compson IV's furnish store for farm tenants in Jefferson, like similar stores across the rural and small-town New South, is "a cavern . . . rank with the blended smell of cheese and kerosene and harness oil and the tremendous iron stove against which chewed tobacco had been spat for almost a hundred years."[25] Faulkner's unconstrained description of the odor of poor rural blacks is employed in *Intruder in the Dust* to reveal the secluded shackles between whites and blacks. After Lucas Beauchamp extracts young Chick Mallison from the cold water of Nine-Mile Branch, he takes the boy to his house to dry his clothes and to warm him. Chick is

> enveloped in the quilt like a cocoon, enclosed completely now in that unmistakable odor of Negroes—that smell which if it were not for something that was going to happen to him within a space of time measurable now in minutes he would have gone to his grave never once pondering speculating if perhaps that smell were really not the odor of a race nor even actually of poverty but perhaps of a condition. . . . He had smelled it forever, he would smell it always; it was a part of his inescapable past, it was a rich part of his heritage as a Southerner; he didn't even have to dismiss it, he just no longer smelled it at all as the pipe smoker long since never did smell at all the cold pipereek which is as much a part of his clothing as their buttons and buttonholes.[26]

Faulkner and Three Towns, Three Counties

When intensely researching the relationship of Faulkner's Jefferson and Yoknapatawpha County to local reality, one must deal with three towns and three counties: the writer's fictional town and county, the historic Oxford and Lafayette County as they existed until the end of Faulkner's life in 1962, and the Oxford and Lafayette County of the present, which are quite different from the town and county the writer knew.[27]

Faulkner, together with his critics, viewed his stories as universal. But are the stories so universal that they are independent of place and time? How vital is the local, the ordinary? Must one comprehend the geography and history of Oxford and Lafayette County of Faulkner's time in order to consummately interpret Faulkner's stories? Cleanth Brooks, among the originators of modern literary criticism, gives an incisive answer to the question. Brooks denounces a type of interpretation that had emerged by the time of Faulkner's death in 1962. "The excessive literalism which converts the fictional into factual events and thus yields 'sociology' is a counterpart of the misguided yearning for universal meanings which produces the perversities of symbol-mongering. Some knowledge of how life is actually lived (and has been lived) in Mississippi would have prevented the writing of much nonsense."[28]

Faulkner could be volatile in discussing his writing. Some of his curt answers to questions about symbolism in his stories seem to support Brooks's approach to criticism. At times, Faulkner left the impression that no hidden meaning lay beyond what he actually wrote. While Faulkner was a writer-in-residence at the University of Virginia, a question-and-answer session between him and Virginia college representatives proceeded toward a sudden conclusion with the second question. Faulkner was asked if the title of *Pylon* refers to Laverne, around whom all the men gravitated, rather than an airplane race marker. Faulkner erupted, "Now there's some more of this erudite professorial symbolism [that] gets into everything. I'm sure that you're quite right. I just hadn't thought of that. I'm glad to know it."[29] This cynical answer about symbolism came from a writer who used *apocrypha* in discussing his work and considered a novel about the return of Christ during the First World War to be his major literary accomplishment.

Calvin Brown Jr. takes a middle-of-the-road position on the relationship of the actual to Faulkner's apocrypha. Maud Morrow, Brown's mother, was born shortly after Maud Butler, Faulkner's mother, and was named for her. The Calvin Browns lived next door to the Murry Falkners on the University of Mississippi campus when Murry was registrar and Calvin and Maud were faculty members. Calvin Jr., a Rhodes scholar who earned degrees in English and was head of the Department of Comparative Literature at the University of Georgia, knew both the young Faulkner and Faulkner's work as intimately as any local. At the conclusion of his detailed discussion of the relationship of the geography of Oxford and Lafayette County to that of Jefferson and Yoknapatawpha County, Brown states:

> Enough has been said here to establish clearly the fact that Faulkner habitually thinks of his characters as moving about Oxford and Lafayette County, and that he often uses the local scene effectively and accurately, though he never bows to it pedantically or slavishly. These facts seem well worth establishing and documenting, and they contribute to an understanding of both Faulkner's methods and of his works. But it is also worth insisting that . . . [t]he aesthetic qualities that have made works like *Absalom, Absalom!*, *Light in August*, and *The Sound and the Fury* a part of world literature are ultimately rooted in their universality rather than in their localization.[30]

Literary criticism has advanced beyond the conservative approach advocated by Brooks and occasionally does not even consider the Mississippi settings of Faulkner's stories. Despite a movement by some critics away from consideration of the geography, history, and culture of Oxford, Lafayette County, and Mississippi, eventually one is confronted with the problem that to comprehensively understand Faulkner there has to be an accurate conception of the setting of his stories. It is in grappling with the setting, one encounters not one town and one county but three of each.

The first town and county are the ones that Faulkner created. During the latter part of his life, Faulkner increasingly spoke of his work as his apocrypha. "Apocrypha" is from the Greek *apokryphos*, meaning hidden or obscure. One definition is a written work that has an obscure or shrouded meaning, which can reveal truth through interpretation.[31] This explanation of apocrypha is tied to Faulkner's idea about literature in continual motion. His stories not only are universal, but they are continually new because they are read by successive generations. Interpretations of Faulkner's works are timeless, for each generation finds not only recently revealed truths but fresh interpretations. Faulkner's stories as apocrypha do not conflict with their being fiction, for fiction often can reveal truth better than fact. However, Faulkner's stories cannot move beyond the places to which they are tied by time. Despite what Faulkner said about his apocrypha having life by the assumption of motion, there is a time boundary beyond which Jefferson and Yoknapatawpha cannot move. They are frozen in time. Essentially, objects are fossilized, characters do not die, and fictional events are an invented history. The town and the county are symbolic. They do not exist and never existed in reality. Oxford and Lafayette County may depict some resemblances to the apocryphal places only because they were geographical sources.

The second town and county with which one must deal in a comprehensive understanding of Faulkner's stories are the ones he knew. Since 1962 considerable changes have occurred in Oxford and Lafayette County, not least the deaths of persons who knew Faulkner. According to Calvin Brown Jr., who was born in Oxford in 1909 and lived there until the early 1930s, "only an old-time resident . . . can get the full impact of Jefferson and Yoknapatawpha County."[32] Oxford and Lafayette County of Faulkner's time now largely exist in historical documents. The Lafayette County jail, described by Faulkner like the one in Yoknapatawpha County, survives only in photographs and films (fig. 2.5). A few persons recognized the importance of the relationship of people, places, and local history as Faulkner knew them to a comprehensive understanding of his fiction. Floyd C. Watkins and Sally Wolff of Emory University studied Oxford and Lafayette County from the 1950s through the 1980s, recording interviews with local persons and taking landscape photographs. They discovered that

[t]he vernacular of a place and time is not easily plotted and mapped. The inflections must be heard. . . .

Remnants of old Lafayette County—houses, bridges, country stores—may still be found, though they are now rapidly disappearing. The words of these people and the pictures provide contexts that deepen our knowledge of Faulkner's everyday life and clearly enhance an understanding of the world in which Faulkner lived and of which he wrote. The artifacts that archaeologists unearth become much more significant with an understanding of how, when, and why they were made. Similarly, details about the lives of whites enhance understanding of their achievements.[33]

The third town and county are those of the present. One of Faulkner's most important geographical legacies is his creation of national and international renown for Oxford and Lafayette County, Mississippi. For many outlanders, and even some locals born since 1962, Oxford and Lafayette County, on which Faulkner based his apocryphal places, have become instead his Jefferson and Yoknapatawpha County. The generations are passing away who have firsthand knowledge of the reality that Faulkner transformed into what he came to view as apocryphal places. Most of the contemporary residents of Oxford and Lafayette County are too young to have known Faulkner. Unfortunately, Jimmy and Murry, Faulkner's nephews who were important to the annual summer Faulkner conferences at the University of Mississippi, died just prior to the one in 2004. Other Falkner family members who remember the Oxford and Lafayette County that the writer knew remain, but their number is diminishing. Estelle died in 1972 and Jill in 2008. The day will come when all who were alive during Faulkner's lifetime are gone. Some members of the older generations rejected both Faulkner and his fiction because his stories were too real and struck sensitive self-esteem. However, children and grandchildren, who did not know the reality, are fascinated by Faulkner's apocrypha because, although it is their heritage, they are not parts of the strange, fascinating southern landscape filled with captivating characters.

By 2000 Oxford had grown into an important city of 12,000, and Lafayette County had a population of 38,744. Almost all of the rural inhabitants were non-farm; less than 1 percent lived on farms.[34] Because of the decline of agriculture and traditional methods of farming, businesses that served a largely rural farm population have vanished, replaced by ones that cater to a growing population of the well educated, including students and faculty of the University of Mississippi and a number of retired persons who have moved to Oxford and rural Lafayette County. Not one hardware store remains on Oxford's courthouse square. The city no longer has a cotton gin, a sawmill, or a gristmill. Seed, fertilizer, and garden implements are purchased in Oxford at discount chain stores. For large tractors and other major farm equipment, farmers travel to Batesville, Como, or other nearby towns in counties where agriculture remains more important than in Lafayette. Persons in the Lafayette County countryside make weekly trips to Oxford to shop for groceries at large chain stores. Restaurants increasingly are dominated by fast-food chains that cater primarily to University of Mississippi students as locally owned restaurants continue to vanish. A large detention center replaced the jail (fig. 10.2).

Figure 10.2. The Lafayette County, Mississippi, Detention Center. The center was constructed a block east of the courthouse square in the 1990s and superseded the small county jail built in the 1960s to replace the one described in Faulkner's stories. Charles S. Aiken, 1999.

Younger Mississippians promote Faulkner's legacy. The annual Faulkner summer conferences at the University of Mississippi are attended by persons from foreign countries and various parts of the United States who are joined by local residents. A Center for the Study of Southern Culture might not have been established at the University of Mississippi if Oxford had not been the home of William Faulkner. Now owned by the university, Rowan Oak is a part of the annual Faulkner conference as well as various seminars and institutes held throughout the year (fig. 10.3).

All that remains of north Mississippi as Faulkner knew it is a framework of the streets, towns, roads, and streams speckled with churches, cemeteries, dwellings, and other landscape objects that survive in the face of change. The most enduring landscape features are place-names that Faulkner replicated in his fiction. Names survive, often devoid of the landscape objects they once denoted. Essentially, only a skeleton of Faulkner's Mississippi endures. Also vanished or altered is much of southern culture as Faulkner knew it. The most profound changes are alterations in the biracial segregated society and in race relations, which have greatly improved since 1962. Oxford and Lafayette County have become parts of the modern Sunbelt South, which has a much-improved image over that of the New South era.

Outlanders, and even locals, who visit Oxford and Lafayette County seeking persons and places of Jefferson and Yoknapatawpha County can go too far in readily accepting the fiction for the authentic. As the years pass, historical Oxford–Lafayette County and fictional Jefferson–Yoknapatawpha County gradually blend toward becoming one. This process, the exact reverse of what Faulkner performed,

Figure 10.3. Renovation and restoration of Rowan Oak in 1982. The 1982 renovation was the first of two; the second one was completed in 2004. Although they may appear unchanged, both the interior and exterior of the house are in better condition than they were at the time of Faulkner's death in 1962. Charles S. Aiken.

is well under way and is a prime example of how geography in fiction becomes accepted as spatial reality. Among the initial efforts to convert the fiction into the reality is Robert D. Oesterling's and Evans Harrington's 1965 motion picture *Faulkner's Mississippi: Land into Legend*. Narrated by Joseph Cotton, the film is promoted as one that "transforms the fiction of William Faulkner's mythical Jefferson and Yoknapatawpha into the reality of Oxford and Lafayette County, Mississippi, with quotations from Faulkner's writings correlated with appropriate scenes." In a 1999 article about the preservation of the railroad depot, the *Oxford–Lafayette County Heritage Foundation Newsletter* declared, "Here William Faulkner met the mail trains when he served as postmaster, and he often wrote about railroads in his novels and stories. Horace Benbow in *Sanctuary*, Mink Snopes in *The Mansion*, Joe Christmas in *Light in August*, and many other Faulkner characters are seen at the depot—not at a depot, but at the Oxford Depot" (fig. 10.4).[35] In a 2000 interview Robert Khayat, chancellor of the University of Mississippi, declared that William Faulkner "taught for a while at the University of Virginia and they have a wonder-

Figure 10.4. The renovated Oxford, Mississippi, railroad station in 2007. The relationship of the station
Faulkner's stories was the principal factor that motivated local citizens to save the structure, which
as built by the Mississippi Central Railroad after the Civil War to replace the one burned by Union
ɔops in 1864. Passenger service through Oxford was discontinued by the Illinois Central Railroad in
41. The station and land surrounding it were sold by the railroad when the tracks through Oxford were
moved in the 1990s. Photograph courtesy of Matthew Davis, Oxford Planning Commission.

ful collection of his work there. But we really *have* Yoknapatawpha County, we
really *have* Jefferson."[36]

In the future, transformation of historic Oxford–Lafayette County into fictional
Jefferson–Yoknapatawpha County will be accelerated by more overt commercial-
ization of Faulkner. If this time comes, one may be able to lodge at the Holston
House, eat at the Blue Goose and Dixie cafes, and tour a reconstructed jail. On a
grander scale I can envision on the outskirts of the city creations of the McCaslin
Plantation and Varner's Crossroads complete to its Littlejohn's Hotel. Some perceptive entrepreneurs have already begun to rent preserved sharecropper shacks
to northern and foreign tourists who want to experience "authentic" Mississippi,[37]
with or without air-conditioning.

Faulkner, a private person, would cringe at the carnal establishment and commercial exploitation of his world, when we remember that he believed there is a
better way for it to live. A primary goal for any artist is "to arrest motion, which
is life, by artificial means and hold it fixed so that a hundred years later, when a

stranger looks at it, it moves again."[38] Faulkner is dead, and the reality from which he created the fictional world of Yoknapatawpha County has all but vanished. But that world, almost as complete as any fictional place can be, from its origin in *Sartoris* to the final, romantic backward glance in *The Reivers*, comes to life—with a bittersweet fragrance of nostalgia that stimulates no desire to return in those who intimately knew the reality—each time Faulkner is read.

NOTES

One. Faulkner's Vanishing South

1. Konigsmark 1999.
2. Cullen 1961, 107.
3. L. King 2006, 107–108.
4. Emily Stone, wife of Phil Stone, one of Faulkner's early mentors, explained the relationship between real and fictional persons: "I had unconsciously been looking in Oxford for Faulkner people and never quite finding them. And yet I knew that what he had written was so right. . . . I was puzzled and disappointed because the people I knew were . . . diluted. . . . And it was a long time before I realized that one of the great sources of Faulkner's power as a writer was the very difference between those diluted persons I saw and the Faulkner characters with their qualities of being more driven, absurd, sardonic, more completely Puritan-ruthless concentrations than were the real persons" (1965, 161).
5. Faulkner's Hometown Upset about Statue of Late Author, *Knoxville News-Sentinel* 1997.
6. Faulkner 1942, Typesetting copy of *Go Down, Moses*, in McHaney 1987, 253.

Two. Geographical Fact into Fiction

1. Blotner 1974, 1:20–91.
2. Gibson 1971, 159–162.
3. L. Q. C. Lamar to A. H. Chapell, May 14, 1850, in Mayes 1896; U.S. Census Office 1864a, 206, 232.
4. Miner 1959, 48–55; M. Brown 1954; *Official Records*, ser. 1, vol. 2, part 1, 370–401. For examples of insights into the Civil War and Reconstruction and their meaning in southern history, see Woodward 1960; D. Doyle 2001, 155–326; and essays in Polk and Abadie 2004.
5. Hartje 1967, 247–270.
6. Captain C. T. Biser (Confederate States Army) 1864, *Official Records*, ser. 1, vol. 2, part 1, 400.
7. McPherson 1988, 854–856.
8. The spelling of the name varies. On several nineteenth-century and early twentieth-century maps the river is the Yoknapatawpha. Eugene W. Hilgard referred to it as the "Yockeney-Patafa" (1860, 296).
9. Hilgard 1860, 296, 306–307.
10. Hathorn [1938], 20–23; Hilgard 1884, part 1, 273–278.
11. Discussions of black residential areas created in small southern towns after the Civil War are in Dollard (1937) and Powdermaker (1939), both of whom studied Indianola,

Miss., using the pseudonyms Southerntown and Cottonville. A discussion of the changes in black residential areas of Mississippi towns produced by the civil rights movement and the War on Poverty is in Aiken 1998, 319–339.

12. Blotner 1974, 1:623–624, 657, 681–682, 803.

13. The one-page map in *The Portable Faulkner* is a redrawn version of the folded insert in *Absalom, Absalom!* (Cowley 1946; Faulkner 1936). Cowley asked Faulkner to revise the map so that it could be reproduced on one page. (Malcolm Cowley to Faulkner, November 10, 1945, in Cowley 1966, 56–61).

14. Faulkner *The Town* 1957, 316.

15. Faulkner *Intruder in the Dust* 1948, 35–36.

16. Faulkner *The Hamlet* 1940, 3–5.

17. Faulkner *The Town* 1957, 316–317.

18. Faulkner *The Reivers* 1962, 95.

19. Faulkner *Intruder in the Dust* 1948, 151.

20. Faulkner *The Hamlet* 1940, 196.

21. Faulkner *The Hamlet* 1940, 182; *The Town* 1957, 292. Faulkner's original title for *Sartoris* (1929) was *Flags in the Dust* (1973).

22. Faulkner *The Unvanquished* 1938, 86.

23. C. Brown Jr. 1962, 652. Brown emphasizes that at the time of Faulkner's death in 1962 much of the Oxford and Lafayette County that the writer knew as a child had been obliterated or altered almost beyond recognition.

24. Faulkner *Sartoris* 1929, 165–166.

25. Faulkner *Sartoris* 1929, 165–166; *Intruder in the Dust* 1948, 49; *Requiem for a Nun* 1951, 239–240.

26. C. Brown Jr. 1962, 653.

27. Miner 1959, 86–88; Faulkner *Absalom, Absalom!* 1936, "Jefferson, Yoknapatawpha Co., Mississippi," map insert.

28. Faulkner quoted in Stein 1956, 141.

29. Blotner 1974, 1:544; Faulkner interview, April 19, 1962, in Fant and Ashley 1964, 57.

30. Faulkner to Harold Ober, November 11 [1954]; Faulkner to Dorothy Olding, June 23, 1960, in Blotner 1977, 373, 445. Faulkner also declined the offer from *Life* because he was offended by an article about him that the magazine published.

31. James B. Meriwether, a Faulkner scholar, assisted editors Saxe Commins and Albert Erskine in finding discrepancies between *The Hamlet*, published in 1940, and manuscripts for *The Town* and *The Mansion*, the second and third parts of the Snopes trilogy, published in 1957 and 1959. "I don't know what you need Meriwether for," Faulkner wrote Erskine. "All I know is two: one to read the mss. and galley, that's you, and tell the other what's wrong, that's me. . . . Do you agree that . . . this volume [*The Mansion*] should be the definitive one, others can be edited in subsequent editions to conform" (Faulkner to Albert Erskine [March 1959] in Blotner 1977, 422, 425–426). Faulkner and his editors are inconsistent in the plural of *Snopes*. Usually the plural is "Snopes" rather than "Snopeses."

32. McHaney 1997. Although Faulkner's map is labeled "Jefferson, Yoknapatawpha Co., Mississippi," it is actually a map of the county rather than the town. (Faulkner *Absalom, Absalom!* 1936, map insert).

33. Blotner 1974, 2:186 notes.

34. Hilgard 1860, 296.

35. Faulkner *The Town* 1957, 312.

36. Faulkner [1927], Flags in the Dust manuscript, 21 (typewritten), 6074, Box IA:3, Faulkner Collection, University of Virginia Library; Faulkner *Sartoris* 1929, 24; *Flags in the Dust* 1973, 21–22.

37. C. Brown Jr. 1962, 657.

38. Faulkner *Big Woods* 1955, 70; *The Reivers* 1962, 72; *Intruder in the Dust* 1948, 164.

39. Another dwelling that Faulkner could have used as a model for Compson's Mile was the Stone-Avant house, home of Phil Stone. The house at the northwest edge of Oxford was shifted to the southeast corner of Jefferson. James M. (Jimmy) Faulkner believed that the Thompson-Chandler house on the street east of South Lamar was the model for the Compson house (James M. Faulkner interview in Wolff and Watkins 1996, 45–49, 53).

40. Faulkner *As I Lay Dying* 1930, 79, 99; *The Mansion* 1959, 32. *Sartor* and *sartorius* in *Webster's New World College Dictionary* 1997, 3rd ed. I thank Thomas McHaney for telling me Faulkner's source for "Sartoris." Also see Taylor 1990, 105–108. Faulkner's source for the name Bayard Sartoris may have been Bayard Taylor, an American poet and journalist.

41. M. Brown 1956, 421–439; Blotner 1974, 1:8–50; Faulkner *Sartoris* 1929, 243–293. The writer reinstated the "u" and used "Faulkner" as his pen name, but throughout his life "Falkner" remained his legal one.

42. G. Buckley 1961.

43. Blotner 1974, 1:341, 528; McAlexander 1977.

44. Faulkner interview, April 19, 1962, in Fant and Ashley 1964, 57.

45. Miner 1959, 86–87; Kerr 1969, 28, 54–55, 246; Kerr miscalculates the size of Sutpen's Hundred, indicating it to have been 6,400 rather than 64,000 acres.

46. Faulkner *Absalom, Absalom!* 1936, 34.

47. Young 1961, 114–137.

48. Sectional Index to the Lands in Lafayette County (Section 7, Township 7 South, Range 4 West), Office of the Chancery Clerk, Lafayette County, Oxford, Miss.

49. Young 1961, 131.

50. Faulkner *The Reivers* 1962, 67–95. The episode was published in the March 31, 1962, issue of the *Saturday Evening Post* as the short story "Hell Creek Crossing." Quotations are from *The Reivers*.

51. For details of an actual trip to Memphis along the Memphis-Oxford Road, see M. Falkner 1967, 69–77. My interpretation of the fictional route disagrees with Calvin S. Brown Jr.'s interpretation. Brown incorrectly identifies the road that crossed the Iron Bridge as the Sardis Road (C. Brown Jr. 1971, 8–10).

52. Riley 1902, 5:348–350; J. Stone 1970, 351–352. The importance of the river link of Wyatt to New Orleans by way of the Mississippi, the Yazoo, and the Tallahatchie is illustrated by Lafayette County planters using New Orleans banks. On March 31, 1850, Wesley Harmon paid his son-in-law William H. Cain's bill for $89.35 (approximately $2,680.00 in 2006 dollars) from Hutchings and Wilcox Merchants with a "draft on New Orleans" (Harmon Collection).

53. The right-of-way for the bridge was granted by Florence Childress to Lafayette County, May 3, 1906. Sectional Index to Lands in Lafayette County (Section 7, Township 7 South, Range 4 West), Office of the Chancery Clerk, Lafayette County, Oxford, Miss.

Three. A Place in the American South

1. Vahanian 1964, 93.
2. Cowley 1946, 9; Kerr 1969, 229–230; Muehrcke and Muehrcke 1974, 318; J. Williamson 1993, 11.
3. Woodward 1960, 34; C. Brown Jr. 1976.
4. Pillsbury 1989; Hart 1976; Zelinsky 1992, 117–125; T. Jordan 1967, 1970. My brief descriptions of the Upland and Lowland Souths are sketches of what are really complex regions.
5. Among the articles and books that treat southern Appalachia are Simple 1901; Kephart 1913; Campbell 1921; Stuart 1938; Caudil 1962; Weller 1966; and Batteau 1990.
6. Buckingham 1842, 2:153–160.
7. Olmsted 1860, 257–261.
8. In 1970 no blacks were enumerated in Dawson and Towns counties, Georgia, and only five in Forsyth and twenty-seven in Fannin (U.S. Bureau of the Census 1975, 10–12).
9. Faulkner *The Town* 1957, 316.
10. Ibid.
11. Faulkner *Intruder in the Dust* 1948, 35–36.
12. Faulkner *The Hamlet* 1940, 3–6.
13. Ibid.
14. Faulkner to Malcolm Cowley, [August 16, 1945], in Cowley 1966, 24–27.
15. Faulkner *Requiem for a Nun* 1951, 227.
16. Faulkner *Absalom, Absalom!* 1936, map insert.
17. Faulkner *The Town* 1957, 316–317; *The Hamlet* 1940, 4.
18. Faulkner *A Fable* 1954, 189–190.
19. Faulkner "Mountain Victory" 1932 in *Collected Stories* 1977.
20. Ibid., 753.
21. Faulkner *Absalom, Absalom!* 1936, 17.
22. Ibid., 220–223.
23. Ibid., 224–232.
24. Friis 1968.
25. Faulkner, May 8, 1957, in Gwynn and Blotner 1959, 130–131.
26. Faulkner *Go Down, Moses* 1942, 44–45.
27. Ibid., 5, 9.
28. Faulkner *Absalom, Absalom!* 1936, 36–42; C. Smith 1996, 50–52.
29. Only one of the eighteen chapters in *The South: Its Economic-Geographical Development* (Parkins 1938) treats cities, and fewer than ten of the 511 pages of *Human Geography of the South* (Vance 1935) are devoted to cities. Cities are virtually ignored in most histories of the South written prior to 1990.
30. For example, Richard C. Wade observed that few places in the world have matched the South's pace in urbanization and that its rate has seemed slow only in comparison with that of the North (1970, 43–69).
31. U.S. Bureau of the Census 1933, 15, 22–25; 1960, passim.
32. Faulkner, May 7, 1957, in Gwynn and Blotner 1959, 125.
33. Faulkner *As I Lay Dying* 1930, 61, 219–220, 235; Faulkner *Light in August* 1932, 1–2.
34. Faulkner *The Reivers* 1962, 94–95.
35. Faulkner "Two Soldiers" 1942 in *Collected Stories* 1977, 81.
36. Faulkner *The Mansion* 1959, 388.

37. Faulkner *Sanctuary* 1931, 226–239.

38. Ibid., 228–229.

39. Ibid., 228–233.

40. Faulkner *The Mansion* 1959, 282–293.

41. Ibid., 284–285.

42. Ibid., 285–289.

43. Ibid., 290.

44. *Memphis, Tennessee, Telephone Directory* 1942; *Polk's Memphis City Directory* 1945, 1349–1350.

45. Blotner 1974, 1:838–839.

46. Miller 1964, 212–213; "Police Will Close Disorderly Houses," *Memphis Commercial Appeal*, April 25, 1940, 17.

47. Faulkner *Absalom, Absalom!* 1936, 174.

48. Faulkner, February 15, 1957, in Gwynn and Blotner 1959, 9–10.

49. Faulkner, April 19, 1962, in Fant and Ashley 1964, 50–51.

50. Irwin 1975, 21.

51. Faulkner 1955 in Meriwether and Millgate 1968, 203.

52. Faulkner *Absalom, Absalom!* 1936, map insert; Cowley 1946, inside front cover.

53. Faulkner "Shall Not Perish" 1943 in *Collected Stories* 1977, 99.

Four. Old South

1. Aiken 1998, 10.

2. United States Works Progress Administration (WPA) Federal Writers' Project 1938, 59; Young 1961, 22–46.

3. Dabney 1974, 3.

4. Faulkner "1699–1945 Appendix: The Compsons" in Cowley 1946, 740–741.

5. Hudson 1976, 55–97; Widmer 1994.

6. M. Smith 1994; Dobyns 1983.

7. Gibson 1971, 3–30; Hudson 1976, 94–116; 1997, 436–437; M. Smith 1994, 270; Bartram 1791, 297.

8. C. Brown 1926, 220.

9. Quoted in C. Brown 1926, 119. In 1913 Calvin Brown photographed a fourteen-foot-high mound at Cornish in southeastern Lafayette County. In 1926 the mound was truncated and a new house stood on it (C. Brown 1926, 4–9).

10. Bartram 1791, 265, 297.

11. Wallace 1999, 335–338.

12. Faulkner "A Bear Hunt" 1934 in *Collected Stories* 1977, 65.

13. Faulkner "Mississippi" 1954 in Meriwether 1965, 12–13. The silver spur is pure fiction. Except for small copper bells (named the "Clarksdale bells"), which were used by the Spanish for decoration on horses and were found in a mound near Clarksdale, no other artifact from the De Soto party has been discovered or identified in Mississippi (Hudson 1997, 465). According to my father, Claude L. Aiken, whose mother, Clara James Blackwell Aiken, was a first cousin of Maud Morrow, Calvin Brown's wife, the Browns' house contained numerous Indian artifacts.

14. Harmontown Community Historical Society 1977, 5; Faulkner "Red Leaves" 1930 in Cowley 1946, 74–104; Hudson 1976, 327–336. Faulkner's source for the burial of a slave

with Issetibbeha might have been an account of the burial of Tattooed Serpent, a Natchez Indian who died in the early 1700s. Eight persons were garroted and buried close to him (Hudson 1997, 434–435).

15. Holt [1935], 25; C. Brown 1926, 7; Blotner 1974, 1:72–73.

16. Faulkner "My Grandmother Millard and General Bedford Forrest and the Battle of Harrykin Creek" 1943 in *Collected Stories* 1977, 667–699.

17. Faulkner *Go Down, Moses* 1942, 36–41.

18. The British strategy for getting the Creeks to cede land in Georgia is discussed by Bartram 1791, 265. DeRosier 1970, 23–28; Wallace 1999, 206–249; Young 1961, 15–21; Gibson 1971, 159.

19. James S. Allen to John A. Eaton, February 7, 1830, quoted in Gibson 1971, 122–123.

20. Gibson 1971, 122–127; Harmontown Community Historical Society 1977, 8; Taylor 1990, 105–108.

21. Clawson 1968, 44–53; Young 1961, 162, 168. Two principal meridians, the Chickasaw and the Choctaw, are employed in the federal survey of north Mississippi. The Tennessee-Mississippi state boundary and the southern border of the Choctaw Cession are base lines.

22. Young 1961, 39–46; Gibson 1971, 159–162.

23. Young 1961, 41–42, 114–125; Gibson 1971, 163–166.

24. Gibson 1971, 163–164; Young 1961, 114–125, 161–171; S. Williamson 2008, Consumer Price Index 2007.

25. Young 1961, 117–118.

26. McAlexander 1986, 8.

27. A. M. Upshaw to Gov. Robert M. Harris, May 15, 1837, Office of Indian Affairs 1824–1881, Chickasaw Agency, National Archives, Washington, D.C., Microcopy 234, Roll 143. House Report no. 271, 27th Congress, 3rd sess., 63, quoted in Gibson 1971, 167.

28. Bowers Reed McIlvaine to Catharine D. McIlvaine [November-December] 1837, in Parsons 1953.

29. Township maps of the Chickasaw Cession, Mississippi, 1833 (Township 7, Range 4 west; Township 6, Range 3 west; Township 6, Range 4 west; Township 8, Range 3 west; Township 7, Range 3 west), Office of the Chancery Clerk, Marshall County; Hathorn [1938], 60–62; Young 1961, 162; Hilgard 1860, 200–201. The store at Mitchell's Bluff in 1833 may have been owned initially by Slone Love or Volner Peel. The firm of Estall and Peel was among the early businesses in Wyatt (Hathorn [1939], 68).

30. Township maps of the Chickasaw Cession, Mississippi, 1833 (Township 7, Range 4 West, Sections 18, 33, 5, 6, 7); Mississippi Deeds Record Book A, 31, 38, 219, Office of the Chancery Clerk, Lafayette County. The La Grange-Hendersonville Road is shown on the 1833 field survey maps, but no ferry is shown where the road crosses the Tallahatchie River. The contemporary name "Toby Tubby" is spelled Tobo Tubby in historical land documents.

31. Hathorn [1938], 50; Simpson Lester, administrator of the estate of Levi S. Harmon, report of rent of land and ferry April 17, 1855 (Harmon Collection).

32. Faulkner "Red Leaves" 1930 in Cowley 1946, 78–79; Faulkner, February 15, 1957, in Gwynn and Blotner 1959, 8.

33. Account from Hutchings and Wilcox for William H. Cain paid by Wesley Harmon with "draft on New Orleans," March 31, 1850 (Harmon Collection).

34. Township maps of the Chickasaw Cession, Mississippi, 1833 (Township 8, Range 3 West), Office of the Chancery Clerk, Lafayette County; Sobotka [1976], 28.

35. Mississippi Deeds Record Book A, Clerk of the Chancery Court, Lafayette County, Oxford, Miss.; Hathorn [1938], 52–54; Young 1961, 163–164, 183.

36. Duncan [1930]; Kendel 1913, 231–232, 263; Holt [1935], 3; U.S. Works Progress Administration, Archives and Special Collections, University of Mississippi; Lloyd 1979, 36.

37. Faulkner *Requiem for a Nun* 1951, 39.

38. Faulkner *Sartoris* 1929, 166, 39.

39. Mississippi Deeds Record Book A, 4, Clerk of the Chancery Court, Lafayette County; Hathorn [1938], 53; Kendel 1913, 263; U.S. Census Office 1864b, 264–269.

40. Hathorn [1938], 27–74; J. Williamson 1993, 77–84.

41. Hathorn [1938], 20–26.

42. Faulkner *Requiem for a Nun* 1951, 3–8, 32–33; *Intruder in the Dust* 1948, 75–76.

43. Faulkner "1699–1945 Appendix: The Compsons" in Cowley 1946, 740; Faulkner *The Mansion* 1959, 334.

44. U.S. Geological Survey, *Natchez, Mississippi, Quadrangle*, 1:62,500, 1965.

45. Faulkner *Absalom, Absalom!* 1936, 7–30; "1699–1945 Appendix: The Compsons" in Cowley 1946, 740; *Intruder in the Dust* 1948, 10.

46. Faulkner *The Mansion*, 1959, 332–337.

47. Faulkner *Requiem for a Nun* 1951, 14–48; Taylor 1990, 9–10, 105–108.

48. Faulkner *Requiem for a Nun* 1951, 21, 29–31.

49. Ibid., 21–22.

50. Ibid., 30–31, 35, 218–220.

51. Ibid., 216–217.

52. Faulkner *Requiem for a Nun* 1951, 227; Aiken 1971.

Five. Civil War

1. Faulkner, April 28, 1958, in Gwynn and Blotner 1959, 249.

2. Blotner 1974, 1:25–32; Duclos 1998, 95–115; J. Williamson 1993, 84–87.

3. Survivors Association of Lamar Rifles [1901]; M. Brown 1940, 45.

4. Faulkner *Sartoris* 1929, 1.

5. Faulkner *Light in August* 1932, 56–57. Van Dorn's actual raid was on Holly Springs, Faulkner's fictional Memphis Junction, in December 1862.

6. Faulkner *Sartoris* 1929, 10.

7. Faulkner *Requiem for a Nun* 1951, 231.

8. Blotner 1974, 1:20–32; Duclos 1998, 134–141. In *Grierson's Raid* Alexander Brown confuses Colonel William Clark Falkner with Colonel W. W. Faulkner of the Twelfth Kentucky Cavalry, a Confederate officer who also fought in Mississippi and Tennessee. John Ford's 1959 motion picture *The Horse Soldiers* (United Artists), starring John Wayne and William Holden, is a fictionalized version of Grierson's raid based on Harold Sinclair's novel *The Horse Soldiers*. Ford's motion picture strayed from both actual facts and the fictional novel. Also see York 2001.

9. Faulkner, April 20, 1962, in Fant and Ashley 1964, 108–109.

10. Faulkner *Absalom, Absalom!* 1936, 341–344; Faulkner in Gwynn and Blotner 1959, 73.

11. Wills 1992, 1; Dasher 1981, 168, 412–413; U. S. Grant 1885, 2:108–109.

12. Blotner 1974, 2:1413; Willis Monroe Lea to Captain Nathaniel W. Lea, July 27, 1864, in M. Brown 1940, 53–54. Upon his return to the Army of Northern Virginia, Willis was killed near Winchester, Va., on September 19, 1864.

13. Wills 1992, 318–378; General N. B. Forrest quoted in Winik 2002, 320–322.

14. Morton 1909; Lytle 1931; Wills 1992, 179–196; Greenhaw 1986; U. S. Grant 1885, *Official Records*, ser. 1, vol. 32, part 1, 610.

15. Faulkner, April 13, 1957, in Gwynn and Blotner 1959, 73.

16. Neely 1997; McPherson 1997; Gallagher 1998.

17. McPherson 1988; 1997, 300–306; Downing 1916, 92–93; *New York Evening Express*, September 21, 1863.

18. Kendel 1913, 228.

19. General U. S. Grant to General H. W. Halleck, November 12, 1862; December 1, 1862, *Official Records*, ser. 1, vol. 17, part 1, 469–470, 471.

20. College Church Congregational and Sessional Records, January 5, 1863.

21. General U. S. Grant, November 9, 1862, Special Field Orders no. 2, *Official Records*, ser. 1, vol. 17, part 2, 331–332; General W. T. Sherman, November 6, 1862, General Orders no. 6, *Official Records*, ser. 1, vol. 17, part 2, 390–391; General-in-Chief H. W. Halleck to General U. S. Grant, November 16, 1862, *Official Records*, ser. 1, vol. 17, part 1, 470–471; U. S. Grant 1885, 1:368–369.

22. General U. S. Grant, December 12, 1862, Special Field Orders no. 21, *Official Records*, ser. 1, vol. 17, part 2, 405.

23. Downing 1916, 86–88.

24. General U. S. Grant to Mary Grant Cramer, December 15, 1862, in Cramer 1912, 95–97; Canton 1960, 335.

25. Hartje 1967, 255–265.

26. U. S. Grant 1885, 1:435–436.

27. U. S. Grant 1885, 1:435–436; General U. S. Grant, report to Colonel J. C. Kelton, December 25, 1862, *Official Records*, ser. 1, vol. 17, part 1, 477–478.

28. Barber 1894, 91–92.

29. Ibid., 90.

30. D. Doyle 2001, 211; Harmon Collection.

31. Colonel Robert C. Murphy, report to Colonel John A. Rawlings, December 20, 1862, *Official Records*, ser. 1, vol. 17, part 1, 508–509.

32. J. Grant 1975, 82–83, 104–109. Julia Grant misidentifies the Walter house as the Walker house (Downing 1916, 89).

33. Downing 1916, 89.

34. Bearss 1979, 313–318; Wills 1992, 202–215; General C. C. Washburn to E. M. Stanton, Secretary of War, June 12, 1864, report of defeat of General Sturgis by General Forrest near Guntown, Miss., *Official Records*, ser. 1, vol. 39, part 2, 106.

35. General W. T. Sherman, June 16, 1864, order to General James McPherson to make inquiries into the recent defeat of General Sturgis at Brice's Crossroads, *Official Records*, ser. l, vol. 39, part 2, 123; General W. T. Sherman, June 24, 1864, message to President Abraham Lincoln, *Official Records*, ser. 1, vol. 39, part 2, 142. Sherman promised Mower the rank of major general if he were successful against Forrest (General W. T. Sherman June 24, 1864, message to General C. C. Washburn, *Official Records*, ser. 1, vol. 39, part 2, 130).

36. Bearss 1979, 237–239.

37. General C. C. Washburn, report to General W. T. Sherman, August 11, 1862, *Official Records*, ser. 1, vol. 39, part 2, 242; Bearss 1962, 452.

38. Bearss 1979, 177–244, 256; General N. B. Forrest [August 1864] to Governor Charles Clark (quoted in Jordan and Prior 1868, 525); Governor Charles Clark to J. A. Seddon,

August 18, 1864, *Official Records*, ser. 1, vol. 39, part 2, 781. Clark states that he has yet to receive a shipment of guns.

39. Bearss 1979, 264–269.

40. Report of Lieutenant-Colonel Edwin Moore to Lieutenant Samuel D. Sawyer, August 26, 1864; report of Colonel James I. Gilbert to Lieutenant James B. Comstock, August 27, 1864; report of Colonel Edward H. Wolfe to Lieutenant James B. Comstock, August 27, 1864; report of Brigadier-General B. H. Grierson to Major J. Hough, September 6, 1864, *Official Records*, ser. 1, vol. 39, part 1, 380–384; Bearss 1979, 264–269.

41. Wills 1992, 237–246; Morton 1909, 217–221.

42. General C. C. Washburn, three dispatches to General A. J. Smith, August 21, 1864; General A. J. Smith, report to General C. C. Washburn, August 24, 1862; General C. C. Washburn, dispatch to Colonel William T. Clark, August 24, 1864, *Official Records*, ser. 1, vol. 39, part 1, 377–378, 468–471. The one-hundred-man cavalry detachment that hand-delivered Washburn's messages to Smith was told by persons along the route from Memphis to Oxford that a Confederate force was in Holly Springs. One by one the Union army units approaching Oxford from the north turned back. For example, the Third Division of the Fourteenth Iowa Infantry moved to within two miles of Oxford. "Here the command was about-faced and line of march taken in the direction of Holly Springs" (Colonel William T. Shaw, report to Major John Hough, August 27, 1864, *Official Records*, ser. 1, vol. 39, part 2, 302).

43. Captain Charles T. Biser, Confederate States Army, report to General S. Cooper, August 31, 1864, *Official Records*, ser. 1, vol. 39, part 1, 400–401; Garner 1901, 32; D. Doyle 2001, 211.

44. General W. T. Sherman, order to General C. C. Washburn, August 19, 1864; General W. T. Sherman, report to General H. W. Halleck, August 20, 1864; General C. C. Washburn, report to General W. T. Sherman, August 27, 1864; General A. J. Smith, special orders to Right Wing, Sixteenth Army Corps, August 27, 1864, *Official Records*, ser. 1, vol. 39, part 2, 270, 274–275, 310–311.

45. Sarah P. Lea to Captain Nathaniel W. Lea, September 3, 1864, in M. Brown 1940, 47–49.

46. General W. T. Sherman, dispatch to General C. C. Washburn, August 24, 1864, *Official Records*, ser. 1, vol. 39, part 2, 296.

47. Faulkner, February 15, 1957, in Gwynn and Blotner 1959, 2.

48. Faulkner *The Hamlet* 1940, 4; *Sartoris* 1929, 223–227; "My Grandmother and General Bedford Forrest and the Battle of Harrykin Creek" 1943 in *Collected Stories* 1977, 667–699.

49. Faulkner *The Unvanquished* 1938, 3–86.

50. Ibid., 93–95.

51. Ibid., 216.

52. Ibid., 103–104.

53. Hirshson 1997, 260–261; Sherman 1875, 2:244–245.

54. Canton 1960, 356–362; Downing 1916, 85; Eaton and Mason 1907, 5–6.

55. Faulkner *The Unvanquished* 1938, 124–128. Union armies were designated by names of rivers, Confederate armies by names of states. Army of the Tennessee [River] was a Union army, and Army of Tennessee, a Confederate army. Faulkner's order should read "Department of *the* Tennessee."

56. Faulkner *The Unvanquished* 1938, 135–213.

57. General U. S. Grant, Special Orders 31, November 27, 1862, *Official Records*, ser. 1, vol. 17, part 1, 526.

58. Canton 1960, 356–362.

59. Parks 1941; Canton 1960, 347–356; Garner 1901, 32.

60. Captain Charles T. Bisser, Confederate States Army, report to General S. Cooper, August 31, 1864, *Official Records*, ser. 1, vol. 39, part 3, 400–401.

61. General N. B. Forrest, Circular to the District of Mississippi, East Louisiana, and West Tennessee, January 24, 1865, *Official Records*, ser. 1, vol. 49, part 1, 930–931.

62. Faulkner *The Unvanquished* 1938, 169–213.

63. McPherson 1988, 854–862.

64. General Robert E. Lee, Farewell to his Army [of Northern Virginia], April 10, 1865, in Brunn and Crosby 1999, 439–440.

65. Survivors Association of Lamar Rifles [1901], 11.

66. Buford in Survivors Association of Lamar Rifles [1901], 71.

67. Coulter 1950, 566.

68. McPherson 1988, 812–813. Also see Jedah Benjamin [1865], "I am lost in Amazement that the Struggle Could have been so Prolonged," in Brunn and Crosby 1999, 440–441.

69. McPherson 1988, 854–858.

70. Downing 1916, 89.

71. Faulkner *Absalom, Absalom!* 1936, 19. A study of a South Carolina community found that the change in the ratio of men ages 15 to 35 to marriageable women declined from 89 to 100 to 60 to 100 as a result of the war (Wilson 1980). Faulkner's use of the term "holocaust" for the American Civil War predates by more than three decades use of the term to portray annihilation of European Jews by the Nazis during the Second World War.

72. Faulkner *Absalom, Absalom!* 1936, 353–354, 184; *The Unvanquished* 1938, 167; Pollard 1866.

73. Faulkner *Absalom, Absalom!* 1936, 68; Faulkner, May 8, 1958, in Gwynn and Blotner 1959, 274. On conscription by the Confederate government, see Moore 1924.

74. Faulkner *Intruder in the Dust* 1948, 194–195.

75. Faulkner *Sartoris* 1929, 8–19.

76. Ibid., 1, 8–19.

77. Faulkner *Light in August* 1932, 459.

78. Faulkner *Absalom, Absalom!* 1936, 345.

79. Faulkner, "1699–1945 Appendix: The Compsons" in Cowley 1946, 741. Resaca, Georgia, forty miles south of Chattanooga, was the site of a battle during General Joseph Johnson's slow fighting retreat toward Atlanta during the summer of 1864. The primary failure at the actual battle of Resaca, which the North won, was by young Union general James B. McPherson, who commanded the Army of the Tennessee. McPherson's flank attack on Johnson through the lightly defended Snake Creek Gap failed when he overestimated the number of Confederates behind the earthworks at Resaca. General Sherman told McPherson, "Well, Mac, you missed the opportunity of your life." McPherson was killed during the Battle of Atlanta when he refused to surrender after accidentally riding behind the Confederate line (McPherson 1988, 744–745, 754).

80. Faulkner *Absalom, Absalom!* 1936, 346.

81. Faulkner *Go Down, Moses* 1942, 288–289.

82. Faulkner *Go Down, Moses* 1942, 286; McPherson 1988, 537.

Six. New South

1. Faulkner *Requiem for a Nun* 1951, 228–262; Blotner 1974, 1:138; C. Brown Jr. 1976, 48; Taylor 1990, 164.

2. Faulkner *Go Down, Moses* 1942, 291.

3. Garner 1901, 122.

4. Ibid., 122–123.

5. Kendel 1913, 271; S. Williamson 2008, Consumer Price Index 2007.

6. U.S. Bureau of the Census 1960, passim.

7. J. Williamson 1993, 85–87; D. Doyle 2001, 211; S. Williamson 2008, Consumer Price Index 2007.

8. Kendel 1913, 233; Estate papers of Wesley Harmon 1860–1871, Harmon Collection; S. Williamson 2008, Consumer Price Index 2007.

9. Faulkner, April 28, 1958, in Gwynn and Blotner 1959, 251.

10. William Faulkner to Robert K. Haas [May 3, 1940] in Blotner 1977, 122–124.

11. Pollard 1866.

12. Mills and Simpson 2003, 27–45.

13. Windberry 1983; Mills and Simpson 2003, xv–xxx, 3–26, 149–162, 183–218.

14. Wilson 1980, 7–17, 171–181.

15. Faulkner *Requiem for a Nun* 1951, 239.

16. Wilson 1980, 26–30. The popularity of "How Firm a Foundation" is revealed in the works of Missouri composer Virgil Thompson. He used the hymn's music as a basis of several of his compositions, including that for the Great Depression pioneer documentary *The River*, a film about floods in the Lower Mississippi Valley. Thompson commented that "How Firm a Foundation" had been played and sung so much that it was almost worn out by the time he used it.

17. Wilson 1980, 32.

18. Cody [1946], 178–179.

19. Faulkner *Requiem for a Nun* 1951, 239–240. In Franklin County, Georgia, the importance of the soldier's staring toward the north is seen in the statue on the small lawn facing the wall of the courthouse.

20. Windberry 1983.

21. U.S. WPA Federal Writers' Project 1938, 255.

22. Wilson 1980, 39; J. Williamson 1993, 81. With the approach of the Civil War Barnard left the University of Mississippi for Columbia College in New York, where he successfully built the scientific university he had begun at Oxford. Barnard College is named for him. Barnard's observatory stands in restored glory on the University of Mississippi campus, void of its telescope, which was the most powerful one created up to the time of the Civil War. Failure of Mississippi to pay for the telescope resulted in its being sold to Northwestern University (Lloyd 1979, 10–11).

23. Faulkner *Intruder in the Dust* 1948, 119; *Requiem for a Nun* 1951, 239–240; Faulkner, April 28, 1958, in Gwynn and Blotner 1959, 249. For the myth that General W. T. Sherman burned Wyatt as told by James M. (Jimmy) Faulkner, see Wolff and Watkins 1996, 115.

24. Faulkner "A Rose for Emily" 1930 in *Collected Stories* 1977, 121; Faulkner, May 20, 1957, in Gwynn and Blotner 1959, 184–185. Apparently, no royalties have to be paid for use of "A Rose for Emily" in textbooks.

25. Faulkner *The Sound and the Fury* 1929, 373–375; Philip A. Stone to Hotchkiss School, December 9, 1955, quoted in Snell 1991, 14–15.

26. Faulkner *Absalom, Absalom!* 1936, 7–9.

27. Faulkner *Requiem for a Nun* 1951, 227.

28. Aiken 1998, 7–10.

29. Blotner 1974, 1:25–32, 69–79.

30. Faulkner *Requiem for a Nun* 1951, 227.

31. Aiken 1998, 29–62.

32. Faulkner *The Hamlet* 1940, 3–8.

33. Ibid., 7.

34. Ibid., 6, 31–32.

35. Nichols and King 1943; Documents concerning the Harmon family, various dates, Harmon Collection.

36. Faulkner *Intruder in the Dust* 1948, 8; Faulkner *The Mansion* 1959, 398; Faulkner *Light in August* 1932, 106–107; Aiken 1998, 154–162.

37. Aiken 1998, 97–132.

38. Sonnichsen 1969; Aiken 1998, 120–130.

39. Faulkner *The Hamlet* 1940, 9–10.

40. Faulkner *The Hamlet* 1940, 9–10; Aiken 1998, 28–39.

41. Faulkner *The Hamlet*, 1940, 21–23.

42. U.S. WPA Federal Writers' Project 1938, 439.

43. Ibid. My father and mother told me of a stop at the big house on Galena plantation on a Sunday afternoon outing in the 1930s. My father held my mother up so that she could peek past a shutter through a window. She saw a large open cabinet filled with chamber pots.

44. Faulkner *Requiem for a Nun* 1951, 33.

45. Faulkner *Absalom, Absalom!* 1936, 187–188.

46. Hilgard 1860, 293.

47. U.S. WPA Federal Writers' Project 1938, 440.

48. Faulkner *The Hamlet* 1940, 196.

49. Blotner 1974, 2:986–987, 1151; Aiken 1998, 5–7; U.S. Bureau of the Census [1948].

50. Faulkner "Barn Burning" 1939 in *Collected Stories* 1977, 3–25.

51. Faulkner *The Mansion* 1959, 90–91.

52. Stoddard 1962; Payne 1982.

53. William Faulkner and Bern Keating quoted in Blotner 1974, 2:1463–1465.

54. Faulkner *Big Woods* 1955, 201, 209, 212.

55. Whittlesey 1929, 162.

56. Mikesell 1976.

57. Aiken 1998, 39–55, 97–113.

58. William Faulkner to Harrison Smith, [February] 1934, in Blotner 1977, 78–79; Faulkner *Go Down, Moses* 1942, 349; Faulkner *Big Woods* 1955, 212. A discussion of wilderness in the American experience is in Nash 1973.

59. The idea of leadership decline and management failure in the South's plantation regions is developed in Aiken 1998, 63–96, 340–375.

60. Faulkner *The Reivers* 1962, 8; "Appendix: The Compsons, 1699–1945" in Cowley 1946, 741–743; *The Hamlet* 1940, 166, 383–415; *The Mansion* 1959, 322. A parallel exists between the shyster Flem, who sold lots from what remained of Compson's Mile, and

Faulkner's early mentor, Phil Stone, who in 1940 began selling small lots on one hundred acres west of his home at the edge of Oxford. The analogy between Stone's enterprise and that of Flem was deliberate. Faulkner dedicated *The Mansion* to Stone. The relationship between Faulkner and Stone became strained in the 1930s when the writer borrowed on his life insurance and loaned his friend the money to help pay his debts. Stone never repaid Faulkner. Stone's real estate development, Oxford's first post–Second World War subdivision, was filled with houses financed by the Federal Housing Authority (FHA) for white middle-class families (Snell 1991, 246–247).

61. Faulkner *The Hamlet* 1940, 3.

62. Faukner *Absalom, Absalom!* 1936, 374–376; "1699–1945 Appendix: The Compsons" in Cowley 1946, 742.

63. Faulkner *Go Down, Moses* 1942, 354.

64. Faulkner, April 24, 1958, in Gwynn and Blotner 1959, 245–246. In a 1955 interview with Cynthia Grenier, Faulkner was asked, "Who are your favorite literary characters in your work?" He named Dilsey and Ratliff. Faulkner's quick little smile to the startled rejoinder of why he did not name Isaac McCaslin hinted that Grenier was entrapped. Faulkner began a rapid series of questions as to why Grenier would put Isaac on the list. He then replied, "Well, I think a man ought to do more than just repudiate" (Meriwether and Millgate 1968, 224–225).

65. On the concept of *masks* of writers see Ford 1969; Hönnighausen 1997. Faulkner never denied fictitious accounts of European combat experiences during the First World War. According to a 1932 article by A. Wigfall Green in the *Sewanee Review*, Faulkner, who at the time could not fly a plane and did not leave North America during the war, had "two enemy planes to his credit and several times barely escaped death" (Green 1932). J. Williamson 1993, 176–185.

66. Blotner 1974, 2:1316–1317, 1410–1414; U.S. Bureau of the Census [1948]. Lafayette County, Mississippi, had 64 plantations in 1940, and Marshall County, Mississippi, had 123 (p. 14).

67. J. Williamson 1993, 116–132.

68. Susie James, "Baker Recalls Faulkner," *Oxford Eagle*, August 6, 1976, 4C.

69. Wilde and Borsten 1976, 310. When Faulkner met Meta Wilde in the 1930s, she was Howard Hawks's secretary, and her last name was Carpenter.

70. William Faulkner to Saxe Commins, [July 2] 1954; [June 18] 1954, in Blotner 1977, 365, 368; Blotner 1974, 2:1509.

71. Blotner 1974, 2:1414.

72. Ibid. Faulkner's costume for the Delta Council meeting is interpreted by some critics as that of a Lafayette County farmer. However, the apparel was not that of a person who worked in the fields, but that of one who owned land but did not closely supervise it.

73. Hodding Carter in Blotner 1974, 2:1417.

74. Faulkner, Address to the Delta Council, 1952, in Meriwether 1965, 126–134.

Seven. Geographical Interpretation of "The Bear"

1. Utley, Bloom, and Kinney 1971.

2. Faulkner "The Bear" in *Go Down, Moses* 1942, 189–331; *Big Woods* 1955, 9–97.

3. Millgate 1966, 201–214.

4. Faulkner *Go Down, Moses* 1942, 196.

5. Faulkner *Absalom, Absalom!* 1936, map insert; Cowley 1946, inside front cover.

6. Faulkner *Go Down, Moses* 1942, 230.

7. J. Faulkner 1963, 90–92; Last Will and Testament of C. F. Cain 1925, Harmon Collection. James Lee Smith, my maternal grandfather, was born in Lafayette County in 1870. While hunting in the Tallahatchie bottom about 1890, he heard a tapping above him in the large tree under which he was standing. Looking up, he saw a panther, which was warning him of its presence by rapping on a branch with its tail.

8. J. Faulkner 1963, 92; Snell 1991, 48–53.

9. Faulkner *Go Down, Moses* 1942, 193.

10. Ibid., 215.

11. Faulkner *Go Down, Moses* 1942, 191, 202–203; Tanner 1942; White 2006.

12. Faulkner *Go Down, Moses* 1942, 315.

13. Ibid., 318–321.

14. Faulkner, March 13, 1947, letter to the editor of the *Oxford Eagle*, in Meriwether 1965, 202–203.

15. James Stone, Legal notice, *Batesville Panolian*, November 15, 1934, 6.

16. Mississippi Secretary of State 1935.

17. Blotner 1974, 1:879.

18. Chain of Titles, Book E, Second District, Clerk of the Chancery Court, Panola County, Batesville, Miss.

19. Faulkner "Lion" 1935.

20. Faulkner *Go Down, Moses* 1942, 315.

21. Faulkner, May 8, 1958, in Gwynn and Blotner 1959, 276–277.

22. Ibid., 273.

23. Howe 1952, 252–259; Beck 1955; Millgate 1966, 202–203.

24. Faulkner *Go Down, Moses* 1942, 254.

25. Ibid., 255–256.

26. Welch 1943, 115–118; Faulkner *Go Down, Moses* 1942, 364.

27. Langsford and Thibodeaux 1939, 12–15; U.S. Bureau of the Census 1902, 432; 1932, 1083–1089; Cobb 1992, 98–229; Aiken 1998, 55–62; Caldwell and Bourke-White 1937; Lange and Taylor 1939; Raper and Reid 1941.

28. Faulkner, May 8, 1958, in Gwynn and Blotner 1959, 277.

29. Blotner 1974, 2:1063–1065; Faulkner "Delta Autumn" 1942.

30. Faulkner *Go Down, Moses* 1942, 335–336.

31. Ibid., 340–342.

32. T. Williams 1955, 191.

33. Faulkner *Go Down, Moses* 1942, 360.

34. Ibid., 342, 353–354.

35. Ibid., 357–365.

36. Faulkner *The Reivers* 1962, 20–21.

37. Aiken 1998, 97–132, 222–228, 340–349.

Eight. Toward the Modern South

1. Faulkner *As I Lay Dying* 1930, 1.

2. E. Davis 1940.

3. Aiken 1998, 99–101.

4. Faulkner *The Hamlet* 1940, 10–11; *The Mansion* 1959, 71. A few cotton houses were left through the twentieth century on some plantations as shelters from sudden rain showers accompanied by lightning.

5. Aiken 1998, 97–132; Mississippi Crop and Livestock Reporting Service 1955, 112; United States Department of Agriculture, Cotton Division, Cotton Harvested Mechanically 1950, 1960, 1967, and 1970; National Cotton Council of America, Number of Mechanical Cotton Pickers on Farms by States 1955–1965 (mimeograph).

6. Mississippi Crop and Livestock Reporting Services 1955, 122–124; U.S. Bureau of the Census 1967; U.S. Department of Agriculture 2002, 424.

7. U.S. WPA Federal Writers' Project 1938, 381; Aiken 1961.

8. Faulkner *Requiem for a Nun* 1951, 244–245.

9. Edgar Brownlee obituary, *Tate County Democrat* (Senatobia, Miss.), March 25, 1981, 1B.

10. U.S. Bureau of the Census 1960, passim; Burford 1963, 38.

11. Neil R. McMillen, December 2, 1994, interview with Dabney Hammer, in McMillen 1997, 103.

12. Aiken 1998, 167–171, 235–237.

13. For examples of critics who believe that by 1942 Faulkner's talent was near its end and what remained was co-opted by a devastating contract with Warner Brothers, see Minter 1980, 192; Singal 1997, 284.

14. Blotner 1974, 1:613–721.

15. Wilde and Borsten 1976, 26–27, 142–149, 319–334. *The Wild Palms* is thought to be based on Faulkner's relationship with Meta Carpenter.

16. Wilde and Borsten 1976, 9; Blotner 1977. In one of his few references to Carpenter, Blotner identifies her among Faulkner's "old . . . California friends." In 1970, six typewritten pages of the manuscript of *Absalom, Absalom!*, with handwritten corrections and the first page dated 1936 and dedicated to Meta Carpenter, were offered for public sale (Blotner 1974, 2:1030, 136 notes).

17. Wilde and Borsten 1976, 310–311.

18. Faulkner to Harold Ober, April 22, 1944, in Blotner 1977, 180–181.

19. Blotner 1974, 2:1096–1098, 1117–1194; Faulkner to Robert Hass [May 3, 1940] in Blotner 1977, 122–123; Dardis 1976, 124–125, 142–144.

20. Faulkner, "1699–1945 Appendix: The Compsons" in Cowley 1946, 737–750.

21. Faulkner to Malcolm A. Franklin [July 4, 1943] in Blotner 1977, 175–176.

22. Blotner 1974, 2:1226.

23. Polk 1997, 132; Shaw 1948; Mailer 1948; Heller 1961; J. Jones 1951.

24. Faulkner *Requiem for a Nun* 1951, 246–247.

25. Faulkner to the editor of the *Commercial Appeal*, March 26, 1950; April 9, 1950, in Meriwether 1965, 203–205. Faulkner read the Memphis newspaper daily.

26. Faulkner to Harold Ober, February 1 [1948]; Faulkner to Robert K. Hass [March 1948] in Blotner 1977, 262–265.

27. Faulkner in Gwynn and Blotner 1959, 141; Thomas McHaney to Charles Aiken, November 22, 2005.

28. T. Davis 1983, 5; Singal 1997, 284; Moreland 2002, 60–69.

29. Cowley 1966, 172.

30. Borstelmann 2001, 98, 266–271; Zangrando 1980, 22–23; Egerton 1994, 494–495.

31. Woodward 1989, 203; 1986, 108–109.

32. Faulkner quoted in Stein 1956, 139; Roper 1997, xi–xii. Also see Lowenthal 1985.

33. Blotner 1974, 2:1276–1277; S. Williamson 2008, Consumer Price Index 2007; Faulkner to Robert K. Hass, April 28, 1940; Faulkner to Harold Ober, February 1 [1948]; Faulkner to Hass [February 22, 1948]; Faulkner to Linton Massey [June 29, 1962] in Blotner 1977, 262–263, 461–462.

34. Aiken 1998, 139–148; W. Jordan 1974, 3–25.

35. Faulkner *Sartoris* 1929, 145–146.

36. Faulkner *The Sound and the Fury* 1929, 34–38.

37. Faulkner *Go Down, Moses* 1942, 359–362. Under Mississippi law at the time, "The marriage of a white person and a negro or mulatto or person who shall have one-eighth negro blood . . . shall be unlawful and void" (*Constitution of the State of Mississippi* 1890, Section 2859).

38. Faulkner "1699–1945 Appendix: The Compsons" in Cowley 1946, 750–756. The accounts of Benjamin (Maury) Compson and the Compson dwelling vary in *The Sound and the Fury* and *The Mansion* from those in *The Portable Faulkner*.

39. Faulkner *Light in August* 1932, 439–440.

40. Zangrando 1980, 5–8.

41. Zangrando 1980, 5–8.

42. Dray 2002, 53–69.

43. Zangrando 1980, 6–8.

44. Blotner 1974, 2:1246; Zangrando 1980, 6–7; Thompson 2001, 191–221. Other writers followed Faulkner with their versions of the anti-lynching theme, including Harper Lee in *To Kill a Mockingbird*, 1960.

45. Faulkner *Intruder in the Dust* 1948, 3, 28–30.

46. Faulkner *Intruder in the Dust* 1948, 74–77.

47. Singal 1997, 248; Brooks 1963, 422–423.

48. Faulkner to Harold Ober, February 1 [1948], in Blotner 1977, 262.

49. Faulkner *Intruder in the Dust* 1948, 203–204. In the expression "the injustice is ours, the South's," Faulkner is equating the South with whites. Faulkner, unconsciously, does not consider that his prose excludes blacks as part of the southern population. On exclusion of blacks as southerners from the discussions, see Aiken 2001, 53–54; Cobb 1996, 10.

50. Faulkner *Intruder in the Dust* 1948, 154–155. Faulkner maintained that it is Gavin Stevens's opinions about race, not his, that are presented in *Intruder in the Dust*. Malcolm Cowley termed such a perspective of Faulkner and other writers "dramatic impersonality" (Cowley 1966), 17–18. Faulkner "Colloquies at Nagano Seminar" 1955, in Meriwether and Millgate 1968, 161.

51. Faulkner *Intruder in the Dust* 1948, 4–14; Carter 2001, 229–230.

52. Faulkner *Intruder in the Dust* 1948, 4–14.

53. Ibid., 7–18.

54. D. Jones 1954–1955, 51; Bogle 1973, vii–xiii; Cripps 1993, 215–249.

55. Cripps 1993, 243–244; Fadiman 1978, 27–28; "Garbo's Favorite Director Left a Valuable Legacy to U. T. Students and All of Tennessee," *Tennessee Alumnus* 2005.

56. Clarence Brown, quoted in the *Commercial Appeal*, March 19, 1949; D. Jones 1954, 52–53.

57. Fadiman 1978, 29.

58. Oliver 1973, 26, 55, 66.

59. Fadiman 1978, 12–13, 80–81.

60. Fadiman 1978, 36–37, 60–61, 80–81; Blotner 1974, 2:1272–1278.

61. Jerry Wald to Clarence Brown, August 17, 1949; John Huston to Clarence Brown, June 6, 1949, *Intruder in the Dust* Scrapbook, File 71, Clarence Brown Collection.

62. "'Intruder' Approved by Memphis Censors: Not up to Ideals Binford Says, But It's O.K.," September 9, 1949; "Oxford's Two-day 'Intruder in the Dust' Premier Party Starts Tomorrow," October 9, 1949, 1; "Premier Ball to Be Tonight," October 10, 1949, 1, *Commercial Appeal*. Cripps 1993, 231; Fadiman 1978, 31. Because of Lloyd T. Binford's odd ideas about which films should not be shown in Memphis, Faulkner named the fictional pimp in Reba Rivers house of prostitution Lucius Binford. The Park theater was built in 1946. Until the Park was annexed by Memphis following the 1950 census, it was less than one block outside the city. The Park showed *The Southerner* and other movies Binford banned in Memphis.

My parents attended the Loew's Palace opening of *Intruder in the Dust*. I remained home with my younger brother who was ill. Curiously, what I remember most is questioning how my parents happened to know the federal district judge from the Northern District of Mississippi, who asked if he might sit with them, and my father's remark about the same cars driving around and around the Lafayette County courthouse during one scene. My parents did not particularly like the movie but were gracious in their comments. They especially enjoyed an evening together, and seeing at the theater so many people they knew.

63. Cripps 1993, 241–244.

64. Harmon 1949.

Nine. From Yoknapatawpha County to the World

1. Aiken 1998, 168–171.

2. Halberstam 1993, 431–441; Huie 1956; Whitfield 1988.

3. "A Surprise—Faulkner Meets the Press," *Memphis Press-Scimitar*, October 12, 1949, 1; Blotner 1974, 1:1294–1298.

4. Hickman 2006.

5. Eastland quoted in Marks 1955; Faulkner, Address to the Southern Historical Association 1955, in Meriwether 1965, 151.

6. Blotner 1974, 2:1596–1597, notes p. 200. In a 1956 interview by Russell Howe, Faulkner identified himself as a "liberal." In answer to the question, "Do you carry a gun?" Faulkner replied, "No," and then added, "But the other liberals in my part of the country carry guns all the time" (Faulkner interview, February 21, 1956, in Meriwether and Millgate 1968, 264).

7. Blotner 1974, 1:52–53, 658–660; 2:992–993; William Faulkner to Robert K. Hass [May 3, 1940] in Blotner 1977, 122–124. Years later, a street in Oxford's Freedman Town was named Callie Barr when the black residential area was cleared of its shacks and unpaved streets and rebuilt with large federal grants.

8. Faulkner interview with Russell Howe, February 21, 1956, in Meriwether and Millgate 1968, 258. Howe transcribed his interview with Faulkner from notes. The primary points of the interview are consistent with what Faulkner wrote, but parts of what Faulkner said may not be correct as to the exact wording. Different versions of the interview appeared in the *London Sunday Times* and *The Reporter*. Privately, Faulkner stated that the

interview was conducted when he had "been drinking so much that week I might have said anything." In a letter to *The Reporter* he qualified the statement that the South was armed to defend segregation and recanted as "foolish" and "dangerous" the statement that "if it came to fighting I'd fight for Mississippi against the United States even if it meant going out into the street and shooting Negroes" (Faulkner, letter to *The Reporter*, April 19, 1956, in Meriwether and Millgate 1968, 265; Blotner 1974, 2:1590–1591, notes p. 199). Percy 1941; General W. T. Sherman, message to General Lorenzo Thomas, June 21, 1864, *Official Records*, ser. 1, vol. 39, part 2, 132.

9. William Faulkner to Estelle Faulkner, January 20, 1960, in Blotner 1977, 440–441; Faulkner, "Address to the Raven, Jefferson, and ODK Societies of the University of Virginia" 1958, in Meriwether 1965, 157.

10. Faulkner, Letter to a Northern Editor, March 5, 1956, in Meriwether 1965, 86–91. *Brown v. Board of Education of Topeka, Kansas*, 349 U.S. 294, 299–301 (1955). Faulkner interview with Russell Howe, February 21, 1956, in Meriwether and Millgate 1968, 258.

11. Faulkner to Paul Pollard, February 24, 1960; Faulkner to Ernest Hemingway, June 28, 1947, in Blotner 1977, 443–444, 251–252. Also see Faulkner, "If I Were a Negro," *Ebony*, September 1956, in Meriwether 1965, 107–112.

12. Faulkner, Address to the Southern Historical Association, November 10, 1955, in Meriwether 1965.

13. Faulkner, "A Letter to the North," *Life*, March 5, 1956. Reprinted in Meriwether 1965, 86–91. Faulkner's original title was "Letter to a Northern Editor."

14. Two hung jury trials resulted in Beckwith going free. Years later, after blacks in Mississippi had their voting rights restored, Beckwith was again tried and was convicted. He died while serving a life sentence for killing Medgar Evers (Massengill 1996).

15. W. Doyle 2003, 101–102, 277–279, 293.

16. Barnett quoted in J. Williams 1988, 208–218.

17. W. Doyle 2003, 65–72.

18. Barnett quoted in J. Williams 1988, 208–218.

19. W. Doyle 2003, 132–133, 146.

20. T. Buckley 1962; Barrett 1965, 123–195; J. Williams 1988, 213–218.

21. Barrett 1965, 123–226; W. Doyle 2003, 280.

22. W. Doyle 2003, 198–201.

23. Ibid., 240–241, 277.

24. T. Buckley 1962.

25. W. Doyle 2003, 298.

26. Blotner 1974, 2:1836–1837; James M. (Jimmy) Faulkner in Wolff and Watkins 1996, 177.

27. Tumin et al. 1958, 149–152; M. L. King 1958, 201; Bartley 1969, 12–20; Faulkner Address to the Southern Historical Association 1955 in Meriwether 1965, 151.

28. W. Doyle 2003, 296.

29. Silver 1964, 6, 162; Turner Catledge Papers.

30. W. Doyle 2003, 250.

31. Caron 2000, 58.

32. Faulkner quoted in Blotner 1974, 2:1833.

33. Faulkner *Intruder in the Dust* 1948; Aiken 1998, 167–282.

34. Aiken 1998, 167–306.

35. Lyndon B. Johnson quoted in Kotz 2005, 336–337.

36. Faulkner interview with Cynthia Grenier, September 1955, in Meriwether and Millgate 1968, 225.

37. Aiken 1998, 273–282.

38. Aiken 1998, 274–282; Mississippi State Department of Education 1989, 64–65.

39. Joint Center for Political and Economic Studies 1991, 10.

40. Katagiri 2001, 128.

41. I was a young faculty member at Memphis State University in the fall of 1962. Several students from the University of Mississippi added my classes late. Most were from Memphis and did not return to Ole Miss.

42. Faulkner "Red Leaves" 1930 in *The Portable Faulkner* 1946, 100. Meredith's quotation does not agree precisely with Faulkner's text.

Ten. Faulkner's Geographical Legacy

1. Faulkner interview with Jean Stein 1956 in Cowley 1958, 141.

2. Faulkner *Sanctuary* 1931, 6–7, 378–380; Faulkner to Mrs. Walter B. McLean [Aunt Bama], September 10, 1925, in Blotner 1977, 19–20.

3. For an example of James Michener's approach to researching the background and setting of a novel, see *Texas*. For an example of James Steinbeck's, see *The Grapes of Wrath*. Faulkner interview with Jean Stein 1956 in Cowley 1958, 141; Faulkner interview with Simon Claxton, March 23, 1962, in Meriwether and Millgate 1968, 279.

4. Blotner 1974, 1:791. Malcolm Cowley to Faulkner, August 9, 1945; Faulkner to Malcolm Cowley [August 16, 1945] in Cowley 1966, 21–27.

5. Faulkner to William F. Fielding [October 7, 1959]; Faulkner to Linton Massey [June 29, 1962] in Blotner 1977, 436–437, 461–462.

6. Ringle 1998, 14–15.

7. Faulkner, February 15, 1957; April 25, 1957, in Gwynn and Blotner 1959, 1, 90.

8. Faulkner *Sartoris* 1929, 6; Hilgard 1860, 296.

9. Faulkner *Go Down, Moses* 1942, 194; *As I Lay Dying* 1930, 41.

10. Blotner 1974, 2:1412–1413; Foote 1977, 43–45.

11. Faulkner *As I Lay Dying* 1930, 35–36.

12. Message from General James R. Chalmers to General Maury, August 20, 1864, *Official Records*, ser. 1, vol. 39, part 2, 787.

13. Faulkner, April 13, 1957; May 30, 1957, in Gwynn and Blotner 1959, 74, 199.

14. Blotner 1974, 1:702.

15. Blotner 1974, 1;702; Faulkner *Light in August* 1932, 441–467.

16. Jackson 2004; White 2006.

17. Aiken 1998, 167–228, 257–282.

18. Agee 1938, Journal, Agee Collection, 2, 20; Agee and Evans 1941; Aiken 1998, 167–282.

19. Woodward 1986, 108–109.

20. Warren quoted in Woodward 1986, 109; Myrdal 1944; Woodward 1955; Kluger 1976. Astonishingly, a group of conservative historians condemned Woodward for practicing *presentism*, use of the past to explain present issues.

21. For analysis of the role and work of the FSA photographers, see Hurley 1972; Stott 1973; Natanson 1992.

22. Foote 1977, 41; Faulkner *Intruder in the Dust* 1948, 5–7.

23. Faulkner, April 28, 1958, in Gwynn and Blotner 1959, 253.

24. Faulkner *Sartoris* 1929, 1; *The Reivers* 1962, 302.

25. Faulkner "1699–1945 Appendix: The Compsons," in Cowley 1946, 746.

26. Faulkner *Intruder in the Dust* 1948, 11–12.

27. I remind the reader that in chapter 2 I discuss Faulkner's drawing from several areas outside Lafayette County and shifting places and events to a Lafayette County geographical base.

28. Brooks 1963, 9.

29. Faulkner, May 12, 1958, in Gwynn and Blotner 1959, 279–280.

30. C. Brown Jr. 1976, 241; McCommons 1978.

31. "Apocrypha," in *Webster's New World College Dictionary*, 3rd ed. For a comprehensive discussion of Faulkner's fiction as his apocrypha, see Urgo 1989.

32. C. Brown Jr. 1976, 2.

33. Wolff and Watkins 1996, 1.

34. U.S. Bureau of the Census 2002. 2000 Census of Population. PHC-1-Mississippi.

35. *Faulkner's Mississippi: Land into Legend*, produced by Robert D. Oesterling and Evans Harrington (Department of Education, University of Mississippi, 1965); *Oxford–Lafayette County Heritage Foundation Newsletter* 1999, 1.

36. Robert Khayat quoted in Vejnoska 2000, M-1.

37. Auchmutey 2001.

38. Stein 1956 in Cowley 1958, 138–139.

BIBLIOGRAPHY

Public Documents

Constitution and Laws of the State of Mississippi, 1890. 1st printing. Possession of Charles S. Aiken.

Lafayette County, Mississippi. Oxford. Office of the Chancery Clerk. County land records, maps, and estate records.

Marshall County, Mississippi. Holly Springs. Office of the Chancery Clerk. County land records, maps, and estate records.

Mississippi Crop and Livestock Reporting Service. 1955. *Base Book of Mississippi Agriculture.* Jackson, Miss.

Mississippi Department of Education. 1989. Public School Enrollment, 1989–1990. Jackson, Miss. Computer printout.

Mississippi Secretary of State. 1934–1935. Charter of Incorporation of the Okatoba Hunting and Fishing Club. Record of Charters. Jackson, Miss.

Official Records of the Union and Confederate Armies. (The War of the Rebellion). 1890–1900. Washington, D.C.: Government Printing Office. (Cited as *Official Records*).

Panola County, Mississippi. Batesville. Office of the Chancery Clerk. County land records and maps.

U.S. Army Corps of Engineers. Sardis Reservoir construction photographs, 1935–1939. Sardis Reservoir land acquisition maps, 1936. Vicksburg District Office, Mississippi.

U.S. Bureau of the Census. 1902. *Twelfth Census of the United States Taken in the Year 1900.* Vol. 6, *Agriculture.* Part 2, *Crops and Irrigation.* Washington, D.C.: Government Printing Office.

——. 1932. *Fifteenth Census of the United States 1930.* Vol. 2, *Agriculture.* Part 2, *The Southern States.* Washington, D.C.: Government Printing Office.

——. 1933. *Abstract of the Fifteenth Census of the United States.* Washington, D.C.: Government Printing Office.

——. [1948]. Special Study: Plantations Based on Tabulations from the Sixteenth Census 1940. Washington, D.C.: Government Printing Office (lithographed).

——. 1960. *Historical Statistics of the United States. Continuation to 1962 and Revisions.* Washington, D.C.: Government Printing Office. Supplements.

——. 1967. *1964 Census of Agriculture,* vol. 1, part 33, *Mississippi,* 263. Washington, D.C.: Government Printing Office.

——. 1975. *Census of Population 1970. Supplementary Report, Race of the Population by County.* Washington, D.C.: Government Printing Office.

U.S. Census Office. 1864a. *Agriculture of the United States: Compiled from the Original Returns of the Eighth Census.* Washington, D.C.: Government Printing Office.

——. 1864b. *Population of the United States in 1860: Compiled from the Original Returns of the Eighth Census.* Washington, D.C.: Government Printing Office.

U.S. Department of Agriculture. 2002. *2002 Census of Agriculture, Mississippi,* www.usda.gov.

Manuscript and Archival Collections

Agee, James. Papers. Special Collections. Hoskins Library, University of Tennessee Libraries. Knoxville, Tenn.

Brown, Clarence. Collection. MS 702. Special Collections, Hoskins Library, University of Tennessee Libraries. Knoxville, Tenn.

Catledge, Turner. Papers. Mitchell Library, Mississippi State University. State College, Miss.

College Church. College Hill, Miss. 1835–1865. Congregational and Sessional Records. Transcribed copy by Gladys M. Morrison and Karl F. Morrison, 1955. Department of Archives and Special Collections, J. D. Williams Library, University of Mississippi.

Faulkner, William. Collection. Department of Archives and Special Collections, J. D. Williams Library, University of Mississippi.

Faulkner, William. Collection. Special Collections, Alderman Library, University of Virginia, Charlottesville.

Harmon Collection. Knoxville, Tenn.

Holt, Minnie Smith. [1935]. Oxford, Mississippi (typescript, 44 pp.). Federal Writers' Project, Works Progress Administration. Department of Archives and Special Collections, J. D. Williams Library, University of Mississippi.

Lafayette County and Oxford Collections. Mississippi Department of Archives and History. Jackson, Miss.

National Cotton Council of America. Cotton Mechanization Files. Memphis, Tenn.

Thorne, William. Collection. Knoxville, Tenn.

U.S. Works Progress Administration, Manuscripts of Federal Writers' Project. Department of Archives and Special Collections, J. D. Williams Library, University of Mississippi.

Newspapers

Athens (Ga.) Observer
Atlanta Journal-Constitution
Batesville (Miss.) Panolian
Commercial Appeal (Memphis)
Jackson (Miss.) Daily News
Memphis Press-Scimitar
New York Evening Express
New York Times
Oxford (Miss.) Eagle
Tate County Democrat (Senatobia, Miss.)

Books and Articles

Agee, James, and Walker Evans. 1941. *Let Us Now Praise Famous Men.* Boston: Houghton Mifflin.

Aiken, Charles S. 1971. The Role of the Eli Whitney Cotton Gin in the Origin of the United States Cotton Regions. *Proceedings of the Association of American Geographers* 8:5–9.

———. 1998. *The Cotton Plantation South since the Civil War.* Baltimore: Johns Hopkins University Press.

———. 2001. Blacks in the Plantation South: Unique Homelands. In *Homelands: A Geography of Culture and Place across America,* ed. Richard L. Nostrand and Lawrence E. Estaville, 53–72. Baltimore: Johns Hopkins University Press.

Ash, Stephen V. 1995. *When the Yankees Came: Conflict and Chaos in the Occupied South, 1861–1865.* Chapel Hill: University of North Carolina Press.

Auchmutey, Jim. 2001. Welcome to the Hotel Mississippi: Shacks Are Chic in Clarksdale, the Crossroads of the Delta Blues. *Atlanta Journal-Constitution,* July 29, K1, K6.

Barber, Lucius W. 1894. *Army Memories of Lucius W. Barber, Company D, 15th Illinois Infantry: May 24, 1861–September 30, 1865.* Chicago: J. M. W. Jones Stationery and Printing Co.

Barrett, Russell H. 1965. *Integration at Ole Miss.* Chicago: Quadrangle Books.

Bartley, Numan V. 1969. *The Rise of Massive Resistance: Race and Politics in the South during the 1950s.* Baton Rouge: Louisiana State University Press.

Bartram, William. 1791. *Travels through North and South Carolina, Georgia, East and West Florida.* Philadelphia: James and Johnson. Repr. edited by Mark Van Doran, New York: Dover Publications, 1928.

Batteau, Allen. 1990. *The Invention of Appalachia.* Tucson: University of Arizona Press.

Bearss, Edwin C. 1962. *Decision in Mississippi: Mississippi's Important Role in the War Between the States.* Jackson: Mississippi Commission on the War Between the States.

———. 1979. *Forrest at Brice's Cross Roads and in North Mississippi.* Dayton, Ohio: Morningside Bookshop.

Beck, Warren. 1955. The New Faulkner. *College English* 17:183–184.

Blotner, Joseph. 1974. *Faulkner: A Biography.* 2 vols. New York: Random House.

———, ed. 1977. *Selected Letters of William Faulkner.* New York: Random House.

Bogle, Donald. 1973. *Tom, Coons, Mulattoes, Mannies, and Bucks: An Interpretative History of Blacks in American Films.* New York: Viking.

Borstelmann, Thomas. 2001. *The Cold War and the Color Line: American Race Relations in the Global Arena.* Cambridge, Mass.: Harvard University Press.

Brooks, Cleanth. 1963. *William Faulkner: The Yoknapatawpha Country.* New Haven, Conn.: Yale University Press.

Brown, Calvin S. 1926. *Archeology of Mississippi.* University, Miss.: Mississippi Geological Survey.

Brown, Calvin S., Jr. 1962. Faulkner's Geography and Topography. *Publications of the Modern Language Association* 78:652–659.

———. 1971. Faulkner's Three-in-One Bridge in *The Reivers. Notes on Contemporary Literature* 1, no. 2: 8–10.

———. 1976. *A Glossary of Faulkner's South.* New Haven, Conn.: Yale University Press.

Brown, D. Alexander. 1954. *Grierson's Raid.* Urbana: University of Illinois Press.

Brown, Maud Morrow. 1940. *The University Greys: Company A Eleventh Mississippi Regiment Army of Northern Virginia, 1861–1865.* Richmond, Va.: Garrett and Massie.

———. 1954. The War Comes to College Hill. *Journal of Mississippi History* 16:22–30.

———. 1956. William C. Falkner, Man of Legends. *Georgia Review* 10:421–439.

Brownlee, Edgar. Obituary. 1981. *Tate County (Mississippi) Democrat.* March 25, 1B.

Brunn, Erik, and Jay Crosby. 1999. *Our Nation's Archive: The History of the United States in Documents*. New York: Black Dog and Leventhal Publishers.

Buckingham, J. S. 1842. *The Slave States*. 2 vols. London: Fisher, Son, and Company.

Buckley, G. T. 1961. Is Oxford the Original of Jefferson in William Faulkner's Novels? *Publications of the Modern Language Association* 76:447–454.

Buckley, Thomas. 1962. Soldiers Beaten; Homes Damaged. *New York Times*. October 2, 24.

Burford, Roger L. 1963. *Net Migration for Southern Counties, 1940–1950, 1950–1960*. Atlanta: Publishing Sevices Division, School of Business Administration, Georgia State University.

Caldwell, Erskine, and Margaret Bourke-White. 1937. *You Have Seen Their Faces*. New York: Modern Age Books.

Campbell, John C. 1921. *The Southern Highlander and His Homeland*. New York: Russell Sage Foundation.

Canton, Bruce. 1960. *Grant Moves South*. Boston: Little, Brown and Company.

Caron, Timothy P. 2000. *Struggles Over the World: Race and Religion in O'Connor, Faulkner, Hurston, and Wright*. Macon, Ga.: Mercer University Press.

Carter, Jimmy. 2001. *An Hour Before Daylight: Memories of a Rural Boyhood*. New York: Touchstone.

Caudill, Harry M. 1962. *Night Comes to the Cumberlands*. Boston: Little, Brown and Company.

Cell, John W. 1987. *The Highest Stage of White Supremacy: The Origins of Segregation in South Africa and the American South*. New York: Cambridge University Press.

Clawson, Marion. 1968. *The Land System in the United States*. Lincoln: University of Nebraska Press.

Cobb, James C. 1992. *The Most Southern Place on Earth*. New York: Oxford University Press.

———. 1996. Community and Identity: Redefining Southern Culture. *Georgia Review* 50, no. 1: 9–24.

Cody, Annie E. [1946]. *History of the Tennessee Division United Daughters of the Confederacy*. Nashville: Cullom and Ghertner.

Coulter, E. Merton. 1950. *The Confederate States of America, 1861–1865*. Baton Rouge: Louisiana State University Press.

Cowley, Malcolm, ed. 1946. *The Portable Faulkner*. New York: Viking Press.

———, ed. 1958. *Writers at Work: The* Paris Review *Interviews*. New York: Viking Press.

———. 1966. *The Faulkner-Cowley File: Letters and Memories, 1944–1962*. New York: Viking Press.

Cramer, Jesse Grant, ed. 1912. *Letters of Ulysses S. Grant to His Father and His Youngest Sister, 1857–78*. New York: G. P. Putnam's Sons.

Cripps, Thomas. 1993. *Making Movies Black: The Hollywood Message Movie from World War II to the Civil Rights Era*. New York: Oxford University Press.

Cullen, John B. 1961. *Old Times in Faulkner Country*. Chapel Hill: University of North Carolina Press.

Dabney, Lewis M. 1974. *The Indians of Yoknapatawpha: A Study in Literature and History*. Baton Rouge: Louisiana State University Press.

Dardis, Tom. 1976. *Some Time in the Sun*. New York: Charles Scribner's Sons.

Dasher, Thomas E. 1981. *William Faulkner's Characters: An Index to Published and Unpublished Fiction*. New York: Garland Publishing.

Davis, Edward Everett. 1940. *The White Scourge*. San Antonio: Naylor Company.

Davis, Thadious M. 1983. *Faulkner's "Negro": Art and the Southern Context.* Baton Rouge: Louisiana State University Press.

DeRosier, Arthur H., Jr. 1970. *The Removal of the Choctaw Indians.* Knoxville: University of Tennessee Press.

Dobyns, Henry F. 1983. *Their Number Becomes Thinned: Native Americans Population in Eastern North America.* Knoxville: University of Tennessee Press.

Dollard, John. 1937. *Cast and Class in a Southern Town.* New Haven, Conn.: Yale University Press.

Downing, Alexander G. 1916. *Downing's Civil War Diary: August 15, 1861–July 31, 1865*, ed. Olynthus B. Clark. Des Moines: Historical Department of Iowa.

Doyle, Don H. 2001. *Faulkner's County: The Historical Roots of Yoknapatawpha.* Chapel Hill: University of North Carolina Press.

Doyle, William. 2003. *An American Insurrection: The Battle of Oxford, Mississippi, 1962.* New York: Anchor Books.

Dray, Philip. 2002. *At the Hands of Persons Unknown: The Lynching of Black America.* New York: Random House.

Duclos, Donald Philip. 1998. *Son of Sorrow: The Life, Works and Influence of Colonel William C. Falkner 1825–1889.* San Francisco: International Scholars Publications.

Duncan, Sallie Belle. [1930]. Early History of Lafayette County. In "Some Early History of Lafayette County, Mississippi, Compiled by David Reese Chapter Daughters of the American Revolution" (typescript). Mississippi Department of Archives and History, Jackson.

Eaton, John, and Ethel O. Mason. 1907. *Grant, Lincoln, and the Freedmen.* New York: Longmans, Green.

Egerton, John. 1994. *Speak Now Against the Day: The Generation Before the Civil Rights Movement in the South.* New York: Alfred A. Knopf.

Fadiman, Regina K. 1978. *Faulkner's Intruder in the Dust: Novel into Film.* Knoxville: University of Tennessee Press.

Falkner, Murry C. 1967. *The Falkners of Mississippi: A Memoir.* Baton Rouge: Louisiana State University Press.

Falkner, William Clark. 1881. *The White Rose of Memphis.* New York: G. W. Carleton and Co.

Fant, Joseph L., III, and Robert Ashley. 1964. *Faulkner at West Point.* New York: Random House.

Faulkner, John. 1963. *My Brother Bill: An Affectionate Reminiscence.* New York: Trident Press.

Faulkner, William. 1929. *Sartoris.* New York: Harcourt, Grace and Company.

———. 1929 *The Sound and the Fury.* New York: Jonathan Cape and Harrison Smith.

———. 1930. *As I Lay Dying.* New York: Jonathan Cape and Harrison Smith.

———. 1930/1977. A Rose for Emily. In *Collected Stories of William Faulkner*, 119–130. New York: Vintage Books.

———. 1930/1946. Red Leaves. In *The Portable Faulkner*, ed. Malcolm Cowley, 74–104. New York: Viking Press.

———. 1931. *Sanctuary.* New York: Jonathan Cape and Harrison Smith.

———. 1932. *Light in August.* New York: Harrison Smith and Robert Hass.

———. 1932/1977. Mountain Victory. In *Collected Stories of William Faulkner*, 745–777. New York: Vintage Books.

———. 1934/1977. A Bear Hunt. In *Collected Stories of William Faulkner*, 63–79. New York: Vintage Books.

———. 1935. Lion. *Harper's Magazine*, December, 67–77.

———. 1936. *Absalom, Absalom!* New York: Random House.

———. 1938. *The Unvanquished*. New York: Random House.

———. 1939/1977. Barn Burning. In *Collected Stories of William Faulkner*, 3–25. New York: Vintage Books.

———. 1940. *The Hamlet*. New York: Random House.

———. 1942. The Bear. *Saturday Evening Post*, May 9, 30–31, 74, 76–77.

———. 1942. Delta Autumn. *Story*, May–June, 46–55.

———. 1942. *Go Down, Moses and Other Stories*. New York: Random House.

———. 1942/1977. Two Soldiers. In *Collected Stories of William Faulkner*, 81–99. New York: Vintage Books.

———. 1943/1977. My Grandmother Millard and General Bedford Forrest and the Battle of Harrykin Creek. In *Collected Stories of William Faulkner*, 667–699. New York: Vintage Books.

———. 1943/1977. Shall Not Perish. In *Collected Stories of William Faulkner*, 101–115. New York: Vintage Books.

———. 1948. *Intruder in the Dust*. New York: Random House.

———. 1951. *Requiem for a Nun*. New York: Random House.

———. 1954. *A Fable*. New York: Random House.

———. 1955. *Big Woods*. New York: Random House.

———. 1955. Address to the Southern Historical Association. In Meriwether 1965, 146–151.

———. 1955. Faulkner in Manila. In Meriwether and Millgate 1968, 119–214.

———. 1957. *The Town*. New York: Random House.

———. 1959. *The Mansion*. New York: Random House.

———. 1962. Hell Creek Crossing. *Saturday Evening Post*, March 31, 22–25.

———. 1962. *The Reivers*. New York: Random House.

———. 1973. *Flags in the Dust*. New York: Random House.

Faulkner's Hometown Upset about Statue of Late Author. 1997. *Knoxville News-Sentinel*, February 18, A8.

Foote, Shelby. 1977. Faulkner's Depiction of the Planter Aristocracy. In *The South and Faulkner's Yoknapatawpha: The Actual and the Apocryphal*, ed. Evans Harrington and Ann J. Abadie, 40–61. Jackson: University Press of Mississippi.

Ford, Mary Ann. 1969. The Metamorphosis of Robert Frost's Masks. M.A. thesis, University of Memphis.

Friis, Herman R. 1968. *A Series of Population Maps of the Colonies and the United States, 1625–1790*. New York: American Geographical Society.

Gallagher, Gary W. 1998. Introduction to *The Myth of the Lost Cause and Civil War History*, ed. Gary W. Gallagher and Alan T. Nolan. Bloomington: Indiana University Press.

Garbo's Favorite Director Has Left a Valuable Legacy to U.T. Students and All of Tennessee. 2005. *Tennessee Alumnus*, Winter, 3A–10A.

Garner, James Wilford. 1901. *Reconstruction in Mississippi*. Repr., Baton Rouge: Louisiana State University Press, 1968.

Gibson, Arrell M. 1971. *The Chickasaws*. Norman: University of Oklahoma Press.

Grant, Julia Dent. 1975. *The Personal Memories of Julia Dent Grant*, ed. John Y. Simon. New York: G. P. Putnam's Sons.

Grant, U. S. 1885. *Personal Memoirs*. 2 vols. New York: Charles L. Webster and Company.

Green, Wigfall A. 1932. *Sewanee Review* 40 (Summer): 299–300.

Greenhaw, Wayne. 1986. "Rommel and the Rebel" is a Solid First Novel. *Atlanta Journal-Constitution*, March 2.

Gwynn, Frederick L., and Joseph L. Blotner. 1959. *Faulkner in the University*. Charlottesville: University of Virginia Press.

Halberstam, David. 1993. *The Fifties*. New York: Villard Books.

Harmon, George. 1949. Faulkner Takes Bow at Oxford Premier of his Novel Film. *Jackson Daily News*, October 12, 1.

Harmontown Community Historical Society. 1977. *Come Reminisce with Us: Harmontown U.S.A.* Como, Miss.

Hart, John Fraser. 1976. *The South*, 2nd ed. New York: D. Van Nostrand.

Hartje, Robert G. 1967. *Van Dorn: The Life and Times of a Confederate General*. Nashville: Vanderbilt University Press.

Hathorn, John Cooper. [1938]. A Period Study of Lafayette County. M.A. thesis, University of Mississippi.

Heller, Joseph. 1961. *Catch-22*. New York: Simon and Schuster.

Hickman, Lisa C. 2006. *William Faulkner and Joan Williams: The Romance of Two Writers*. Jefferson, N.C.: McFarland and Company.

Hilgard, Eugene W. 1860. *Report on the Geology and Agriculture of the State of Mississippi*. Jackson, Miss.: E. Barksdale.

———. 1884. *Report on Cotton Production in the United States*. 2 parts. Washington, D.C.: Government Printing Office.

———. 1907. *Soils*. New York: Macmillan.

Hirshson, Stanley P. 1997. *The White Tecumseh: A Biography of General William T. Sherman*. New York: John Wiley and Sons.

Hönnighausen, Lothar. 1997. *Faulkner, Masks and Metaphors*. Jackson: University Press of Mississippi.

Howe, Irving. 1952. *William Faulkner: A Critical Study*, 2nd ed. New York: Vintage Books.

Hudson, Charles. 1976. *The Southeastern Indians*. Knoxville: University of Tennessee Press.

———. 1997. *Knights of Spain, Warriors of the Sun: Hernando de Soto and the South's Ancient Chiefdoms*. Athens: University of Georgia Press.

Huie, William Bradford. 1956. The Shocking Story of Approved Killing in Mississippi. *Look*, January 24, 46–49.

Hurley, F. Jack. 1972. *Portrait of a Decade: Roy Stryker and the Development of Documentary Photography in the Thirties*. Baton Rouge: Louisiana University Press.

Irwin, John T. 1975. *Doubling and Incest/Repetition and Revenge, A Speculative Reading of Faulkner*. Baltimore: Johns Hopkins University Press.

Jackson, Jarome A. 2004. *In Search of the Ivory-Billed Woodpecker*. Washington, D.C.: Smithsonian Books.

Joint Center for Political and Economic Studies. 1991. *Black Elected Officials: A National Roster, 1990*. Washington, D.C.: Joint Center for Political and Economic Studies Press.

Jones, Dorothy B. 1953–1954. William Faulkner: Novel into Film. *Quarterly of Film, Radio, and Television* 8:51–71.

Jones, James. 1951. *From Here to Eternity*. New York: Charles Scribner's Sons.

Jordan, Terry G. 1967. The Imprint of the Upper and Lower South on Mid-Nineteenth-Century Texas. *Annals of the Association of American Geographers* 57 (December): 667–690.

———. 1970. The Texan Appalachia. *Annals of the Association of American Geographers* 60 (September): 409–427.

Jordan, Winthrop D. 1974. *The White Man's Burden: Historical Origins of Racism in the United States*. New York: Oxford University Press.

Jordan, Thomas, and J. P. Prior. 1868. *The Campaigns of Lieut.-Gen. N. B. Forrest's Cavalry*. New Orleans: Blelock and Co.

Katagiri, Yasuhiro. 2001. *The Mississippi State Sovereignty Commission: Civil Rights and States' Rights*. Jackson: University Press of Mississippi.

Kendel, Julia. 1913. Reconstruction in Lafayette County. *Publications of the Mississippi Historical Society* 13:223–271.

Kephart, Horace. 1913. *Our Southern Highlanders*. New York: Outing Publishing Company.

Kerr, Elizabeth M. 1969. *Yoknapatawpha: Faulkner's "Little Postage Stamp of Native Soil."* New York: Fordham University Press.

King, Larry. 2006. *In Search of Willie Morris: The Mercurial Life of a Legendary Writer and Editor*. New York: Public Affairs.

King, Martin Luther, Jr. 1958. *Stride toward Freedom: The Montgomery Story*. New York: Martin and Row.

Kluger, Richard. 1976. *Simple Justice: The History of Brown v. Board of Education and Black America's Struggle for Equality*. New York: Alfred A. Knopf.

Konigsmark, Anne Rochell. 1999. Newcomers Flooding Mississippi Landmark. *Atlanta Journal-Constitution*, April 11, H5.

Kotz, Nick. 2005. *Judgment Days: Lyndon Baines Johnson, Martin Luther King Jr., and the Laws that Changed America*. Boston: Houghton Mifflin.

Lange, Dorothea, and Paul Schuster Taylor. 1939. *An American Exodus: A Record of Human Erosion*. New York: Reynal and Hitchcock.

Langsford, E. L., and B. H. Thibodeaux. 1939. *Plantation Organization and Operation in the Yazoo-Mississippi Delta*. U.S. Department of Agriculture, Technical Bulletin 682. Washington, D.C.: Government Printing Office.

Lee, Harper. 1960. *To Kill A Mockingbird*. Philadelphia: Lippincott.

Lloyd, James B. 1979. *The University of Mississippi: The Formative Years*. University, Miss.: Department of Archives and Special Collections, University of Mississippi.

Lowenthal, David. 1985. *The Past Is a Foreign Country*. New York: Cambridge University Press.

Lytle, Andrew Nelson. 1931. *Bedford Forrest and His Critter Company*. New York: G. P. Putnam's Sons.

McAlexander, Hubert. 1977. General Earl Van Dorn and Faulkner's Use of History. *Journal of Mississippi History* 40 (Fall): 357–361.

———. 1986. Flush Times in Holly Springs. *Journal of Mississippi History* 48: (February): 1–13.

———. 2000. *A Southern Tapestry: Marshall County Mississippi, 1835–2000*. Virginia Beach, Va.: Donning Company Publishing.

McCommons, Pete. 1978. Closeup: Calvin Brown [Jr.]. *Athens (Ga.) Observer*, March 8, 10–12.

McElfresh, Earl B. 1999. *Maps and Mapmakers of the Civil War*. New York: Harry N. Abrams, Inc.

McHaney, Thomas L. 1977. Yoknapatawpha: A Domain of Words. In *Faulkner in Venice*, ed. Rosella Mamoli Zorzi and Pia Masiero Marcolin. Proceedings of the Language, Stylistics, Translations Conference, November, University of Venice, Ca'Foscari. Venice: Marsilio, 2000, 89–99.

McHaney, Thomas L., ed. 1987. *Go Down, Moses: Typescripts and Miscellaneous Typescript Pages*. New York: Garland Publishing.

McIlvaine, Bowers Reed. 1837. Letters to Catherine Dumesnil McIlvaine. In *Letters on the Chickasaw Removal of 1837*, ed. John E. Parsons, 273–283. New York Historical Society Quarterly, July 1953.

McMillen, Neil R., ed. 1997. *Remaking Dixie: The Impact of World War II on the American South*. Jackson: University Press of Mississippi.

McPherson, James M. 1988. *Battle Cry of Freedom: The Civil War Era*. New York: Oxford University Press.

———. 1997. From Limited War to Total War in America. In *On the Road to Total War: The American Civil War and the German Wars of Unification, 1861–1871*, ed. Stig Förster and Jörg Nagler, 295–309. Washington, D.C.: German Historical Institute and Cambridge University Press.

Mailer, Norman. 1948. *The Naked and the Dead*. New York: Rinehart.

Marks, Jack. 1955. Senatobia Meeting Boosts Segregation. *Commercial Appeal*, August 14, sec. 1, 7.

Massengill, Reed. 1996. *Portrait of a Racist*. New York: St. Martin's.

Mayes, Edward. 1896. *Lucius Q. C. Lamar: His Life, Times, and Speeches, 1825–1893*. Nashville: Publishing House of the Methodist Episcopal Church, South.

Memphis, Tennessee, Telephone Directory. 1931, 1942. Birmingham, Ala.: Southern Bell Telephone and Telegraph Company.

Meriwether, James B., ed. 1965. *Essays, Speeches and Public Letters of William Faulkner*. New York: Random House.

Meriwether, James B., and Michael Millgate, eds. 1968. *Lion in the Garden: Interviews with William Faulkner, 1926–1962*. New York: Random House.

Mikesell, Marvin W. 1976. The Rise and Decline of "Sequent Occupance": A Chapter in the History of American Geography. In *Geographies of the Mind*, ed. David Lowenthal and Martyn J. Bowden, 149–169. New York: Oxford University Press.

Miller, Francis Trevelyan, and Robert S. Lanier, eds. 1911. *Photographic History of the Civil War*. New York: Review of Reviews Co.

Miller, William D. 1964. *Mr. Crump of Memphis*. Baton Rouge: Louisiana State University Press.

Millgate, Michael. 1966. *The Achievement of William Faulkner*. New York: Random House.

Mills, Cynthia, and Pamela H. Simpson, eds. 2003. *Monuments to the Lost Cause: Women, Art, and the Landscapes of Southern Memory*. Knoxville: University of Tennessee Press.

Miner, Ward L. 1959. *The World of William Faulkner*. New York: Pageant Book Company.

Minter, David. 1980. *William Faulkner: His Life and Work*. Baltimore: Johns Hopkins University Press.

Moore, Albert Burton. 1924. *Conscription in the Confederacy*. New York: Macmillan.

Moreland, Richard C. 2002. Faulkner's Continuing Education: From Self-Reflection to Embarrassment. In *Faulkner at 100: Retrospect and Prospect*, ed. Donald M. Kartiganer and Ann J. Abadie, 260–288. Jackson: University Press of Mississippi.

Morton, John Watson. 1909. *The Artillery of Nathan Bedford Forrest's Cavalry*. Nashville: Publishing House of the Methodist Episcopal Church, South.

Muehrcke, Phillip C., and Juliana O. Muehrcke. 1974. Maps in Literature. *Geographical Review* 64 (July): 317–318.

Myrdal, Gunnar. 1944. *An American Dilemma: The Negro Problem in America*. New York: Harper and Row.

Nash, Roderick. 1973. *Wilderness and the American Mind*, rev. ed. New Haven, Conn.: Yale University Press.

Natanson, Nicholas. 1992. *The Black Image in the New Deal: The Politics of FSA Photography*. Knoxville: University of Tennessee Press.

Neely, Mark E., Jr. 1997. Was the Civil War a Total War? In *On the Road to Total War: The American Civil War and the German Wars of Unification, 1861–1871*, ed. Stig Förster and Jörg Nagler, 229–294. Washington, D.C.: German Historical Institute and Cambridge University Press.

Nichols, Ralph R., and Morton B. King Jr. 1943. *Social Effects of Government Land Purchase*. Bulletin 390, Agricultural Experiment Station, Mississippi State College.

Oliver, Deborah Lynn. 1973. Survey of American Critical Reaction to the Film Career of Clarence Brown. M.A. thesis, University of Tennessee, Knoxville.

Olmsted, Frederick Law. 1860. *A Journey in the Back Country*. New York: Mason Brothers.

O'Neill, William L. 2001. Fanning the Flames: Longstanding Methods of Curtailing Fires May Encourage Them Instead. *New York Times Book Review*, May 13, 21.

Oxford–Lafayette County Heritage Foundation. 1999. Save the Depot Project. *Oxford–Lafayette County Heritage Foundation Newsletter*, Fall, 1.

Parkins, A. E. 1938. *The South: Its Economic-Geographical Development*. New York: John Wiley and Sons.

Parks, Joseph H. 1941. A Confederate Trade Center under Federal Occupation: Memphis, 1862 to 1865. *Journal of Southern History* 7 (August): 289–314.

Payne, Stephen J. 1982. *Fire in America: A Cultural History of Wildland and Rural Fire*. Princeton, N.J.: Princeton University Press.

———. 1997. *Vestal Fire: An Environmental History, Told through Fire, of Europe's Encounter with the World*. Seattle: University of Washington Press.

Percy, William Alexander. 1941. *Lanterns on the Levee: Recollections of a Planter's Son*. New York: Alfred A. Knopf.

Pillsbury, Richard. 1989. Cultural Landscape. In *Encyclopedia of Southern Culture*, ed. Charles Reagan Wilson and William Farris, 533–541. Chapel Hill: University of North Carolina Press.

Polk, Noel. 1997. *Outside the Southern Myth*. Jackson: University Press of Mississippi.

Polk, Noel, and Ann J. Abadie, eds. 2004. *Faulkner and War: Faulkner and Yoknapatawpha 2001*. Jackson: University Press of Mississippi.

Polk's Memphis City Directory. 1945. St. Louis, Mo.: R. L. Polk and Company.

Pollard, Edward A. 1866. *The Lost Cause: A New Southern History of the War of the Confederates*. New York: E. B. Treat and Company.

Powdermaker, Hortense. 1939. *After Freedom: A Cultural Study in the Deep South*. New York: Viking Press.

Raper, Arthur F., and Ira De A. Reid. 1941. *Sharecroppers All*. Chapel Hill: University of North Carolina Press.

Riley, Franklin L. 1902. Extinct Towns and Villages of Mississippi. *Publications of the Mississippi Historical Society* 5:311–383.

Ringle, Ken. 1998. Faulkner between the Lines: The Author Was Hard to Read, Even in Person. *Virginia*, Spring, 12–17.

Roper, John H., ed. 1997. *C. Vann Woodward: A Southern Historian and His Critics*. Athens: University of Georgia Press.

Shaw, Irwin. 1948. *The Young Lions*. New York: Random House.

Sherman, William T. 1875. *Memoirs of General William T. Sherman*. 2 vols. New York: D. Appleton and Co.

Silver, James W. 1964. *Mississippi: The Closed Society*. New York: Harcourt, Brace and World.

Simple, Ellen C. 1901. The Anglo-Saxons of the Kentucky Mountains. *Geographical Journal* 17:588–623.

Sinclair, Harold. 1955. *The Horse Soldiers*. New York: Harper and Brothers.

Singal, Daniel J. 1997. *William Faulkner: The Making of a Modernist*. Chapel Hill: University of North Carolina Press.

Smith, Chesley Thorne. 1996. *Childhood in Holly Springs: A Memoir*. Lafayette, Calif.: Thomas-Berryhill Press.

Smith, Marvin T. 1994. Aboriginal Depopulation in the Postcontact Southeast. In *The Forgotten Centuries: Indians and Europeans in the American South, 1521–1704*, ed. Charles T. Hudson and Carmen Chaves Tesser, 257–275. Athens: University of Georgia Press.

Snell, Susan. 1991. *Phil Stone: A Vicarious Life*. Athens: University of Georgia Press.

Sobotka, C. John Jr. [1976]. *A History of Lafayette County, Mississippi*. Oxford, Miss.: Rebel Press.

Sonnichsen, C. L. 1969. The Sharecropper Novel in the Southwest. *Agricultural History* 43 (April): 249–258.

Stein, Jean. 1956. William Faulkner. In Cowley 1958, 119–141.

Stoddard, H. L. 1962. Use of Fire in Pine Forest and Game Lands of the Deep Southeast. In *Proceedings of Tall Timbers Fire Ecological Conference*, 1:31–42. Tallahassee, Fla.: Tall Timbers Research Station.

Stone, Emily Whitehurst. 1965. How a Writer Finds His Material. *Harper's Magazine*, November, 157–161.

Stone, James H. 1970. The Economic Development of Holly Springs during the 1840s. *Journal of Mississippi History* 32:341–361.

Stott, William. 1973. *Documentary Expression and Thirties America*. New York: Oxford University Press.

Stuart, Jesse. 1938. *Beyond Dark Hills*. New York: E. P. Dutton.

Survivors Association of Lamar Rifles. [1901]. *Lamar Rifles: A History of Company G, Eleventh Mississippi Regiment, C.S.A.* Oxford, Miss.: privately printed.

Tanner, James Taylor. 1942. *The Ivory-Billed Woodpecker*. Report no. 1. Washington, D.C.: National Audubon Society. Repr., New York: Dover Publications, 1966.

Taylor, Herman E. 1990. *Faulkner's Oxford: Recollections and Reflections*. Nashville: Rutledge Hill Press.

Thompson, Julius E. 2001. *Black Life in Mississippi: Essays on Political, Social, and Cultural Studies in a Deep South State*. New York: University Press of America.

Tumin, Melvin M. et al. 1958. *Desegregation and Resistance and Readiness*. Princeton, N.J.: Princeton University Press.

United States. Works Progress Administration. Federal Writers' Project. 1938. *Mississippi: A Guide to the Magnolia State*. New York: Viking Press.

Urgo, Joseph R. 1989. *Faulkner's Apocrypha: A Fable, Snopes, and the Spirit of Human Rebellion*. Jackson: University Press of Mississippi.

Utley, Francis Lee, Lynn L. Bloom, and Arthur F. Kinney, eds. 1971. *Bear Man and God: Eight Approaches to William Faulkner's "The Bear."* 2nd ed. New York: Random House.

Vahanian, Gabriel. 1964. *Wait without Idols*. New York: George Braziller.

Vance, Rupert B. 1935. *Human Geography of the South*. 2nd ed. Chapel Hill: University of North Carolina Press.

Vejnoska, Jill. 2000. Revival at Rowan Oak. *Atlanta Journal-Constitution*, October 29, M1–M4.

Wade, Richard C. 1970. An Agenda for Urban History. In *The State of American History*, ed. Herbert J. Bass, 43–69. Chicago: Quadrangle Books.

Wallace, Anthony F. C. 1999. *Jefferson and the Indians: The Tragic Fate of the First Americans*. Cambridge, Mass.: Belknap Press of Harvard University Press.

Welch, Frank J. 1943. *The Plantation Land Tenure System in Mississippi*. Agricultural Experiment Station Bulletin 385. State College: Mississippi State College.

Weller, Jack E. 1966. *Yesterday's People*. Lexington: University of Kentucky Press.

Wells, Lawrence. 1986. *Rommel and the Rebel*. New York: Doubleday.

White, Mel. 2006. The Ghost Bird. *National Geographic*, December, 142–157.

Whitfield, Stephen J. 1988. *A Death in the Delta: The Story of Emmett Till*. New York: Free Press.

Whittlesey, Derwent. 1929. Sequent Occupance. *Annals of the Association of American Geographers* 19 (September): 162–165.

Widmer, Randolph J. 1994. The Structure of Southeastern Chiefdoms. In *Forgotten Centuries: Indians and Europeans in the American South, 1521–1704*, ed. Charles Hudson and Carmen Chaves Tesser, 125–155. Athens: University of Georgia Press.

Wilde, Meta Carpenter, and Orin Borsten. 1976. *A Loving Gentleman: The Love Story of William Faulkner and Meta Carpenter*. New York: Simon and Schuster.

Williams, Juan. 1988. *Eyes on the Prize: America's Civil Rights Years, 1954–1965*. New York: Penguin Books.

Williams, Tennessee. 1955. *Cat on a Hot Tin Roof*. New York: New Directions Books.

Williamson, Joel. 1993. *William Faulkner and Southern History*. New York: Oxford University Press.

Williamson, Samuel H., 2008. Six Ways to Compute the Relative Value of a U.S. Dollar Amount, 1790–2007. Institute for the Measurement of Worth, http://www.measuringworth.com.

Wills, Brian Steel. 1992. *A Battle from the Start: The Life of Nathan Bedford Forrest*. New York: Harper Collins.

Wilson, Charles Reagan. 1980. *Baptized in Blood: The Religion of the Lost Cause, 1865–1920*. Athens: University of Georgia Press.

Windberry, John J. 1983. "Lest We Forget": The Confederate Monument and the Southern Townscape. *Southeastern Geographer* 59 (May): 107–121.

Winik, Jay. 2002. *April 1865: The Month that Saved America*. New York: Perennial.

Wolff, Sally, and Floyd C. Watkins. 1996. *Talking about William Faulkner*. Baton Rouge: Louisiana State University Press.

Woodward, C. Vann. 1951. *Origins of the New South, 1877–1913*. Baton Rouge: Louisiana State University Press.

———. 1955. *The Strange Career of Jim Crow*. New York: Oxford University Press.

———. 1960. *The Burden of Southern History*. Vol. 9 of *A History of the South*, ed. E. Merton Coulter and Wendell Holmes Stephenson. Baton Rouge: Louisiana State University Press.

———. 1986. *Thinking Back: The Perils of Writing History*. Baton Rouge: Louisiana State University Press.

———. 1989. *The Future of the Past*. New York: Oxford University Press.

York, Neil Longley. 2001. *Fiction as Fact: The Horse Soldiers and Popular Memory*. Kent, Ohio: Kent State University Press.

Young, Mary Elizabeth. 1961. *Redskins Ruffleshirts and Rednecks: Indian Allotments in Alabama and Mississippi, 1830–1860*. Norman: University of Oklahoma Press.

Zangrando, Robert L. 1980. *The NAACP Crusade against Lynching, 1909–1950*. Philadelphia: Temple University Press.

Zelinsky, Wilbur. 1992. *The Cultural Geography of the United States*. Rev. ed. Englewood Cliffs, N.J.: Prentice-Hall.

INDEX

McElroy's Grocery, 12
McGehee plantation, 177–179; map of, 178
McHaney, Thomas, 188
McIlvaine, Bowers Reed, 68
McKinley, William, 125
McLean, Alabama Leroy (Aunt 'Bama), 218
McMillen, Neil, 181
McPherson, James B., 100
McPherson, James M., 112–114
Madison Avenue (Oxford, Miss.), 26–27
Magnolia Rifles, 82
Maiden aunts, 82, 120, 124–127, 129–131
Mailer, Norman, 186
Main Street (Memphis, Tenn.), 49, 50, 51, 53
Malaria, 44, 74, 171
Mallison, Charles, Jr. (Chick): and awareness of blacks, 227; Faulkner's interpretation of, 215; perception of battle of Gettysburg by, 115–116; role of, in *Intruder in the Dust*, 187–188, 192, 194–200, 202; mentioned, 21, 214, 216
Manassas, Va., first battle of, 85, 87
Mansion, The (Faulkner), 136, 186, 188, 219, 232
Marshall County, Miss., 31, 67, 75, 83, 88, 91, 93, 100, 144, 145
Maryland, 116, 117
Maury County, Tenn., 73
Mayer, Louis B., 197
Meadowfill, 79
Memphis, Tenn.: descriptions of, by Faulkner, 48–53; Forrest's raid on, 104–105; map of, 52; photographs of, 49, 50, 54; mentioned, 1, 2, 11, 21, 32, 33, 35, 41, 44, 45, 68, 86, 87, 89, 91, 93, 101, 102, 106, 110, 123, 150, 153, 155, 159, 161, 168, 177, 180, 181, 182, 185, 187, 193, 201, 204, 210, 222
Memphis and Charleston Railroad, 93, 97, 109
Memphis-Jefferson Road, 32
Memphis Junction, 18, 27, 31, 159, 161
Memphis-Oxford Road, 11, 32, 33, 36, 64, 65, 69, 135, 141, 143, 148, 160, 180; photograph of, 35
Memphis State University (University of Memphis), 216

Merchants and Farmers Bank, 12, 86, 226
Meredith, James, 209, 214, 217
Metro-Goldwyn-Mayer (MGM), 190, 197, 199, 200
Mexican-American War, 87
Michener, James A., 219
Middleton, Tenn., 29
Milam, J. W., 203
Millard, Rosa (Granny), 64, 107–112, 114–115
Minnesota, 102
Mississippi: maps of, 60, 78; migration from, 181, 201
Mississippian tradition, 58
Mississippi Board of Trustees of Institutions of Higher Learning, 209
Mississippi Central Railroad, 2–3, 11, 23, 35, 71, 75, 93, 97, 100, 102, 104, 105, 106, 109, 117, 122, 233. *See also* Illinois Central Railroad
Mississippi Freedom Summer, 213, 216
Mississippi National Guard: 108th Armored Cavalry Regiment, 209; 155th Infantry Division, 209; Troop E, 108th Armored Cavalry Regiment, 211; mentioned, 210, 213, 214, 216
Mississippi River, 51, 57, 97, 171, 172, 180, 223
Mississippi state militia, 104
Mississippi State Sovereignty Commission, 213, 216
Mississippi State University, 213
Mississippi: The Closed Society (Silver), 213
Missouri, 91, 101, 180
Miss Reba's brothel, 50, 53
Mitchell, Wyatt C., 32, 35, 69, 71, 73
Mitchell's Bluff, 69; photograph of, 71
Mobile and Ohio Railroad, 93, 97
Mohataha, 79, 80, 81
Moketubbe, 32, 36, 79
Moler College of Beauty Culture and Barbering, 53
Montgomery, Ala., 193
Morris, Willie, 3, 5
Mottstown, 27
Mower, Joseph A., 102
Muir family, 40
Mulberry Street (Memphis, Tenn.), 53

Mules, 1, 107, 109, 110, 111, 140, 149, 176, 179; photograph of, 136
"My Grandmother Millard and General Bedford Forrest and the Battle of Harrykin Creek" (Faulkner), 107
Myrdal, Gunnar, 225

Naked and the Dead, The (Mailer), 186
Nashville, Tenn., 125, 198
Natchez, Miss., 46, 67, 79, 179
Natchez Trace, 65
National Association for the Advancement of Colored People (NAACP), 193–194, 197, 207, 208, 216
National cemeteries, 124, 125
National Velvet (film), 198
Nazi, 185
Negroes. *See* blacks
Nelson's department store, 1, 27; photograph of, 14
Neshoba County, Miss., 213, 216, 224
New Albany, Miss., 2, 8, 33
New Deal, 11, 147, 223
New Hope Church, 29
New Orleans, La., 11, 45, 48, 71, 181, 187, 194
New York, Mississippi, and Arkansas Land Company, 67
New York, N.Y., 48, 91, 154, 155, 179, 183, 193, 194, 204
New York Times, 213
Nine Mile Branch, 196, 227
Nobel Prize for Literature, 2, 6, 203, 204, 212, 224
Nolan's store, photograph of, 133
Norfolk-Southern Railroad, 2
North, the, 21, 88, 112, 113, 114, 172, 181, 195, 196
North America, 58, 63, 118, 149
North Carolina, 39
North Lamar (North St.; Oxford, Miss.), 12, 26, 75
North Mississippi College, 9, 23, 28
Northwest Mississippi Junior College, 205
No Way Out (film), 197

Oak Grove Christian Church (Church of Christ), 135

Ober, Harold, 184, 187, 195
O'Connor, Flannery, 225
Odum, Howard, 225
Oesterling, Robert D., 232
Ohio River, 179, 180
Okatoba Hunting and Fishing Club, 166
Oklahoma (Indian Territory), 67, 81
Old Ben (the bear), 158–159, 163–164, 166
Oldham, Lida Estelle. *See* Faulkner, Lida Estelle Oldham Franklin
Olive Branch, Miss., 33
Origins of the New South (Woodward), 189
Orne, Edward, 32, 67, 69
Oscars (Academy Awards), 198, 201
Oxford, Miss.: "battle of," 209–215, 216, 217; burning of, by Union army, 105; courthouse square of, 1, 5, 15, 11, 26, 74, 75, 77, 165, 210, 230; Freedman Town, 15, 22, 137, 138; interpretation of, as three towns, 227–233; maps of, 13, 42, 76, 95, 138; photographs of, 6, 12, 14, 15, 16, 17, 77, 94, 143, 232, 233; mentioned, 1, 2, 3, 5, 6, 8, 9, 11, 15, 16, 18, 22, 23, 93, 96, 97, 100, 102, 104, 106, 111, 118–120 passim, 123, 125, 129–131 passim, 147, 149, 154, 155, 161, 165–166, 177, 179, 182, 183, 198, 201, 205, 206, 214, 216, 222
Oxford, Miss. (fictional), 28
Oxford Eagle, 165, 201
Oxford Inn, 105, 123
Oxford-Lafayette County Heritage Foundation Newsletter, 232

Panola, Miss., 104, 105
Panola County, Miss., 161, 166, 169, 177, 178
Paris, France, 218, 219
Paris, Miss., 28
Paris, William, 214
Parks plantation, 147; photograph of big house on, 148
Patterson, Elizabeth, 199, 201
Patton Hardware, 11
Pawnshop on Beale Avenue (Memphis, Tenn.), 53; photograph of, 54
Peabody, Lucius Quintus, 80, 81, 221
Pearl Harbor, Hawaii, 184
Pearl River valley, 224

Sea Island cotton region, 175
Sears Roebuck, 194
Second Manassas, Va., battle of, 87, 116
Second Mississippi Infantry Regiment, 82, 86
Second World War, 47, 51, 57, 79, 127, 131, 180–181, 183, 185–187, 188–189, 192, 197, 201, 223; battles of, 184, 187
Segregation, 180, 181, 191, 192, 194–199, 202, 205, 207–208, 209, 212, 213, 215, 216, 224, 225, 231
Selma, Ala., 224
Seminary Hill, 27
Senatobia, Miss., 104, 179, 205
Sequent occupance, 150–151
Seventh Mississippi Cavalry, 87
Sharecroppers, 139, 140, 149, 167–168, 174, 178, 179, 180, 233; sharecropper novels, 139–140
Sharpsburg (Antietam), Md., battle of, 117
Shaw, Irwin, 186
Shegog, Robert, 16
Shegog-Bailey house, 16, 29, 45, 105, 143. *See also* Rowan Oak
Shenandoah Valley, 113
Sherman, William T., 9, 89, 90, 93, 94, 97, 102, 105, 106, 129–130, 206; march of, across Georgia, 108, 109, 113
Shiloh (Pittsburgh Landing), Tenn., battle of, 9, 88, 109, 117, 125, 126, 211, 221
Shumann, Laverne, 228
Siam, 208
Signal, Daniel, 188
Silver, James W., 186; *Mississippi: The Closed Society*, 213
Sixth Iowa Division, 96
Slaves, and slavery, 9, 39, 42, 45, 63, 65–67 passim, 69, 71, 75, 78, 80, 101, 106–109 passim, 120, 122, 123, 130–133 passim, 135, 140, 145, 150–152 passim, 158, 163, 167, 172, 175, 180, 185, 193, 206, 212, 224
Smith, Andrew J., 9, 93, 102, 104–105, 106, 123, 211–212, 222; map of failed Mississippi campaign of, 103
Smith, Edmund Kirby, 113
Smith, Harrison (Hal), 222
Smith, Lillian, 225
Snopes, Abner (Ab), 111, 140, 149

Snopes, Eula Varner, 152
Snopes, Flem, 50, 52,
Snopes, Mink, 41, 48, 49–51, 53, 149, 188, 232
Snopes, Virgil, 49–51, 53
Snopes, Wesley, 177
Snopes family, 20, 21, 151, 156
Snopes trilogy, 220
"Snow" (Faulkner), 184
Soil erosion, 145, 147, 151, 221, 223; photographs of, 146
Sound and the Fury, The (Faulkner), 129, 180, 188, 191, 220, 228
South, the: Modern South era, 6, 57, 131, 175–202, 212, 213, 215, 216, 231; New South era, 5, 6, 57, 119–157, 174, 175, 178, 180–187, 188, 191, 206, 224, 226; Old South era, 8, 46, 57–81, 118, 119, 120, 123, 129, 131, 132–133, 134, 141, 145, 147, 150, 168, 175, 177, 180; rural and urban, 47–53, 184; Upland and Lowland, 38–46, 133, 149, 224, 225; Upland and Lowland, map of, 39; mentioned, 1, 9, 112, 113, 116, 125, 126, 189, 194, 195, 208, 218, 222
South America, 155
South Atlantic and Gulf Coastal Plain, 38
South Carolina, 175
Southerner, The (film), 185
Southern Historical Association, 189, 205, 208
Southern Horrors (Wells), 193
South Lamar (South St.; Oxford, Miss.), 12, 75
Soviet Union, and Soviets, 184, 189, 209
Speak Now Against the Day (Egerton), 189
Stearns, DeWhitt, 123
Stein, Jean, 218
Steinbeck, John, 219; *The Grapes of Wrath*, 139
Stevens, Gavin, 18, 187–188, 192, 194–196, 202, 214, 215
Stevens, Temple Drake. *See* Drake, Temple
Stevens family, 48–49
St. Louis–San Francisco (Frisco) Railroad, 11, 161; map depicting, 163
Stockholm, Sweden, 204
Stone, James ("General"), 161; hunting camp of, 161, 166, 174; photograph of

hunting lodge of, 173; railroad stop of, 161, 174
Stone, Philip Avery (Phil), 130, 183
Stone, Rosamond Alston (Miss Rosie), 130
Story, 169
St. Paul, 15
Strange Career of Jim Crow, The (Woodward), 189, 225–226
Strider, Clarence, 203
Stryker, Roy, 226
Stuart, James E. B. (Jeb), 116, 117, 118
Student Nonviolent Coordinating (SNCC), 224
Sturgis, Samuel G., 101
Sullivan, R. L., 166
Summers, Jill Faulkner. *See* Faulkner, Jill
Summers, Paul D., Jr., 155
Sutpen, Clytemnestra (Clytie), 152
Sutpen, Henry, 88, 114, 195
Sutpen, Thomas, 31, 32, 44, 45, 46, 80, 90, 114, 115, 130–131, 151, 172, 195
Sutpen family, 40, 45
Sutpen's Hundred, 18, 31, 32, 79, 145, 151

Tallahatchie County, Miss., 166, 203
Tallahatchie River: map of land holdings in river bottom, 161; river bottom, 11, 36, 40, 61, 62, 64, 69, 106, 135, 154, 158–159, 161, 164; river valley, 11, 35, 64, 93, 223; mentioned, 18, 29, 32, 33, 65, 67, 71, 74, 75, 78, 91, 100, 104, 105, 128, 134, 173, 180, 222
Tate County, Miss., 33, 64, 139, 143, 147, 148, 178
Tate house, photograph of, 143
Tate Merchandise Company, 11
Taylor, Elizabeth, 198
Taylor, John, 65–66, 79, 80
Taylor, Miss., 29, 66
Taylor, Paul, 139
Tennessee, 8, 9, 38, 40, 41, 43, 44, 87, 88, 89, 91, 93, 97, 101, 109, 113, 115
Tennessee River, 65
Third Street (Memphis, Tenn.), 53
Thompson, Jacob, 105
Thompson's Calvary, 83
Tidewater, 44, 45
Till, Emmett, 203, 205, 216

Tobacco Road (Caldwell), 139
To Have and Have Not (film), 185
Town, The (Faulkner), 186
Tractors, 147, 151, 177, 179, 221, 230
Treaty of Dancing Rabbit Creek (1830), 57
Treaty of Pontotoc Creek (1832), 57, 66, 118
Truman, Harry S., 181
Tubby, Toby (Tobo), 63, 64, 65, 69; Toby Tubby Creek, 33, 64; Toby Tubby ferry, 36, 64, 65, 69
Tuberculosis, 58, 82
Tulane University, 154
Tull, Vernon, 177
Tunica County, Miss., 61, 182
Tupelo, Miss., battle of, 102
Twelfth Wisconsin Cavalry, 87
Twentieth Century-Fox, 197
"Two Soldiers" (Faulkner), 184
Tyro, Miss., 33

Ulster Scots, 38
Umbey, Il Lap Pah, 32
Union, the, 39, 43, 44, 90, 94, 96, 110, 113, 114, 125
Union army (Federal army): fictional invasion of Mississippi by, 107, 108, 109–110, 111; historical invasion of Mississippi by, 90, 91, 93, 94, 96, 97, 100, 101, 104, 105, 106, 118, 128, 211, 217; mentioned, 9, 22, 31, 43, 64, 80, 85, 89, 113, 115–117 passim, 124. *See also* U.S. Army
Union County, Miss., 33
Union Navy, 111
Union Station (Memphis, Tenn.), 51
United Artists, 197
United Daughters of the Confederacy (U.D.C.), 125–128
University Greys, 83, 85, 86, 88, 125, 217
University of Georgia, 125, 228
University of Memphis (Memphis State University), 216
University of Mississippi (Ole Miss): Center for the Study of Southern Culture, 231; during Civil War, 83, 96, 105, 112, 118; integration of, 209–217; photograph of students of, 84; mentioned, 1, 2, 8, 11, 12, 28, 29, 63, 75, 128–129, 182, 228, 230, 232

Wright's Sanitarium, 204, 212
Writers at Work (ed. Cowley), 190
Wyatt, Miss., 27, 33, 35, 36, 69, 71, 73, 77, 93, 130, 135; map of, 72
Wyatt Crossing, 35
Wyman, Jane, 198
Wyott, 27, 32, 33, 36
Wyott Crossing, 32, 33

Yankees, 44, 45, 88, 100, 107, 108, 110, 117
Yazoo Delta (Yazoo Basin), 21, 41, 150, 156, 161, 164, 166, 168, 169–174, 182, 203, 223; photograph of log train in, 165. *See also* Delta
Yazoo River, 71

Yearling, The (film), 198
Yellow Fever, 44, 74
Yellow Leaf Creek, 11, 27
Yocona (hamlet), 23, 27
Yocona River, 9, 26, 74, 91, 104, 222; river bottom, 61, 75
Yoknapatawpha County, Miss.: jail of, 23, 80, 81; map of, 19; as microcosm of South, 5, 37, 41–42, 45, 53, 55, 218; population of, 24, 42
Yoknapatawpha River (Yockeney-Patafa River), 9, 18, 27, 78, 107, 221; river bottom, 11. *See also* Yocona River
Young, Stark, 177
Young Lions, The (Shaw), 186